PIECES OF EIGHT

UNIVERSITY PRESS OF FLORIDA

Florida A&M University, Tallahassee
Florida Atlantic University, Boca Raton
Florida Gulf Coast University, Ft. Myers
Florida International University, Miami
Florida State University, Tallahassee
New College of Florida, Sarasota
University of Central Florida, Orlando
University of Florida, Gainesville
University of North Florida, Jacksonville
University of South Florida, Tampa
University of West Florida, Pensacola

PIECES OF EIGHT

More Archaeology of Piracy

Edited by
Charles R. Ewen and Russell K. Skowronek

University Press of Florida
Gainesville · Tallahassee · Tampa · Boca Raton
Pensacola · Orlando · Miami · Jacksonville · Ft. Myers · Sarasota

Copyright 2016 by Charles R. Ewen and Russell K. Skowronek
All rights reserved
Printed in the United States of America on acid-free paper

This book may be available in an electronic edition.

21 20 19 18 17 16   6 5 4 3 2 1

A record of cataloging-in-publication data is available from the Library of Congress.
ISBN 978-0-8130-6158-0

The University Press of Florida is the scholarly publishing agency for the State University System of Florida, comprising Florida A&M University, Florida Atlantic University, Florida Gulf Coast University, Florida International University, Florida State University, New College of Florida, University of Central Florida, University of Florida, University of North Florida, University of South Florida, and University of West Florida.

University Press of Florida
15 Northwest 15th Street
Gainesville, FL 32611-2079
http://www.upf.com

To the memory of Kenneth J. Kinkor (1954–2013), dedicated historian of the *Whydah* and willing collaborator with all.

Contents

List of Figures ix

List of Tables xiii

Preface xv

Acknowledgments xvii

1. Setting a Course toward an Archaeology of Piracy 1
   Russell K. Skowronek

2. Blackbeard's *Queen Anne's Revenge* and Its French Connection 15
   Mark U. Wilde-Ramsing and Linda F. Carnes-McNaughton

3. Revisiting the *Fiery Dragon* 57
   John de Bry and Marco Roling

4. Black Bart's *Ranger* 93
   Chad M. Gulseth

5. The Wreck of the *Quedagh Merchant*: The Lost Ship of Captain William Kidd 110
   Frederick H. Hanselmann and Charles D. Beeker

6. Plundering the Spanish Main: Henry Morgan's Raid on Panama 132
   Frederick H. Hanselmann, Tomás Mendizábal, and Juan G. Martín

7. Ireland's Golden Age of Piracy: History, Cartography, and Emerging Archaeology 165
   Connie Kelleher

8. Shiver Me Timbers!: The Influence of Hollywood on the Archaeology of Piracy 193
   Russell K. Skowronek and Charles R. Ewen

9. Signaling Pirate Identity 208
   Heather Hatch

10. Artifacts That Talk Like Pirates: Jolly Roger Iconography and Archaeological Sites   228
    Kenneth J. Kinkor

11. Pirates as Providers   239
    Kathleen Deagan

12. Recognizing a Pirate Shipwreck without the Skull and Crossbones   260
    Courtney Page and Charles R. Ewen

13. Parting Shot   274
    Charles R. Ewen

References Cited   281

List of Contributors   308

Index   311

Figures

1.1. *An Attack on a Galleon* by Howard Pyle   11
2.1. Location map for the wreck of the *Queen Anne's Revenge*   16
2.2. French frigate circa 1700   19
2.3. *Queen Anne's Revenge* site plan with excavation units   21
2.4. Inspecting an X-ray image   23
2.5. Compilation of alignment maps   25
2.6. *Queen Anne's Revenge* site plan with overlay   27
2.7. Swivel gun   28
2.8. Breech block   30
2.9. Gold jewelry pieces   32
2.10. Coin weight and stemware   33
2.11. Global origins pie chart   34
2.12. Stern post with draft marks   38
2.13. Drawing of bell   39
2.14. Windowpane   39
2.15. Drawings of storage jar elements   42
2.16. Saintonge vessel sherd   43
2.17. Clyster and marks   45
2.18. Mortar and pestle   46
2.19. Set of weights and close-up of marks   47
2.20. Possible nesting weight lid and finial   48
2.21. Porringer and marks   49
2.22. *Queen Anne's Revenge* sword handle after recovery   50
2.23. Boxwood handle   52
2.24. Buckles, links, and wooden button   53

Figures

3.1. Map with survey areas in the harbor and Pirate Bay region 64
3.2. Historical map of 1847 projected over Google Earth satellite images 65
3.3. Chart with *Fiery Dragon* photo mosaic and plotted measurement grid 68
3.4. Chart showing *Fiery Dragon* excavation sections and plotted hull parts 70
3.5. Artifact overview per section 72
3.6. Two Chinese porcelain cups 75
3.7. Examples of the phoenix motif 77
3.8. Three Chinese white porcelain figurines 78
3.9. Carved wooden statue of a female 80
3.10. Carved stone statue of a female 81
3.11. Ivory piece inscribed "INRI" 82
3.12. Schematic topside view of the cannon found at the "channel wreck" site 84
3.13. Intact wine bottle 86
3.14. Porcelain sherds of the "channel wreck" 87
3.15. Lead gaming piece marked "X" 88
3.16. A 1730 manuscript on Madagascar that yielded important historical data on the pirates of Sainte-Marie Island 89
3.17. A 1733 map of Sainte-Marie Island harbor 90
4.1. Captain Roberts with the *Ranger* and *Royal Fortune* at Whydah Road, January 11, 1722 94
4.2. The *St Agnes*, captured in the mouth of the Senegal River and renamed *Ranger* and later *Little Ranger* 95
4.3. Sir Chaloner Ogle, 1681–1750 96
4.4. *An Exact Plan of Chocolata Hole and the South End of the Town of Port Royal in Jamaica* 101
4.5. Areas excavated by Marx and Hamilton at Port Royal 103
4.6. Site plan of the *Great Ranger*, Port Royal, Jamaica 106
5.1. Rendering of Captain William Kidd by Howard Pyle 111
5.2. Contemporary portrait of William Kidd by Sir James Thornhill 113
5.3. Close-up of Kidd's testimony to Lord Bellomont and the details of the ship and its cargo 115

Figures · xi

5.4. Site map of the *Quedagh Merchant* shipwreck   118
5.5. Main concentration of guns on the *Quedagh Merchant* shipwreck site   120
5.6. Exposed keel or keelson prior to recovery of the cannon   123
5.7. Cross section of the teak sample   124
5.8. Exposed section of the ship's hull   125
5.9. Image of the rabbeted seam and a fastening hole   126
5.10. Cannon outline with measurements   128
5.11. Rabbet seam with peg   128
5.12. Interpretive guide in Spanish for the Captain Kidd Living Museum in the Sea   130
6.1. Woodcut of Henry Morgan   134
6.2. Depiction of Morgan and his men attacking Portobelo   138
6.3. Castillo de San Lorenzo   145
6.4. Excavation of the Cabildo at the base of the iconic bell tower   152
6.5. Sword uncovered during the excavations of the Cabildo   153
6.6. Traces of fire on the excavated steps of the Cabildo   154
6.7. Aerial image of the Castillo de San Lorenzo, Lajas Reef, and the mouth of the Chagres River   155
6.8. Two divers raise a small gun from the seafloor   157
6.9. Image of a gun with concretions removed   158
6.10. 2011 site map   161
6.11. Photo mosaic of the shipwreck site   162
7.1. A 1612 John Hunt Chart 4, showing southwestern coast of Munster   166
7.2. Detail of Dutch ships from 1612 John Hunt Chart 4   168
7.3. Crookhaven Harbour, County Cork   169
7.4. Detail from 1612 John Hunt Chart 4, depicting William Hull's fortified house and Black Castle   174
7.5. Dún na Séad Castle overlooking Baltimore Harbour   175
7.6. Detail from 1612 John Hunt Chart 4, depicting Dún na Séad Castle in Baltimore   176
7.7. Rockfleet Castle in County Mayo, home to "pirate queen" Gránuaile   177

7.8. Dutchman's Cove, Castlehaven, with rock-cut steps and lantern niches   180

7.9. Canty's Cove near Dunmanus Bay   181

7.10. Pirate steps at Gokane Point, Crookhaven   183

7.11. Recording broken swivel gun on Dunworley Bay wreck site prior to recovery for conservation   184

7.12. View of Leamcon looking out toward Long Island and the south Atlantic   186

7.13. Sherd from the handle of a seventeenth-century Tuscan oil jar   189

7.14. Stone mooring post at Leamcon with evidence of rope wear at base   190

7.15. Basal remains of the "Long Dock" quay and steps at Leamcon Harbour   191

10.1. Wax seal with wounded heart motif   231

10.2. Pewter plate   232

11.1. Locations of study sites shown on the 1764 Puente map   249

11.2. Trends in the origins of tableware ceramics in St. Augustine households, 1650–1760   250

12.1. Approximate location of the wreck of *Queen Anne's Revenge* on James Wimble's 1738 map of eastern North Carolina   262

12.2. Approximate location of the wreck of *Whydah* off the coast of Cape Cod on Cyprian Southack's map of the New England coast   263

12.3. Approximate location of the wreck of HMS *Invincible*   264

12.4. Location of the wreck of *Henrietta Marie*   266

12.5. Graphic representation of artifact frequencies for each shipwreck by category   270

12.6. Graphic representation of the logarithm of artifact frequencies for each shipwreck by category   270

12.7. Artifact frequencies by ship   271

12.8. Logarithm of artifact frequencies by ship   271

Tables

3.1. Category Overview of the Artifact Materials of the *Fiery Dragon* 72

3.2. Category Overview of the Artifact Materials of the Channel Wreck 85

4.1. *Great Ranger* Artifacts 108

9.1. Use of Flags by Golden Age Pirates 217

9.2. Frequency of Occurrence of Design Elements on Pirate Flags, 1700–1723 225

11.1. Ceramics Occurring as Tablewares in St. Augustine Households, 1650–1750 243

11.2. Political Events and Related Periods for the Legal Entry of English and French Goods into St. Augustine 246

11.3. Sites and Households Used in This Study 247

11.4. Terminus Post Quem Groups for Archaeological Deposits Used in This Study 248

11.5. Imported European-Tradition Tablewares in Eighteenth-Century St. Augustine Households 252

12.1. Categories Used to Organize Artifact Assemblages and Artifact Types in Each Category 261

12.2. Artifact Frequencies for Each Shipwreck (in Percentages) 269

12.3. Logarithm of Artifact Frequencies for Each Shipwreck 272

Preface

In Rudyard Kipling's short story titled "The Man Who Would Be King" Danny Dravot and Peachy Carnahan, two seasoned veterans of Queen Victoria's army, draw up a contract and swear an oath of friendship to cross the Hindu Kush and become "Kings of Kafiristan." This audacious plan sprang from their hubris, based on their past experience and successes. We have enjoyed similar success in our undertaking (and we both lived to make the sequel).

More than a dozen years ago at the Society for Historical Archaeology annual meeting, then being held on RMS *Queen Mary* in Long Beach, California, we fell upon the idea of a scientific examination of piracy. At that time this undertaking was perceived by some as akin to treasure hunting or at least smacked of populism. Nonetheless, we were both thirty years into our careers, confident in our ability to weather the inevitable criticism that would target the study—*and* we were tenured. Whatever the outcome, we were ready to take on the challenge.

X Marks the Spot: The Archaeology of Piracy (2006) was successful right out of the gate. While there were critics in the archaeological community, the interested public flocked to the book. As those familiar with academic publishing will attest, scholarly books (not to mention edited volumes from university presses) often have difficulty in selling out their initial press runs. We had no problem. The hard-bound printing sold out within a year of its release and is found in public and collegiate libraries and in classrooms across North America and Europe. This was followed by two more paperback printings. The book has been recognized as an archaeological best seller in Europe. It continues to do well nine years after its release.

Over the years we have been honored to give dozens of lectures on the topic of the archaeology of piracy at venues such as the Witte Museum in San Antonio, Texas; the School for Advanced Research, Santa Fe, New

Mexico; the Science Museum of Minnesota, St. Paul; the Columbia River Maritime Museum in Astoria, Oregon; Flagler College in St. Augustine, Florida; the North Carolina Museum of History in Raleigh; the Graveyard of the Atlantic Museum in Hatteras, North Carolina; the South Florida Museum in Bradenton; the University of North Carolina at Greensboro; Princeton University; and the following places in California: the Porterville College Cultural Historical Awareness Program; the Stanford Archaeology Center, Stanford University; the National Endowment for the Humanities Landmarks of American History and Culture Workshops for School Teachers Institute in Monterey, sponsored by California State University, Monterey Bay; Santa Clara University in Santa Clara; and Cabrillo College in Aptos.

Through the years we have continued our research on the topic of pirates and piracy both in the field (such as at Bath and Beaufort, North Carolina) and in our offices. At scholarly conferences we have presented our work and asked to serve as discussants on a growing number of panels by others who have joined us in this great adventure. As more pirate sites were discovered around the world, it became clear to us that it was time to complete a companion volume to *X Marks the Spot*. When we undertook this new endeavor some people asked if *Pieces of Eight* was simply a retitled second edition. What a scurvy question! The book you hold builds on and expands the information published nine years ago. We hope that you find it informative.

In closing we note that our friendship, like that of Danny Dravot and Peachy Carnahan, only improves with time and with the knowledge that we can count on each other through thick and thin.

Acknowledgments

Any publication is the result of the efforts of more than the authors or editors. Thus, it is not just the actors on stage but the people behind the scenes who bring such endeavors to reality.

This volume and its forerunner and companion *X Marks the Spot: The Archaeology of Piracy* was conceived more than a decade ago in a frigid swimming pool in Long Beach, California during the Society for Historical Archaeology annual meeting on the RMS *Queen Mary*. Meredith Babb, director of the University Press of Florida, approached us about creating the first serious archaeologically focused "look" at piracy. She envisioned books with titles like *X Marks the Spot* and, yes, *Pieces of Eight*. You might say "an accord was struck" and we embarked on this voyage of discovery. It has been a journey fraught with the dangers associated with working on topics which lie in the nether region between scholarly enquiry and sensationalism. Since its publication in 2006, *X Marks the Spot* has been well received by our colleagues and the broader public. Soon others began to contact us about their work and we began to muse about a companion volume with Meredith's title, *Pieces of Eight: More Archaeology of Piracy*, the book you hold in your hands today. We hope it will find a prominent place in the archaeological study of the illicit behaviors associated with piracy and smuggling.

First we wish to acknowledge Ken Kinkor, historian for the *Whydah* project. In 2003, during the Society for Historical Archaeology meeting in Providence, Rhode Island and in the midst of a howling snowstorm on Cape Cod, Ken opened the *Whydah* Museum in Wellfleet and welcomed us in from the storm. For several hours he sheparded us through their exhibits and told us of their work. Nearly a decade later when *Pieces of Eight: More Archaeology of Piracy* was being "storyboarded" we convinced him to join us, not knowing he was ill. Ken carried through and provided us with his chapter. Sadly, he passed away before this book was published. We dedicate this volume to his memory.

"Everything is improved with editing" is an adage which every scholar should have tattooed on their fist. The University Press of Florida found excellent reviewers for the draft manuscript of this book, including: J. Barto Arnold III, past president of the Society for Historical Archaeology and one of the pioneers of underwater research in the United States; Donny Hamilton, professor at Texas A&M University and contributor to *X Marks the Spot* on the topic of Port Royal, Jamaica; and Dr. Steve Dasovitch of Lindenwood University in Missouri, who is a rising star in underwater research. Their thoughtful and very helpful observations, comments, and critiques helped us to avoid embarrassing oversights and outright mistakes. Thank you for your help.

Next we wish to heartily thank Kathy Lewis, the copy editor for this and many of our other books with the University Press of Florida. It is always a pleasure to work with such a professional. Thank you.

The bibliography and index for this volume were created by Simon Goldstone, a graduate assistant in the anthropology program at East Carolina University. The index created by our friend Anita Cohen for *X Marks the Spot* was used as the starting point for the one in the current volume. We wish to thank both of them for their diligence and attention to detail.

In addition to Meredith Babb, the aforementioned director of the University Press of Florida, we are indebted to Rachel Doll, our publicist and exhibits coordinator, and Eleanor Deumens, the project editor for this book. Thank you for all of your help and the gentle kick in the pants when needed.

Finally, we want to thank those of you who have supported our endeavors through speaking invitations and the purchase of our books. Those accolades mean a lot to academics laboring in state universities. Our families have often carried the brunt of our absences surrounding these studies: please be advised we could never, ever, have done this without you. A special mention to our parents who saw the drafts, but did not live to see the completed project. Thank you.

1

Setting a Course toward an Archaeology of Piracy

RUSSELL K. SKOWRONEK

The heavily laden merchant vessel easily nosed its way through the low waves of the open sea. On board the crew members busied themselves with the myriad details associated with taking a vessel to a distant port. Twenty-four hours a day they had courses to lay, meals to prepare, and a vessel to be maintained. The crew, numbering thirty or fewer, was barely adequate to manage the ship. It was small because every extra hand who was not absolutely necessary to shipboard operations would cut into the profits to be realized from the cargo, which the owners of the vessel were loath to do. Merchant sailors, usually poorly paid, do not have a vested interest in defending the cargo of their employers. Arming a merchant ship might be an option, but it had both positive aspects and major drawbacks. An armed vessel could be defended, thus better ensuring the successful delivery of a cargo. The cargo carried would be less and costs would rise, however, as space would need to be allocated for weapons and ammunition and the men who would serve in this defensive capacity as well as their belongings and victuals.

The waters that the vessel traversed were said to be infested with pirates. Any concern was mitigated by the realization that the merchant vessel was large and the crew members were vigilant for strange vessels. To avoid running afoul of this danger, the captain steered a course that would carry them far beyond the coast, where sheltered coves and inlets might hide the miscreants. Other vessels might pass unnoticed on the horizon, however, or smaller fishing boats might bob on the swells. Under cover of darkness small, swift boats might appear, carrying heavily armed men desperate to sustain themselves through thievery. Approaching from the stern, the crews of these boats would clamor over the counter rail and seize control of the undefended ship. The captured vessel and crew might be set free once the ship was plundered of both mundane, personal items (watches, rings, clothing, shoes) and ship's stores as well as more valuable cargo. At other times the ship might be kept, with hostages taken for ransom.

Vignettes such as this might easily characterize the activities of Somali pirates in the twenty-first century: the 2008 hijacking of the *Sirius Star* (an oil tanker carrying 2 billion gallons of oil) and the *Faina* (a cargo ship filled with munitions, tanks, and anti-aircraft guns) and the 2009 capture of the *Maersk Alabama*, a container ship made famous in the 2013 film *Captain Phillips* with Tom Hanks (Heintzelman and Rainey Marquez 2013:8–11; Phillips with Talty 2010; Sekulich 2009:276–77). These were all unarmed merchant vessels with fewer than three dozen crew members. More than $6 million was paid as ransom for the first two vessels and their crews. The four pirates who captured the *Maersk Alabama* did not fare as well: they were either captured or killed.

The Russians have had a naval task force in the Indian Ocean conducting pirate patrols. In retaking vessels they have killed pirates and taken others to Russia and sometimes to Kenya and other states in the region for trial. It is suspected that many simply "disappeared" and returned to Somalia (Rivkin and Ramos-Mrosovsky 2010). In 2009 Russia hinted that its navy would "take no prisoners" (Hellmer 2010). In May of 2010 the Russian oil tanker *Moscow University* was captured by Somali pirates. It was retaken by the Russian navy, wounding one pirate. Articles dated May 12, 2010 (Anonymous 2010a, 2010b) reported that the ten captured pirates were dead, following their release by the Russian navy after they were returned to their boat. A seven-minute video titled *Without a Trial* was posted in May 2010, purporting to show what happened in the wake of that action. In the film some two dozen Somali pirates, one of whom is wounded, are held at gunpoint on their boat. The videographer shows AK-47s, handguns, Molotov cocktails, and a long boarding ladder. The pirates are then handcuffed to the boat. In the last scene, ostensibly shot from the deck of the Russian destroyer, the boat appears to explode, taking the pirates with it. Is it real or a hoax? In any case these accounts all underscore the dangers associated with piracy.

The International Chamber of Commerce International Maritime Bureau has reported more than 5,000 pirate attacks since 1992 (Skowronek 2006). Currently it is estimated that those represent an annual loss to the global economy of $15 billion in losses, insurance premiums, and delays (Sekulich 2009:80). Off Somalia alone 179 ships were captured by pirates between 2005 and 2012. To free these vessels and their crews an estimated $400 million in ransoms was paid. The average pirate received about $30,000. This is more than fifty-four times the $550 per year income of the average Somali (Harress 2013).

While merchant vessels might command greater ransoms, pirates are known to be ecumenical in their attacks. In the middle of October 2009 Paul and Rachel Chandler's 38-foot yacht was taken by pirates and stripped of everything of value. The couple was then held for ransom (Hassan and Lawless 2009). The Chandlers were released 388 days and $440,000 later, following beatings and imprisonment (Gettleman 2011). Another example was the capture in April 2009 of the French yacht *Tanit* and its five crew members in the Gulf of Aden. Fearing that the pirates were about to take the hostages ashore to be held for ransom, French commandos retook the boat, killing two of the five pirates and the owner of the yacht (Hellmer 2010).

These contemporary accounts of piracy are almost identical to historic acts of piracy. Eighteenth-century 200-ton merchant ships had small crews numbering between thirteen and seventeen (Leeson 2009:10). In 1821 the *Zephyr*, a merchant brig with a crew of fifteen (carrying coffee, arrowroot, dyewood, and indigo and passengers including women and children) set sail from Jamaica to London. A few days into their voyage they were overtaken by pirates sailing a schooner. Ten heavily armed men cowed the crew and passengers and began their search of the vessel. In addition to confiscating portions of the cargo and some of the ship's stores including water, livestock, sails, spars, and other rigging items, they ransacked the living quarters, took earrings from the children, and threatened and beat the captain into surrendering his cash (Smith 2011: 13). They then forced the first mate, Aaron Smith, to accompany them for the next year. After witnessing and being victim of various tortures, he escaped his captors, was imprisoned in Havana, and later was tried and acquitted of piracy in London (Smith 2011).

A century earlier, in June 1722, fisherman Philip Ashton was working the cod fishery off the coast of Nova Scotia, three hundred miles northeast of Marblehead, Massachusetts, his home port. Ashton and his five fellow crew members were in their schooner at the end of a day of fishing when four pirates sailing with Edward Low boarded the vessel. The pirates took food and clothing and forced Ashton and his compatriot Joseph Libbey, like Aaron Smith a century later, to leave their schooner and join the pirates on their brigantine the *Rebecca* (Flemming 2014). Unlike Libbey, Ashton did not join the pirates. He remained a captive or "forced" man for nine months until he made his escape in March 1723 while part of a "watering party" on Roatan Island in the Bay of Honduras. There he survived for sixteen months and finally returned to Marblehead in June 1725, some three years after being captured. As this was happening Libbey, his onetime fisher friend turned pirate, was captured. A month later, in July 1725, he was hanged in Newport, Rhode Island, for piracy. While it is debatable whether modern international law permits the execution of pirates by naval task forces without benefit of trial, in the eighteenth century captains had the right to hang the pirates (Turley 1999:46). Between 1716 and 1726 more than four hundred pirates were hanged following capture by the Royal Navy (Rediker 1987:283).

Studying Pirates and Piracy in the Past

In order to study piracy it is necessary to define it. Many terms are commonly used as cognates, including buccaneer, corsair, and privateer. These terms are often used interchangeably, but there are differences between them.

Webster (1981: 867) defines a "pirate" as one who commits robbery on the high seas or makes unauthorized use of another's idea or invention. A more colorful definition comes from the nineteenth-century *Pirate's Own Book*: "Piracy is an offence against the universal law of society. As, therefore, he has renounced all the benefits of society and government, and has reduced himself to the savage state of nature, by declaring war against all mankind, all mankind must declare war against him" (Maritime Research Society 1924:x). In other words, pirates robbed ships. Not all those who robbed ships were bad, however, at least not in the eyes of their home country. Some were accorded special honors.

A "privateer" is a mariner licensed by a sovereign state to attack enemy shipping. Privateers carried what are known as letters of marque, which made the privateers an auxiliary to the regular navy of the state. Letters of marque permitted the bearer to prey upon the shipping of an enemy country and split the prize with the authorizing government (Cordingly 1995:xvii). This makes the difference between privateers and pirates a matter of perspective. Sir Francis Drake was knighted by his government as a hero of the realm but at the same time was viewed as a dreaded pirate by the Spaniards living in the Caribbean, upon whom he preyed. Captain William Kidd went to the Indian Ocean carrying a letter of marque as an

English privateer. Upon his return some chicanery took place: his letter was conveniently lost or misfiled, to be rediscovered two hundred years later. Without the letter he was deemed a pirate for his actions and hanged at Execution Dock at Wapping in 1701 (Zacks 2002). "Corsair" is of French origin, meaning one who runs or hunts or pursues. It usually is used in reference to those sailing from ports such as Tripoli in North Africa, historically known as the Barbary Coast. "Buccaneer" is a corruption of the French word *boucanier*. When the Spanish abandoned the western third of Hispaniola in the latter half of the sixteenth century, French smugglers occupied the uninhabited region. Their subsistence was largely based on the hunting of wild cattle that were plentiful in the area. The meat from these cattle was smoked over grills called *boucans* and sold to passing ships. Before long these *boucaniers* were supplementing their income by preying upon some of the passing ships (Konstam 1999:74). The term later was anglicized into "buccaneer." Tortuga Island, off the northern coast of Haiti, became one of the early pirate lairs in the Caribbean. When the British captured Jamaica, the buccaneers or "Brethren of the Coast" made Port Royal their home. With these definitions we can now begin the investigation of piracy.

In the study of piracy it is not enough to cherry pick passages from the documentary record to explain illicit activities in the past. As scientists we draw upon many lines of evidence from contemporary and historic acts of piracy and seek patterns, which begin to explain social and material phenomena. What were the patterns of behavior adopted by pirates? Why did pirates do things the way they did? And what artifacts and other physical remains might result from pirate actions and groups? Taken together, the methods of history, anthropology, and archaeology are a powerful way to study pirates and piracy in the past. To paraphrase Robert Schuyler (1977), this kind of research uses the written word, the spoken word, observed behavior, and preserved behavior.

The written word includes accounts such as contemporary letters and bureaucratic reports, maps, newspapers, vital records, deeds, probate inventories, census data, ethnohistorical accounts, and quantifiable documentary evidence. All are especially useful for understanding where piracy took place in the past, the nature of the act of piracy, the people who were pirates, and their place in culture. Such materials have enormous descriptive value in providing a picture of the community and the concerns of portions of the populace. For example, using contemporary documents Michael Kwass (2014) has told the story of Louis Mandrin, a smuggler of calico and tobacco into early eighteenth century France. Captured, condemned, and executed by French authorities, Mandrin has been characterized as a "Gallic Robin Hood" for his undermining of royal authority through smuggling. Kwass considers the hidden connections of illicit commerce, criminality, and revolt.

Peter Leeson (2007, 2009), a professor at George Mason University, has examined through the lens of economics the labor conditions that led seafarers to piracy and how that in turn created a "democracy" of sorts within a pirate crew. He considers how developing a fierce reputation by flying the skull and crossbones or torturing captives made good economic sense. These sorts of analyses of documentary evidence can provide a perspective on the options available to past peoples. They do have limitations, however, which often can be addressed by an analysis of other lines of evidence.

Oral history, once a mainstay of history, fell out of favor at the end of the nineteenth century as a weaker form of evidence associated with preliterate societies. As a result it passed into the realm of anthropologists and folklorists. By the last third of the twentieth century social historians had begun to turn to oral histories and the evidence provided by other social scientists to study the past. Oral history can fill in the gaps on particular subjects about which little or no information is available. Oral history can complement both documentary and archaeological records with human experience and perception (Newland 1997). In this way we can draw upon the descriptions of modern piracy for a better understanding of past phenomena.

Other accounts also shed light on the place of pirates and piracy. Ben Dixon MacNeill (1958:58–64) recorded a very different image of Blackbeard on the Outer Banks of North Carolina in the 1920s. Two hundred years after the death of the pirate, there was "a very lively belief that Captain Teach was a right considerable fellow." He was said to have maintained a respectable house in Bath and to have made gifts to the church and to the first library in North Carolina. Perhaps most importantly, "he preferred the hospitality of the simple folk across the Inlet from Portsmouth to the brawling thieves who built their warehouses and defrauded" the local Hatteras people. "And, anyhow, what if he was a pirate? He was a respectable pirate and a good neighbor when he was around the community" (MacNeill 1958:61).

Oral histories collected by MacNeill detail Teach's bravery and the unfair advantage of Lt. Robert Maynard in his surprise attack. After Teach died in the battle, it is reported that his head hung from the bowsprit of Maynard's ship on its return to Virginia (Rankin 1960:58–59). The accounts suggest that after the battle Maynard fled the region for fear of reprisals at the hands of the local inhabitants.

"'He slunk out of here,' an Islander will say, near two and a half centuries afterward, and he says it as if it happened no longer ago than last week" (MacNeill 1958:63).

Observed behavior, ethnology, and the comparison of similar phenomena or analogies are another valuable way to study the past. For example, studies of bandits in Sardinia and the Mafia in Sicily have shown that the mid-nineteenth century ascendancy of the Italian nation-state with its unified civil and criminal codes played a significant role in shaping the perception of outlaws (Anderson 1965; Moss 1979). The result was that outlaws or bandits who were glorified or at least accepted in their native districts were feared as raiders outside the area. These outlaws walked an ambiguous line between the poverty of their neighbors and the wealth of others. Successful bandits stand out as people who evolved from poverty to relative wealth and acquired power in spite of existing government. The more successful bandits are, the more extensive is the protection granted to them, and the more they make themselves respected (Blok 1972; Hobsbawm 1972). In regard to the creation of a Robin Hood–like myth Eric Hobsbawm points out:

> The myth-making or otherwise distorting capacities of the human memory are well-known, and not confined to bandits. The significance of such information is, that it shows (a) the selectivity of the bandit myth (some bandits are "good" whereas others are not), (b) the bandit myth (high moral status, "good" actions) actually formulated by the policeman who fought the bandit, and therefore also (c) the myth of the "good" bandit. It seems simplest to assume that there is some relation between a bandit's real behavior and his subsequent myth. There is, of course, also some evidence that certain bandits have genuinely attempted to play the Robin Hood role. (Hobsbawm 1972:505)

Finally, behavior preserved in the archaeological or material record, when systematically and comparatively considered, will allow us to discern piracy in the absence of the documentary, oral, and ethnographic records. Lest we forget, the most successful pirates are those that we do not know. They are the ones who survived and never had their stories told.

Scholars continue to struggle over the primacy of the material, written, and spoken records. Documents may be overvalued in the face of contradictory material evidence or may be unsystematically and uncritically used.

Oral histories and ethnographic and ethnohistorical accounts associated with the direct historic approach to studying the past may be taken as unchanging traditions. Finally, there are continuing misperceptions regarding the nature of "science" and "history" as being separate and not comparable (Feinman 1997).

Today the archaeological, ethnographic, documentary, and spoken records are powerful methodologies for the examination of history through the lens of historical archaeology (Little 2007). By using these complementary and nonexclusive data sets we can get a more accurate and unbiased view of past peoples and their associated cultures.

Can an Archaeology of Piracy Exist?

A decade ago the answer would have been easy: no. Pirates have captured popular imagination for more than 125 years as a broadly drawn caricature. In the past decade Disney films have regenerated the genre for a new century and new generations through Johnny Depp and the *Pirates of the Caribbean* franchise. While pirates have long captured the popular imagination, only a handful of historians have tried to separate fiction from fact. Archaeology was remarkably silent on this topic. The reasons for this silence varied. Such sites were often the target of treasure hunters or those seeking some tangible evidence of past nefarious activities. Scholars in academic institutions were fearful of any research topics that might be scorned by senior colleagues as being less than worthy and sensational pursuits. In cases involving pirates and piracy, the goal was to explain the presence of certain exotic artifacts as evidence of illicit behavior. These researchers had no goal of creating a larger explanatory model for the identification of such behaviors in the archaeological record.

This approach (or lack thereof) was forever changed in 2006 with the publication of *X Marks the Spot: The Archaeology of Piracy* (Skowronek and Ewen 2006). Now in its third printing, it continues to be well received the world over. Our book, written with an educated popular audience in mind, has become the primary means for professional archaeologists and the public to learn about real pirates. As a result a growing number of archaeologists are now examining the footprint left by pirates and asking more nuanced questions about their place in society.

Archaeologists asked: "What is a pirate and how would you recognize a pirate site"? *X Marks the Spot* brought terrestrial and underwater archaeologists of the early modern era together and simply asked them, leaving documentary evidence aside, what physical evidence they had for piracy and related illicit behavior. Three categories of sites were identified. First were staging sites or bases colloquially termed "lairs." Next were the ships used by pirates. Last were the players themselves, the victims and other willing participants in these nefarious activities.

Lairs

Land bases were for staging attacks, the sale of stolen goods, or simple rest and relaxation. Pirates are opportunistic thieves. In modern Somalia or Indonesia they may fish or farm and occasionally prey on passing vessels to supplement their meager resources. But with success comes change. The port of Eyl in Somalia now has hotels and restaurants. The inhabitants show their newfound wealth by driving Mercedes and building villas (Kennedy 2009). Captured ships are anchored in the harbor, awaiting the payment of ransom. The fast pursuit boats are maintained and modified by teams of mechanics (Blair 2008). History offers parallels. The work of Daniel Finamore (2006) in the Barcaderas of Belize and J. David McBride on nearby Roatan in the Bay of Honduras shows that logwood cutters in the seventeenth and eighteenth centuries would attack ships and return to their secure retreat where they could enjoy their gain without fear of reprisal. In the middens associated with these communities are found ceramic artifacts usually associated with high-status individuals rather than with manual laborers.

Two of the most famous lairs were Ile de la Tortue (Tortuga) off the north coast of Hispaniola (modern Haiti) and Ile Sainte-Marie, an island off the east coast of Madagascar in the Indian Ocean. Both served as main staging bases in the late seventeenth and early eighteenth centuries. From documentary accounts, these were truly international communities where individual rights, equitable division of revenues, and democratic decision-making were the norm. To date little terrestrial archaeological work has been done at either site, although work was done on shipwrecks in the harbor at Saint Marie (de Bry 2006). If the pattern seen by Finamore in the Barcaderas continues, archaeologists might expect to find evidence of an egalitarian society with associated maritime industries and fortifications at these pirate sites.

Transshipment locales are another category of terrestrial sites. At these sites, located away from communities, stolen or smuggled goods were lightered from mother ships to smaller boats and barges. Grande Terre Island (in the Gulf of Mexico south of New Orleans, Louisiana) is one such place (Exnicios 2006). There Jean Lafitte and his brother Pierre operated a small establishment that according to reports was home to 250 to 1,000 people. Mundane goods including soap, paper, iron, rope, cloth, window glass, salt, coffee, and cocoa were off-loaded from merchant ships or from captured vessels for smuggling into New Orleans. Thus it was a location far from legitimate points of egress to the Mississippi River. Archaeology at the site reveals glass and ceramic artifacts, like those found in the middens of Barcaderas, which are more appropriately associated with affluent elites than with working commoners.

Finally, there are the famous pirate ports such as Port Royal, Jamaica. Books and films have portrayed this town as a rollicking pirate lair. For decades, Donny Hamilton has studied the community and concluded that it was "a mercantile center first and a pirate port second" (Hamilton 2006:15). As he points out, as the de facto capital of English Jamaica, Port Royal was also the port for legitimate privateers representing England. In times of peace merchants supplied Spanish America, and in times of war privateers based in Port Royal raided the same ports on the Spanish Main. Except for what may be the remains of captured pirate ships, nothing has been found in the ruins of Port Royal that can be attributed to either privateering or piracy. The parallels to Eyl in Somalia are striking. Originally a port dedicated to the fishing industry, Eyl was transformed following the collapse of the Somali government in the early 1990s. Now it serves as a hub for this illicit activity. Connie Kelleher's work in Ireland (chapter 7) is another example of this phenomenon. At the beginning of the seventeenth century many pirates shifted their base of operations from southern England to southern Ireland. She notes that in addition to ports Ireland had "coastal access points" for clandestine activities, which served as vantage points to observe the coast and provided easy access to the sea for attacks and escape routes via pathways and stairways in the event of discovery.

Pirate Ships

In popular culture the pirates who leapt from Rafael Sabatini's pen sailed in the square-rigged vessels *Arabella* (*Captain Blood*) and the *Black Swan* (*Black Swan*). In the more recent *Pirates of the Caribbean* franchise, Captain Jack Sparrow's *Black Pearl* is also depicted as a heavily armed warship large enough to take on a Spanish galleon or a British warship. While pirates did have well-armed "mother" ships, in reality those vessels were not regularly employed in the active capture of other vessels unless the pirates were certain that there would be little or no fighting. A successful pirate,

Figure 1.1. *An Attack on a Galleon* by Howard Pyle (from Pyle 1921).

like a successful thief, can take a prize without being hurt or captured and rapidly escape.

This point is underscored in the century-old artwork of Howard Pyle. His 1905 painting *An Attack on a Galleon* shows a small open boat with six men sailing up on the stern of a grand vessel, where they will join another similarly sized vessel whose crew is swarming up the victim's starboard stern quarter (figure 1.1). These were open unarmed boats, but they were fast and manned by pirates who were heavily armed. If there was resistance, they would make a rapid withdrawal. If the ship was taken, they robbed it and carried the booty away to the mother ship. The recent film *Captain Phillips* depicts the modern equivalent of these sorts of capture. Based on the book *A Captain's Duty* (Phillips with Talty 2010) the container ship *Maersk Alabama* with a crew of thirty is captured by four armed Somalis who climb aboard from a fast, open boat powered by an outboard motor. The pirates planned to rob the ship and collect a ransom and then return to the mother ship. Instead they ran afoul of the U.S. Navy and were killed or imprisoned.

Identification of pirate ships is not easily accomplished. The find does not include a preserved black flag emblazoned with a skull and crossbones or a keg containing hooks or peg legs or parrot skeletons. Thus far the identification of such vessels has been based on a combination of documentation and a constellation of positive and negative material evidence. For example, in recent years a number of "pirate" ships have been identified and excavated. These include John Bowen's *Speaker* (1702, Mauritius: Lizé 2006), Samuel Bellamy's *Whydah* (1717, Cape Cod: C. Hamilton 2006), Edward Teach's *La Concorde* or *Queen Anne's Revenge* (1718, North Carolina: Rodgers et al. 2005; Wilde-Ramsing 2006), and William Condon's *Fiery Dragon* (1721, St. Marie Madagascar: de Bry 2006). Now the initial observations are being further refined with the discovery of Captain William Kidd's *Quedagh Merchant* by Frederick H. Hanselmann and Charles D. Beeker (chapter 5), work on Bartholomew Roberts's *Ranger*, dating from 1722 and lying in Port Royal, Jamaica (chapter 4; D. Hamilton 2006), and continued work on Blackbeard's *Queen Anne's Revenge* (chapter 2) and the *Fiery Dragon* (chapter 3).

Each of these would best be seen as a "mother ship." They were similar in size: about thirty to thirty-five meters in length, weighing between 300 and 450 tons, with armament consisting of thirty to forty guns. Most of these vessels had previously been employed in the West African slave trade and were built for speed to ensure the survival of their "perishable" cargo. With such speed and armament pirate ships could easily overtake potential prizes or outrun most naval vessels.

The ships would carry the same sorts of victuals and personal items found on normal ships of the era. What might be missing are more mundane cargo items or other accoutrements. For example, modern Somali pirates often claim to be fishers; yet when searched their ships contain neither nets nor fish. Instead AK-47s, rocket-propelled grenades, Molotov cocktails, and ladders to scale the sides of container ships are found in plenty (Burnett 2002; Phillips with Talty 2010). Pirate ships, like naval vessels, had many different armaments with which to conduct their business. Merchant ships, if armed, would probably only carry a single size of weapon, for guns and ammunition took valuable cargo space. What might set pirate ships apart from regular naval ships was a lack of standardization in such weaponry.

With this evidence in hand Courtney Page and Charles R. Ewen (chapter 12) take the first step toward formulating a pattern for recognizing pirate-associated shipwrecks.

Victims and Smuggling

Contemporary historic accounts often lament pirate attacks on communities. For example, attacks against Santo Domingo in Hispaniola and St. Augustine in Florida in 1586 were attributed to "El Pirata Draque." In an age when nations lacked navies Francis Drake was a privateer (an official representative of England). Privateer Henry Morgan sacked Panama City a century later (Patel 2013). Evidence of these attacks is found as a burnt layer of building rubble in the sites. Frederick H. Hanselmann, Tomás Mendizábal, and Juan G. Martín (chapter 6) elaborate on the attack on Panama. Their work not only details the terrestrial evidence for the raid but also identifies a scatter of guns thought to be associated with Morgan's 1671 raid as part of the Río Chagres Maritime Cultural Landscape. After repeated attacks by pirates, privateers, and navies of all flags, elaborate fortifications were constructed in Spanish, Portuguese, French, Dutch, Danish, and English port towns.

Smuggling was another issue. The movement of unsanctioned goods is clearly not documented. Today drugs, art, exotic animals, and animal by-products move clandestinely through porous frontiers to buyers willing to pay a premium for such things. Smuggling is most visible archaeologically at the transshipment sites, where such items are lightered for easier moving. Once contraband moves into a community it can only be identified as an aspect of illicit trade if researchers have excellent control both spatially and temporally over the materials. What may be legitimate commerce one year may become illicit the next after the declaration of war or embargos. Thus the discovery in seventeenth-century St. Augustine, Florida, of ceramics made in France might be evidence of illicit trade. The same ceramics form eighteenth-century contexts are evidence for normal trade under the Bourbon kings of France and Spain (Skowronek 1992). Often some artifacts do not align with expected activities of such sites. Assessing the effect of pirates and smugglers is also problematic (Skowronek and Ewen 2006). Kathleen Deagan (chapter 11) revisits this issue and discusses how pirates and smugglers served as "providers" in Spanish St. Augustine.

Pirate Identity and the Archaeological Record

The pragmatic views of pirate ships, lairs, smuggling, victims, and their associated artifacts represent an opportunity to examine piracy and other illicit activities from an archaeological perspective. With this evidence in hand a return to the documentary record sheds further light on the lives of these remarkable persons. Heather Hatch (chapter 9) and Kenneth J. Kinkor (chapter 10) examine identity through varied iconography. Flags emblazoned with hearts, skulls, and hourglasses may represent Protestant/Puritan ideas relating to death. Spoons and plates engraved with blazing stars or compass and square design elements might represent Masonic symbols or simply the doodles of a bored sailor. Edward Kritzler's (2008) *Jewish Pirates of the Caribbean* suggests that in the future others may wish to search for "codes" representing other faiths.

The telling and retelling of stories can color the expectations of both the public and scholars. As a result archaeologists are often faced with a conundrum when asked by the general public to tell the "real" story of pirates. Some are captivated by popular tales, which have been repeatedly retold in books and films. The editors of this book consider images of piracy in fiction, history, and archaeology and how these stereotypes influence archaeological interpretation (chapter 8).

Toward an Archaeology of Piracy

Who were these people? Were they earlier versions of organized crime lords or drug smugglers? How would you recognize them? Do they have specialized clothing or technology that is different from that of their peers? Do they eat different foods or sail different ships? The answer is nuanced and requires drawing analogies from modern acts of illicit behavior. Pirates could be as invisible in their world as gangsters may be in our own. The most successful pirates are the ones that we do not know. They were never caught and lived out their lives in privacy as "legitimate" businesspeople. Their brotherhood was at once fearsome to outside authorities and friendly to their neighbors. Today archaeology is revealing patterns that illuminate the unrecorded world of the story of piracy.

Time and tide wait for no one. Let us now set sail to further explore the archaeological evidence of life in the world of pirates.

2

Blackbeard's *Queen Anne's Revenge* and Its French Connection

MARK U. WILDE-RAMSING
AND LINDA F. CARNES-MCNAUGHTON

Chapters 9 and 10 in *X Marks the Spot* (Wilde-Ramsing 2006; Lusardi 2006) reported evidence gathered during the early years of the *Queen Anne's Revenge* shipwreck project. The initial assessment of the shipwreck involved remote sensing instruments, exploratory trenching, and mapping of all exposed remains to attain a preliminary understanding of the extent and layout of the shipwreck. The initial retrieval of artifacts from 1997 to 2004 was limited to artifacts likely to reveal age, origin, or ownership, including several iron cannon from the ship. Artifacts were primarily recovered from test excavations and the emergency recovery of a portion of the ship's hull. By 2004 approximately twenty thousand individual items from the wreck site had been recovered, cleaned, and analyzed. The bulk of these items were lead shot or ballast stone. While this recovery and site examination gathered considerable data and several thousand artifacts, it was only a sampling (less than 3 percent of the total assemblage) that provided a limited view of site 31CR314 lying in Beaufort Inlet, North Carolina (figure 2.1).

At that time no definitive artifact had surfaced that positively identified the ship as *Queen Anne's Revenge*, which is still the case today. From its discovery, authorities have been careful not to declare that Blackbeard's flagship had been found; conversely, this supposition then became the investigation's working hypothesis (Wilde-Ramsing and Ewen 2012:112). While the shipwreck's identity was occasionally challenged (Cashion 1998; Rodgers et al. 2005; Lusardi 2006), these claims focused on the lack of conclusive evidence. There was, however, an even greater lack of contrary evidence upon which to reject the working hypothesis. Furthermore, no other candidate was found during extensive historical research that conformed

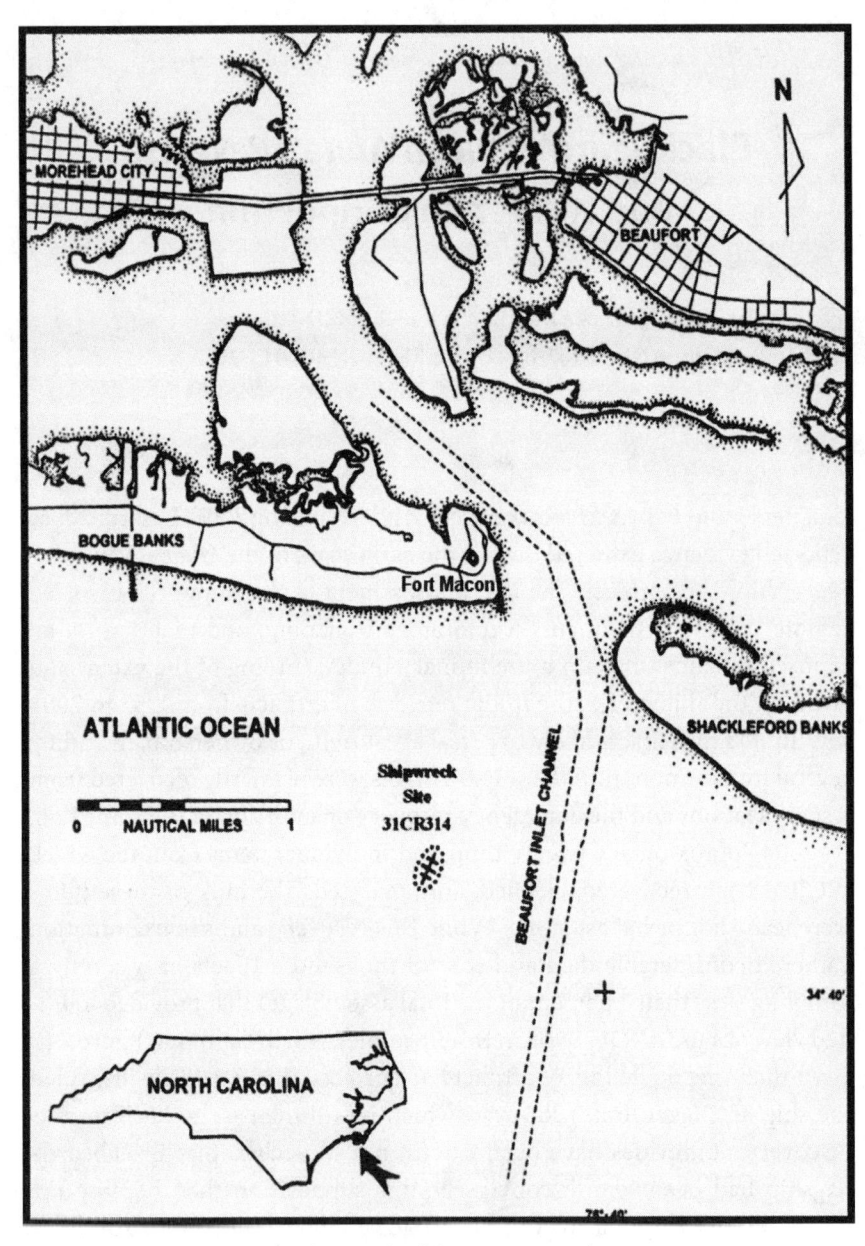

Figure 2.1. Location map for the wreck of the *Queen Anne's Revenge*.

to the basic characteristics of the Beaufort Inlet shipwreck, a heavily armed vessel dated to the first half of the eighteenth century.

What has changed since the essays were written for *X Marks the Spot* is the retrieval of a great deal more of the ship's remains and subsequent cultural and scientific analysis. The body of evidence at this time gathered from site 31CR314 demonstrates beyond reasonable doubt that it represents Blackbeard's flagship, *Queen Anne's Revenge* (*QAR*) (Wilde-Ramsing and Ewen 2012). Research contributing to this conclusion was mined from *QAR*'s rich maritime assemblage, now consisting of hundreds of thousands of individual artifacts. A wide spectrum of applied studies have focused on artifact and site attributes, both physical and cultural, which have a bearing on the shipwreck's age, size, national affiliation, function, and circumstance of loss.

It is our intention in the following pages to provide a historical briefing on the known service of *QAR* (formerly *La Concorde*), followed by a summary of archaeological investigations since 2005 and new evidence concerning the character of the vessel, its service period, and the activities of the crew. The research presented later in the chapter focuses primarily on the vessel's ties to France, for it is this cultural affiliation that not only most clearly supports *QAR* identity but provides a window into one of the most compelling aspects of the ship's history.

It is not a surprise that English pirates, only a few years removed from their sanctioned looting of French and Spanish vessels during Queen Anne's War, would choose to prey on the slave ship *La Concorde* out of Nantes, France. Perhaps it is also tenable that the pirates would conscript French sailors from their surrendered ship to supplement operations with their professional skills. Archaeological examination of the French goods might provide some sense of the English pirates' attitudes and treatment of the vessel and those that they forced to sail with them against their will. What French items did the pirates retain as part of the ship's property and what did they choose to discard and replace with their own? And what can we determine about the status of the French sailors: were they treated as prisoners or good company? After all, one of archaeology's greatest strength is to provide voices for disenfranchised and undocumented stories. Fortuitously, the low-impact grounding yet forced and rapid abandonment during the loss of *QAR* accentuates our ability to detect emotion and instinct (Wilde-Ramsing 2009:192–94). In this case, focusing on the French connection can reveal something about both captors and captives.

Historical Summary

The anatomy of a wooden ship, constructed of sawn planking, held together with fasteners of iron or wood, sealed with coatings of pitch and tar, motivated by a matrix of ropes, pulleys, and cleats, and propelled by pieces of sailcloth and the natural forces of wind and water, was a subject well known to sailors and pirates alike. As a means of transport wooden ships were considered vital elements of geographically dispersed social, political, and economic systems of the world for several centuries. Warships imposed political force; cargo vessels existed for commerce; and passenger ships reflected the social structure of the period. Nautical researchers have long considered the ship to be an operational system consisting of interrelated components made up of crew, equipment, passengers, and cargo. Once wrecked, the ship would yield clues about its function, its people, and the floating community that it contained (for example, Muckelroy 1978:215–25).

Throughout the seventeenth and eighteenth centuries many of these wooden ships were engaged in the transatlantic "Triangle of Trade," moving people, cargo, and cultures among the three primary destinations of Europe, Africa, and the Americas. Ships originating in Europe carried manufactured goods to exchange for human cargo in Africa and then moved the slaves along the "middle passage" into the Caribbean and northward to America, finally returning to Europe with products of the New World, such as sugar, rum, tobacco, and naval stores. *La Concorde* was one of these ships, a successful slaver that was later captured by pirates seeking plunder.

French historian Jacques Ducoin (2001) conducted archival research on a particular slave ship named *La Concorde de Nantes*. He summarized a compendium of French slave trade expeditions that described three separate voyages of *La Concorde*, compiled by Jean Mettas (1978:16, 37, 56). Originating out of the port of Nantes, the ship was acquired by René Montaudoin in 1710 and operated as a privateer vessel during the period of Queen Anne's War (figure 2.2). Ducoin's research also concluded that the same ship was used for the 1713 and 1715 voyages from France to Africa and Africa to the Caribbean islands. Thus it became fully immersed in the Triangle of Trade enterprises until its third voyage of 1717 (Dosset 1718; Ernaut 1718). Eyewitness accounts of the November 28, 1717, capture of this vessel by an English pirate identified by the French as Edouard Titche (also written Teach or Thatch, widely known as Blackbeard) were found in a letter from the "governor" of Martinique, Charles Mesnier (1717). Historical

Figure 2.2. French frigate circa 1700 (from Boudriot and Bertia 1993).

research also reveals that Blackbeard immediately renamed the stolen ship *Queen Anne's Revenge*, perhaps as a form of political satire intended to annoy the English queen's successor, King George I of Hanover (Butler 2000: 35).

For several months *QAR* served as Blackbeard's flagship, which he used to raid and plunder numerous ships throughout the Caribbean (Lawrence 2008). As the flotilla made its way up the Atlantic seaboard in the spring of 1718, the pirate captain boldly sealed off the British port of Charles Town (present-day Charleston), South Carolina, and for more than a week prevented shipping traffic from entering or leaving. During that time Blackbeard seized several vessels and detained a number of influential citizens, thereby provisioning his fleet with food, liquor, clothing stripped off their victims, and a large supply of medicine. In addition, the pirates took the collective sum "of about 1500 pounds of sterling, in gold and pieces of eight," nearly half a million U.S. dollars (South Carolina Court of Vice-Admiralty 1719:8).

As *Queen Anne's Revenge* approached Beaufort Inlet less than a week after leaving Charles Town, it was battle ready—a floating fortress armed with forty cannon and a force of at least 150 sailors, armed fighting men, and nonskilled laborers. Among the crew were fourteen Frenchmen from

La Concorde, ten of whom had been forced to join the pirates when Blackbeard took the ship because of their professional skills; the others apparently came along of their own volition.

About June 9, 1718, on its approach to Beaufort Inlet (formerly Topsail Inlet) and the village of Beaufort, the flagship was run aground on a submerged sandbar. Efforts to free it were exhausted within a few hours. Then a rescue vessel became stuck, and the call to "abandon ship" echoed across the water. From that moment, as crew and portable cargo were removed from the stricken vessel, the wooden ship began its final journey of transformation from the systemic world into the archaeological record. As strong inlet tides, steady offshore winds, and sinking sands continued for days and weeks, the ship was transformed into tattered sails, rotted timbers, and decomposing organics. As the wrecking process continued, the ship suffered many changes of state until the remains became completely submerged. Heavier objects sank rapidly, lighter objects drifted away, and others were snagged and buried, until eventually all elements had reached equilibrium with the underwater environment.

Archaeological Summary

Confronted with the challenges of sustainable funding and the ravages of coastal storms threatening to scour and disperse the remains of *Queen Anne's Revenge*, recoveries in May 2005 and May 2006 were carried out under the auspices of a stratified sampling program during which twenty-three test units were fully excavated (Wilde-Ramsing 2005). Within each of these 5 × 5 foot excavations, archaeologists mapped and recovered all visible artifacts and sampled and panned sediments for extremely small artifacts.

As funding improved and permanent staff was hired, the quest to complete total recovery of all *Queen Anne's Revenge* artifacts and their associated archaeological data began. Expeditions have taken place during fall months in 2006, 2007, 2008, 2010, 2011, and 2012. A total of forty weeks has been spent on site during this period, with the remainder of each year committed to cataloging and analyzing the recovered materials in the conservation laboratory. Excavation and recovery began at the offshore or south end of the wreckage, where archaeologists anticipated a distinct edge in artifact distribution because of the dominant seabed currents that constantly move sediment and artifacts shoreward. Continuing the 5 × 5 foot excavations, units were explored during stratified sampling, as excavations moved

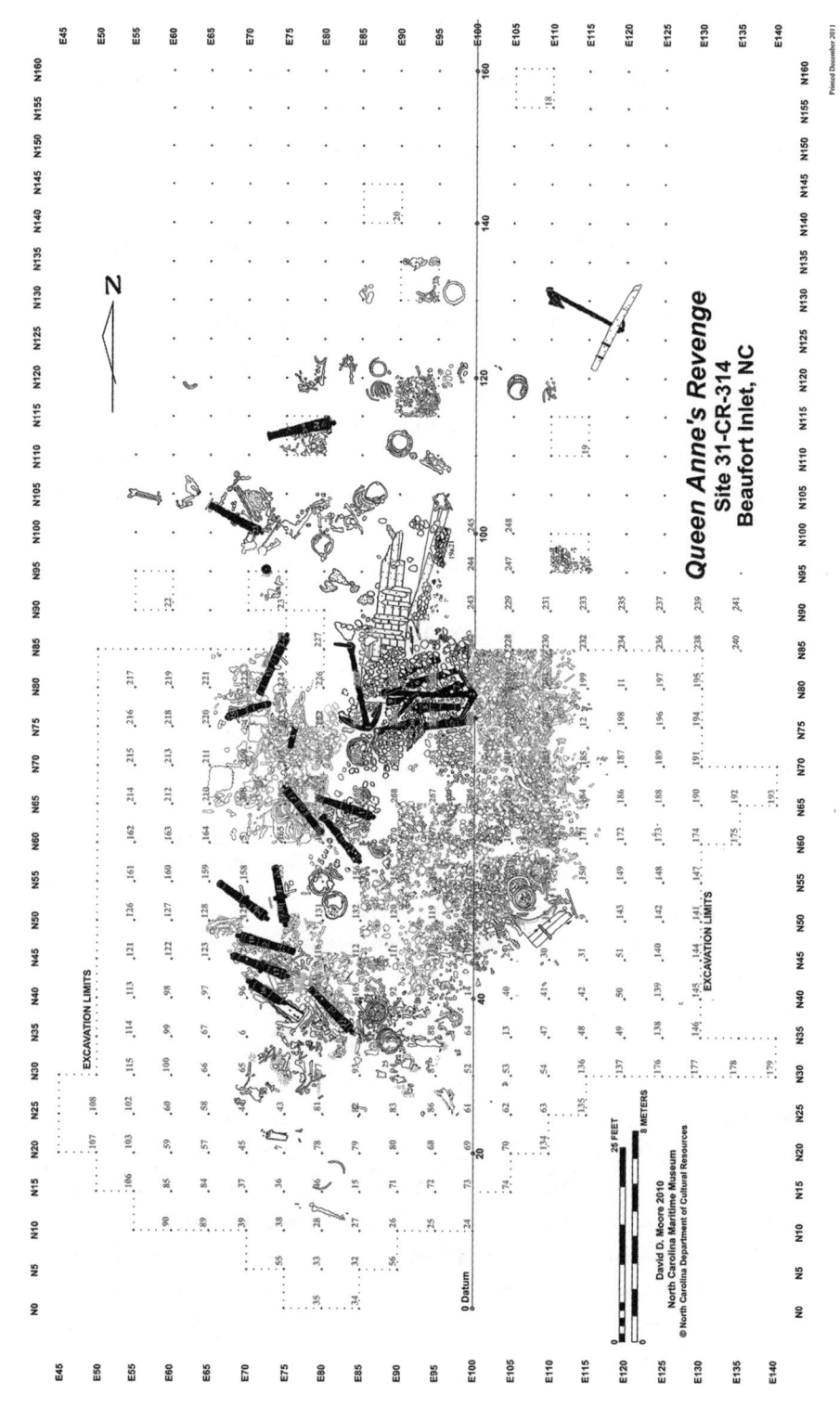

Figure 2.3. *Queen Anne's Revenge* site plan with excavation units.

shoreward and outward to the margins, where cultural materials waned to insignificant numbers. By the end of 2011 recovery passed the halfway point in terms of area covered and artifact recovery, with 224 units excavated (figure 2.3).

The cultural layer ranges in depth from several feet to a few inches below the seabed. As eighteenth-century materials are reached during excavations, archaeologists employ a 3-inch induction dredge system to bring all sediment surrounding and underlying artifacts to the deck of the recovery vessel, where the slurry flows over baffles of a gravity-fed sluice and into fine-mesh screens. After removing small artifacts from the sluice and screens, the remaining dredge spoils undergo further recovery by hand panning to retrieve microscopic evidence. This results in nearly complete recovery of shipwreck-related items, such as specks of gold, fragments of lead, and glass bead fragments.

Individual artifacts, groups of redundant artifacts, concretions, and unit sediments are tagged with identification numbers to denote their location on the site. Artifacts are immediately returned to water in temporary storage tanks until they can be transported to the *Queen Anne's Revenge* Conservation Laboratory on the campus of East Carolina University for permanent wet storage and eventually taken through the documentation, analysis, and conservation process.

The most intensive and expensive phase of the *QAR* project occurs after recovery because of the artifacts waterlogged and salt-impregnated condition. Making the conservator's task even more difficult, the majority of artifacts arriving at the laboratory are covered with a heavy layer of corrosion and marine growth known as concretion. While some artifacts can be identified protruding from the conglomerate, most can only be revealed through meticulous and labor-intensive cleaning. An important interim step is the use of X-radiography, which enables researchers to "see" inside concretions and identify lead shot, glass beads, nails, and other iron fittings, items of pewter and copper alloy, and gold flakes (Welsh and Wilde-Ramsing 2008) (figure 2.4). Based on X-rays and the physical cleaning of a sample of concretions recovered from *QAR*, each concretion is expected to produce an average of 100 individual artifacts (Southerly et al. 2007:10). The preliminary analysis has now allowed researchers access to 280,762 individual artifacts, which is a fourteen-fold increase over what was reported in the chapters in *X Marks the Spot* (Sarah Watkins-Kenney, personal communication, 2011).

Figure 2.4. Inspecting an X-ray image.

Summary of Findings

Historical accounts place the grounding of *Queen Anne's Revenge* on the outer bar of Beaufort Inlet. No navigational charts from the second decade of the eighteenth century are available to indicate exactly what channel alignment the pirates faced as they attempted to steer through the inlet. The Moseley (1733) and Wimble (1738) charts recorded not long after the event, however, provide an idea of possible channel alignments, with a general orientation entering the inlet from the southwest. The two historic charts are remarkably similar to highly accurate hydrographic maps recorded in 1911 and 1930 (figure 2.5). In both the eighteenth-century and twentieth-century map sets, the throat of the inlet remained stable while the channel alignment moved further west in time. When the *QAR* wreck site is placed on them, it shows that no matter which side of the channel the vessel grounded on, the location matches historical accounts reporting it stranded on the bar at the seaward entrance to historic Beaufort Inlet.

The wreckage of *Queen Anne's Revenge* lies between twenty-two and twenty-six feet deep today, although it likely grounded in nine to twelve feet of water based on the ship's estimated draft. Coastal geologists addressed this discrepancy by examining how energetic forces of the nearshore environment impact a ship's deterioration (McNinch et al. 2001; Trembanis and McNinch 2003; McNinch et al. 2005; McNinch et al. 2006). Using a time series of high-resolution bathymetric surveys coupled with data from an onsite current meter and previous research conducted on submerged mines for the military, a predictive scour-burial model for *QAR* was developed. In a scour-burial sequence, ships that sink onto unconsolidated seabed sediments, regardless of size, will begin to settle when they are subjected to sufficient bottom flow. The mechanism for their burial begins with increased undercutting of sediments on the lee side as they obstruct current flow. When flow is sufficient, scoured areas will become large and deep enough that the obstruction will settle into the depression. In doing so the wreckage becomes level with the seabed and no longer restricts current flow. After currents subside, sediments fall out of suspension and fill the scour pit to complete the burial cycle. The scour-burial sequence is repeated when current flow becomes strong enough to suspend sediments around ship remains, making them an obstruction again (Trembanis and McNinch 2003:4–5; McNinch et al. 2006:4–5).

Cartographic studies demonstrate that several times over the past three centuries the Beaufort Inlet channel migrated across the 31CR314

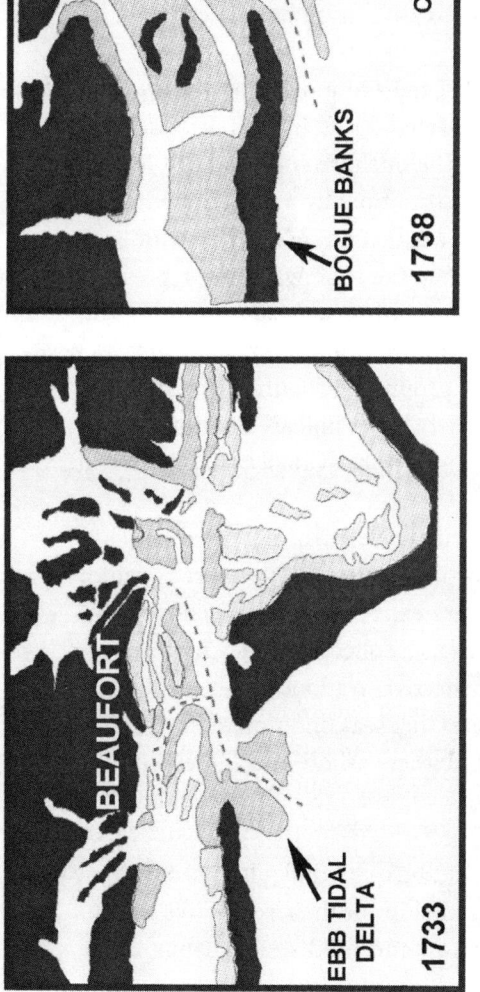

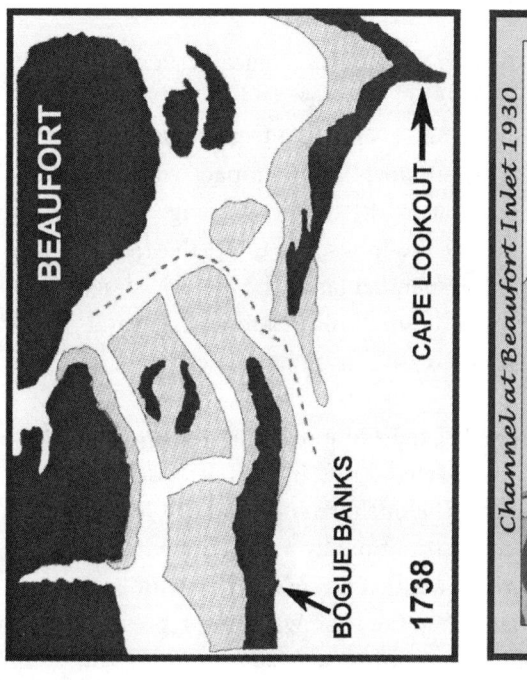

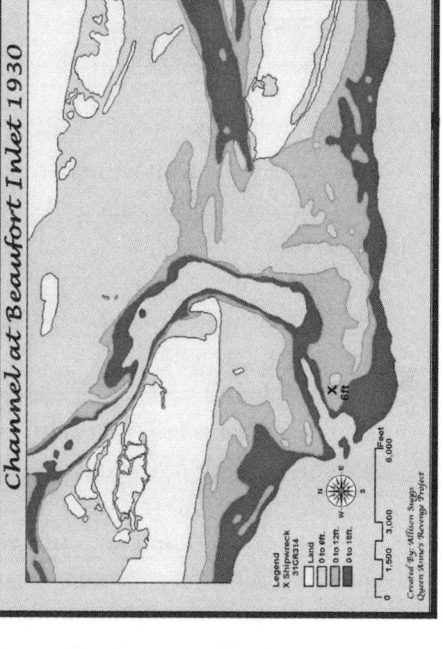

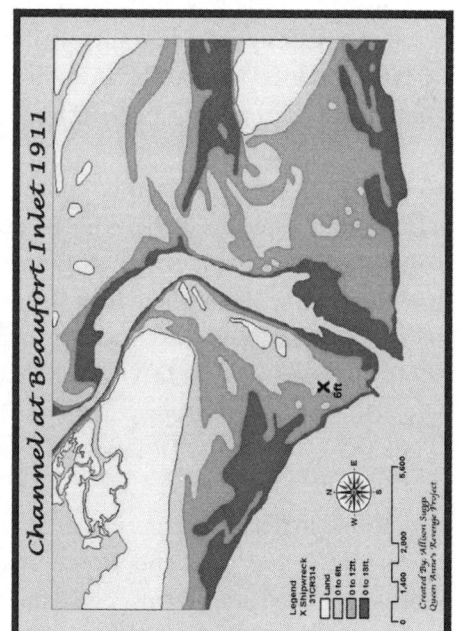

Figure 2.5. Compilation of alignment maps.

shipwreck, exposing it to intense tidal currents (Wells and McNinch 2001). When the inlet channel passed over the wreckage, seabed currents would have moved the remains below its grounding depth to the natural channel depth of twenty feet or deeper.

Magnetic gradiometer surveys together with archaeological test excavations determined that the *QAR* wreckage is contained within an area no more than two hundred feet in length and seventy-five feet across (Lawrence and Wilde-Ramsing 2001). This supports a low-impact wrecking event rather than a catastrophic loss that might scatter wreckage across great distances on the seafloor. Wreckage lies in a south to north orientation, parallel to the inlet channel and perpendicular to the historic shoal. This indicates that during loss the vessel did not broach and end up parallel to the beach, as would have been the case during heavy seas (Wilde-Ramsing and Ewen 2012).

Artifacts found within the confines of the site indicate that the vessel was pointed shoreward, as would be expected for an incoming vessel that miscalculated and hit the outer shoals. The offshore end has been identified as the vessel's stern based on items traditionally associated with the ship's officers, including pewterware, scientific and medical instruments, and gold dust. Conversely, a large anchor at the shoreward end represents the ship's main anchor, once located on the ship's starboard bow. Cannon lie in paired sets along the site's western edge, indicating that the vessel rolled onto its port side sometime after grounding (figure 2.6). Over fifty lead strips used to patch leaks in the vessel's lower hull are distributed longitudinally throughout the site, providing further evidence that the vessel deteriorated in place.

In all, 183 separate iron hoop fragments have been recovered, and another 18 complete sets have been recorded in situ. While there is minor debate about whether some of these were extra hoops in the cooper's inventory, a portion of them likely were in use; collectively they represent as many as 150 barrels and barriques (hogsheads) (Watkins-Kenney 2006:29–34). The presence of intact casks indicates that sea conditions at the time of wrecking were not strong enough to wash them ashore and agrees with the low-impact loss of *QAR* reported by eyewitnesses (South Carolina Court of Vice-Admiralty 1719).

While it has been argued that it would be quite difficult to separate an armed merchantman and a pirate-based ship on their respective assemblage of tools, equipment, personal items, and food stuffs (Babits 2001), some aspects of the assemblage recovered from *QAR* hint at a few possible

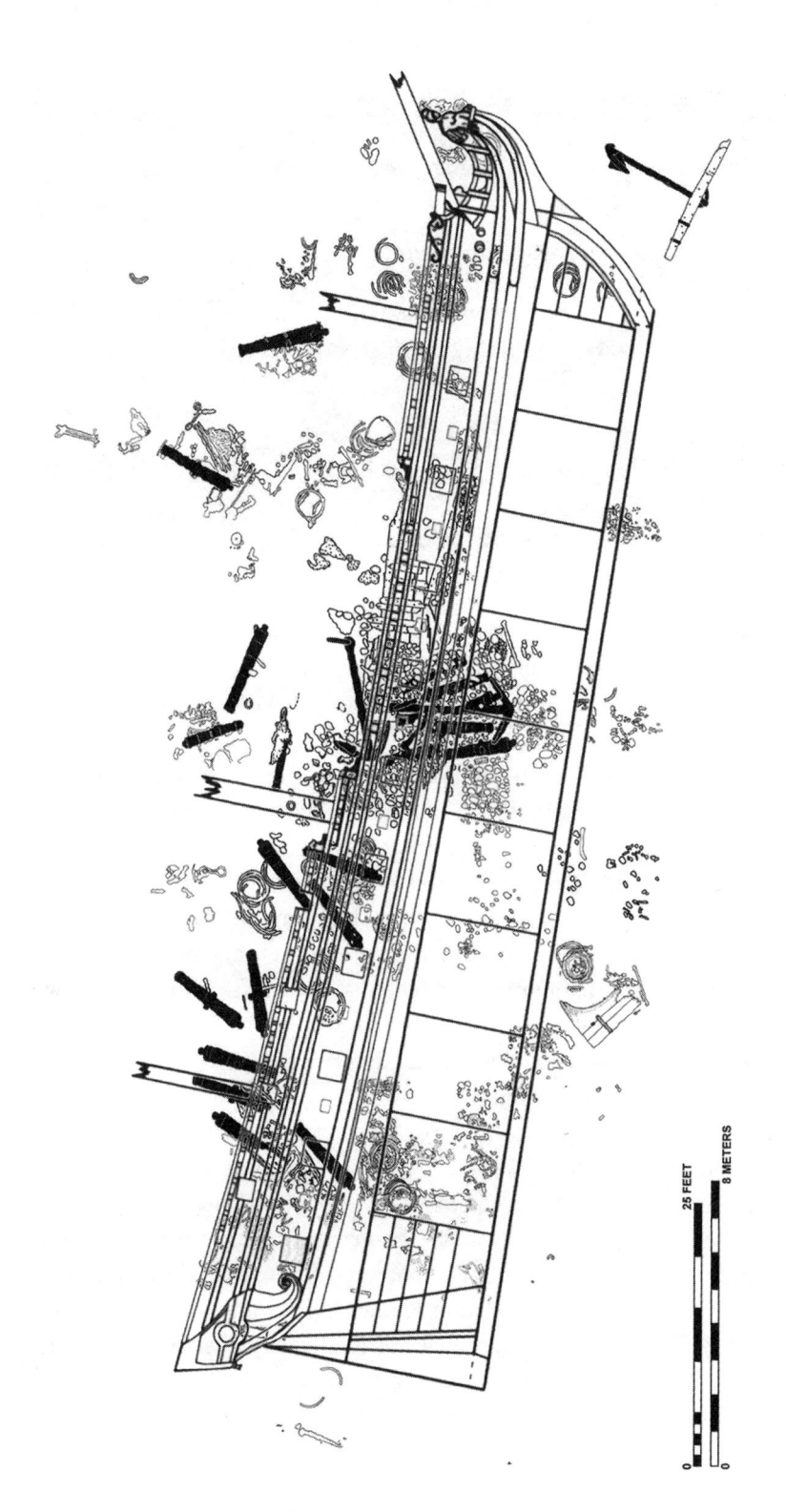

Figure 2.6. *Queen Anne's Revenge* site plan with overlay.

Figure 2.7. Swivel gun.

differences. The most compelling evidence involves the ship's armament and associated ammunition, which somewhat diverge from the military norm. Furthermore, such an armed vessel would have been out of place for the period in the nascent and militarily nonstrategic Carolina port of Beaufort, unless it is a pirate ship (Butler 2000:5). In the seventeenth and early eighteenth century colonial North Carolina was known as a pirate hideout because of its myriad of inlets and waterways, deep water harbors for careening vessels, and proximity to major shipping lanes (Butler 2000:26). The ship's iron cannon include seventeen six-pounders, four four-pounders, and five small carriage-mounted cannon. The only swivel-mounted gun is a brass cannon that may have served as the ship's signal gun (Brown 2007). Collectively the *QAR* assemblage conforms to the armament of a late seventeenth to early eighteenth century English sixth-rate ship or French light frigate (Henry 2009) (figure 2.7).

The five recovered and cleaned iron cannon were manufactured either in England or in Sweden (Henry 2009). Four were found loaded, indicating that the vessel was prepared for battle. Three contained a single round shot with wadding holding it in place and evidence of a powder charge at the breech. A fourth cannon, C-19, contained a bundle of three iron bolts placed in front of its shot and charge. Known as *langrage*, this was not standard naval practice but a contrivance commonly employed by pirates, privateers, and desperate merchantman (Falconer 1780:171). Several variations of bar-type shot, which are the more traditional projectile used to slash through rigging and sails, have also been recovered from the wreckage. The vast majority of the ninety loose cannon shot recovered so far, however, are solid iron balls corresponding in diameter and number to the *QAR* cannon, mostly six-pounders. The single exception is a 24-pound cannon ball that may represent a postwreck intrusion fired from nearby Fort Macon during the American Civil War (Henry 2008).

Radiography and concretion removal have revealed two iron breechblocks or chambers for swivel guns, known as slings or murderers (Brown 2009). Their use was common throughout the sixteenth, seventeenth, and early part of the eighteenth century. Although crude in appearance, these guns were sophisticated, sturdy, easy to make and use, and highly effective.

> The breechloading swivel gun's ability to be aimed and fired relatively rapidly and its small size made it the weapon *par excellence* for close range, anti-personnel fire in much the same way that the machine gun has been used since the beginning of the 20th century. It was used extensively on ships but was also found to be useful on fortifications and castles where it was ideal in close-fighting against boarders, or even mutinous crews. (Brown 2009:4)

When firing these guns, several breechblocks were made ready by filling them with powder and kept dry with wooden tompions until put into action. The cannon would have been loaded with different sorts of projectiles, sometimes single shot, but more likely "base and burr" or hail shot (Brown 2009: 5) (figure 2.8).

Lead shot is relatively abundant on *QAR*, with 220,000 individual pieces recovered so far for a total weight of 353.5 pounds. Unlike iron shot, which was distributed throughout the site and mirrored the position of cannon, lead shot appears to be concentrated in the vessel's stern, indicating the location of the ship's armory or gun room. Most numerous are "Rupert method" drop shot, which were manufactured by using a technique first reported in 1665 and continued until the invention of shot towers about 1769. Rupert shot are typically imperfect and thus more likely to be used as hail shot for personal arms such as blunderbusses or in cannon, as described above for breechloaders. Lead shot produced in two-part molds are also present in significant amounts and generally found in association with drop shot. Most of the molded shot have a diameter of less than 0.33 inches and are classified as buckshot, which is also intended for multiple shot loads or packed shot (Henry 2008). Historical accounts during Blackbeard's final battle reported that "Teach fired some small Guns, loaded with Swan shot, spick Nails, and pieces of old Iron, in upon Maynard, which

Figure 2.8. Breech block.

killed six of his Men and wounded ten" (Lee 1974). Canvas material has been found in association with lead shot, nails, and sherds of glass in *QAR* concretions and may represent cannon bag shot assembled for antipersonnel loads (Wilde-Ramsing 1998: 59). Such was the case on the 1717 pirate ship *Whydah*, which had a cannon loaded with two hemp bags containing lead shot (C. Hamilton 1992: 271–72).

Studying a large sample of recovered *QAR* ballast stones weighing a total of 2,703 pounds, geologists found them to be relatively homogeneous and evenly distributed across the site. Over 80 percent were of three major types: microporphyritic basalts, porphyritic volcanics, and hornblende gabbros (Callahan et al. 2001). Using the known travels of *La Concorde*, on both sides of the Atlantic, to examine the potential source(s) of ballast, only the islands of the Caribbean matched the age, composition, and variation of the rocks recovered from the *QAR* shipwreck. Specifically, the ballast assemblage appears to have originated from somewhere along the Lesser Antilles island chain between Hispaniola and Grenada (Miller et al. 2007). The French slave trading port of Martinique, *La Concorde*'s destination before being intercepted by pirates, lies in the middle of this area.

During the eighteenth-century slave trade, it was not uncommon to find the presence of beads and clay tobacco pipes on board a ship for use among the slaves during Middle Passage. Overseers and slave traders on board the ships offered men and boys tobacco pipes to smoke topside to enjoy after meals (or in place of meals). Thus these items, as a "reward incentive," served to assuage their feelings for manipulations by the traders and handlers and to placate the conditions of their enslavement and prepare them for Western culture and customs (Handler 2006). Seventeen white clay pipe fragments (bowls and stems) perhaps of English or Dutch origin have been recovered, though more appear now in concretions. Their presence on board ship testifies to the popularity of tobacco smoking as a nascent commodity during the early eighteenth century slave trade.

Only four beads were initially recovered through laboratory and sediment processing, but now hundreds of glass beads are being seen in X-rays, as they remain locked in concretions. Portable, desirable, and durable, beads find their way into many archaeological sites. So far all glass beads from *QAR* are small to medium in size. The predominant color for these tube-drawn glass beads is bright gold, most with a thick patina, matching Kidd and Kidd Type II a 19 (Kidd and Kidd 1982). A few opaque white beads have also shown up, along with a few black beads. Most of these beads date to the 1680s to 1780s period of manufacture, and all but the one described below are likely from Venetian or Dutch glasshouses.

One medium-sized bead of powdered glass construction, with an oversized central perforation, has been identified as African in origin. Under a microscope the matrix is granular and pale cream to yellow in color, although severely degraded (it was first identified as a wooden bead). This type of bead has been documented from African slave graves in New York, ca. 1690s–1710s (Bianco, DeCorse, and Howson 2006). The source is thought to be Ghana or the west coast of Africa.

Other evidence of the African slave trade has been found on *QAR*, documenting its initial use as a French slave trade vessel. Gold nuggets and gold dust have been recovered through sediment processing, and components of leg-shackles, called bilboes, provide more evidence of the ship's former enterprise. Two pieces of gold jewelry from the wreck not only testify to the presence of African gold ornaments but have been snipped into pieces, a common practice among pirates for dividing up the booty. The item on the left in figure 2.9 is a gold ring band, cast and carved in an ornate baroque or rococo pattern, and the item on the right is a piece of an Akan gold bead. Akan gold beads were and are still a national symbol of the Asante and Gold Coast populations of Africa. The gold dust recovered so far from *QAR* (less than an ounce in weight) is but a tiny portion of the twenty pounds

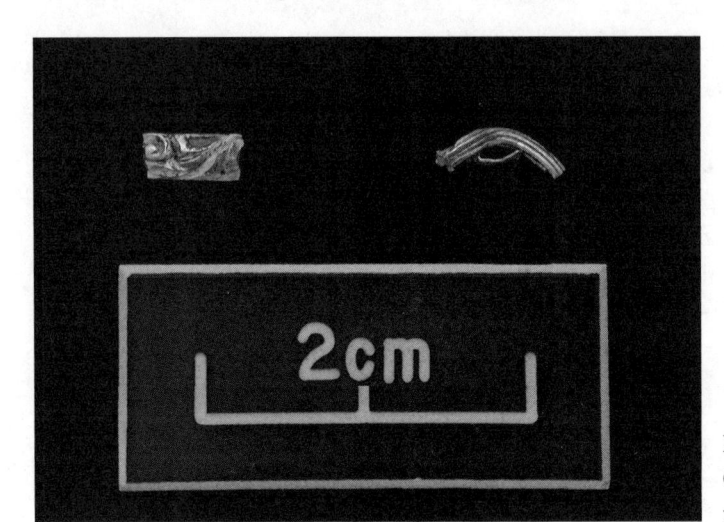

Figure 2.9. Gold jewelry pieces.

purported to have been on board the wreck prior to the grounding event on Beaufort Inlet, indicating that Blackbeard and his crew were able to remove most valuables in ample time.

With the exception of a few intrusive artifacts, the *Queen Anne's Revenge* artifact assemblage is made up of late seventeenth and early eighteenth century items. Key among them are relics with absolute dates: a bronze bell with "1705" cast in block numerals opposite the inscription "IHS Maria" (Wilde-Ramsing and Ewen 2012) and a Swedish cannon with the numerals "713" on its left trunnion, which represent its manufacture in 1713 (Brown and Smith 2005; Henry 2009:8–10).

Two other items, a coin weight and a coronation glass, tie vessel operations to the middle of the second decade of the eighteenth century. The coin weight, which was used to authenticate the weight of gold guinea coins, bears the bust of the English monarch Queen Anne. The weight was cast during her reign from 1702 to her death in 1714. The body portion of a molded stemware wine glass, embellished with embossed tiny crowns and diamonds, has also been found (figure 2.10). This unique piece was produced to commemorate Queen Anne's successor, King George I (of the House of Hanover), dates to ca. 1714, and likely served as a coronation souvenir (Carnes-McNaughton and Wilde-Ramsing 2008:13–14).

Many other items provide a general period for their manufacture. All five cannon and a blunderbuss barrel were made prior to 1718 (Henry 2009). This includes one iron six-pounder cannon with the numerals "173" crudely chiseled lengthwise along its breech. While this was once thought to be a possible date of 1730 or 1737 (Rodgers et al. 2005:30; Lusardi 2006:202), the angular, single cone shape and the more angular muzzle swell of cannon C3 indicate that this piece is a Swedish finbanker manufactured between 1675 and 1700. This implies that the numbers represent the cannon weight or identification mark rather than a manufacture date (Brown and Smith 2005).

Another class of well-represented artifacts is pewter flatware. At least thirty flatware plates, dishes, and chargers have been recovered and bear marks from four different London pewterers, all of whom were in business during the late seventeenth to the second quarter of the eighteenth century (Watkins-Kenney 2008). The earliest was John Stiles, who began in 1689 and remained in business until ca. 1730. The most recent was Timothy Fly, with his mark registered from 1712 to 1736. The others were Henry Sewdley from 1709 to ca. 1739 and George Hammond from 1695 to ca. 1709 (Watkins-Kenney 2008). A pewter spoon exhibits the distinct style (curved handle end with a raised pip on the top and abbreviated rat-tail handle terminal on the underside of the bowl) attributed to the House of Hanover

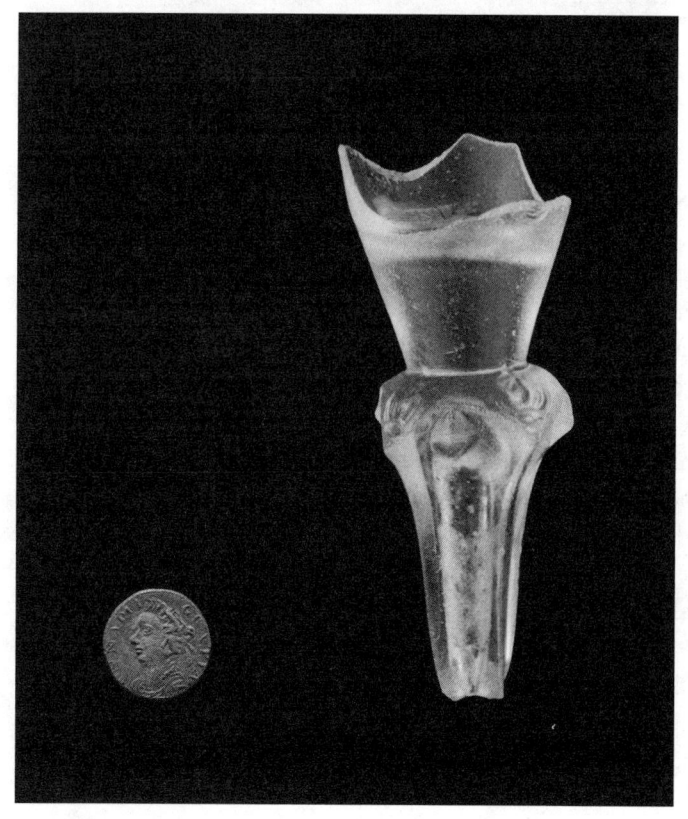

Figure 2.10. Coin weight and stemware.

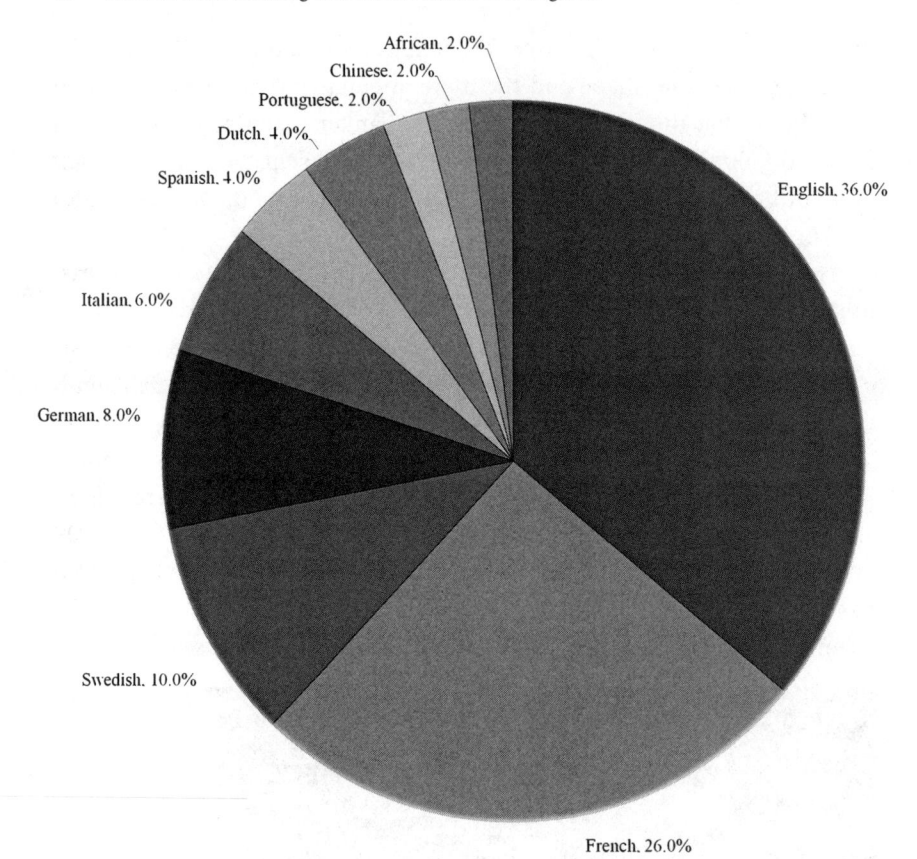

Figure 2.11. Global origins pie chart.

and dates from 1710 to 1730 (Carnes-McNaughton 2008). A silver handle from a large basting spoon, ironically shaped like a cannon tube, was found among the wreckage. It is missing its bowl portion, but this style of spoon dates from the late 1690s to the 1710s (Moore 1987:24; Snodin 1982:35).

The remaining dates of manufacture come from a collection of ceramic vessels, glass bottles, tobacco pipes, and clothing items. Several intact squat wine bottles date from the 1690s to the 1710s, with one example matching the profile of a "body sagging down on itself and the base spreading, a profile ungallantly known . . . as the Queen Anne shape" (Noel Hume 1969:64, 68, 1970:33). Various features exhibited on seventeen clay tobacco pipe fragments, including hole diameter, bowl design, and spur characteristics, place their manufacture from 1680 to 1750, with a mean date of 1711 (Carnes-McNaughton 2007b). Carnes-McNaughton (2007a) has identified several datable clothing items. Two different styles of shoe buckles, one of silver and the other a copper alloy, were made from 1690 to 1720. A two-piece brass button can be assigned to the period ca. 1700 to 1720.

Collectively, manufacturing dates from forty-five individual or classes of artifacts show that none began production after *QAR*'s sinking in 1718 and provide a mean date of 1708. Artifact use-life would have varied depending on durability and composition of the artifact. For instance, ceramic tableware would last a few years (Miller 2000:1), while pewterwares might remain viable for several decades (Hornsby et al. 1989). Viewing the datable assemblage as a whole, it is reasonable to conclude that *QAR* was lost within a decade or so of the mean artifact date 1708 and shortly after 1713 to 1715, based on cannon C-19 and the King George I coronation glass of 1714.

Not surprisingly, artifacts found on the early eighteenth century vessel in Beaufort Inlet represent a variety of international sources, including English, German, Chinese, Caribbean, Italian, Spanish, Swedish, African, Dutch, and French. As noted, among the items so far analyzed are wine bottles, glassware, tobacco pipes, coin weights, small weapons, silver spoons, and pewter platters from England, silver coins and olive jars from Spain, salt-glazed stoneware jugs from Germany, oil jars and glass beads from Italy, hand-painted porcelain from China, cannon from Sweden, and powdered beads, gold dust, and jewelry from Africa. Identifiable artifacts from *QAR* most frequently represent England and France as manufacturing centers (figure 2.11).

The French Connection

At the time the *X Marks the Spot* essays were written only one artifact, a urethral syringe, had been positively identified as French based on its manufacturing mark (Lusardi 2006). It was felt that the link to French artifacts would be key evidence conclusively connecting the Beaufort Inlet wreckage to *Queen Anne's Revenge* due to its former service as the French privateer and slave ship *La Concorde*. With only a single item to show, Lusardi (2006:217) used the lack of evidence to state: "It seems improbable that of the thousands of artifacts recovered from a French slaver, only one single item can be definitively identified as being French." Over the past five years the recovery of more evidence and a higher level of analysis have now revealed a strong French connection.

At present approximately 26 percent of the artifacts analyzed indicate a French origin of manufacture. The following discussion specifically focuses on ties to France, for it is this cultural affiliation that not only most clearly supports the vessel's identity but also provides a glimpse into how the English pirates viewed their newly captured ship and its conscripts. Augmenting the historical research done by Ducoin and others, an examination of these French connections is laid out here, beginning with the ship's structural elements and then highlighting galley goods, medical equipage, small weapons, and personal gear.

This evidence is illuminated by the low impact of the wrecking event, which presented minimal risk of personal injury or danger to the pirates once on board the ship but some urgency to escape while the opportunity was at hand. Under these circumstances it appears that as the pirates abandoned their ship they carried off accessible items that they deemed useful, such as small weapons, personal gear, tools, and valuables. The French may have been less able or willing to take their personal goods with them as they headed into unknown territory.

The Ship

The time and place of *La Concorde*'s specific construction still remains unknown. The vessel first appears on July 21, 1710, as a French frigate of 300 tons, armed with twenty-six cannon, owned by the prominent Nantes businessman René Montaudoin. The Montaudoin family was heavily invested in ships that were engaged in the slave trade throughout the eighteenth century and also sponsored privateering vessels during Queen Anne's War (Burgot 2008). The conversion from privateer to armed merchantman, as occurred in the case of *La Concorde* and other Montaudoin-owned ships, demonstrates the fine line between privateering and transporting enslaved Africans to the New World, both of which required vessels that balanced size, speed, power, and crew size.

While the origins of most ships owned by René Montaudoin are known through government documents (as stated above), this is not the case for *La Concorde*. Critical government records that might have shed light on where Montaudoin first obtained the ship have not been located (Ducoin 2001:18). Three possible origins for *La Concorde*'s construction have been proposed and are considered here: (1) a naval vessel; (2) a foreign prize captured by French privateers; or (3) a merchantman built locally (Ducoin 2001). Ducoin considers the third option to be most probable: *La Concorde* was built at commercial yards for service as a French privateer. Purpose-built French frigates were of light construction and designed for speed (Ducoin 2001:16–17).

What remains of the *QAR* hull lies pinned under a concentration of ballast, cannon, and anchors and consists of frames (futtock and/or floors), thick hull planking, and thin outer planks that served as sacrificial sheathing to protect the ship from marine fouling and shipworm damage. It is unclear whether the hull section, relatively flat in profile and missing characteristic features such as keel/keelson portions or evidence of gun ports, represents the vessel's bottom or side (Moore 2001:49). While appearing nondiagnostic, the dimensions of the timbers and their fastening pattern provide pertinent clues regarding the vessel's size, build, and place of construction. The twenty-four frame components represent eleven pairs (of futtock/futtock or floor/futtock), with individual timbers averaging seven inches sided and ca. eight inches molded with room and space measuring approximately twenty-two inches. Hull planks range in width from 10.25 inches to 13.75 inches and exhibit a relatively uniform thickness of 2.75 inches. Planks were fastened with a combination of one iron spike and one wooden treenail per frame. This fastening pattern may distinguish construction by French shipwrights rather than those in England, based on late seventeenth and early eighteenth century shipbuilding practices (Moore 2001:54). Newsom and Miller (2009:5-6) identified the wood used for construction as a type of oak "conforming closely to European species and some elements as Scotch pine, a species common in Scandinavia."

The frame size, along with recorded room and space relative to the thickness of the bottom planking, represents a relatively lightly built vessel (Moore 2001: 62). These construction features are consistent with characteristics reported for the French frigate *La Concorde*. The ship was reportedly part of a class of vessels that measured less than 100 feet in length with a breadth of 28 feet, displaced 270 tons, and was armed with twenty-five to thirty guns (Boudriot and Bertia 1993:52–53).

Brought to the surface in 2007, the lower section of the ship's stern is a large composite piece made up of the sternpost, which held the rudder and the stern knee that once joined it to the keel. On one side near the lower gudgeon strap are two deeply carved draft marks and the lowest depth mark, "VI" (figure 2.12). The measured distance between the two incised marks is 12.79 inches, which matches the traditional French foot (*pied*), instead of an English/Dutch foot of 12 inches or the Spanish foot (*pie*) of 10.97 inches. This further supports the vessel's French construction.

A bronze bell was one of the first items brought up on the day of discovery. As previously described, it has the date "1705" cast in block numerals

Figure 2.12. Stern post with draft marks.

opposite the inscription "IHS Maria" (figure 2.13). It may be the ship's main bell, yet disappointingly was not engraved with the ship's name, *La Concorde*. The religious inscriptions "IHS" and "Maria," however, were typical for French bells of the early eighteenth century. A smaller brass bell without markings was retrieved more recently from the stern section and likely served as the watch bell (Wilde-Ramsing and Wilde-Ramsing 2008: 27).

Architectural items such as window glass have also been recovered. These glass panes, made using the blown or crown method, exhibit the distinctive central bull's-eye or pontil scar. Each pane measures approximately four inches in width, but the length remains undetermined because of breakage. Finished edges were purposefully snipped. Lead caming, also found on the wreck site, was used to hold these individual panes into a window frame, providing light in the captain's quarters or stern section of the ship. Invented in the Rouen region of France in the early fourteenth century, this technique later spread across Western Europe (found in York

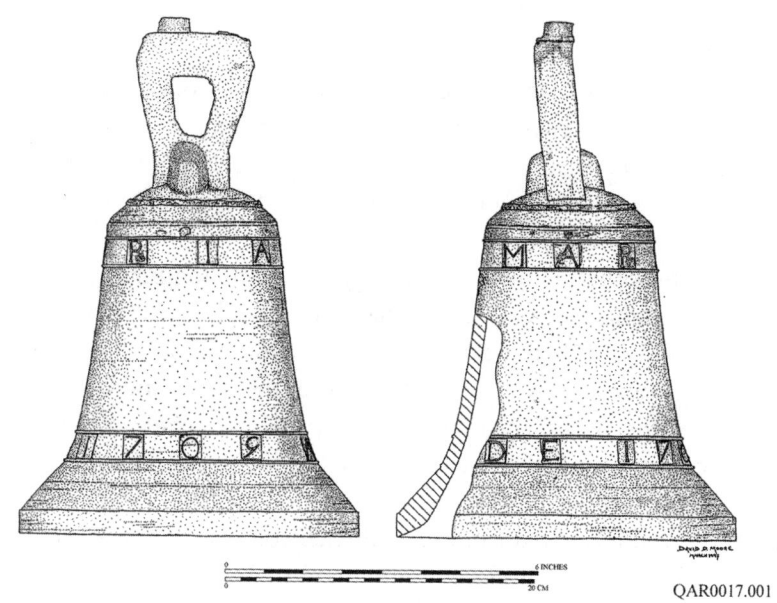

Figure 2.13. Drawing of bell.

as early as the fifteenth century). The color and composition of these glass panes, a unique blue-green, match a collection of French flacon bottles also found in the wreckage, strongly suggesting the same region of wood-fired furnaces of Gresigne in Languedoc or the crown glass factories of Normandy (Carnes-McNaughton and Wilde-Ramsing 2008) (figure 2.14).

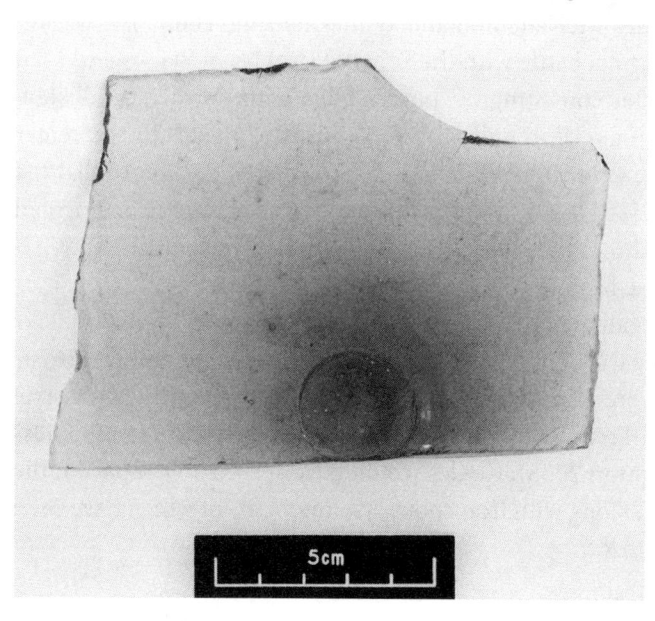

Figure 2.14. Windowpane from *Queen Anne's Revenge*.

Vessel Operations

A second class of artifacts relate to vessel operations or communal crew activities. Those of French manufacture represent items that were probably part of *La Concorde*'s accoutrements that were not discarded after the English pirates took over operations but most likely continued in use to support everyday shipboard activities.

In tandem with the French window glass, the predominant bottle type found in the archaeological record is flacon case bottles also manufactured in France from ca. 1710 to 1750 (Carnes-McNaughton and Wilde-Ramsing 2008:3–7). The distinctive blue-green color of the panes and bottles, represented by lips, necks, square bases, and panels, results from a mixture of sand, calcium, and alkali flux, produced in the wood-fired furnaces of glasshouses in Languedoc, France. Examples of whole bottles of the same type have been recovered from early French colonial land sites in North America (for example, Trudeau, Louisiana; Fort Michilimackinac, Michigan; and Louisbourg, Nova Scotia) and in other eighteenth-century shipwrecks (such as the *Machault*). The Louisbourg inventories record *flacons* as most often containing oil (*buille*), perhaps reflecting their original use. An examination of bottle contents and legible labels recovered during Louisbourg excavations indicates contents other than oil. *Flacons* also held a variety of liquids representing laboratory, apothecary, and household products as well as toilet water, perfumes, and occasionally spirits (Harris 2000:241; Carnes-McNaughton and Wilde-Ramsing 2008:7). It was reported that in his final battle with the British Royal Navy Blackbeard used handmade grenades consisting of "bottles filled with powder, small shot, and pieces of iron and lead and ignited by fuses worked into the center of the bottle" (Lee 1974:116). While there is no concrete evidence that the numerous quart-sized *flacons* were used in this same manner, documented evidence clearly shows that Blackbeard had the knowledge and materials to produce and use Molotov cocktails for combat purposes.

Among other galley goods found were copper kettles used for cooking communal meals. Copper rivets used for kettle patches and fragments of a lug handle were also found. Comparative analysis indicates the style of kettle used on French colonial sites of the same period (1680–1700s) (Carnes-McNaughton 2008). Kettles would have served a vital part in the cook's equipment, along with iron cookpots, fragments of which have been recovered from *QAR*.

Carnes-McNaughton (2008) identified evidence of large storage jars similar to an intact example found on the 1717 French shipwreck at St. Malos (*Natierre*) that would also have been used to haul food items aboard large ships and may have served as onboard cisterns in the galley. More than fifty fragments of a single oil jar have been recovered on the *QAR* site. This large earthenware jar, lead-glazed on the interior and unglazed on the exterior, is estimated to be about twenty-four inches high and twelve inches in diameter. Possible sources of these large jars are the Bito region of France and Montelupo region of Italy. A few sherds exhibit the telltale signs of white paint on the exterior surface. These markings have been interpreted as a pattern painted on the jar in preparation for a raffia grass or woven harness to facilitate easier handling or hauling once the jars were filled with liquid and were heavy (figure 2.15).

Although common sailors, crew, and pirates would likely have dined on wooden plates/bowls or treenwares, or perhaps even on pewter plates, a few specialized tablewares may have been reserved for captains or elite guests, such as the French surgeons. A bowl rim of green-glazed earthenware found on the wreck was made in the Saintonge region of France, from the 1700s to the 1750s. Intact examples found on land sites (such as Old Mobile, Trudeau, and Louisbourg) provide useful comparative data. Also found were sherds of another type of Saintonge lead-glazed earthenware dish representing a second piece of tableware (figure 2.16). This small eating plate was coated with a green (copper oxide) glaze over a white slip on the upper surface and unglazed on the bottom. Similar eating plates have been found in Old Mobile, a French colonial town. The newest vessel is a piece of slip-trail decorated lead-glazed earthenware found on *QAR* in 2010. It is represented by a rim sherd from a bowl and exhibits a unique "circle and dot" decorative motif, made in the Saintonge region. One whole example was found at the Trudeau Site in Louisiana. The "circle and dot" design was popular in France during the 1680s to early 1700s and is not often found on American sites. Another tiny sherd of earthenware from the site exhibited a polychrome slip of marbled design on what may be a bowl interior. A similar bowl found at the Trudeau site provided useful comparative data; but, given the small size of the sherd, the French origin of this ceramic dish remains speculative. These four vessels represent distinct consumption behaviors most likely associated with a French table (Carnes-McNaughton 2008).

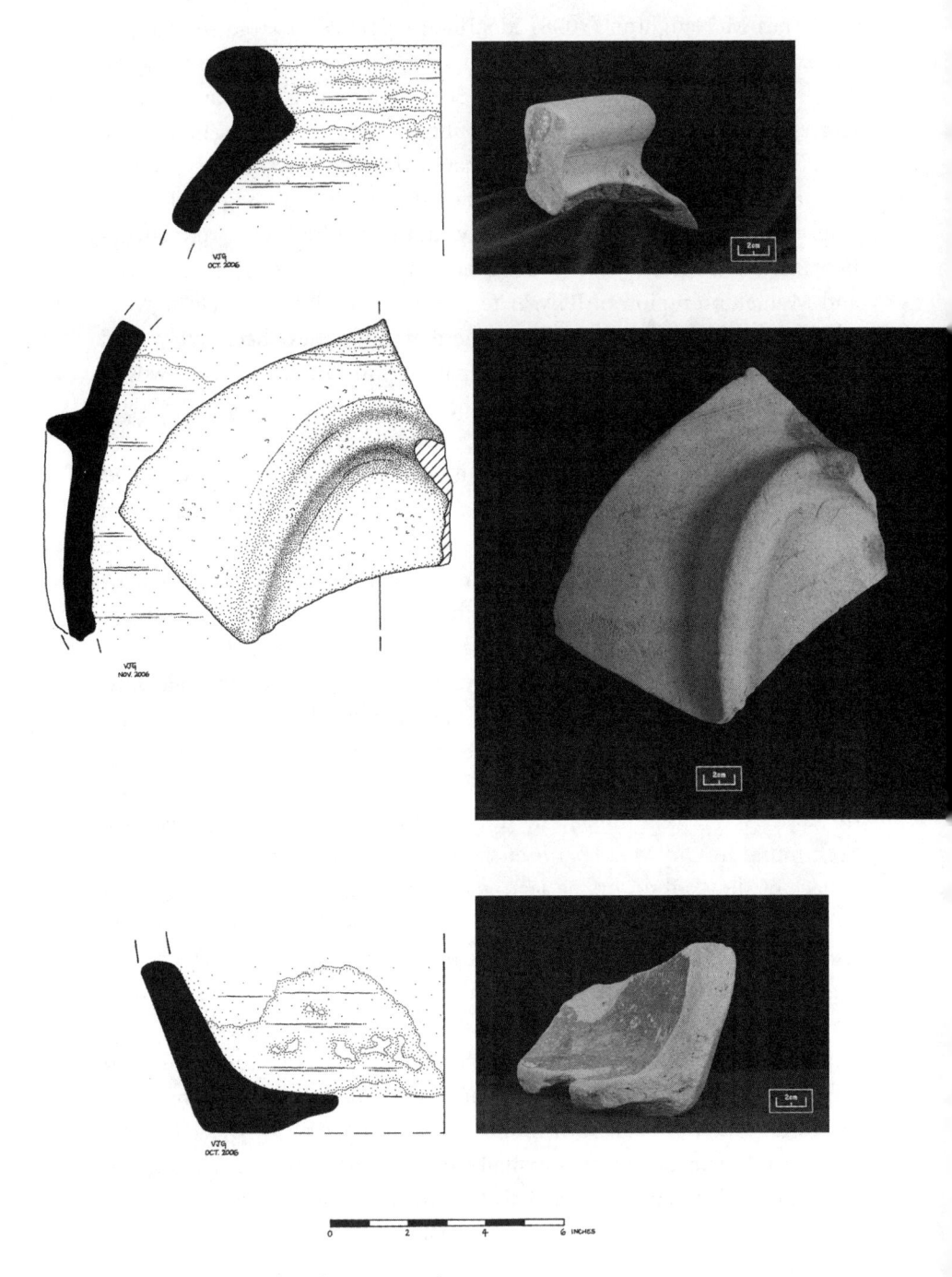

Figure 2.15. Drawings of storage jar elements.

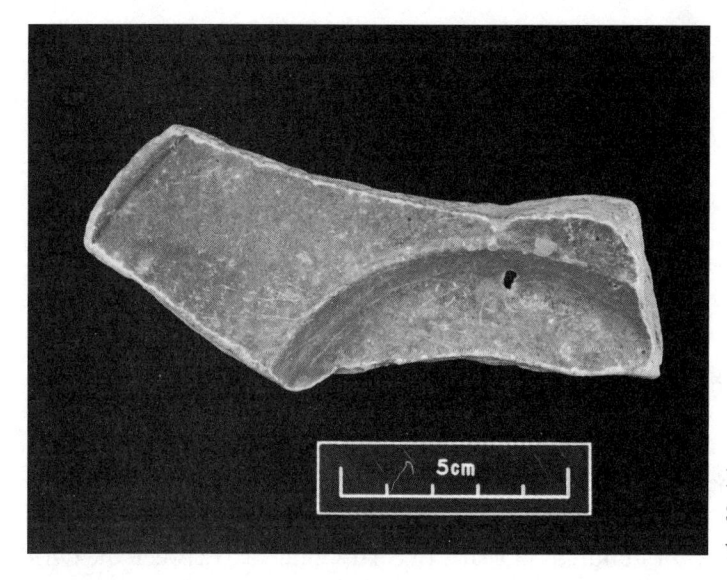

Figure 2.16. Saintonge vessel sherd.

Professional Tools and Instruments

One of the most significant groups of items coming off *QAR* relates to the surgeon's kit and the medicine chest, requisites for any oceangoing operation. The duty of the surgeon was to administer to the wounded, infirmed, and diseased, whether they be captains, crew members, or cargo, in the case of slave ships. The number of surgeons placed on ships depended on the number of persons to treat and duration of the voyage. The medicine chests were well stocked with drugs, ointments, medicaments, and instruments for treating sick persons (according to *The Sea-Man's Vade Mecum* 1707). The surgeon was not to leave the vessel in which he was engaged before the voyage was completed, under pain of loss of his wages or heavy fines. Typical ailments for the sailors (pirates or otherwise) were fevers, sunburns, boils, itch, gout, gripes, flux, pox, stones, consumption, infections, wounds, and the ever-present "foul disease." Treatments included all extremes, from bleeding and amputations to topical or digestive treatments for minor afflictions. Ceramic galley pots filled with unguents, salves, balms, and potions were on board. Glass bottles filled with liquid libations or digestion tonics filled the medicine chest. Tools included lancets for bleeding, porringers for bleeding basins, glass cups, clysters, syringes, saws, picks, surgical knives, pliers, forceps, probes, extractors, needles, guts for suturing, and straps. To grind or crush compounds or ingredients needed for medicines, a mortar and pestle were essential. Some set of scale weights would have been included in the surgeon's gear to measure out concoctions and medicines. After 1717 the ship's surgery may also have included a screw tourniquet invented by French surgeon Jean-Louis Petit, used to stem the bleeding during amputations (from Pirates of the Caribbean 2011). Numerous items related to the surgeon's equipage and medicines have so far been found on QAR.

One of the ceramic vessels found in the archaeological record is represented by four pieces of a tin-enameled pink-bodied earthenware apothecary jar or galley pot, fitted together. Jars of this type were used for the storage of ointments, unguents, or other medicinal compounds. The pinkish paste and general shape of this pot suggest a French origin, dating from about 1700 to 1750.

Nearby, in the stern of the vessel's wreckage, parts of two pewter clysters were found during the excavations. A clyster is a large pump syringe used to administer medical enemas to the afflicted, as documented through many cultures for hundreds of years. In correspondence between the QAR conservators and scholars of French pewter, several interesting and datable manufacturing marks have been identified. Philippe Boucaud (2010) identified a cylinder mark on one clyster as being made in Rouen in the year 1698. The second mark on this piece represents a duck and is symbolic of the Canu family of pewterers, who operated between 1659 and 1701. *Canu* (cane) became a phonic joke on the French word for duck (*canard*): hence the mark (figure 2.17).

Early in the excavations a pewter urethral syringe was found. The mark was identified as a Paris trademark and first reported in *X Marks the Spot* (Lusardi 2006: 209). The angled funnel or nozzle and distinct maker's mark on the plunger point to St. Laurent Chatelain (a saint who was grilled and martyred, thus the grated icon). The date of manufacture is 1707. Traces of mercury have also been detected through chemical analysis of this artifact; mercury was a popular treatment for venereal diseases, common among sailors and pirates alike. Interestingly, syphilis was also called the foul disease but was called the French disease by the British and the Italian disease by the French during the eighteenth century. At that time doctors believed that gonorrhea and syphilis were the same illness, with the former being an early stage of the latter. In any case, the foul disease was a very real life threat to pirate crews. This fact alone may be the reason why Blackbeard kidnapped and held for ransom members of Charleston's important families to swap for needed medical supplies for his crew members and why he kept the three French surgeons as hostages after his takeover of *La Concorde*.

Figure 2.17. Clyster and marks.

An intact mortar and pestle, the apothecary's essential tools, were recovered from the *QAR* wreckage in the mid-ship area (figure 2.18). This cast brass tool set was used to grind ingredients and prepare compounds for treatment of the ill and afflicted. The mortar measures four inches tall and five inches in diameter. No manufacturing marks provide an origin for these two pieces of medical equipment.

Adding to the surgeon's kit were two sets of nested weights commonly used by medical practitioners, chemists, and merchants to measure medicine, compounds, and sometimes precious metals. The principle behind these weight sets was the compact assemblage of graduated cups fitted tightly into each other, with the largest "master cup" forming the outer base and often having a hinged lid to keep other cups intact. The weight of the largest cup is equal to the sum of all the other smaller cups; and the weight of the second largest cup equals the sum of all the smaller cups. The graduated weight-system continues in descending order for each subsequent cup down to the final weight, which is a disc. One set of three cups was found and then later a nearly complete set of seven cups. Historian Diana Crawford-Hitchins with the *Mary Rose* shipwreck project, in her

46 · Mark U. Wilde-Ramsing and Linda F. Carnes-McNaughton

Figure 2.18. Mortar and pestle.

correspondence with *QAR* conservator Wendy Welsh, has commented on the maker's marks found in this second set. Numbers 1, 2, 4, and 8 appear on the interior base of these cups, along with one or multiple fleur-de-lis (flower of the lily) stamps. Fleur-de-lis are cultural symbols with several origins (the symbol of Christ and the Trinity as seen in fifteenth-century stained glass windows of Belgium and heraldic shields of the Middle Ages or the sign of an iris as seen in Florence, Italy). The fleur-de-lis has come to be associated primarily with French culture since the thirteenth century. Welsh's research also located a set of similar weights found on the shipwreck the *Maidstone* (Maisonneuve 1991). Further research on the weights suggests that the touchmark on the master cup consisting of a shield and central dot flanked by the initials "N" and "C" represents the town of Montpelier, France, as the manufacturing source (figure 2.19). Bruno Kisch's encyclopedic volume on *Scales and Weights* (1965:155–59) illustrates French weights of round shape with marked denominations of 8, 4, 2, and 1, with a shield and dot touchmark accompanied by fleur-de-lis stamps as being made in Montpelier since the 1600s.

Blackbeard's *Queen Anne's Revenge* and Its French Connection · 47

During the 2011 field season, a flat disc-shaped lid for a set of nested weights was found and may match this set. Hinge and fitting elements found in earlier excavations may also be part of this set, as well as a cast brass finial of a small cockerel (figure 2.20). The cockerel, which possesses multicultural symbolisms, has become the nationalistic symbol of France, formerly known as the country of Gaul (as a play on *Gallus gallus*, the rooster genus and species name). Without a pronounced comb, this brass cockerel could prove to be a hen, suitable for sitting atop a set of nested weights.

A crushed pewter porringer, possibly used for medical purposes, was recently recovered in the excavations. Once cleaned, it yielded important data on manufacturing and its country of origin. Original decorative morphology of this double-handled bowl was suggested by the cable-like motif

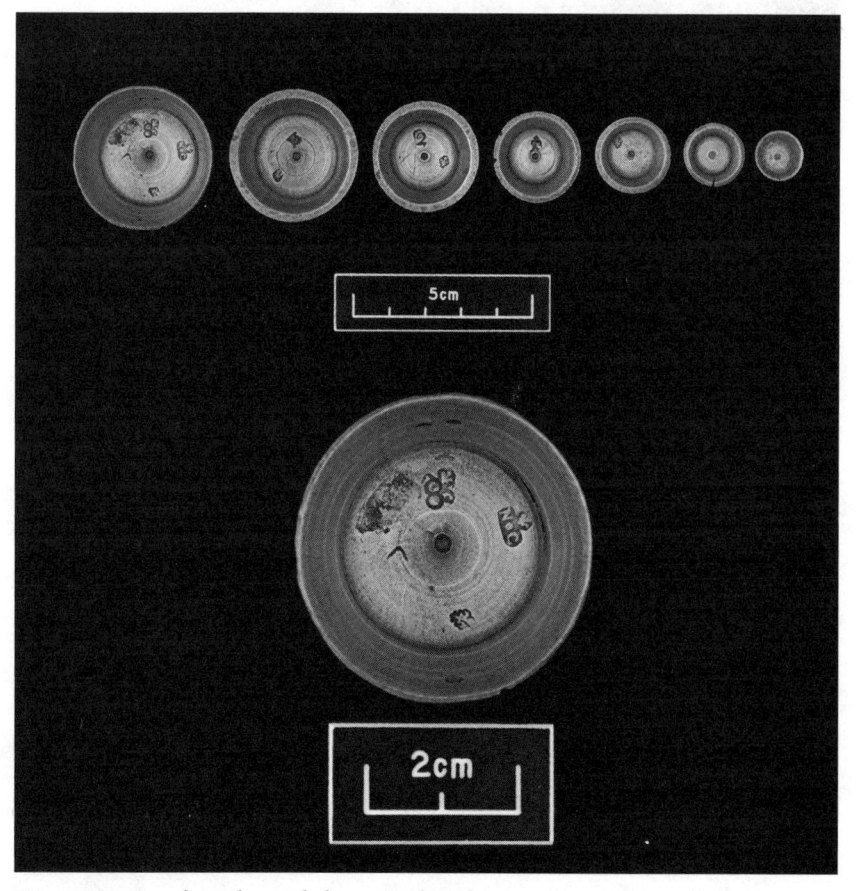

Figure 2.19. Set of weights and close-up of marks.

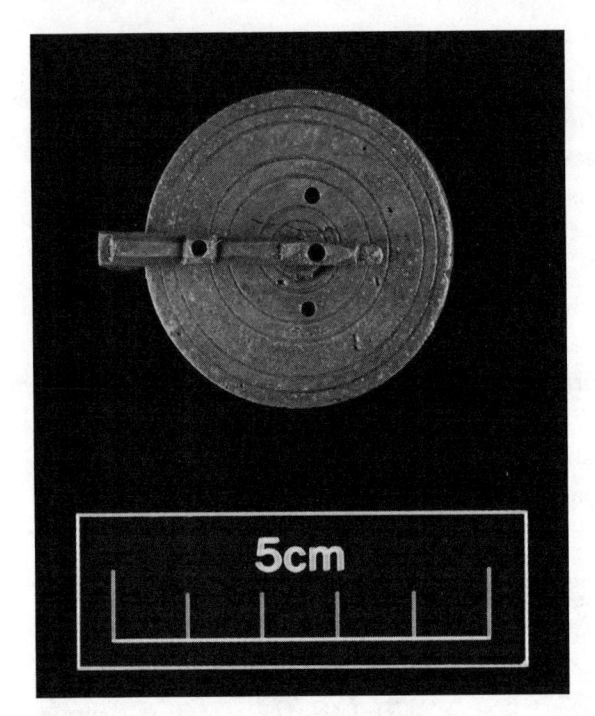

Figure 2.20. Possible nesting weight lid and finial.

applied to the footring and rim (figure 2.21). Once bowl-shaped, the object had been purposefully crushed over a round cylindrical object exactly five inches in diameter, perhaps serving as a lid for a canister of food. Tiny gnaw marks from rats were identified around the rim of the porringer. A maker's touchmark was visible on one handle (bearing the initials "I M" separated by a fleur-de-lis set within a cartouche). The double-stamped initials "D V" found on the exterior base were likely the owner's mark. French pewter specialist Philippe Boucaud provided illustrations of similar porringers made in eastern France, with the same ornate scrollwork handles and location of touchmarks, dating from the 1675 period to early 1700s. While the initials "I M" (or "J M": "I"s and "J"s were interchangeable during this era) on the handle could not be identified, the cable-like trim on the base and rim of the porringer was a recurrent feature of wares made in the town of Metz since about 1600 (Boucaud 2011). Some historical evidence suggests that double-handled porringers have also been used as bleeder basins.

Personal Items

Whether they relate to the French sailors who were along for the voyage aboard *Queen Anne's Revenge* or were of interest to the pirates and were retained during the capture of *La Concorde*, personal items manufactured

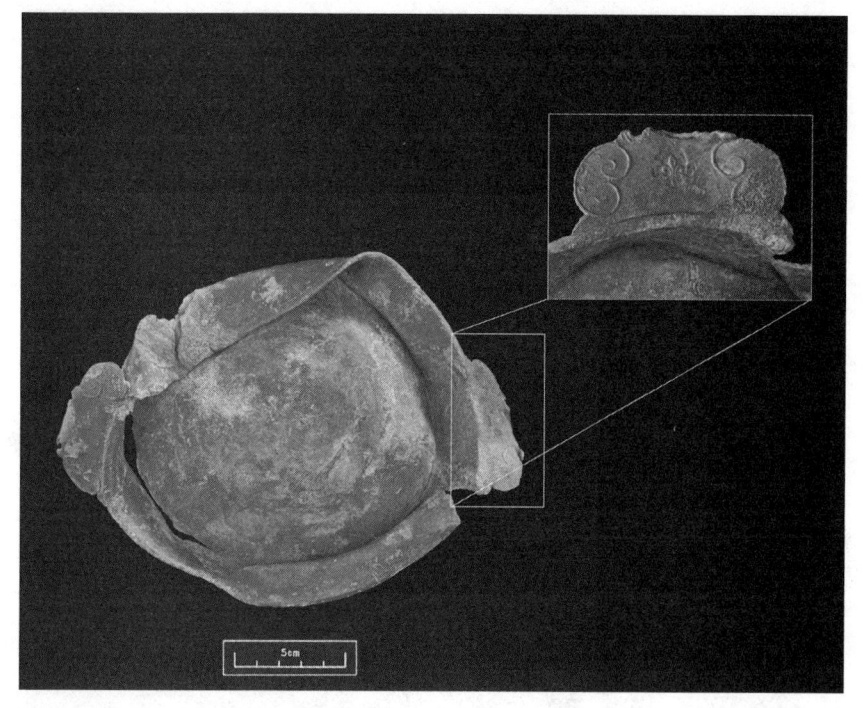

Figure 2.21. Porringer and marks.

in France were also represented in the archaeological record. Arms and armament are considered personal gear, along with the clothing items that have been found.

One of the most spectacular finds is a small cast and carved item, called a quillon block, which served as part of a short sword or bladed weapon. A washer separated the block from the blade end (most of which is gone). The handle, secured with a ferrule, fitted into the opposite end. A chain was substituted for a knuckle guard and fastened to the pierced hole in the quillon block at one end, with the nose or pommel knob at the other end. The design, cast and then finely carved on each side of the quillon, exhibits the Romanesque bust of a male figure in the center, framed by baroque (or its later variant rococo after 1710) foliage and scrollwork. Each side is slightly different in tooling. Research for this design was found in a sword guard recovered on the *Machault* shipwreck, which shows a similar Romanesque or draped bust of a male, possibly a monarch. Experts on French weaponry agree that there is a strong possibility that this male figure may represent Louis XV, the child monarch who took the throne at the age of five in 1715 (David Leyoden and Michel Petard, personal communication,

Figure 2.22. *Queen Anne's Revenge* sword handle after recovery.

2010). Replicas of the *Machault* sword refer to it as the Royal Sword. Portraits of "Louis le Bien Aimée" (Louis the Beloved) appear on numerous sword styles throughout his reign.

In addition to this uniquely decorative quillon block, a sword handle or grip composed of a stag horn ("hartshor") handle topped with an embossed metal pommel was found on the site (figure 2.22). The design of the copper-alloy pommel is composed of four alternating diamond-shapes, two fleur-de-lis, and two cherub faces, encircling a central hole (finial missing). Two pommels matching this exact motif have been recorded so far. One was purchased by/for a museum from an eBay seller (who declared it to be English, ca. 1680s–1690s, though no provenance data were provided), while the other pommel was excavated from a battlefield site of the French-Chickasaw War (French marines who fought a band of Chickasaws in 1736 at the town site of Ackia) near Tupelo, Mississippi (Smith et al. 2013). The decorative motif and the documented context of the second pommel strongly suggest that it is also of French manufacture. These short swords were preferred weapons on board ships for close fighting and served as gentlemen's weapons (also called court swords) among the elite.

Another unique artifact was found in the wreckage, which has yet to be positively identified by country of origin. It consists of the cylindrical wood and pewter handle from a dirk or hunting knife. Dirks are short thrusting daggers commonly found among sailors or naval personnel. Used as a boarding weapon and functional dagger, it was easily stowed and kept handy. The everyday dirk could be used for fighting, eating, and recreation. It was also more affordable than a sword or hanger. Analysis of the wood revealed a provisional origin of European boxwood impregnated with some type of oil or paint (Lee Newsom, personal communication, 2011). The carved decorative pewter fittings exhibit diamond-shaped motifs and three-lobed floral incised designs, along with zigzag border treatments (figure 2.23). While the exact origin of this bladed weapon is not yet known, the European boxwood handle indicates a northern European source. Newsom has also identified a boxwood knife handle from the French explorer Robert de La Salle's ship *Belle* lost in 1686.

Clothing Items

Among the personal gear that survived the wrecking episode are clothing items: buttons and buckles (figure 2.24). A few indicate French connections. A wooden button constructed from a small wooden disc with a central hole and convex underside was found in the wreckage. This plain

Figure 2.23. Boxwood handle.

core was often covered with a matrix of silk, wool, or golden threads in a decorative pattern. Decorative fasteners of this type were part of a French cottage craft known as passementerie and included tassels, rosettes, and pompoms as ornaments. Few intact examples of the decorative threadwork survive. It has a broad date of manufacture during the seventeenth and eighteenth centuries. Similar style wooden cores have been found on the *Machault* shipwreck site.

Decorative sleeve-links were another type of clothing fasteners commonly found on colonial land and shipwreck sites. Two pairs have so far been recovered from the *QAR* site and are in excellent condition. Similar examples of link sets were found on the *Machault* and at the Trudeau Site of the same French colonial period. These items are usually associated with gentlemen's attire and were not likely the garb of a common sailor or pirate crew.

Despite the abandonment of the ship, crew members likely wore or took what clothing items they could carry off. Although the wearing of shoes by sailors or passengers was often problematic (depending on their attitude and safety, availability, and weather factors), these buckles may attest to some shoes being lost in the shuffle. Another intact silver buckle, dating to

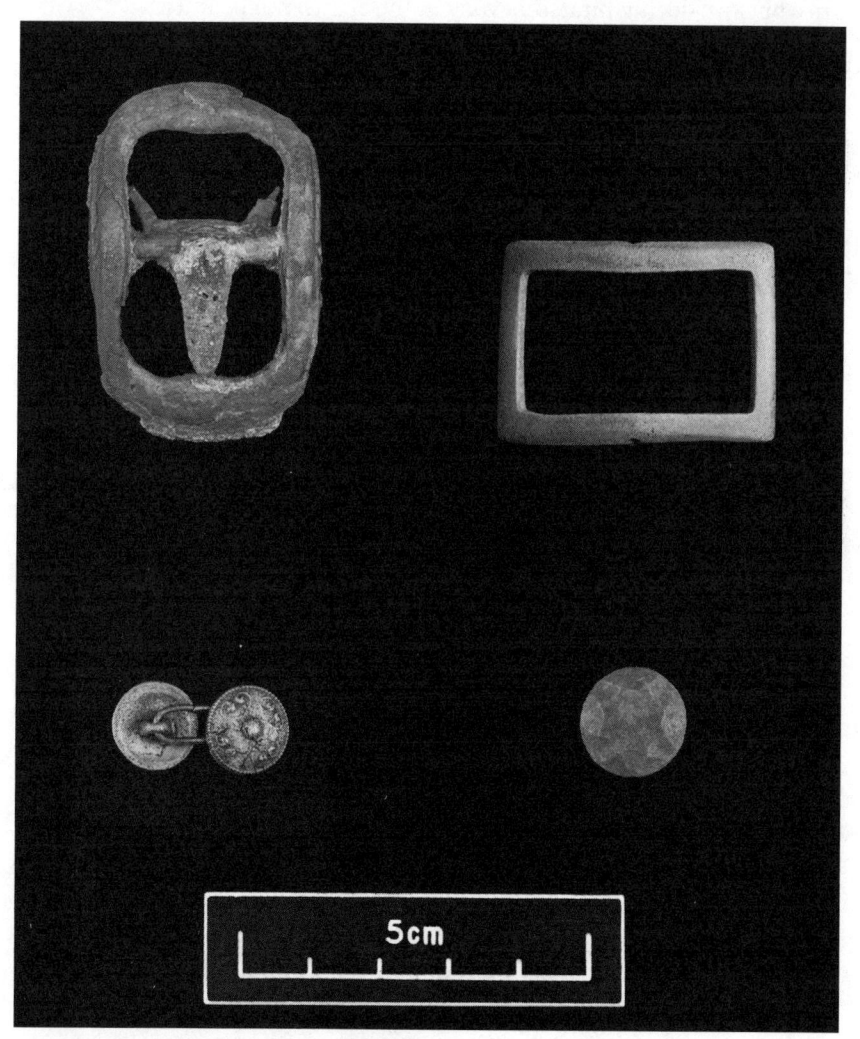

Figure 2.24. Buckles, links, and wooden button.

the 1690–1720 period, was identified by its oval frame, loop chape, single spike, prong tang, and size. The source of manufacture cannot be determined. Another simple rectangular buckle frame and of the simplest construction is likely of French origin. Made of copper alloy, it survives on many French and Spanish sites in Florida and Louisiana. Buttons and buckles matching these found on the *QAR* have been found on the shipwrecks of *Machault* and *Whydah*. Also recovered in the wreck was a somewhat "fancier" buckle with a stud-chape design, complete with a rectangular cartouche and initials on the stud face; this may be identifiable with further conservation. These stud-chape fasteners were used for shoes, spurs, and knee buckles during pirates' heyday in the eighteenth century.

Collectively these few clothing items represent the common fasteners of the day, suitable for French attire on land or sea. Their loss and subsequent discovery in the shipwreck not only testify to the level of ongoing scientific recovery of artifacts at this site but also provide evidence of the personal expressions of eighteenth-century century fashion among the wearers (or captors). As is often the case, the everyday mundane details of life aboard *QAR* were obscured, neglected, or not fully comprehended as significant until archaeologists took a closer look at this segment of seagoing society.

Final Thoughts

As Wilde-Ramsing and Ewen (2012) argue in their article "Beyond Reasonable Doubt: A Case for *Queen Anne's Revenge*," circumstantial evidence clearly supports identity of wreck site 31CR314 lying in Beaufort Inlet as the pirate Blackbeard's abandoned flagship. Considering the loss of this large, heavily armed, early eighteenth century ship in the forgotten space along the coast of the fledgling North Carolina colony, other potential candidates for the wreckage simply do not exist. The "smoking blunderbuss" has not been found, but perhaps that is not surprising in the case of this shipwreck, because it was not a catastrophic loss and personal items were removed. While pirates are portrayed as living a different life on the high seas, the truth is that any differences in the archaeological record will be subtle because life aboard ships (whether they sought to carry commerce, defend the sea lanes, or prey on unsuspecting ships, sanctioned or not) operated under restrictions and a code of command and ethics.

The identification is strengthened by a strong representation of French manufactured goods that neatly suggest that *QAR* was *La Concorde* at the time of capture. A few clues, such as the fastening pattern and draft marks from the ship, point to French construction. The French sailors themselves, however, and what they left behind in their haste to abandon ship are most telling.

In his report to authorities after the capture of *La Concorde*, Lt. François Ernaut (1718) reported:

> The said pirates retained by force ten men of their crew, namely Charles Duval, from Port Louis, pilot; Jean Dubois, Gascon, surgeon major; Marc Bourgneuf, second surgeon, from La Rochelle; Claude Deshayes, third surgeon; Esprit Perrin, master carpenter, married at Pellerin; René Duval, second carpenter from Nantes; Jean Puloin Callerfas; Guillaume Creuzet, sailor from Brest; Georges Bardeau, second cook; Jean Jacques, gunsmith and also a black passenger Trompette, married at St. Malo, whose name the aforesaid does not know; and the aforesaid also said that four of the crew, including the chamber boy, already mentioned [Louis Arot of Nantes, aged fifteen, who had told the pirates that *La Concorde*'s captain and officers each had hidden gold powder, which they consequently handed over], surrendered of their own free will to the pirates, namely: Nicollas Pommeraye from St. Malo, skipper of lifeboats; François Deruet from La Rochelle, sailor; and Julien Joseph Martesang called La Mornayx, volunteer from St. Per en Mer.

The Frenchmen joined a crew of an estimated 150 English pirates aboard the newly named vessel *Queen Anne's Revenge*.

The French assemblage recovered from *QAR* contains medical instruments that were most likely the possessions of the surgeons Dubois, Bourgneuf, and Deshayes. Surgeons and doctors were regular members of ships, needed to treat the captain, crew, and the human cargo in the case of a slave ship. Being men of status, their equipage, clothing, furnishings, and eating habits were often "fancier" or more refined than those of the normal crew. The French-manufactured clothing artifacts found on *QAR* include silver buckles and gilded buttons. Of the few weapons left aboard, some were decorative short swords or dirks that the French once carried. The Saintonge tablewares were part of *La Concorde*'s accoutrements and most likely continued to be used by the French surgeons and perhaps Blackbeard and his officers for dining purposes. They may have used the stemware to drink wines and pewter flatwares to eat. *La Concorde*'s second cook Bardeau remained in the galley and continued the use of French-made storage jars and copper cooking ware to prepare foods familiar to his compatriots.

As recovery and analysis continues on *Queen Anne's Revenge*, a stronger link will be made between specific artifacts and their French owners or others in the pirate crew. Could the initials "D V" on the bottom of the porringer belong to Charles Duval, the pilot from Port Louis, or perhaps his compatriot René Duval, the carpenter from Nantes? We may never know for sure, but the finds reported here and the many more to surface will certainly further illuminate the last week, days, and hours of the vessel's final voyage. In doing so, the *QAR* shipwreck project, under the direction of the North Carolina Department of Cultural Resources and its many partners, is providing the most thorough record of an early eighteenth century ship of this size anywhere in North America.

3

Revisiting the *Fiery Dragon*

JOHN DE BRY AND MARCO ROLING

After a ten-year hiatus, from the beginning of October until mid-November of 2010, a team of archaeologists and remote-sensing specialists revisited the wreck site of the pirate ship tentatively identified as the *Fiery Dragon*, a large sailing vessel scuttled in 1721 in the natural harbor of Sainte-Marie Island, off the northeast coast of Madagascar. During previous expeditions conducted in 2000, the archaeological team discovered a number of seventeenth-century and eighteenth-century pirate shipwreck sites. One of these wrecks was initially thought to be the *Adventure Galley*, commanded by the infamous pirate William Kidd, but a small site excavation revealed artifacts of a later date than the time of sinking in 1698. Further historical research suggested a ship known to have been lost in the immediate vicinity in 1721, which was a likelier candidate given the location and spectrum of artifacts, and the wreck site was accordingly tentatively identified as the *Fiery Dragon* of Captain Christopher Condent, also known as William Condon (de Bry 2006:106).

The primary goal of the 2010 expedition was to investigate this wreck site further in order to obtain more evidence on the nature of the wreck, confirm its identity, and discover whether its debris field might overlap one or more times immediately on top of adjacent wrecks. At least seven shipwrecks are known to have taken place in and around the harbor of Ilot Madame at Sainte-Marie during the Golden Age of Piracy, so the expedition of 2010 also focused on conducting a high-tech geophysical remote sensing survey of the harbor area in an attempt to locate submerged cultural resources.

The island of Sainte-Marie of Madagascar was discovered by Arab seafarers in the twelfth century and by Europeans in the sixteenth century. It lies between twenty-six and thirty kilometers to the east of the Great Red

Island and is some seventy kilometers long with a width that varies between one to six kilometers. The island is a tropical paradise, sparsely populated. Pirates made their home there between 1650 and 1725. They used Sainte-Marie as a base from which to launch raids on Portuguese vessels and ships of the East India companies of England, France, and Holland and the richly laden Indian Mogul ships that sailed to India, Mocha, and Jeddah, the port of the Holy City of Mecca.

Madagascar had become a choice destination for English and other European merchants because slaves were cheaper than on the African continent and there was a great demand on the part of the native inhabitants for firearms as well as for all sorts of Western merchandise. Sainte-Marie became a base for pirates for a variety of reasons. It was the place of choice to water ships and take on supplies after having crossed the Cape of Good Hope and the perfect spot to wait out the monsoon winds (Rogozinski 2000: 55). Sainte-Marie offered an excellent anchorage with a naturally protected bay, and an islet at the entrance of this bay made a natural harbor and a place to careen ships. Careening was the process of leaning a ship on its sides or alternatively on a gently sloping beach, in order to clean, repair, and caulk the hull. This was especially necessary in warm subtropical and tropical waters where wood from the hull was often attacked and eaten by teredo worms (*Teredidae eulamellibranchiata*). This worm-like creature, actually a bivalve mollusk, uses its greatly reduced shell to bore tunnels into wood. In the age of wooden sailing ships this was a tremendous problem that often led to sinking.

The strategic location of the island made it an ideal location from which to launch raids on ships sailing back to Europe, loaded with rich cargoes of gold, precious stones, Chinese blue-on-white export porcelain, silk, spices, and drugs from India and the Far East. As early as the 1660s merchants from England were making the long and perilous journey to Madagascar. In 1675 a ship from Boston came to trade with the Malagasy natives. Pirates were not far behind, arriving in the region about 1684 (Ritchie 1986:83).

Piracy had become a major problem in the Caribbean. Tired of being attacked and robbed by those lawless people of the seas, the European colonial powers had decided not only to protect themselves better but to hunt down pirates aggressively and mercilessly. The Spanish treasure fleets became increasingly larger, better armed, and better protected and as a result suffered fewer losses. No such organized fleets sailed the Indian Ocean, leaving poorly protected ships at the mercy of roving marauders. Piracy had been practiced in this part of the world for centuries, but the uncertainties of tropical weather patterns, the fury of typhoons, and the treacherous crossing of the Cape of Good Hope were of much graver concern to seafarers than isolated acts of piracy. The establishment of European/American pirate companies in the 1680s introduced a new element of danger that would have a devastating economic impact on the region. Because the vast majority of pirates were English, Indian and Chinese authorities felt that all pirates were English. Whenever a ship was attacked and taken those authorities retaliated by closing down the counters of the English East India Company, putting the personnel under house arrest, and even sometimes imprisoning them. Until given monetary reparation for their losses by the English Crown, those counters would remain closed, resulting in heavy financial losses.

Christopher Condent and the *Fiery Dragon*

Christopher Condent, also known as William Condon, John Condent, Congdon, Connor, and Condell (Ken Kinkor, personal communication, 2000), is said to have been a native of Plymouth, England. As the Caribbean became too dangerous for those sea marauders, Condent, along with other pirates, migrated to the safer and often more lucrative Indian Ocean. The career of Condent and his pirate crew sheds light upon the origin of the *Fiery Dragon*, where it was built, when it was captured, the circumstances under which it was scuttled at Saint Marie, and thus also what can be expected to have remained aboard the ship. The following chain of events is reconstructed, based on different historical sources, given the absence of satisfactory secondary-source accounts.

Around April or May 1718 Captain Condent took over twenty vessels of the salt fleet at the Cape Verde island of Maio, as well as a former Dutch privateer at St. Jago, after a short fight in which the Dutch captain was killed. Condent renamed the Dutch ship *Flying Dragon* and made it his flagship, leaving his old sloop to a mate (Johnson 1972: 582). The original name of the Dutch ship is not given in this account. One possibility is that it was an outward-bound Dutch East Indiaman (a commercial European ship trading with India and the Far East) called the *Meiboom* taken at one of the Cape Verde islands. This 36-gun vessel was converted to a pirate vessel, most of the crew joined the pirates, and six of the ship's cannon were a short time later transferred to a captured English ship near the African coast. The *Meiboom* was then renamed *de Zeebloem* (Dutch National Archives [DNA]:1.05.01.02.104, fols. 58a–58b). Another possibility is that

Flying Dragon was a Dutch West India Company frigate named *Kroonprins van Pruijssen* taken together with several English ships near the Cape Verde islands. Some cannon were transferred to this frigate along with all three hundred men, after which they continued their journey, leaving some Dutch sailors with an old English ship (Paesie 2008:66). Condent then sailed to the coast of Brazil, where he conducted numerous raids. He sailed to the Azores and the Guinea coast from June to September 1718, taking a number of Portuguese, English, and Dutch vessels. Sometime in 1719 the pirates attacked *Compagnies Welvaren*, a Dutch West Indiaman frigate, and the English ship *Fame* at Luengo Bay on the southwest coast of Africa (Johnson 1972:583). *Fame* deliberately ran aground to avoid capture, but the marauders took the Dutchman and renamed it *Fiery Dragon*, fitting it out with forty cannon, twenty brass swivel guns, and even three manportable coehorne mortars that could lob exploding shells onto the decks of opposing ships. With 320 men and small arms for twice that number, the ship was as well manned as it was well armed.

Condent continued to capture prizes around West Africa and headed for South Africa in 1720. The next rich prize came near the Cape of Good Hope in February with the capture of the 24-gun, 400-ton *Maison d'Autriche* (House of Austria), homeward bound to Ostend in the Austrian Netherlands from Canton, China, under the command of former English East India Company captain James Nash (or Naish) and with a large cargo of Kangxi porcelain (1662–1722) and a consignment of gold (Gill 1961:17–18).

After taking yet another Dutch East Indiaman, the marauders then made for Madagascar. At Sainte-Marie, Condent recruited members of local black tribes as well as hardened career pirates residing on the island and set sail for the coasts of Arabia, Persia, and India. A pirate ship thought to be *Fiery Dragon* thereafter captured three "Moorish vessels" and a Dutch East India Company ship in the Gulf of Persia (Leibbrandt 1896:282).

In August 1720 near Mumbai, Condent struck it rich, capturing a 500-ton Hajji ship belonging to the son-in-law of Abdul Ghafur of Surat, homeward-bound from Jeddah. One of the richest vessels ever taken by pirates, it was worth "12 lakhs of rupees" (ca. £123,000) according to East India Company reports. Other sources put the value of the gold, drugs, spices, and silk at £150,000. There were also diamonds, rubies, and emeralds reported aboard, and its owners demanded restitution from the East India Company in the amount of twenty lakhs of rupees (ca. £205,000) (India Office Records [IOR]:218–19, 239–41; Rogozinski 2000:208). Once the Indian ship had been fully looted, Condent and his crew returned to the safety and idyllic life of Sainte-Marie Island. They sold stolen goods such as silk and spices to crooked merchants in exchange for liquor, gunpowder, and other supplies (Public Record Office, Colonial Office Papers [PRO CO] 77/16, fols. 291–96).

While Condent and his crew divided the rich booty and celebrated their good luck, the *Crooker*, a type of English vessel called a snow, sailed into the small harbor to take on water. Perhaps inebriated and with a bit too much celebrating under their belt, the crew of the *Fiery Dragon* boarded the *Crooker* and seized its supply of alcoholic beverages. Condent ended up compensating the master of the *Crooker*, Captain Baker, for the spirits taken by his exuberant crew. They engaged in a most civilized, if not friendly, conversation during which Baker revealed that the French governor of Bourbon (present-day Reunion Island) was offering a pardon to any pirate giving up his trade. A royal decree had given the island a legitimate right to pardon pirates and even encourage them to settle on the island, requiring only that they turn over or destroy their ship and turn over their weapons and ammunition. In return for a small fee each former pirate would be allowed to bring in one black slave and settle on the island to lead a righteous and honest life. Condent was very interested in this offer, especially after having taken such a rich prize, knowing full well that he would be allowed to keep his ill-gotten fortune. He asked Captain Baker to return to Bourbon and inquire as to the validity of this pardon offer. Condent was not unknown to Governor Joseph Beauvollier de Courchant, who was more than happy to see this menace off the water and under control and quickly agreed to a general pardon for Condent and his men.

In February 1721 Condent and thirty-two of his crew left Sainte-Marie for Bourbon Island, scuttling the *Fiery Dragon* as it lay at anchor just before departing. It is not clear what truly transpired, however, and it is quite possible that the 135 crew members disagreed as to whether to accept the pardon and retire to Bourbon or continue their piratical activities. Perhaps a scuffle broke out, resulting in the inadvertent and premature burning of the *Fiery Dragon* (PRO CO 77/16, fols. 291–96). This scenario would explain why so much cultural material remained on the ship. When an English squadron called into port at Sainte-Marie's the following year, Captain Clement Downing reported finding "the Ruins of several Ships and their Cargoes piled up in great Heaps, consisting of the richest Spices and Drugs" (Downing 1737:46).

Condent distinguished himself while on Bourbon Island, acting as a negotiator for the governor of the island when pirates under John Taylor and "La Buze" took over a disabled Portuguese ship, *Nostra Senhora de Cabo*, which had sought refuge on the island after weathering a devastating storm, and took the viceroy of Portuguese India hostage. Condent managed to persuade the pirates to release the viceroy, thus gaining the governor's respect and friendship. In 1722, after marrying the governor's sister-in-law, Condent sailed for France in November and settled down in the port city of Saint-Malo on the Normandy coast, where he became a successful and respectable businessman and ship owner (Johnson 1972:584). While the name of William Kidd became synonymous with the word "pirate," he had a short career and was one of the less successful pirates who roamed the Indian Ocean. Yet Condent, relatively unknown, was the second most successful scoundrel that ever lived: he committed one of the largest robberies in history and literally got away with murder.

Other Shipwrecks in Sainte-Marie Island

In the course of several years' robberies throughout the Indian Ocean, the pirates of the *Mocha Frigate*, with forty guns, under the command of Captain Robert Culliford and the *Soldado*, with twenty guns, under the command of Captain Richard "Dirk" Chivers, had captured Chinese, English, French, Indian, Japanese, Malayan, Persian, Portuguese, and Siamese vessels. These included not only rich ships on a pilgrimage to Mecca (so called Hajji ships) but also China traders with rich cargoes of Kangxi blue-on-white export porcelain.

On September 23, 1698, a Turkish-owned 600-ton Hajji ship known as *Great Mahomet* (in Turkish *Yüce Muhammetc*) was homeward bound to Surat, India, from the port of Jeddah on the coast of Arabia. It was attacked north of Mumbai by two European pirate vessels under the command of Robert Culliford of the forty-gun *Mocha Frigate* and Richard "Dirk" Chivers of the twenty-gun *Soldado*. The sea battle that followed was unusually violent. At least twenty pirates were killed, while over three hundred of the passengers and crew of the pilgrim ship died, according to Ibrahim Khan, one of the owners of the vessel who was then aboard. Another owner, Hussein Hamedan, declared that the pirates had tortured Indian merchants to reveal the hiding places of their treasure. As was often the case for important Hajji ships returning to India from pilgrimage to Mecca, *Great Mahomet* was immensely rich. In addition to the £130,000 (equivalent today to $65 million) in gold, *Great Mahomet* was also carrying personal possessions, devotional objects, religious souvenirs, and other baggage of approximately six hundred Hajj pilgrims from a wide range of social strata.

By the time the pirates had captured the Indian ship, *Soldado* had become completely unseaworthy, so the two ships took their prize to the coast, released the Indian captives, and proceeded to share their ill-gotten booty. According to some testimony each man of the 250 men of two crews received a share worth £700 to £800 (about £375,000 today), in gold, jewels, and other valuables. The crew of the *Soldado* transferred the cannon and some of the men to *Great Mahomet*, which was renamed *New Soldado* and put it under the command of Chivers, and then sunk their own vessel (Rogozinski 2000:141). Some sixty women were kept on board the pirate ship as captives to be taken to the pirate base at Ile Sainte-Marie, while the rest of the Muslim crew and passengers were put aboard the ship's launches to make for shore as best they could. After attacking several other ships off the coast of India, the pirate flotilla arrived at the harbor of Ile Sainte-Marie on January 29, 1699.

Shortly after their arrival, the pirates were surprised by the approach of a powerful Royal Navy squadron that had set sail from England on a pirate-hunting expedition under the command of Commodore Thomas Warren. *Great Mahomet* and *Mocha Frigate* were hurriedly sunk by the pirates across the entrance to the bottle-necked harbor in order to block passage by the naval squadron.

Methodology in Searching for Shipwrecks

Before starting to locate shipwrecks using nonintrusive methods, such as towing side scan sonar behind a small motorboat, it is important first to define a survey area in order to be able to plan a systematic and feasible research. Determining the exact survey area at Sainte-Marie was done during the first expedition week by combining historical sources, maps, and accurate geographical images. By using photographs of maps and charts of the seventeenth and eighteenth century found in French archives and projecting them on top of satellite images using Google Earth software, it became easier to predict where shipwrecks would most likely be found and how to delimit the survey area.

The harbor of Ilot Madame (originally named Ile aux Cayes, from the Spanish *cayo* [rock], the islet was renamed Ilot Madame in 1820 in honor the French king's daughter) and Pirate Bay are both likely to hold several shipwrecks of the Golden Age of Piracy. To locate the remains of these vestiges by performing nonintrusive, nondestructive survey methods it is important to limit the survey area as much as possible, although the harbor and bay by themselves are not extremely large. The harbor area, roughly delimited by drawing an imaginary latitude line between the tip of Ilot Madame and Sainte-Marie Island proper, is about eight hectares, of which only four hectares that are deeper than two meters can be surveyed. Pirate Bay is about forty-two hectares, of which only twenty-two hectares can easily be investigated (figure 3.1).

Today a causeway constructed during World War II separates the harbor and bay. The western part of this causeway is built on top of the so-called bottleneck of the channel east of Ilot Madame into the bay. When a detailed map created by lieutenants Laurent de Venancourt and Cornette de Venancourt in 1847 is projected over the satellite image it immediately becomes clear where the bottleneck is located and why this causeway was later built exactly here. This was the narrowest entry point into Pirate Bay, only forty meters across and six to eight meters deep.

Apart from showing detailed geographical features and structures such as buildings and fortifications, the map is also surprisingly accurate for bathymetry. Dotted lines and crosses indicating reefs or rocky areas point to relatively shallow areas. These shallow areas on the map may also indicate

Figure 3.1. Map with survey areas in the harbor and Pirate Bay region.

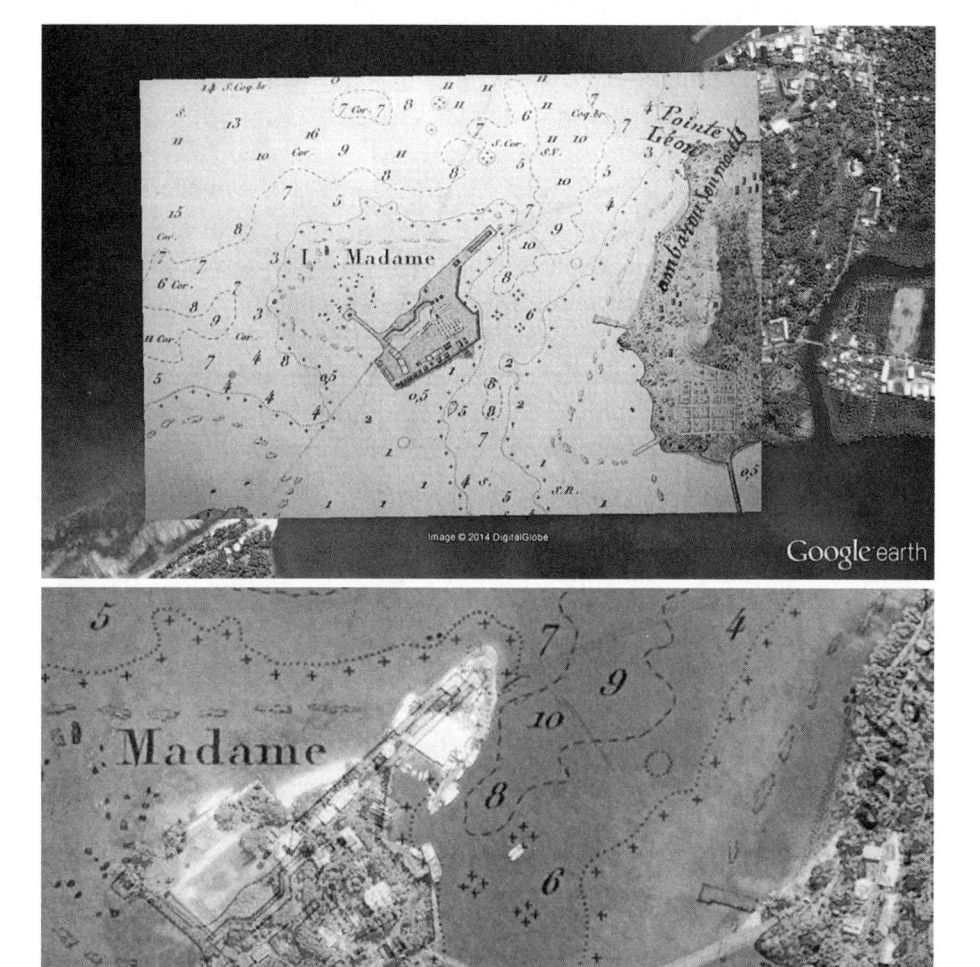

Figure 3.2. Historical map of 1847 projected over Google Earth satellite images.

submerged obstructions such as shipwrecks. Plotting the exact location of the shipwreck tentatively identified as *Fiery Dragon*, sunk in the harbor area in 1721, shows that one of the sets of cross marks indeed matches up with this wreck site. The map is easily projected without much distortion over the current satellite image using present landmarks, which indicates that mid-nineteenth-century French cartographers were capable of creating detailed and reliable maps that are still of use today (figure 3.2).

The Ilot Madame harbor area was surveyed during two days, using a boat with a Humminbird 1197c side imaging sonar. Individual sonar images were recorded together with their GPS positions. The survey was performed by running the boat in parallel tracks with a few meters interval. Scanning the harbor area in several directions resulted in a set of points of interest. Subsequent visual underwater inspection was conducted by diving on these locations. A nineteenth-century shipwreck was found, with some remaining structure protruding above the sediment. As the harbor area bottom is covered with a layer of fine silt and sand, most shipwreck remains are covered and cannot be seen by the sonar. But piles of ballast stones only slightly higher than the surrounding area can be detected with the help of the side scan sonar, indicating buried wrecks below them.

One target located a short distance to the southeast of the *Fiery Dragon* site turned out to be just such an area with a visible ballast deposit. The ballast deposit itself could be from the seventeenth or eighteenth century by first estimate, but a heavy anchor chain lying across it is of a more recent period. Plotting the GPS position on Google Earth and projecting it over the historical map of 1847, it became clear that this site is located exactly in the middle of the inner channel and a little to the north of the bottleneck, thus effectively blocking the entrance to the bay.

The location of this ballast pile is consistent with the historical record of the *Mocha Frigate* and *Great Mahomet* being hastily scuttled in the channel. An initial visual dive inspection of the area of the ballast deposit did not lead to the recovery of any datable artifacts, but the team decided to investigate this site further during the course of the expedition.

It was not possible to survey the bay area because no facilities were present to launch an engine-powered boat. The bay is blocked by a causeway without any lock chamber or passable bridge. One promising location in the bay was determined first on the historical map and then located by using landmarks on Ilot Madame. That particular site is neither deep nor far from the islet's eastern shore, so it was surveyed by two team members snorkeling and free diving on it. A ballast pile was found, consisting of rounded river rocks, but no artifacts were observed. This effectively demonstrated the accuracy and usability of the 1847 historical map as a historically reliable source.

The 2010 investigation of the remains of the shipwreck tentatively identified as the *Fiery Dragon* focused on several historical and archaeological questions. The first goal was to find further evidence to confirm the findings of the expedition in 2000 that this shipwreck does represent the *Fiery*

Dragon. To accomplish this it was important to collect diagnostic artifacts in order to determine a terminus ante quem and verify that it did not indicate a date after 1721. It was decided to survey the ballast mound intensively and record and recover any artifacts for identification and reliable dating (figure 3.3). This was also a rescue archaeology operation, as the chance of unauthorized diving in the harbor area increased as soon as the expedition team was present and at work.

Small test units were set up in and around the ballast mound in order to get a better understanding of the spatial relationship between artifacts and categories of artifacts and to expose more of the remaining hull structure. Apart from these intensified surveys, a more detailed excavation was undertaken in order to expose part of the hull elements and to understand the orientation of the wreck, how much of it is still extant, and, if possible, the nationality of the ship by studying the method used for hull construction. An excavation was conducted in 2000 at the southeast side of the ballast mound, so it was deemed logical to continue working there.

A basic measurement system was put in place by defining control points around the site, making use of stakes put down in 2000 that are still present. Each control point from A up to F was marked by an attached floater hovering two to three meters above the control point. This makes navigation underwater easier, especially when taking into consideration the prevailing low visibility close to the bottom from stirred-up silt. Control point A was secured to a cannon south of the ballast mound that does not appear to be associated with the wreck site but provides a solid and fixed point underwater. Enough distances between the control points were carefully measured and copied into the ArcGis software to obtain an accurate overview of the measurement system. The photo mosaic created in 2000 was used in both Google Earth and ArcGis software as a base map on top of which the measurement system could be projected.

After setting up the basic measurement system a rigid 2×2 m PVC grid was constructed and secured underwater to the southeast sloping side of the ballast mound. It was not possible to pinpoint precisely the location where the excavation of 2000 took place because the previous team had reburied the site by putting back the ballast stones from where they had been moved in order to protect the wreck from being looted. As it turned out, during the course of two weeks of underwater excavation the grid was only 1 m west of the 2000 test area. Besides the grid, all other sections where artifacts were collected for analysis and dating were carefully mapped in order to establish individual location and section. Special finds

Figure 3.3. Chart with *Fiery Dragon* photo mosaic and plotted measurement grid.

were accurately measured in situ to control points in order to record their position in ArcGis.

The grid area was excavated almost completely by using a Venturi underwater dredging system and by hand, exposing futtocks, planking, and spaces between them. Because the excavation was on the side of the ballast mound, the outside end was exposed easily. But moving into the ballast mound created a thread of collapsing sides, as the hull slopes downward and the excavation depth increases to 1.5 m. Having ballast rocks on top required careful planning for extending the excavation area, removing stones when needed.

The purpose of extending the grid southward and westward was to get closer to the keelson, which might provide additional clues as to the basic construction of the ship and where it was built. As historical accounts identify the *Fiery Dragon* as a former Dutch East Indiaman, it is vital to understand the differences between the techniques of the major shipbuilding countries of Europe like England, France, and Holland in order to recognize specific features of the remaining hull structure. Starting hull analysis from the keelson is the best way to find out how the ship was built and what framing technique was employed.

Eighteen sections were defined On the *Fiery Dragon* site. Fifteen sections were intensely surveyed, and small test units were created to collect artifacts for identification and dating and to expose parts of the hull structure. The excavation area itself consisted of the grid (section S001) and adjacent sections S004 and S008. This area of 10 m^2 was excavated to 80 percent of the outer hull planking.

Hull Structure

At least four pairs of double frames joined tightly together were exposed. One single structural timber, possibly a futtock (labeled HP002) with a pointed edge, displayed fasteners to which a second futtock was once attached (figure 3.4, down left quadrant where futtock HP002 points out). Between the double frames is a small space of about 10 to 15 cm, creating cavities that capture sediment and artifacts. The timbers themselves measure roughly 25 × 20 cm across. They are at a slight angle, going down and underneath what may be a set of crossbeams that are oriented almost at a 90-degree angle with the timbers (figure 3.4: HP009, timber pointing to the top and bottom).

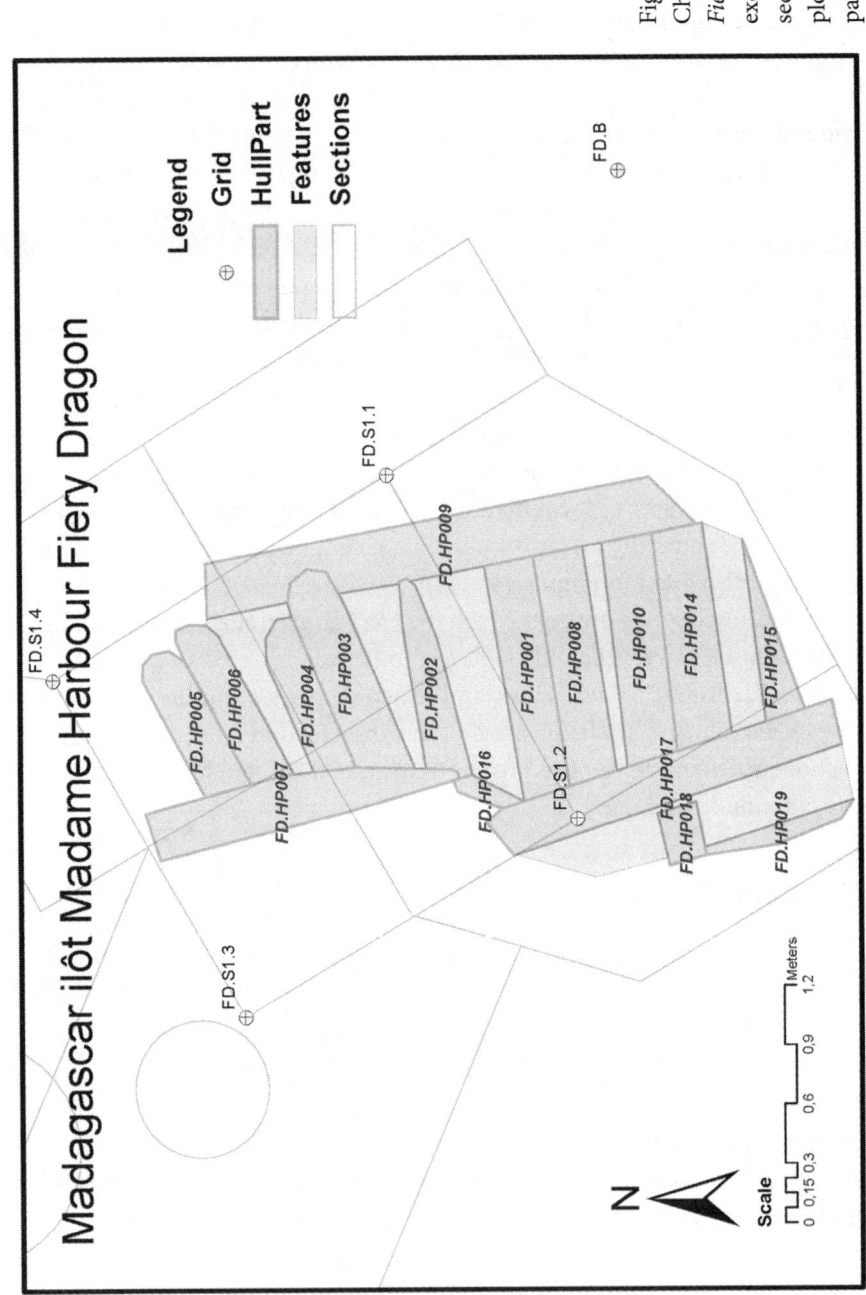

Figure 3.4. Chart showing *Fiery Dragon* excavation sections and plotted hull parts.

These crossbeam structures are at a level some 20 cm higher than the futtocks and likely to be from another structure such as a collapsed deck. Too little was uncovered to understand the origin and extent of these upper structures. Edges of futtocks are found north and south of the test area, all with the same bearing of about 260 degrees.

Assuming that these futtocks led to the keelson of the wreck, this keelson is expected to be pointing in a 350-degree direction in a north to south orientation. The wreck is therefore fairly parallel to the shoreline of Ilot Madame. Thus it is unlikely that the ship sunk with either bow or stern pointing to the shallow careening spot. The favored hypothesis currently is that the ship was probably towed from the careening spot and subsequently sunk in the channel. It is not possible at this point at this time to say how the ship is oriented in terms of bow and stern. The way the ship went down is not known: all sorts of scenarios are possible. The ballast mound itself does not provide any clue at this point as to whether it is in the middle and center of the ship or more toward the bow or stern. This can only be established once the keelson is reached and followed in either direction to locate remains of the bilge housing (turn of the bilge) or the bow or stern itself.

The photo mosaic of the site provides another theory as to why the ballast mound is round rather than elongated, as is normally the case. Ballast stones are also found east of the *Fiery Dragon* and do not seem to correlate to it. It is therefore conceivable that below the wreck lies another wreck at an angle of 90 degrees (thus pointing toward Ilot Madame's shore) that is propping up part of the *Fiery Dragon* wreck above the seabed at the point where the two wrecks overlap. This theory can be proved or disproved when the keelson is located. This will make it clear whether the keelson is lying flat or is distorted at some point along its course.

Artifact Statistics

Nearly two thousand artifacts were collected on the *Fiery Dragon* site over the course of twenty days of diving (table 3.1). Chinese blue-on-white export porcelain sherds, followed by other ceramics, form by far the largest group of artifacts. Together they make up 88 percent of the cultural assemblage.

Cowry shells have been found by the thousands, especially within the grid, but were not counted individually because this would make a disproportionately large group. The many almonds (recorded as "Seed") were also not counted individually. No packing material was found.

Table 3.1. Category Overview of the Artifact Materials of the *Fiery Dragon*

	Number of Artifacts	Percentage
Porcelain	1526	76.6
Ceramics	228	11.4
Glass	58	2.9
Bone	49	2.5
Concretion	42	2.1
Copper alloy	16	0.8
Iron	15	0.8
Lead	13	0.7
Cowry shells	11	0.6
Seed	7	0.4
Semiprecious stone	6	0.3
Dental	5	0.3
Stone	4	0.2
Wood	3	0.2
Gold	2	0.1
Tin alloy	2	0.1
Building ceramics	2	0.1
Pipe Clay	2	0.1
Ivory	1	0.1
	1992	100.0

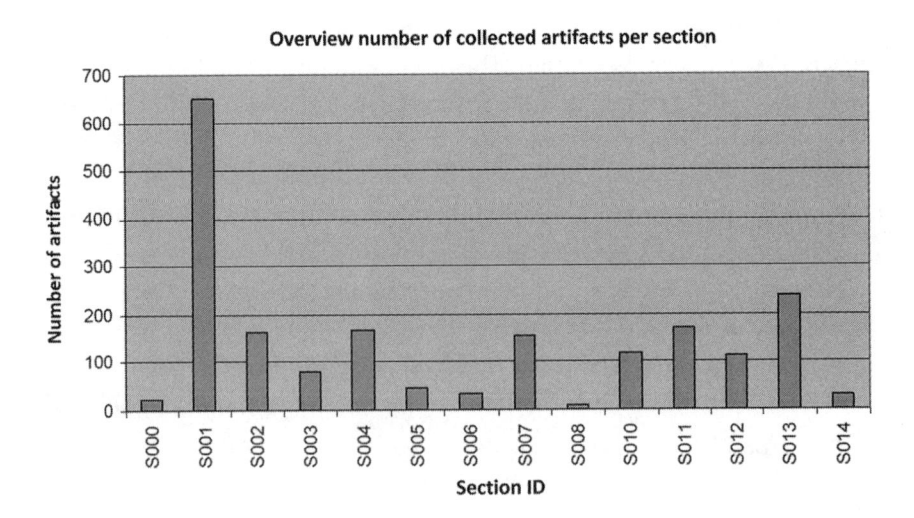

Figure 3.5. Artifact overview per section.

Section S001 has provided the most artifacts (figure 3.5). This is the primary excavation area within the 2 × 2 m grid. Together with adjacent sections S004 and S008 to the south and southwest end of S001 they capture over 40 percent of the artifacts found.

Coins

Two coins were found in section S004 less than a meter apart and at the level of the futtocks. They date to 1689 and 1650 and support the date of scuttling the *Fiery Dragon*.

Austrian Ducat 1689

obverse: LEOPOLD[VS]:D[EI].G[RATIA].R[OMANORVM].I[MPERATOR].S[EMPER].A[VGVSTVS].G[ERMANIAE].H[VNGARIAE].B[OHEMIAE].REX K B
(with depiction of the king)
In English:
Leopold, by the Grace of God, Roman Emperor, always Augustus, of Germany, Hungary, and Bohemia, King (with depiction of the king) ("K B" indicates the mint of Kremnitz, Austria)
reverse: AR[CHIDVX].AV[STRIAE].DV[X].BV[RGVNDIAE].M[ARCHIO]:MO[RAVIAE]:CO[MES]:TY[ROLIS] 1689
(with depiction of Virgin Mary)
In English:
Archduke of Austria, Duke of Burgundy, Margrave of Moravia, Count of Tyrol 1689

Dutch Ducat 1650
obverse:
CONCORDIA.RES P AR[VAE].CRES[CENT].
WEST [FRIESLAND] ✿ 16 50
(depiction of a standing knight with sword and seven arrows in a
   bundle; minted in Enkhuizen by Diederik van Romond)
In English:
Work together to accomplish more
West Friesland (indicates the mint of Enkhuizen, Holland) ✿
   (a five-leaved flower indicates the mint master from 1649 to 1680)
   1650

reverse:
MO[NETA]ORD[INUM] / PRO.VIN[CIARUM] /
   FOEDER[ATARUM] / BELG[II].AD / LEG[EM].IMP[ERII]
(depiction of a decorated square with text)
In English:
Coin of the States of the United Provinces of the Netherlands according to the law of the Empire

Chinese Export Porcelain

The porcelain cups and ware fragments found in situ on the wreck site tentatively identified as the *Fiery Dragon* are extremely varied in styles as well as vessel types and suggest provenience from more than one ship taken as a prize and haphazardly loaded crates (figure 3.6). Fragments from platters, plates, bowls, cups, and lids are scattered across the site but seem to be

Figure 3.6. Two Chinese porcelain cups (artifacts MAD.2010.FD.A000003 and MAD.2010.FD.A000004).

more numerous on the east portion of the wreck. Some vessels have lobed rims, others scalloped. The most common decorations are flower and vegetal motifs, while a few fragments display landscape scenes with pagodas (houses) and bodies of water. Fewer have animals, usually birds, such as the double-headed phoenix. None depict human figures. Geometric designs were also incorporated on some ware fragments, mixed with floral and vegetal motifs. Careful examination revealed traces of "ghost" patterns left by polychrome paint that had been applied over the glaze following the firing process. The over-glaze enamel paint did not resist long-term immersion in seawater, but the ghost image that it left allows for the possibility of sketching the patterns and visualizing what the vessels looked like prior to saltwater immersion.

All the fragments and two intact cups appear to have been fired in the kilns of Jingdezhen, in the province of Jiangxi, in southern China during the Kangxi period (1662–1722). This is indicated by the shape of the foot, the decorative patterns, and the high quality of the porcelain. Stoneware had been produced in Jingdezhen since the tenth century, but the city made its reputation thanks to the introduction of *qingbai*, a white porcelain with a blue glaze that adheres perfectly and requires only a single firing. During the Song Dynasty (960–1279), potters from Jingdezhen began to exploit a new deposit called *gaoling*, thirty kilometers northeast of the city, which provided exceptionally fine clay, thus making the city's fortune. This refractory clay is feldspar formed of silica and alumina originating from the decomposition of an eruptive crystalline rock. In order to use this material in the manufacture of porcelain, it must be mixed with a substance known as *baidunzi*, which has the same structure as *gaoling* but is less decomposed. Once pulverized, the resulting mixture is made into small blocks and placed in pits to decompose over a period of several years. At the end of the decomposition period, the material has become flexible and malleable. During firing, the *baidunzi* melts to form a sort of cement that coats the kaolin particles. Mixed in equal proportions, the two components produce a beautifully pure white medium. The new genre, called blue-on-white, was created when an iridescent decoration made of cobalt oxide was added directly to the unfired surface using a brush. The entire piece was then coated with a special glaze and fired. The grayish cobalt oxide pigment would then turn blue during the firing process. Thanks to this very dense glaze, the blue-on-white decoration was inalterable (Desroches 1992).

The great Chinese export porcelain trade emerged during the reign of the Emperor Wanli (1573–1619), during the Ming Dynasty era. Blue-on-white porcelain is also designated as Kraak, from the Dutch *kraakpoorselein*, used to designate the first Chinese export porcelain originally transported by carrack, a Portuguese type of ship (Castro 2005). The quality and style of blue-on-white export porcelain from Jingdezhen is reflected in the porcelain material found on the wreck of the *Fiery Dragon*. The port-city of Guangzhou (Canton) is located south-southwest of Jingdezhen. Guangzhou, strategically situated on the Xi Jiang River, became an active and important port trading with India and the Muslim world as early as the seventh century and started trading with Europe from 1514 on. The first East India Company trading office was established there in 1684. It was the main port from which Chinese export porcelain was being shipped to Europe.

There is another tantalizing, if not exceptional, clue as to the identity of this particular wreck. Several porcelain shards have a double-headed eagle or phoenix motif repeated three times and separated by foliage (figure 3.7). Originally this motif was thought to be associated with the Augustinian Order (Jean-Paul Desroches, personal communication, February 2000). Thirty years after the first Jesuits arrived in Macao, three Spanish Augustinians came there on November 1, 1586, to establish a convent. On August 22, 1589, by order of Philip II of Spain, who then also reigned over Portugal, the Portuguese Augustinians took over the Convent of Our Lady of Grace. The

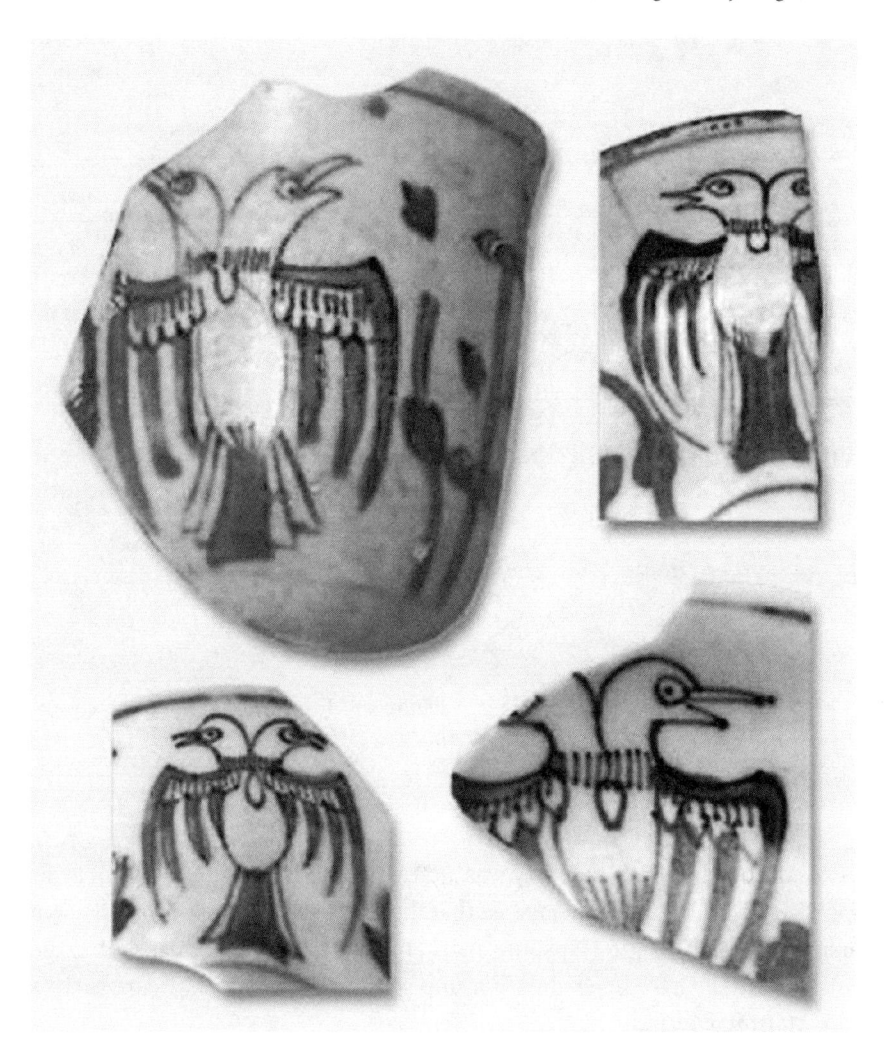

Figure 3.7. Examples of the phoenix motif.

heraldic device of the Saint Augustinian Order is a phoenix surmounted by a vegetal crown, standing on a heart pierced by two arrows. Only three Chinese porcelain objects adorned with the double-headed eagle are known, all three from the Wanli period (1573–1619).

The presence of this porcelain on Sainte-Marie Island is surprising because such items were thought to have been manufactured exclusively for the Macao market. We are dealing with a pirate ship, of course, which could explain why the cargo would not be typical of the cargo of an East Indiaman. There may be another explanation for this decoration. The coat of

Figure 3.8. Three Chinese white porcelain figurines.

arms of the Hapsburg Dynasty was a crowned phoenix with a coat of arms on its chest. It is quite conceivable that those porcelain fragments represent a special order for the Hapsburg market rather the Macao one. This cargo may originally have been aboard a ship seized by the *Fiery Dragon*, such as the *Maison d'Autriche*.

Two small molded figurines made of plain white porcelain and the fragmentary lower portion and base of a third one were found during the excavation (figure 3.8). The smaller of the two whole or partially complete figurines represents a small person or a child, apparently female, wearing a buttoned coat and holding a pet (possibly a cat) in her right arm. She is standing next to a tree trunk against which a bouquet of flowers is resting. This particular piece was manufactured from a single mold. The piece is about 5.2 cm high, with a maximum pedestal diameter of 3.5 cm. The larger piece appears to have been shaped from two pieces molded separately. The figurine itself appears to have been glued to the pedestal with barbotine, although this cannot be confirmed until the figure undergoes a careful cleaning process (Goddio and Saint Michel 1999:136, 138). This particular piece depicts a smiling Asian man, most likely Chinese, wearing a dome-shape hat. He appears to be sitting, although encrustation makes it difficult to determine this with any degree of certainty. His head is tilted to his right, and he is looking to his left. The man is holding an object on what appears to be a tray; his hands and portions of the pedestal are broken and missing. The piece is about 8 cm, with a maximum pedestal diameter of 4.8 cm. The third figurine consists of the feet and part of the lower legs of a central figure. The remnants of two small feet are seen at the left side of the central figure, while a Fu dog is seen sitting next to its right foot. The piece is about 1.5 cm high, with a maximum pedestal diameter of 5.4 cm.

Shells

Large quantities of cowry shells were found on the wreck, many cemented to the ribs of the ship. A number of the cowries have been identified as *Cypraea chinensis* (Indo-Pacific), *Cypraea walkeri* (Seychelles Island and Maldives Islands), *Cypraea helvola* (Indo-Pacific), *Cypraea gracilis* (Indian Ocean), *Cypraea erosa* (Indo-Pacific), *Cypraea arabica* (Indo-Pacific), *Cypraea lynx* (Indian and west and central Pacific Oceans), and *Cypraea talpa* (Indian and central Pacific Oceans). Other species have yet to be identified, but these species were found to be the most numerous. The *Fiery Dragon* is known to have had a large quantity of cowries on board as other pirate ships in Sainte-Marie undoubtedly did. Cowries were widely used in the region to trade as well as to purchase slaves.

Other Organic Material

Wood used in the construction of the *Fiery Dragon* has been tentatively identified in situ as *Quercus* spp. (European white oak), most probably *Q. robur* or *Q. petraea*. This wood, found on numerous wrecks, played a major role in European commerce and warfare and was the most commonly used wood throughout the history of seafaring (Steffy 1994). It is slightly lighter than *Q. alba* (American white oak).

Two types of seeds found on the lowest level of the *Fiery Dragon* test unit have been tentatively identified as cf. *Prunus* sp. and *Myristica fragrans* (nutmeg). The latter seed is from the spice nutmeg, a tropical, dioecious evergreen tree native to the Moluccas or Spice Islands of Indonesia, and may have come from the large Mogul ship taken near Mumbai on August 18, 1720. This spice was much appreciated and in demand in Europe. A

French Royal Ordinance dated September 9, 1726, directed French ship captains to bring back a variety of exotic plants, fruits, and spices whenever possible (de Bry 2006:127). Nutmeg was part of the extensive list given to sea captains sailing to the Americas, Africa, and the Orient.

Cf. *Prunus* sp. is from the Rosaceae family and closely resembles cf. *Prunus dulcis* the (almond). The seeds examined do not appear to have the exterior pericarp shell present, which would greatly aid in identification as it contains the diagnostic pitting around the shell surface, but seem to represent the middle mesocarp shell that encircles the kernel or almond. This seed also looks much like that of the apricot *Prunus armeniac*, also called the Chinese almond (Donna Rhule, personal communication, January 5, 2011).

Sculpture

A special find from the *Fiery Dragon* is a carved wooden statue. This piece is made of a tree branch with the grain centered vertically. The statue height is about 10 cm, with a base between 5 and 6.2 cm (figure 3.9).

It is a sculpture of a woman wearing a mantle and robe. Her arms are pointing forward and toward each other; but the hands are broken off, so it is not clear if they are touching. The head is slightly bent to the left. The

Figure 3.9. Carved wooden statue of a female.

Figure 3.10. Carved stone statue of a female.

general impression of this carved wooden statue is of a madonna. There are no signs of painting, gold plate, or other decoration. The lower sides and back are decorated with rows of round objects.

Another sculpture was made of a small piece of dark gray stone, probably slate. The artifact is 5.7 cm high, approximately 2 cm wide, and only 1 cm thick. It is a fairly flat piece. The back side is slightly hollowed with a small hole at waist height, most likely to attach the sculpture to another object. The statue is not very detailed and rather roughly cut (figure 3.10).

Inscription

A notable find on the *Fiery Dragon* is a small rectangular piece of ivory with an inscription consisting of the four letters "INRI" (figure 3.11). This is the abbreviation of "Iesus Nazarenus, Rex Iudaeorum" (Jesus of Nazareth, king

82 · John de Bry and Marco Roling

Figure 3.11. Ivory piece inscribed "INRI."

of the Jews). The inscription most likely was attached to a small crucifix, although no marks indicate how it was fastened. The ivory piece measures 44 × 14 × 2 mm. The letters are incised into the ivory. Traces of gold still present in the engraving indicate that the letters were fully gilded.

Archaeological Research of the "Channel Wreck"

After the discovery of the ballast mound in the channel, surveys were conducted in order to get an initial idea of the size and orientation of the site. The distribution of ballast rocks pointed to an almost east-to-west orientation of the assumed wreck. A basic measurement system was established underwater, consisting of two control points connected by a straight base line. The line started at the chain in the center of the ballast area and ended at a well-secured and stable piece of wood sticking out of the bottom some 11.5 m west of the starting point. Distances between the control points and points A and F of the *Fiery Dragon* site were carefully measured and copied into the ArcGis software to get an accurate overview of the measurement system and spatial relationships.

Initially no hull structure was visible and hardly any artifacts were visible. The next stage in the survey was to scan the bottom with metal detectors in order to locate any large objects like cannon and cannonballs. As this wreck site could be either the *Mocha Frigate* or the *New Soldado* (formerly known as the *Great Mahomet*), which were purposely wrecked in a hurried fashion, part of the cargo and a substantial amount of ordnance could be expected (assuming no subsequent salvage). Metal detector survey indeed indicated a number of hot spots. One was these chosen as section S001 for further excavation. By using a water jet to blow overburden of about 30 cm of sand and silt away, a large iron cannon was located together with a concretion of cannonballs and glass objects, including an intact bottle and several large fragments of green glass. Only a few porcelain sherds were found around the site.

Based on the size and shape of the cannon, the bottle, and decoration of the porcelain sherds the site can tentatively be placed in the second half of the seventeenth century. This tentative dating fits well with the reported scuttling of both above-mentioned ships in 1699. By moving ballast rocks aside along the base line, a test unit of about 3 × 3.5 m was created (section S002). Excavation revealed part of the inner structure of a hull, but few datable artifacts.

Site Significance

As evidenced by the *Whydah* wreck site (1717), vessels employed as maritime predators carried a broader cross-cultural selection of artifacts than did their merchant or naval counterparts. The archaeological and historical significance of the site therefore cannot be taken lightly or underestimated. For example, in addition to valuables in the form of gold coins and jewelry left behind by pirates who were under extreme pressure to sink their ships to block the entrance to the bay at the Bottle Neck, it is virtually certain that some Islamic objects that would be of enormous significance today were left behind by the pirates, who most likely had no interest in them. The Islamic objects that the archaeological team expects to encounter on the wreck of *Great Mahomet*, in particular, could represent the most unique and significant religious assemblage from the Holy Cities of Mecca and Medina ever found within the context of a shipwreck. Similarly, the known career of the *Mocha Frigate* in the eastern Bay of Bengal and Indonesian waters establishes a reasonable expectation of encountering, for example, extremely rare Southeast Asian artifacts.

The Cannon

The cannon found in S001 was fully exposed and documented but was not recovered for conservation reasons (figure 3.12). The cannon is heavily concreted and made of iron. It is a muzzle-loading gun measuring 2.4 m in length. The chase, reinforce, and vent field are not clearly visible because of concretions. The shape of the button and the cascabel at the rear portion of the cannon are visible.

The cascabel is round (not inward curved as in figure 3.12) and appears to be textured with large grape-like shapes. The muzzle is similarly textured, suggesting a form of decoration. The button extending outward from the cascabel measures 17 cm in diameter. The measured distances along the cannon D1 and D2 are approximately 1.4 m and 1 m. Diameters at points A, B, and C are 30, 26, and 45 cm. Note that all measurements are influenced by the concretions, so the actual dimensions of the cannon can vary.

The diameter of the trunnions on each side is about 16 cm, with the trunnions placed closer to the lower portion of the cannon. The cannon was

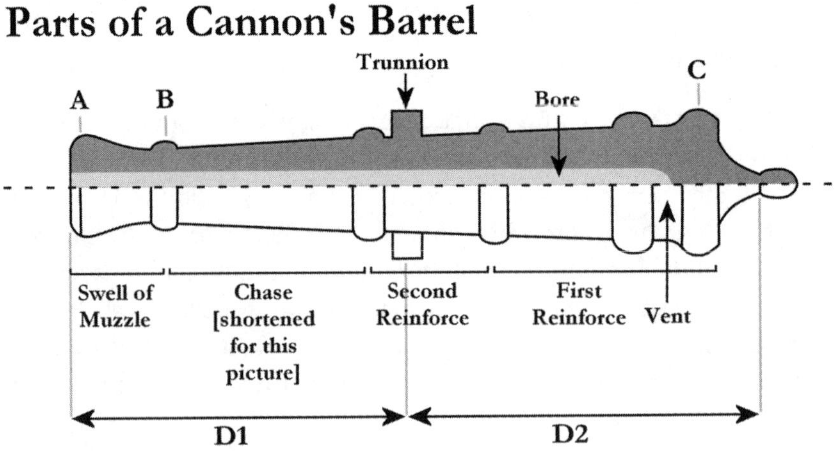

Figure 3.12. Schematic topside view of the cannon found at the "channel wreck" site.

lifted by using airbags in order to shift it aside. Bags with a total capacity of over 2,150 kg were needed to lift the cannon. It was not possible to measure the bore because of concretion. Based on the preliminary weight and length of the cannon, it is likely that it is a six-pounder. Placement of the trunnions on the lower portion of the cannon instead of the center line suggests a date in the second half of the seventeenth century. In the original design of cast cannon, the normal position of the trunnion was just forward of the point of balance of the gun (to give some degree of breech preponderance) and probably originally was merely a crosspiece lashed beneath the piece. As a general rule the older the gun, the lower the center line of the trunnions (Caruana 1994: 5).

Artifact Categories

Sixty-nine artifacts were recovered from this site (table 3.2). The relatively great number of twenty-seven glass artifacts is due to the fact that several pieces belong to the same glass vessel. At least four individual specimens of bottles were found: two with a round bottom, one square (gin case bottle), and one fully intact bottle with an oval bottom (figure 3.13). This oval bottle can be dated to the second half of the seventeenth century. Besides the bottles, a piece of a drinking glass was found and a small piece of what appears to be window glass were found.

A number of concretions were also found. Some concretions contain iron cannonballs, obvious from the shape and size. Other concretions have unknown contents pending postrecovery conservation and analysis.

Table 3.2. Category Overview of the Artifact Materials of the Channel Wreck

Material	Number of Artifacts
Glass	27
Concretion	15
Ceramics	8
Lead	7
Porcelain	7
Bone	1
Iron	1
Stone	1
Tin alloy	1
Copper alloy	1

Figure 3.13. Intact wine bottle.

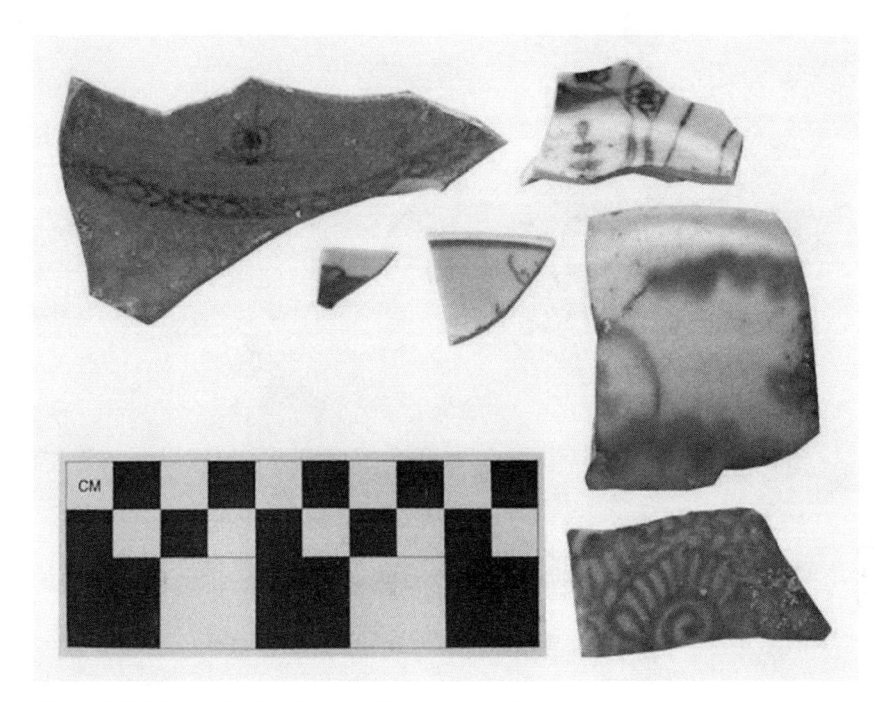

Figure 3.14. Porcelain sherds of the "channel wreck."

Seven pieces of porcelain were collected from the wreck site surface (figure 3.14), so these pieces may be intrusive and cannot be used for accurately dating the site. Although further analysis is required, the pieces do not seem to be of a later date than those found on the *Fiery Dragon* and are consistent with identification as *Great Mahomet* or *Mocha Frigate*.

Seven pieces of lead have been found on this site so far. Three of them have been identified as lead shot. Two pieces have a diameter of about 14 to 15 mm; the third is about 9.5 mm. One of the larger ones has a small triangular piece of lead attached to it, indicating that it was cast but that the sprue had not yet been trimmed to make it usable.

Two pieces of lead are rectangular, and another one is almost square. This last piece is 21 × 23 mm and has a large "X" mark incised on one side (figure 3.15). It could have been used as a gaming piece. Similar pieces were found on the pirate shipwreck *Whydah* (1717) off Cape Cod, Massachusetts.

Figure 3.15. Lead gaming piece marked "X."

Hull Structure

The exposed structure consists of a heavy timber 50 cm wide, lying flat, with four smaller beams of around 15 cm wide attached underneath it at a 90-degree angle pointing outward. The areas between the four beams are open and by using the Venturi could be cleared down to 1 m to expose a continuous space underneath that is filled completely with loose sediment. The structure does not have any visible distortion, so it is possible that the lower hull section of the ship sunk into the sediment and is thus preserved intact. No outer hull features such as like futtocks, knee joints, floor planking, or keelson were observed within the excavation area, although such features may be found at a deeper level. The exposed heavy timber is considered to be parallel to the center line of the hull and oriented with a bearing of 280 degrees, thus pointing toward the shore in an almost east to west direction. This supports the idea that the ship was sunk across the channel as a means of blocking it.

A Pirate's Life for Me

A manuscript located in the Service Historique de la Défense archives in Vincennes (Paris) yielded important and interesting clues as to how pirates lived on the island of Sainte-Marie (figure 3.16). The author of the book,

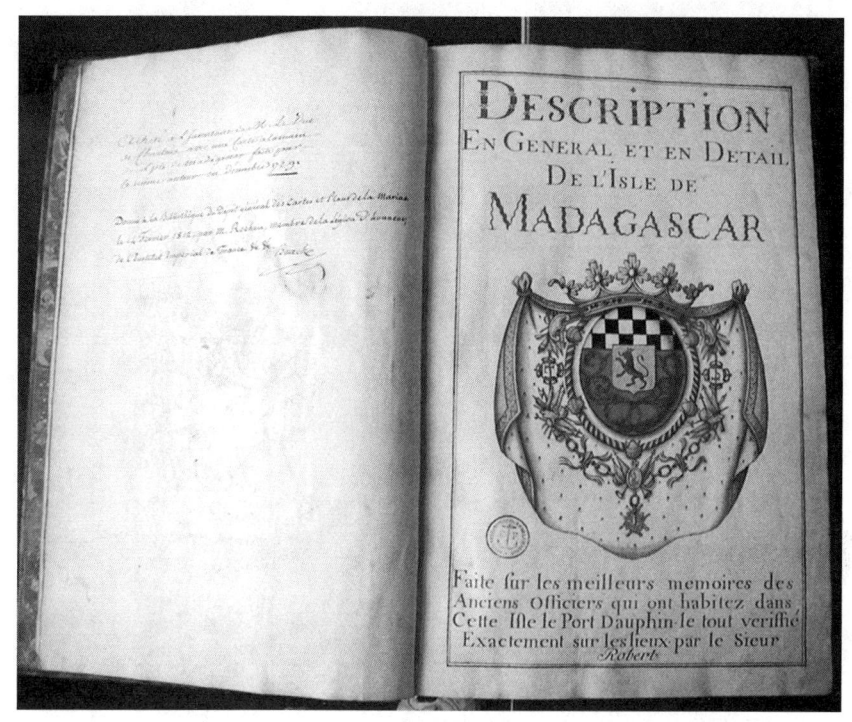

Figure 3.16. A 1730 manuscript on Madagascar that yielded important historical data on the pirates of Sainte-Marie Island (courtesy Service Historique de la Défense, Vincennes).

the Sieur Robert, actually gathered testimonies from various individuals over a period of several years in the 1720s while he was in Madagascar and claims that they were all reliable eyewitness accounts. Robert indicates that much of the east coast of the Big Island was frequented by pirates who had settled there over the course of over a decade, more specifically in the area of Manghabé, known today as the Baie d'Antongil, north-northwest of Sainte-Marie Island.

The small island of Sainte-Marie became the pirates' headquarters and principal base of operation, benefiting from a natural harbor that could accommodate four to five large vessels, with a place to careen ships, and an islet in the middle of a shallow bay that could be used at a retreat and stronghold (figure 3.17). This island is known as Ile aux Forbans (Pirate Island). The pirates lived well, with each captain owning his own house or bungalow on stilts. The houses could be identified by individual silk pennants of various colors bearing individual marks or symbols flown above each dwelling.

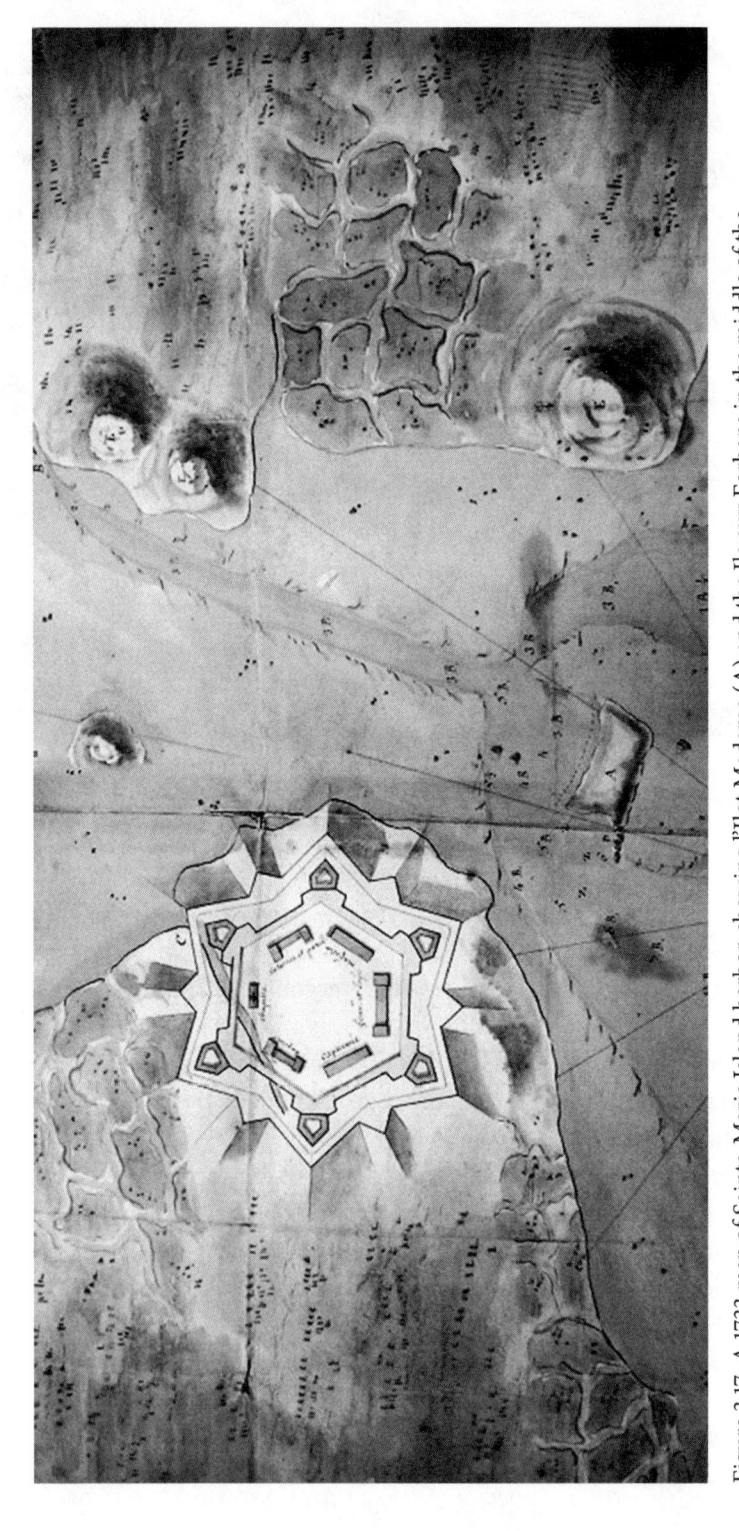

Figure 3.17. A 1733 map of Sainte-Marie Island harbor, showing l'Ilot Madame (A) and the Ile aux Forbans in the middle of the bay in the upper center section of the map. The fort feature on top of the hill overlooking Ilot Madame is proposed, not actual.

Most of the pirates had a local black woman as wife or mistress, on whom they lavished presents. The observer reported seeing many of those women dressed in long Indian silk dresses with gold and silver embroideries and wearing gold earrings, bracelets, and necklaces, some with diamonds of considerable value. But not all women were well treated by the pirates. The pirates often threatened to send them back and replace them. Some of the women took revenge by poisoning their companions and fleeing to the main island on pirogues, carrying with them all of their gold, precious stones, and other valuables. Robert states that more than eighty pirates were thus murdered. He writes that the pirates owned a considerable quantity of diamonds: one reported weighing 64 karats, others between 20 and 30 karats, and numerous ones weighing between 10 and 20 karats. But however rich they were, the pirates were lacking many necessities. This caused visiting merchants, many from Boston and New York, to make their fortune by selling merchandise at exorbitant prices and being paid in gold, diamonds, and slaves.

Robert also mentions the capture of the rich Portuguese East Indiaman *Senhora de Cabo* near Ile Bourbon (present-day Reunion Island) by John Taylor and Olivier La Buse. The viceroy of Portugal (Count Ericeira) and the archbishop of Goa were traveling on board, with the viceroy carrying a fortune in diamonds and exotic Asian products. The ship was subsequently brought to Sainte-Marie Island and modified from a three-deck vessel to two and a half decks and its armament reduced to sixty guns. The modification cost the pirate dearly, paid for in gold and diamonds. But Taylor and La Buse along with their crew had made a colossal fortune. This prize combined with a few others ships plundered shortly before represented the largest booty ever taken, totaling nearly $500,000,000 in today's money. Each crew member received from one to forty-two diamonds, depending on their size (Rogozinski 2000:215).

The 2010 expedition has contributed to the exposure of only a small part of the wreck of the *Fiery Dragon*. Further research is needed in order to understand the architecture and origin of the ship, the way it came to rest on floor of the natural harbor of Saint Marie, the cargo, and objects that remain. Future expeditions will focus on the continued excavation of the wreck. The first aim is to expose part of the hull, including the keelson and other parts of the structure.

The "channel site" still needs to yield additional clues as to the ship's origin date and other factors that might determine whether it is the *Mocha Frigate* or the *Great Mahomet*. Only a minute part of the wreck site was investigated, so a large-scale excavation should be conducted in order to expose a cross section of the hull. A bigger survey of the area should reveal the extent of the site. Apart from these two wreck sites, others are still to be found and mapped. At least five other shipwrecks from the Golden Age of Piracy are likely to be present in the harbor area and in the vicinity of the careening spot off Ilot Madame. In order to locate and record these wrecks a more extensive systematic survey should be undertaken to map the entire harbor area as well as part of Pirate Bay.

Based on the excavation and survey results in terms of number of artifacts found in 2010, subsequent expeditions are expected to yield an exponentially greater amount of material culture. This requires careful planning and organization of conservation work. The local museum at Ilot Madame is neither equipped nor organized at this time to conserve artifacts of an organic nature such as wood and bone. Future expeditions will therefore focus on development and improvement of the local museum as a place to secure, conserve, and exhibit material culture from submerged environments. This will benefit both the local community and the expedition team. A refurbished museum housing a permanent exhibition on pirates of Madagascar will provide a major tourist attraction that make a significant contribution to the local economy as well as to the knowledge of the cultural history of Sainte-Marie and Madagascar in general. It provides the unique opportunity to house and curate this cultural heritage and provide an educational tool within reach of the actual wreck sites. Having a permanent research base set up at the museum will ensure that the process of excavation and conservation of artifacts can be made more effective and efficient. It also can lead to empowerment of local researchers and build up the capacity for research and conservation.

A multiyear project at Sainte-Marie can be envisioned if these goals are to be fulfilled. With the excellent collaboration of the authorities of Madagascar and the local community at Sainte-Marie Island, such a project can be expected to be successful in recovering and preserving an important cultural heritage for future generations.

4

Black Bart's *Ranger*

CHAD M. GULSETH

Wherever we want to go, we go. That's what a ship is, you know. It's not just a keel and hull and a deck and sails. That's what a ship needs. But what a ship is . . . what the Black Pearl really is . . . is freedom.

Captain Jack Sparrow (*Pirates of the Caribbean*)

Armed with the finest of pistols, dressed in the fanciest attire, and festooned with a diamond-studded cross and gold chains, Captain Bartholomew Roberts had his throat torn out by a broadside of grapeshot from a Royal Navy man-of-war. His lifeless body was wrapped in chains and sent to the depths. The rest of his pirate crew had a date with the gallows. This intense and gruesome final battle, followed by the mass hanging of fifty-two men, exemplifies the risks that many of these sailors were willing to take in order to live a life of crime and freedom on the high seas (Atkins 1723; Johnson 1972).

For the last two and a half centuries we have been captivated by the legends of pirates. Whether it is a historical account like that of Captain Charles Johnson or a fictional tale like Robert Lewis Stevenson's *Treasure Island*, people have been fascinated with the high-seas marauders of the seventeenth and early eighteenth centuries, known as the Golden Age of Piracy. The men and women from this time conjure up thoughts of flintlock pistols and cutlasses, eye patches and parrots, and gratuitous amounts of rum. Fact or fiction, the stories of pirates have been researched and rewritten time and time again. The material remains and archaeology of these Golden Age villains seem to be the next chapter of their lives that has yet to be told. Here is what remains of history's most successful pirate: Captain "Black Bart" Roberts.

Born in Pembrokeshire, Wales, Roberts captured and plundered more than four hundred ships in less than three years, carving out his place in

94 · Chad M. Gulseth

Captain Bartho. Roberts *with two Ships, Viz. the* Royal Fortune *and* Ranger, *takes 11 Sail in* Whydah Road *on the Coast of* Guiney, *January* 11th 1722/4.

Figure 4.1. Captain Roberts with the *Ranger* and *Royal Fortune* at Whydah Road, January 11, 1722 (Johnson 1972).

history as the single most successful pirate captain. He inherited the ship *Royal Rover* from pirate Captain Howell Davis, who was killed in an ambush on the island of Princes in 1719 (Johnson 1972). Throughout his pirating career, Roberts commanded nine vessels in all. The *Royal Fortune*, *Little Ranger*, and *Great Ranger* were the three ships under his command (figure 4.1) during his final battle with the Royal Navy's Captain Chaloner Ogle of His Majesty's Ship *Swallow*, a fourth-rate fifty-gun man-of-war. The tale of Captain Roberts and his final days is riveting, packed with violence and action. It is even more exciting, however, that the three ships that he last commanded before his death are still within our grasp today.

"Fit Her for a Sea Rover"

Four-hundred leagues off Africa, the crew of the *Good Fortune* voted. They deserted Captain Roberts and left the company of the *Royal Fortune* during the night (Johnson 1972:173). The men were sad to see the swift brigantine go, but they fell to windward and sailed near the Senegal River, where French cruisers patrolled to protect the gum trade. Two "cruisers" (one with ten guns and sixty-five men and one with sixteen guns and seventy-five men) gave them chase (Johnson 1972:196), likely a sloop and light frigate. They both surrendered as soon as Roberts ran up the Jolly Roger. *Comte de Thoulouze*, the sixteen-gun vessel, was refit and mounted with twenty-four guns and renamed *Ranger*, while the smaller ship named *Ranger* (formerly the *St Agnes*) was renamed the *Little Ranger* (figure 4.2). The smaller vessel was used as their store ship.

They spent six weeks cleaning and refitting, drinking, and whoring. At the beginning of August 1720 they sailed along the coast of Africa, leaving a wake of destruction (Johnson 1972:198). Captain Michael Gee of the *Onslow* likely struck a deal with the pirates for the exchange of his vessel (British National Archives and Maritime Museum [BNA] T 70/4:24). The *Onslow* was a fine frigate of the British Royal African Company of 410 tons, with twenty-six guns and fifty men. It was headed for Cape Coast Castle and

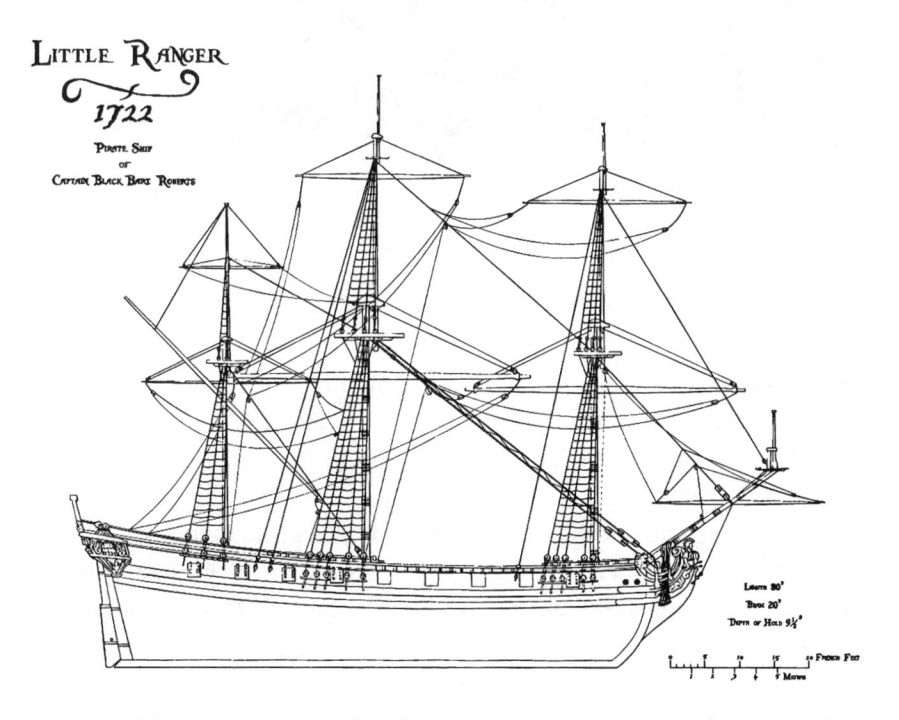

Figure 4.2. The *St Agnes*, captured in the mouth of the Senegal River and renamed *Ranger* and later *Little Ranger* when the larger *Comte de Thoulouze* was acquired and renamed *Ranger*.

Figure 4.3. Sir Chaloner Ogle, 1681–1750 (BNA ADM 1/2242).

then to Whydah to collect slaves for Jamaica. Onboard were copper bars, muskets, looking glasses, cloth, pewter, and a dozen other types of trade goods. The insurance paid £6000.0.0 (BNA T 70/1225:13). Roberts likely found a new hat aboard, listed as a present on the ship's cargo manifest. "Beav hatt laced & red Feather" (BNA T 70/922:91). This matches Johnson's description of Roberts "being dressed in a rich crimson damask waistcoat and breeches, a red feather in his hat" (Johnson 1972:212). Captain Gee was given the old French vessel *Royal Fortune*, though they continued to use this name aboard *Onslow*, which had been renamed *Royal Fortune* after its capture.

The pirates "fell to making such alterations as might fit her for a sea rover, pulling down her bulkheads, and making her flush, so that she became, in all respects, as complete a ship for their purpose, as any they could have found" (Johnson 1972:199). The new *Royal Fortune* was mounted with forty guns and along with the 24-gun *Ranger* continued to wreak havoc along the west coast of Africa.

On January 11, 1722, *Royal Fortune* and *Ranger* sailed into Whydah Road, accompanied by fiddles, fifes, drums, and horns, Jolly Rogers, cutlasses, pistols, and cannon. Roberts made a grand spectacle of his crimes. This was the most dashing and daring of all pirate robberies. Captain Ogle (figure 4.3) of the HMS *Swallow* writes:

> On my arrival at Whydah I was informed that two Pyrate ships, one of forty and another of twenty-four guns commanded by one Roberts had been there, and sailed about twenty-six hours before: I found ten sail of ships in the road, two of which were English, three French, and five Portuguese, they had all ransomed at the rate of eight pounds weight of gold each; an English ship, for refusing to ransom the pyrates had been burnt with a considerable number of Negroes aboard. The Pyrates being informed that a French ship they had taken sailed well and had formerly been a privateer of St Malo, did, notwithstanding a ransom paid for her, carry her away with a design to fit her for their service and quit their twenty-four gun ship: Therefore I judged they must go to some place in the Bite to clean and fit the French ship, before they would think of cruising again; which occasioned me to stretch away into the Bite, and look into those places which I knew had a depth of water sufficient for his Majesty's Ships.
>
> On the 5th of February at daylight, I saw Cape Lopez bearing W.S.W. about three leagues; and at the same time discovered three ships at anchor under the Cape, which I believed to be the Pyrates, two of them having pendants flying. I was obliged to haul off N.W. and W.N.W. to clear the Frenchman's Bank, the wind at S.S.E. and in less than an hour one of the three got under sail and gave me chase; and I to give her fair opportunity of coming up with me without being discovered, kept on the same course, with the same sail aboard I had when I first saw her: About eleven that morning she got within gunshot of me and fired several chase guns, under English colors and a black flag at her mizzen-peek; soon afterwards being come within musket shot, I starboarded my helm and gave her a broadside, and in an hour and an half's time she struck and called for quarter, we having disabled her very much, and shot down her main-top-mast; she proved to be the French ship they had taken out of Whydah Road,

and had put into her 32 guns and 132 men, 23 of whom were Blacks, she had 26 men killed and wounded the, Captain's name was Skyrm, who had a leg shot off; the prisoners informed me, that the two ships they left at anchor under the Cape were Roberts in the 40 gun ship, and the other 24 gun ship they had that morning quitted for the prize. The 6th ditto in the night, I left the prize, having put her into the best condition for sailing so short a time would allow of, and ordered her away to the island Princess. I made the best of my way to windward again, in order to descry the two ships that remained at anchor under Cape Lopez. On the 9th ditto in the evening, I made the Cape, and saw two ships stretching-in under the land about five leagues distance, having day-light enough, I was obliged to stand off and on all night, and in the morning I stretched in under the Cape, where I saw at anchor three ships, the biggest of them with Jack, ensign, and pendant flying, whom I lay up with 'till I got within random shot, when the wind took me ahead and made two trips, in which time she slipped and got under sail and came down upon me, with English ensign and jack, and a black pendant flying at her main-top-mast-head, and I showed her a French ensign, when she came within pistol shot I hoisted my proper colors and gave her a broadside, which she returned, and endeavored to get from me, by making all the sail she could, but in less than two hours shot her main-top-mast down, and then she struck, her mizzen-top-mast being shot away some time before: The captain, whose name was Roberts, was killed, his prize (formerly called *Onslow*, and since by the Pyrates the *Royal Fortune*) had 40 guns mounted and 152 men, 25 of whom were Negroes. The next day I plied back again for the Cape, in order to take out the 24 gun ship the Pyrates had quitted, and to restore to the third (which was a ship freighted by the African Company-Hill Commander), such provisions as the Pyrates had robbed him of, together with his surgeon and four men, Roberts having seized her the day before I took him, as she was coming to under the Cape to water; but anchoring again under the Cape the 12th ditto, I found ther only the Pyrate ship of 24 guns without anybody aboard her, all the men's chests being broke open and rifled, which occasions me to believe that by the speedy sailing of the above said Company's third ship, which had but a very small quantity of water provisions aboard two days before, they must have robbed her otherwise could not possibly have sailed so soon. The Pyrates informed me that they had left in their chests aboard a considerable quantity of gold, but not above 10 ounces of it we found aboard her. (BNA ADM 1/2242)

This section of the letter to the Admiralty gives us some important details about Roberts's pirate ships. It verifies the names of all of his vessels and their armament. The letter also describes *Great Ranger* as being a French ship from St. Malo that would need to be refit for pirating. Then Ogle describes how he separated Roberts's forces by luring the 32-gun *Great Ranger* away from the other two pirate vessels and fired a surprise broadside down the length of their hull. This made *Great Ranger* the most heavily damaged vessel throughout these engagements.

After fifty-two pirates were hanged at Cape Coast Castle, Ogle sailed with his three pirate prizes across the Atlantic, stopping to sell prize goods in Barbados and then sailing to Port Royal, Jamaica, to sell the rest.

Port Royal and the 1722 Hurricane

HMS *Swallow* arrived in Port Royal on August 14, 1722. Lt. Isaac Sunn was placed in charge of removing goods from the pirate vessels to be sold on shore (BNA ADM L/S/564). Sunn began with *Royal Fortune*. From August 16 until August 27, they removed several longboats full of prize goods and took off three long boats full of water. There is no fresh water in Port Royal, so it has to be gathered on the main part of the island. Removing water from the pirate vessels would have saved them a considerable amount of time and effort.

Before Sunn could finish salvaging the pirate prizes, a hurricane struck the island on August 28, 1722. John Atkins, the *Swallow*'s surgeon, published a very vivid description of the 1722 hurricane:

> Within it was worse, for the waters sapping the foundations, gave continual and just apprehensions of the houses falling, as in effect half of them did, and buried their inhabitants . . . Wrecks, and drowned men were every where seen along shore, general complaints of loss at land which made it a melancholy scene, and to finish the misfortune, the slackness of the sea-breezes, calms, and lightning, stagnating waters, broods of insects thence, and shock or two of earthquake that succeeded to the hurricane, combined to spread a baneful influence, and brought on a contagious distemper, fatal for some months through the island. (Atkins 1723:238–41)

Atkins wrote that only six of the fifty sailing ships in the harbor survived the storm, with their masts and booms were blown away. The governor of Jamaica, Sir Nicholas Lawes, wrote a letter to the Colonial Office about a month after the hurricane, detailing a list of all the ships in and around Port Royal and Kingston during the hurricane. This list gives the names of seventy-three vessels, of which fifty were lost, as Atkins said. Eleven rode out the storm, two more were stranded on shore, and ten of the lost vessels were salvaged (BNA CO 137/14:178–82).

Among the casualties of this hurricane were the *Royal Fortune* and *Little Ranger*. They were blown across the harbor and splintered to pieces on the rock of Saltpond Hill. The *Great Ranger*, however, was one of the few vessels to have survived the storm (BNA ADM 51/954). Nevertheless, it was heavily damaged. Sailors of the Royal Navy salvaged what they could to repair the *Swallow*, including water butts, puncheons, and even two spars used for yards. Ogle's crew continued to salvage the *Great Ranger* until about mid-October and then sold it to someone in Port Royal (BNA ADM L/S/564). Ogle received £5364.9.9 sterling for the sale of the *Great Ranger* and other effects, though he never shared any spoils from this venture with his crew (BNA ADM 1/2242/5).

The 1724 Map

Less than two years after the hurricane of 1722, HMS *Launcestone* was anchored at Port Royal. The ship's 1st Lt. James Cascoigne drafted a map that contains both features of land and water with *An Exact Plan of Chocolata Hole and the South End of the Town of Port Royal in Jamaica* (figure 4.4). This map was drafted for captains approaching Chocolata Hole, with the north arrow pointing to the bottom left of the chart.

Until 1735 Port Royal did not have a proper wharf for careening large vessels. But smaller vessels were able to careen at Chocolata Hole. Marked as "N the wreck of the *Lewis Hulk*" in the center of the chart, this ship was used by the Royal Navy to pull ships over on their sides to be cleaned and repaired. The *Hulk* was deliberately sunk at this location in 1703 for this purpose (Pawson and Buisseret 2000:173).

Two other wrecks are identified on this map. "O the wreck of a Galeon taken by James Littleton Esq (since a Flagg Officer)" and "P the wreck of the Ranger a pirate ship taken by Capt Chaloner Ogle (since Knighted)." The discovery of this map by Donny Hamilton (2006:24–25) in 1982 is what triggered the present research on the *Ranger*. Several historical accounts

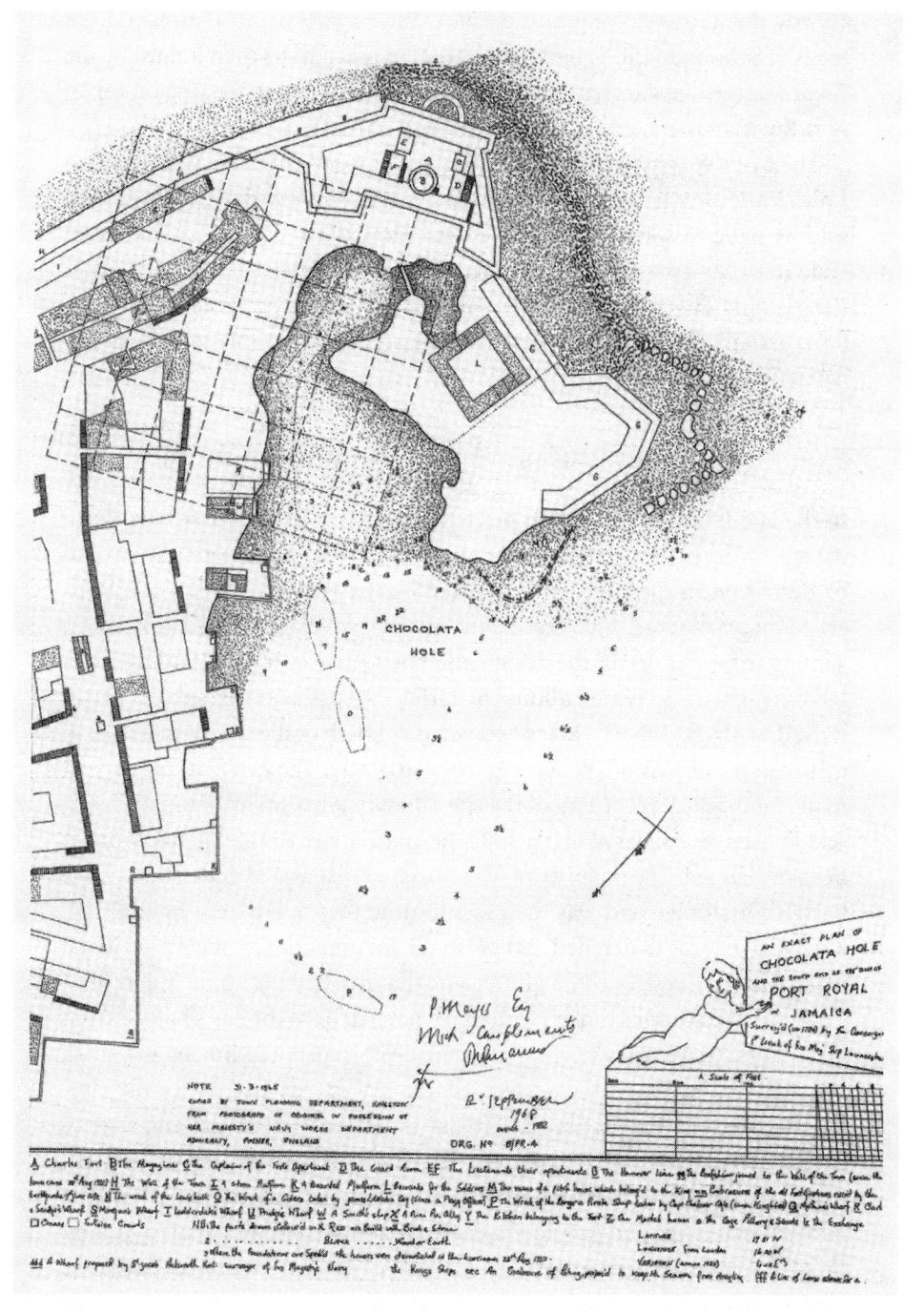

Figure 4.4. *An Exact Plan of Chocolata Hole and the South End of the Town of Port Royal in Jamaica* (Cascoigne 1724).

already detail the sinking of the *Little Ranger* with *Royal Fortune* on the rocks of Saltpond Hill. Therefore, if this map is accurate, then it must be the *Great Ranger* that survived the 1722 hurricane that is now resting on top of Port Royal's sunken city.

The *Great Ranger* was the most heavily damaged ship in battle, survived a hurricane after having all its masts and rigging blown away, and was then sold by Ogle to someone in Port Royal. How did it end up in Chocolata Hole less than two years later? Perhaps the person who bought the *Great Ranger* only did so in order to salvage the ship, as opposed to repairing it for sea. Only the archaeology of this shipwreck will be able to help us understand what happened.

Marx Excavations, 1966–1968

In the late 1960s plans were in place to dredge up a portion of Port Royal harbor for large cruise ship docking. Much of the underwater city would be destroyed in the process. Supported by the Institute of Jamaica, Robert Marx was tasked with producing an accurate chart of the sunken city, gaining information on the design and construction of the buildings, and recovering the surviving building materials and artifacts for later display in museums (Marx 1968:3). Marx excavated as much of the underwater city in this region as he could, collecting many artifacts. The haste of this project made methodical recording of the site difficult. Also, many of today's treatments used to conserve artifacts from marine environments had not yet been developed. The majority of what had been excavated ended up in large barrels for storage and was then lost to time (Marx 1968:15). In addition, almost all of Marx's detailed and personal documentation of his Port Royal work was later destroyed in a hurricane that flooded his home in Florida.

Marx's excavations took place along what had been the city's harbor front on Fishers Row (figure 4.5). He used an airlift to bring sediment and small artifacts to a barge on the surface, where it was screened by locally contracted workers. Marx utilized standard units of measurement and a series of polygons in his drawings to outline structural remains and shipwrecks that he discovered. His preliminary reports identified the location by a circle with a letter and provided a list with a description of artifacts found there. Roman numerals I, II, III, and IV corresponded with the depth of the artifact below the sea floor. "I" indicated artifacts uncovered just below the surface to a depth of two feet, "II" indicated two to four feet, "III" indicated

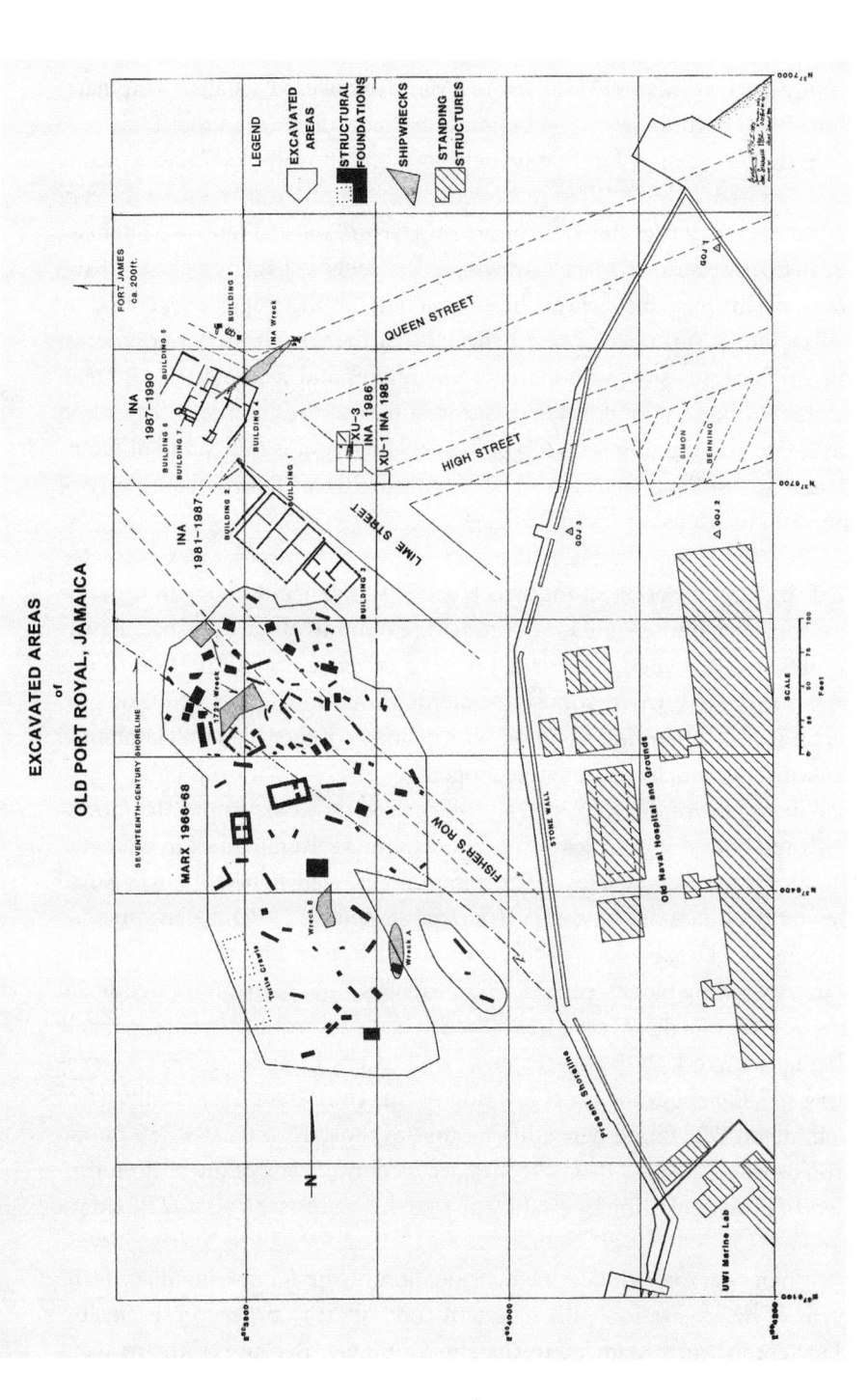

Figure 4.5. Areas excavated by Marx and Hamilton at Port Royal (D. Hamilton 2006).

four to seven feet, and "IV" indicated anything found between seven and nine feet (Marx 1968:25).

In March of his 1967 dig season Marx uncovered what he originally thought were timbers from a building. He later discovered that they were from the wreck of a ship that he believed sank during the 1722 hurricane, so he named it the "1722 Wreck." Unknown to Marx at the time, he had found the remains of Roberts's pirate ship *Great Ranger*. Figure 4.5 has been created from four of Marx's drawings that included the wreckage of the *Ranger*. This map shows how the two sections of the ship are separated by ballast and tree timbers. Marx believed that the tree timbers were part of the ship's cargo as dyewood. The other squares and rectangles in the map are the outlines of brick walls that were a part of the city before it sunk in 1692. Because the ship is on top of the sunken city, it is difficult to differentiate many of the artifacts associated with the *Great Ranger* from those of sunken Port Royal.

The *Great Ranger* had been broken into two large pieces. Marx estimated that the larger section of the wreck was fifty-five feet long, with only the keelson, keel, frames, and lower futtocks remaining. Because he had no way to preserve the wood, he decided only to excavate a small portion of this ship in order to uncover some information about the ship's identity and protect it from further deterioration. The majority of the ship's hull contained ballast rock, which was concreted together with 150-lb mortar balls, which had been part of the ship's ballast. Marx used crowbars to pry the mortar balls and ballast apart, excavating a hole to the keelson ten feet in diameter. He recovered four whale's teeth, cannonballs, lead musket balls, a small pewter tea pot, a pewter tankard, a large stoneware Dutch bellarmine jug, buttons, buckles, cooking utensils, intact bottles, and hundreds of rigging parts, including blocks, pulleys, and deadeyes. One of the more significant artifacts that he discovered was a French écu coin from 1721, appropriately dating the wreck to the hurricane in 1722 (Marx 1973:201–2, 239). Marx is very specific about the exact location of this coin: "One French silver Ecu coin dated 1721 found beneath a mound of those 11" diameter, 150 pound iron mortar balls and ballast stones, wedged into some of the bottom timbers of this wreck, which certainly proved this wreck sank after 1721" (Marx 1968:68).

When Marx concluded his investigation of the *Ranger* he filled in the areas of his excavation with sediment and ballast in order to prevent further teredo worm damage to the ship's timbers. Because of the artifacts recovered by Marx and the history that he discovered, the plans to dredge the harbor for cruise ships were canceled and the underwater city was saved.

Pirate Hunting

During the summer of 2012 three other students from Texas A&M's Nautical Archaeology Program and I were given a permit from the Jamaica National Heritage Trust to conduct and archaeological survey of the shipwreck *Ranger* in Port Royal harbor and search the far side of the harbor for the *Royal Fortune* and *Little Ranger*. We had a limited budget and only thirty days to complete our objectives. We flew out of Houston, with two carry-on bags and two checked bags of fifty pounds each. This included our clothing, SCUBA gear, computers, cameras, tapes, lines, reels, and other miscellaneous archaeology gear.

The *Great Ranger* was not difficult to relocate; it is right where 1st Lieutenant Cascoigne drew it in 1724 and where Donny Hamilton (2006:19, fig. 2.4) accurately plotted it on his excavation plans at E304700 N1984279. We started by running a baseline along a longitudinal timber, which later proved to be the ship's keelson. The keelson measured exactly one French foot wide, identifying it as a French-made vessel. Next we divided the ship into six quads labeled A to F. We each mapped our own quads with the same scale, and within a week we had a nice site plan going. We used a two-inch water dredge and a paintbrush to clear some of the overburden to record the ends of the floor timbers as accurately as possible. To further our accuracy, we took direct measurements from our data and input them into Site Recorder 3H. The Site Recorder web, photographs, videos, scale drawing, and notes were all used to create an overall site plan of the *Great Ranger* (figure 4.6).

Like a forgotten ghost, the wreck is a small mountain in the center of the large depression left by Marx's excavation. Only 10 m of the pirate ship has been left reasonably undisturbed. A mound of rock and eight mortar balls are all that remain of the ballast. A local Jamaican diver named Emmanuel Blake told me how he helped Robert Marx remove twenty-six of these mortar balls from the wreck site and placed them by the seawall in the late 1960s. The Jamaican Coast Guard recently pulled the balls out of the sea, and the Jamaica National Heritage Trust has placed them in freshwater storage for conservation.

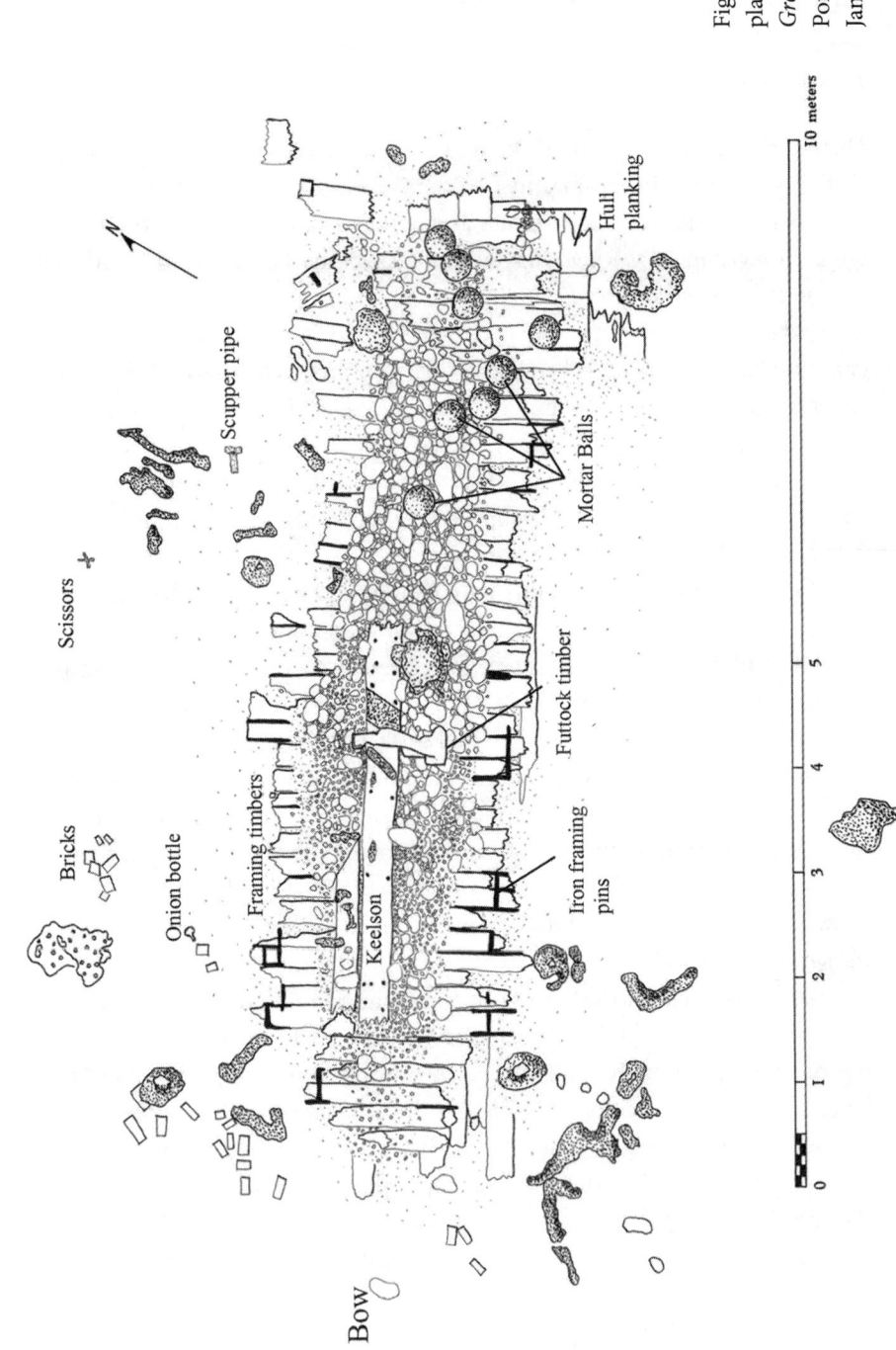

Figure 4.6. Site plan of the *Great Ranger*, Port Royal, Jamaica.

Guarded by spotted moral eels, stingrays, and scorpion fish, thirty-seven large, tightly spaced framing timbers peek out from the mound of rock and sand. A number of these floor frames were joined with large framing pins. These iron fasteners are 3–3.5 cm in diameter and run through two and sometimes three frames at a time. This type of fastening system in a heavily framed frigate would have given the ship a sturdy hull and is not unlike the construction of the French colonial ship *La Belle* and Blackbeard's pirate ship *Queen Anne's Revenge*.

A disarticulated ship timber was discovered on top of the ballast pile. Retaining a framing pin similar to those found in the floor timbers, this timber apparently had been previously excavated from the port side of the wreck and then set on top of the site. This timber was loose on the site, so it would be difficult to believe that it had remained there for forty-five years, since the Marx excavations. Nevertheless, we brought the timber to the surface for a better look. After we recorded it in detail, it was returned to the ship with the other artifacts discovered and reburied on the starboard side, nearly amidships.

Artifacts

The main object of surveying the *Great Ranger* was to test the truth of the 1724 map on the ground. Without a complete excavation or at least a trench this would be incredibly difficult. In order to collect as many data as possible while making a minimal impact on the site itself, we used a small water dredge to help remove the sand that covered some of the prominent features of the wreck. The spoil was collected in a mesh bag attached to the end of the exhaust hose. In all six bags of spoil were removed from the site and sifted through a ¼" screen. Only two pipe stems were found in the spoil. These two pipe stems made up 10 percent of the entire assemblage of twenty artifacts found during our investigation (table 4.1).

Eight of the twenty artifacts were pieces from the ship itself, including the futtock timber, a portion of a rigging block, iron fasteners, a treenail, and a lead scupper pipe. The lead scupper was taken back to the Texas A&M Conservation Research Laboratory (CRL) for conservation and further study. With a few simple measurements of the scupper pipe, it was easy to determine that the thickness of the hull was approximately 20 cm. This artifact is similar to the scupper pipes found on HMS *Dartmouth* (Lavery 1987:66). The *Great Ranger* scupper did not have a leather flap to prevent

Table 4.1. *Great Ranger* Artifacts (2012)

Artifact #	Description	Y (Base Line)	X	Z (Vertical from Datum)
1	Onion bottle	4.48	2.04	surface
2	Futtock	6.25	0.00	surface
3	Onion bottle	7.48	4.57	surface
4	Rigging block	4.10	0.75	surface
5	Wood fragment	4.68	0.95	surface
6	Iron fastener	12.40	1.25	top 5 cm
7	Pipe stem	10.38	0.60	upper 5 cm
8	Pipe bowl	10.14	0.90	upper 5 cm
9	Bottom of bottle	12.00	0.55	0.66
10	Treenail	11.26	0.77	0.60
11	Iron concretion	12.40	1.25	top 5 cm
12	Glass bottle bottom	6.40	1.50	0.57
13	Pipe bowl	12.07	1.05	top 5 cm
14	Pipe stem	Quad E		
15	Pipe stem	Quad E		
16	Fastener hollow	10.58	0.14	surface
17	Scupper pipe	9.00	1.52	surface
18	Ceramic	11.43	-0.06	top 5 cm
19	Scissors	8.03	2.92	surface
20	Cloth	5.25	-0.21	under ballast rock

water from entering the ship, however, as those on *Dartmouth* did and appears more crudely constructed.

Some of the other artifacts found during the survey were more likely to be intrusive to the site. On the first dive I discovered a whole onion bottle on the surface of the wreck. Another was later discovered in the same fashion. It is difficult to believe that these whole onion bottles had just been sitting on the surface of the wreck since the 1720 and had been missed by archaeologists and divers for decades. It seems more likely that a storm had kicked them up out of the sunken city and that they were deposited on the wreck site. Whether or not the scissors that we found belong to the *Great Ranger* is also debatable, though their stylistic attributes are more closely related to the 1720s than to the great earthquake of 1692 (Noël Hume 1969:268). I would like to think that a pirate might have cut his hair with them.

Of the twenty artifacts found, only six were recovered for conservation. The two onion bottles were taken by the Jamaica National Heritage Trust to be conserved in Kingston. The lead scupper pipe, the "modern" cloth, the scissors, and a diagnostic sherd of red earthenware were taken back to CRL in Bryan, Texas. Once the research and conservation of these artifacts was completed, they were sent back to the Heritage Trust in Jamaica.

Conclusion

Based on archaeology, could we definitively say that the "1722 Wreck" discovered by Robert Marx (1968) is the remains of the pirate ship *Great Ranger*? No. Without the 1724 map as well as Marx's and Dr. Hamilton's excavation plans we would probably never know the identity of this vessel. Marx found the 1721 French coin and the keelson is exactly one French foot in width, but that information gives only a date and country of origin. A dendrochronological study of the ship's timbers would damage the site and likely give us this same information. I believe that it is more telling to look at the entire picture. The Royal Navy was salvaging the heavily damaged *Great Ranger* after the hurricane. Someone in Port Royal bought it at very low cost. In less than two years the *Ranger* was drawn on a map as a navigational hazard. Today there is a shipwreck site right where the 1724 map says it should be. The *Lewis Hulk* also was intentionally sunk in this same location. Archaeological research yields no sign of any cupreous metal remaining on the site and a few remnants of charred wood. It is quite obvious that this wreck was salvaged and intentionally sunk. The area in which it is located is too shallow for an anchorage, let alone a good spot to anchor with a hurricane looming on the horizon, ruling out Marx's original thought. Taking all these factors into account, is this 10-m-long pile of floor frames, ballast rocks, and eight mortar balls the only material evidence that we have left of the great Captain Bartholomew Roberts? No: the *Royal Fortune* and *Little Ranger* are still waiting to be discovered just across the harbor.

5

The Wreck of the *Quedagh Merchant*

The Lost Ship of Captain William Kidd

FREDERICK H. HANSELMANN AND CHARLES D. BEEKER

Piracy grows everyday in this part of the world . . . and there is no help for it.

Richard Coote, Earl of Bellomont, September 7, 1699 (The National Archives
of the United Kingdom, Colonial Office [TNA CO] 5/860, fol. 278)

Among the names associated with the most notorious figures in the history of pirates, Captain William Kidd can be found at the top of the list. Most do not know the true story of Captain Kidd and how he went down in history as an infamous pirate (figure 5.1). At the dawn of the Golden Age of Piracy, Kidd was sanctioned by England as a privateer to hunt pirates and to quell pirate activity in the Indian Ocean. He would eventually capture the *Quedagh Merchant*, a move that would brand him a pirate and lead to his eventual execution. Kidd abandoned the *Quedagh Merchant* off the coast of Hispaniola in 1699, where it remained lost in its watery grave. Archaeologists are excavating and researching a shipwreck off the southern coast of the Dominican Republic and have found that the archaeological research matches the historical records, which positively prove that the wreck of the *Quedagh Merchant* has been found after 300 years.

Historical Overview

William Kidd became a captain and first made a name for himself as an English privateer, fighting against the French for control of the West Indies from 1689 to 1691. With his newfound wealth and reputation, Kidd married a wealthy widow and became a merchantman, sailing from New York and Boston to the English colonies in the Caribbean, with the task of occasionally running off foreign privateers and ne'er-do-wells. Kidd became a noted

Figure 5.1. Rendering of Captain William Kidd by Howard Pyle (1921).

gentleman, well connected to the colonial government of New England, living in a house on Pearl Street in New York City, and owning real estate in other areas of New York (Zacks 2002) (figure 5.2). While in London in 1695, Kidd entered into a business venture of sorts involving the governor of New England, Lord Bellomont, a prominent colonial merchant, and four Whig lords and members of Parliament (British Library [BL] 70036, fol. 72; Zacks 2002). King William was rumored also to have been involved, as Kidd's letter of commission bore the king's seal. Kidd, backed by his investors, was to hunt and capture any pirates and enemy vessels, sharing the profits of their spoils according to the articles of agreement. He commissioned a ship, the *Adventure Galley*, and set sail for the Indian Ocean on September 6, 1696.

For almost two years Kidd and his crew battled the elements in search of pirate and enemy vessels. Much to the chagrin of naval officers, he avoided the attempts of the Royal Navy to press-gang members of his crew (Zacks 2002). Although this endeared him to his crew, many of the men began to grumble about the difficulties of life at sea and the lack of any prize. As the days dragged on, Kidd's crew grew more restless and mutinous. The situation came to a head when the gunner William Moore publicly accused him of ruining the crew and Kidd hit him over the head with a wooden bucket in a fit of anger. Moore died the next day (Zacks 2002). The crew members remained in the same spirits yet ceased to voice their opinion publicly. Their luck changed when the men in the *Adventure Galley* saw the masts of the *Quedagh Merchant* off in the distance and gave chase. The crew members of the *Quedagh Merchant* knew that they were greatly outgunned by their opponent's thirty-four cannon and gave up without a fight on January 30, 1698. Although the captain was English, Kidd rationalized that the French flag and the vessel's French pass justified the capture. It was this French pass that also listed the ship's name as *Cara Merchant*. According to Kidd's testimony, it was commissioned under a consortium of Armenian merchants. Referring to the ship as *Cara Merchant*, the French East India Company pass states that it left harbor on January 14, 1698, and was flying French colors.

Kidd then made berth at St. Mary's Isle off Madagascar, as the *Adventure Galley* was taking on water and was no longer seaworthy. Anxious to lay claim to their shares, the majority of his men mutinied and looted the *Adventure Galley*, taking four cannon from the ship in the process (Anonymous 1701). Kidd later testified to Bellomont that he and the remainder of his crew then outfitted the *Quedagh Merchant*, reloading it with bales of silk and satin, forty tons of saltpeter, seventy to eighty tons of scrap iron,

Figure 5.2. Contemporary portrait of William Kidd by Sir James Thornhill (courtesy of The Children's Museum of Indianapolis).

and the remaining thirty cannon from the *Adventure Galley* in addition to the twenty already aboard the *Quedagh Merchant*, with thirty mounted and twenty in the hold (TNA CO 40774, fol. 197). Kidd renamed the vessel the *Adventure Prize* and set sail for the West Indies.

The capture of the *Quedagh Merchant* would prove to be Kidd's undoing. Unbeknownst to Kidd, almost half of the cargo belonged to Muklis Khan, a nobleman in the court of the grand Mogul (BL 40774, fol. 86; Zacks 2002). Adding to the brewing scandal was the fact that the trade had been brokered by the English East India Company. The Mogul issued threats to the English East India Company and sent letters to London denouncing English pirates, with Kidd on the top of the list (BL 40774, fol. 86). According to the president of the Old English East India Company, Kidd had become a "thorn in their side" and there were many "to desire that Kidd might be made an example of" (BL 40744, fol. 183v). Kidd's backers began to distance themselves from him and disavow any knowledge of his exploits.

Rounding Cape Horn and making the arduous voyage across the Atlantic with only a skeleton crew, Kidd was greeted in Anguilla with the shocking news that he was wanted for piracy. He sailed through the Greater Antilles, constantly seeking an inconspicuous place to berth the *Adventure Prize* and trading a bit with local merchants in order to acquire provisions. Kidd eventually decided to return to New England and attempt to clear his name. He left the *Adventure Prize* on the leeward side of Catalina Island (TNA CO 5/860, fol. 197) under the care of a merchant named Henry Bolton, purchased the sloop *St. Antonio* from him, and sailed to New England under the assumption that he would soon return for the *Adventure Prize*. Bolton later testified that the vessel was in the river across from Catalina Island (TNA CO 5/860, fol. 174–75). According to one witness, nearly three months after Kidd's departure the vessel was burned and set out to sea (BL 40774, fol. 183). Kidd was never to return. His case became the political scandal of the day. The Tories charged that the king and the majority party, the Whigs, supported and funded piracy. Kidd was railroaded at his trial in England, where he was accused of giving the four cannon to known pirates as a gift. The French passes from the *Quedagh Merchant*—which he had given to Bellomont—did not surface until more than 200 years later (Anonymous 1701). Kidd was hanged for piracy on May 23, 1701. Even during his execution his luck ran bad. The rope around Kidd's neck broke, and he fell to the ground alive. He was then hanged a second time. Kidd's body was tarred and hung in an iron gibbet to demonstrate the perils of piracy.

Archaeological Investigations

Since Kidd first reported the location of the vessel in 1699, people have searched for the *Quedagh Merchant*. While Kidd was locked in solitary confinement in England, Lord Bellomont sent Captain Nathaniel Cary to Hispaniola, who searched in vain for the ship (TNA CO 5/860, fol. 375). Legend of Kidd's buried treasure also led many to attempt to find his documented spoils. Even today modern treasure hunters have searched in the Dominican Republic for the lost treasure vessel. It was a snorkeler, however, who found a conglomerate of cannon and contacted the Dominican Republic's Oficina Nacional de Patrimonio Cultural Subacuático (ONPCS). Indiana University was requested to investigate the site and noted shipwreck cargo attributes that suspiciously matched records of the *Quedagh Merchant*. One of the main factors in successful historical archaeological research is the amount of primary source documentation available. In the case of the *Quedagh Merchant*, this documentation is crucial to understanding the shipwreck. A wide variety of letters and documents exist on Captain Kidd and his exploits. One document in particular provides a great deal of information essential to the identification of the wreck site. On July 3, 1699, Kidd held council with the Earl of Bellomont, the governor of New

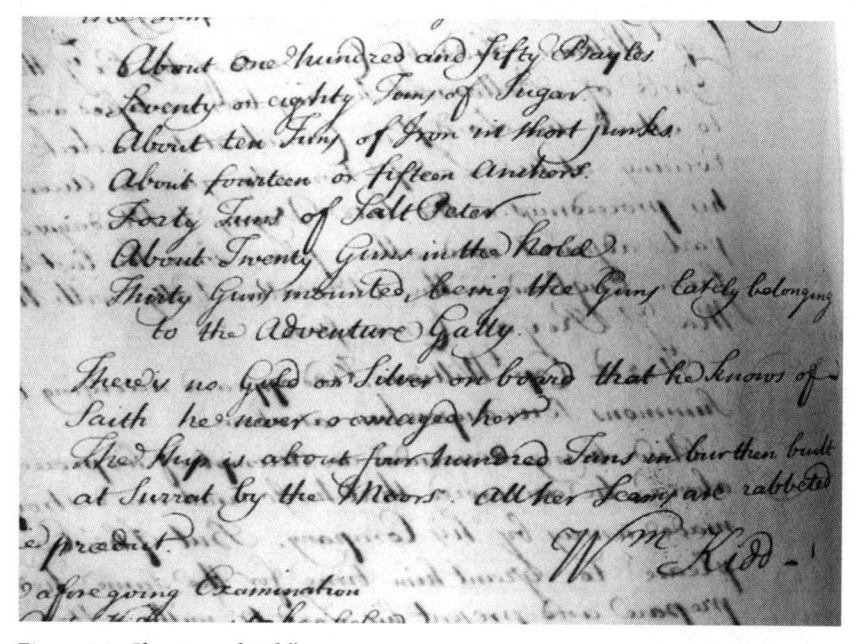

Figure 5.3. Close-up of Kidd's testimony to Lord Bellomont and the details of the ship and its cargo (TNA 5/860, fol. 197).

England, upon his return from Hispaniola. Document number 5/860 found in the Colonial Office Papers under Massachusetts Governor's Documents in the Public Records Office in the National Archives in London, England, provides incredible data regarding *Cara Merchant* and its cargo. The following is the transcript of Kidd's testimony that day (figure 5.3).

Boston, New England
Monday 3 of July 1699

Capt. William Kidd by command of his Excellency the Earle of Bellomont having been notified and required to attend his Lordship in Council at six o'clock this evening at his Lordship's house to give an account of his proceedings with late voyage to Madagascar, parts adjacent and other places since his last departure from England in the Adventure Gally with his Magesty's Royal Commission.

The said Capt. William Kidd appeared according to the Summons served upon him as above.

Also being demanded an account of his proceedings of above he answered that his Journal was destroyed and made away by his Company. But if his Excellency would please to grant him time for the same he would prepare and present his Lordship with a Narrative thereof in writing.

Being further demanded an account of the Ladeing onboard his Sloop now lying within this Port and on board the ship which he saith he left at Hispaniola.

Saith. There is on board the Sloop first
Forty Bayles containing Callico's Silke muslin, striped and plain.
Five or Six Tons of refined Sugar contained in bags.
About Forty pound weight in coin and of bar Gold
About Eighty pound weight in bar silver

All which he saith he purchased at Madagascar with the Powder, Small arms and other furniture belonging to the Adventure Gally whereof he was late Commander.

And Further Saith,
That about forty two or three days since he left a ship on the South

side of Hispaniola in the possession of Henry Bolton of Antigua Merchant and about twenty two men which ship he brought
Last from Madagascar. And that there is on board the same the Several Goods following first
About one hundred and fifty bayles
Seventy or eighty Tons of Sugar
About ten Tons of Iron in short junks
About fourteen or fifteen anchors
Forty Tons of Salt Peter
About Twenty Guns in the hold
Thirty Guns mounted being the Guns lately belonging to the Adventure Gally
There is no gold or silver on board that he knows of saith he
The Ship is about four hundred tons in burthen built at Surrat by the Moors. All her seams are rabbeted.

The present
W. Kidd

The aforegoing Examination of Capt Kidd was taken before his Excellency and Council
J Addington Secretary (TNA CO 5/860, fol. 197)

Kidd's testimony outlines three main features related to the analysis and interpretation of the shipwreck of the *Quedagh Merchant*: the ferrous artifacts—the quantity and spatial arrangement of cannon, anchors, and unidentifiable iron conglomerate; the vessel's origins; and the specific characteristics of the ship's hull construction.

Methodology

In June 2007 the team of archaeologists from Indiana University was requested to investigate a previously unknown shipwreck off the coast of Catalina Island. A baseline was laid, and the site was mapped using offsets and photo documentation. The team returned to the site twice in 2007 for further assessments of both the cultural and biological resources. Archival research was initiated in 2007 and is ongoing. Much of the historical documentation provides information that the wreck is the *Quedagh Merchant*. The first season of excavation took place in May and June 2008 (Beeker

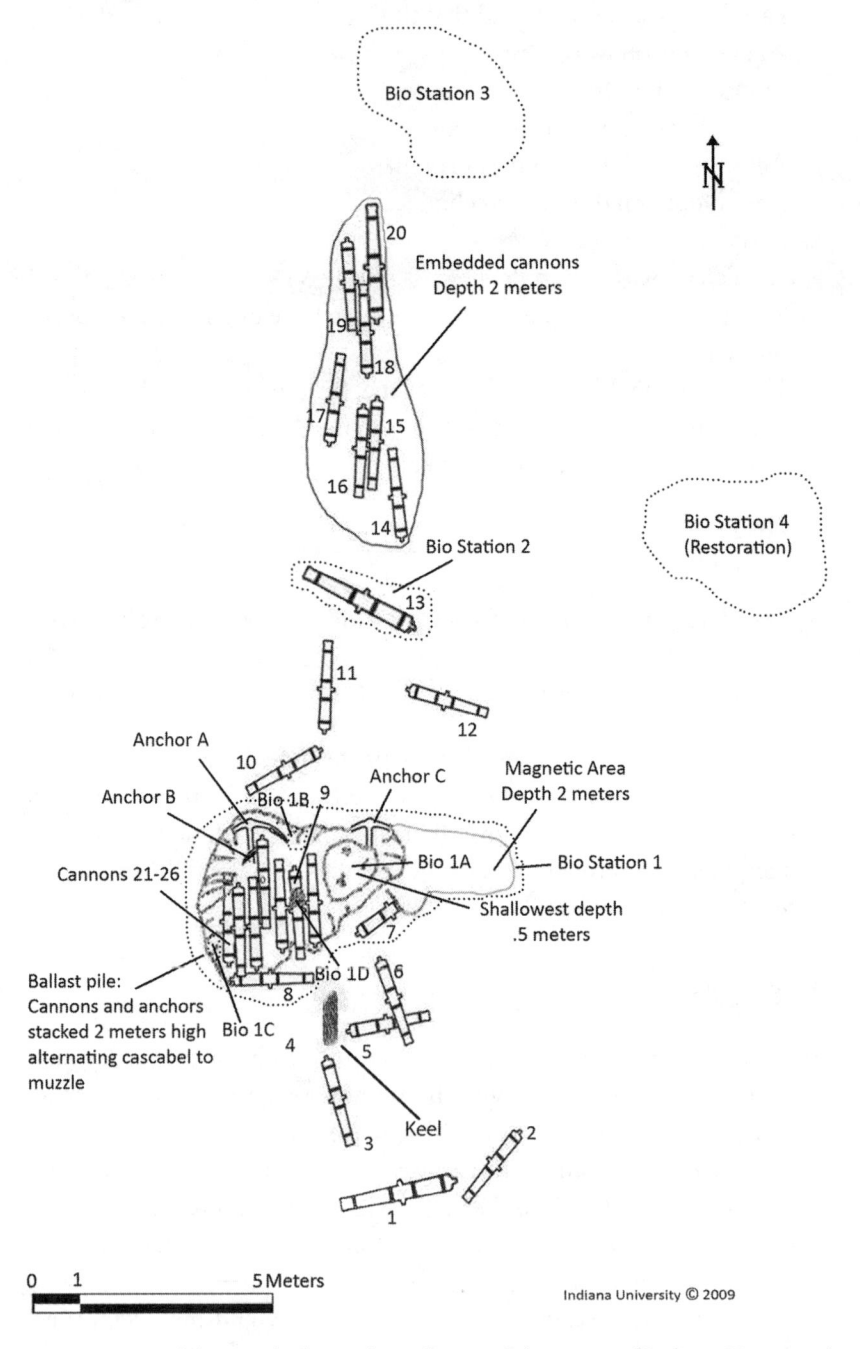

Figure 5.4. Site map of the *Quedagh Merchant* shipwreck (courtesy of Indiana University).

and Hanselmann 2009). One cannon was selected for recovery, freed from the bedrock using air chisels, and transported for treatment at the ONPCS Conservation Laboratory in Santo Domingo. Wood samples were recovered for analysis, and other smaller artifacts were excavated and are currently undergoing treatment. Due to the close proximity to shore, the adjacent shoreline of Catalina Island was surveyed and mapped. Test pits were excavated in the sand contained in solution crevices within the iron shore, which yielded a number of ballast stones, as noted in the overall site map (figure 5.4). Test excavations in the area of the removed cannon have yielded iron pins and nails as well as a section of lower hull remains.

The Shipwreck

The seventeenth-century shipwreck of the *Quedagh Merchant* is relatively intact: although the upper hull structure and ship's components are not within the assemblage, much of the heavy cargo in the hold and the hull structure are firmly embedded in the seafloor. The shipwreck consists of twenty-six cannon, three large anchor crowns protruding from underneath a 2-m high pile of cannon, and a large encrusted magnetic anomaly seaward of the pile. The majority of the cannon are arranged as cargo in the hold, alternately stacked muzzle to cascabel. There are two distinct piles of cannon, with several disarticulated cannon between the piles and on the southernmost limit of the site. Under the main 2-m-high cannon pile we believe that there are additional cannon and other scrap metal (figure 5.5). Kidd testified to loading the guns from the *Adventure Galley* onto the *Quedagh Merchant* at Madagascar (TNA CO 5/860, fol. 197). The exposed anchor crowns and one fluke and other metallic anomalies identified are indicative of the ten tons of scrap iron. Functional anchors would not be stored beneath the cannon, as they would need to be easily accessed in the event of a storm. Kidd indicated that he had fourteen to fifteen anchors (TNA CO 5/860, fol. 197), so additional anchors are anticipated to be documented within the pile. Wooden hull remains were also discovered underneath the recovered cannon, possibly the keelson or keel of the vessel. A section of the hull was excavated in a trench close to the main pile of cannon. The wreck is situated in 3 m of water, only 25 m from the rocky shoreline of the island, which explains why those that searched for the ship never found its remains. The wreck site of the *Quedagh Merchant* is a semidiscontinuous site in a high-energy zone with a large amount of wave action; any lighter

1699 *Cara Merchant*
Catalina Island, Dominican Republic

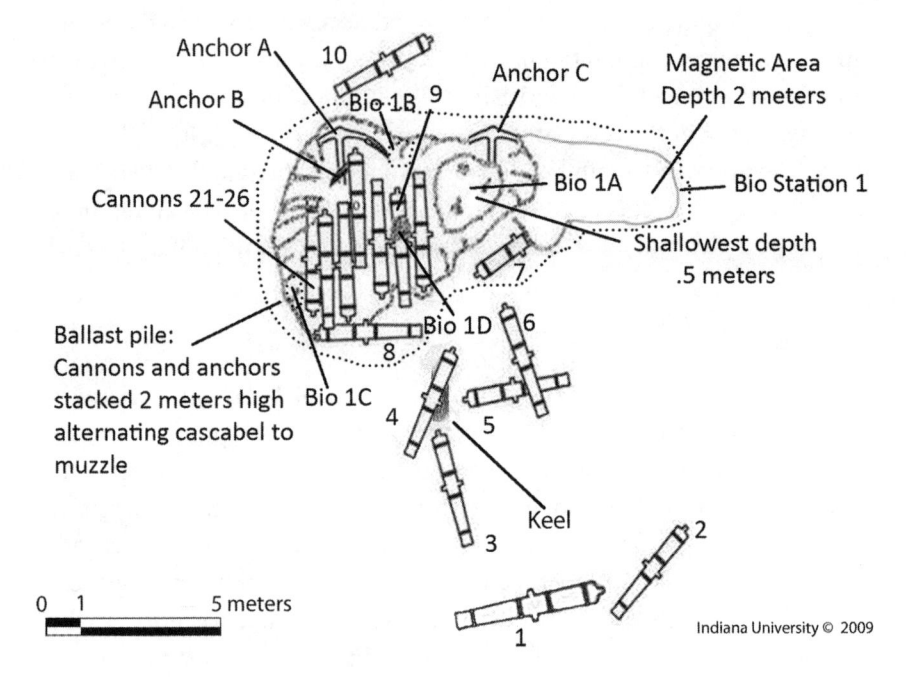

Figure 5.5. Main concentration of guns on the *Quedagh Merchant* shipwreck site (courtesy of Indiana University).

artifacts were carried out to sea or were washed into the rocky shoreline, along with the burned upper ship's structure.

Site Formation

In the formation of a shipwreck site, transformations affect a ship and its contents as it shifts from a functional object to an archaeological context (Muckelroy 1978). The remains survive the process of extracting filters and scrambling devices, which include forces such as seabed movement, disintegration, and material loss to salvage. These variables play a determining role in what survives and what does not. This process results in two types of sites: continuous and discontinuous (Muckelroy 1978). A continuous site forms when the vessel sinks intact and becomes trapped, waterlogged, and buried in the seabed. A discontinuous site forms when the ship and the objects it contains are scattered over a large area. The heavier objects settle on the ocean floor and the less dense objects are carried away, in a pattern characterized by a lack of the vessel's architectural framework (Muckelroy 1978). Based on the combination of the lack of upper hull structure and the intact cargo of the hold, we define this site as semidiscontinuous.

The wreck's assemblage and associated contemporary accounts suggest a theory of the wrecking process of the ship. Kidd left the vessel on the protected west side of the island. Bolton then took it upriver in order to ransack it out of sight, set fire to it, and set it adrift. The vessel was carried by the wind and current until it grounded near the eastern shore of Catalina Island. The goods were removed before it was set on fire (BL 40774, fol. 183). Bolton could have salvaged the mounted cannon but might not have wanted to put forth the effort required to remove the cannon in the hold, which remained in the burning vessel. Another theory would have Bolton burning the vessel out of fear of the Spanish, with the deployed cannon still in place on the burning vessel and then falling overboard as it burned. This would have made the vessel lighter so that it would travel further toward the island before sinking. In either case, the *Quedagh Merchant* grounded on the windward side of Catalina Island on a seafloor of coralline bedrock. For over 300 years the elements ate away at the wreck until only the cannon and other heavy artifacts were concreted to the coralline rock, pinning the remaining hull beneath. Miraculously, the wreck of the *Quedagh Merchant* remained untouched by salvors and looters prior to its archaeological study.

Ferrous and Other Artifacts

The ferrous artifacts and features located on the site provide the initial evidence to identifying the wreck as the ship that Kidd abandoned in 1699. One diagnostic feature of the shipwreck site is the arrangement of the cannon, stacked as cargo in the hold, alternating from cascabel to muzzle. The scatter pattern gives no evidence of deployed cannon, suggesting a scuttled vessel. Kidd collected and stored cannon, "with 20 some cannons from the *Quedagh Merchant* placed in the hold and 30 cannons from the Adventure Galley deployed" (TNA CO 5/860, fol. 197). This amount of artillery is far greater than what a merchant vessel would carry. The cannon also have a variety of lengths, the majority measuring 1.8–2.1 m, with few of matching lengths. Only three cannon are 2.44 m in length. The assumption is that the three largest cannon were loaded into the cargo hold of the *Quedagh*

Merchant from the *Adventure Galley*. The documentation of these three matching "Great Guns" along with the twenty-odd eclectic cannon of the *Quedagh Merchant* on the site further indicates that the cannon of the *Adventure Galley* were mixed with those of the *Quedagh Merchant* and provided the initial evidence that this was Captain Kidd's lost ship.

Beneath and around the main pile of cannon are obvious broken anchors and metallic anomalies. Kidd testified that the *Quedagh Merchant* also held "about ten Tons of Iron in short junks" (TNA CO 5/860, fol. 197). This scrap iron would be placed in the very bottom of the hold, for it would retain its value even if wet. The cannon would not function properly if they were submerged, however, which is why they would have been stacked on top of the iron.

In the age of global seafaring, colonization and increased resource accumulation led to further cross-cultural networking and trade. Exotic luxury foods figured largely in maritime trade and also constituted a major portion of captured goods from merchant ships. Food items such as sugar and spices could be sold for a handsome profit upon arrival in a port friendly to pirates. As noted, pirates were interested in profiting from all manner of trade goods. One of the most important was sugar. As stated in Kidd's testimony, the *Quedagh Merchant* held seventy or eighty tons of sugar, which was still a luxury good in England and in high demand at the time (Mintz 1986).

Bolton would have much to profit by removing the remaining trade goods, especially the sugar. This theory can be bolstered by the gap between the two piles of cannon. Spatial analysis of the site indicates that the ship had much more room for other goods. Kidd testified to carrying the sugar and forty tons of saltpeter onto the *Quedagh Merchant* on St. Mary's Island following the mutiny (TNA CO 5/860, fol. 197). The actual distribution of the site's features also indicates areas where the sugar may have been stored. Each pile of cannon would be directly under the cargo hold hatch on the upper deck, as these are not easily maneuvered by hand. Bags of sugar are much easier to move than cannon. The sugar would most likely have been stored between and around the cannon piles.

Origins of the Vessel

While the spatial distribution of the ferrous features of the site are somewhat circumstantial, Kidd's testimony that the *Quedagh Merchant* was built at Surat and had all seams rabbeted offers historical details that provide much harder evidence. In attempting to identify the origins of the vessel, three physical aspects were analyzed: samples of the wooden hull remains, the ballast stones, and the ship's hull construction.

Wood Sample Analysis

One of the most diagnostic features of the site is the keel or keelson that was uncovered during the excavations in the 2008 season (figure 5.6). Again, Kidd's testimony directly relates to the discovery and subsequent analysis of the discovered hull remains: "The Ship is about four hundred tons in burthen built at Surrat [Surat] by the Moors" (TNA CO 5/860, fol. 197). While excavating a cannon for recovery and conservation, what might be the keel or keelson was discovered beneath layers of coralline rock. Along with the cannon, a sample of the wood was removed and sent to three laboratories for analysis. Each came back with the same conclusion on the identification of wood: teak (figure 5.7). Teak (*Tectona grandis*) is indigenous to Thailand, Myanmar, Laos, and India.

According to Kidd, the *Quedagh Merchant* was built at Surat, a city in west India. Teak is recognized "as the finest of all timbers for naval purposes and is excelled by none because of its complete resistance to water

Figure 5.6. Exposed keel or keelson prior to recovery of the cannon (courtesy of Indiana University).

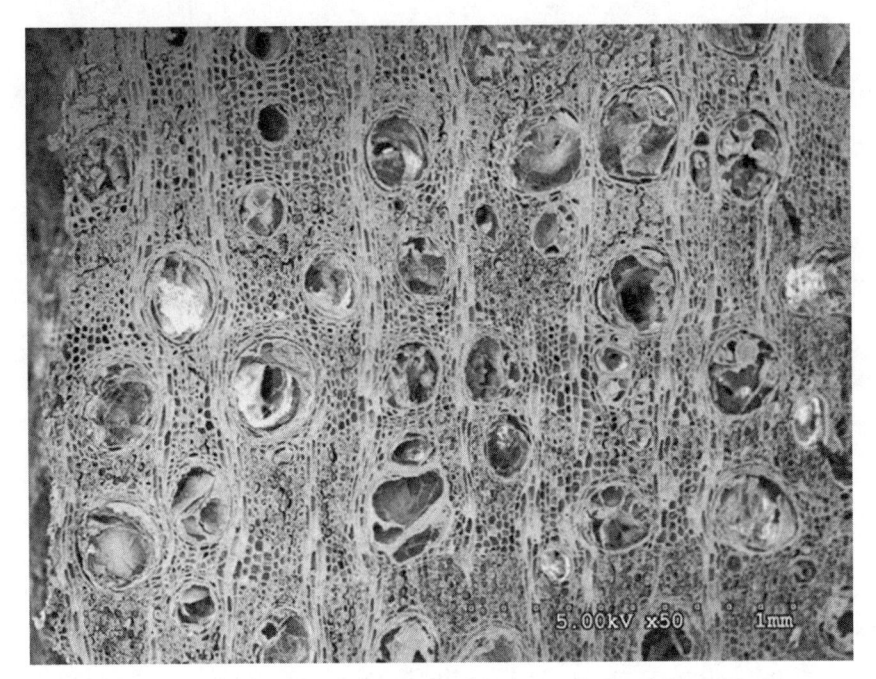

Figure 5.7. Cross section of the teak sample (courtesy of Indiana University).

and worm" (Wadia 1957:183). In 1802 Anthony Lambert, a merchant in Calcutta, noted the durability of teak and its proximity to Surat: "The excellence of teak for the purpose of ship building and its durability are too well known to require any description; although it must be observed that Pegue teak is not reckoned equal to what grows on the Malabar Coast, and near Surat" (Mookerji 1962:181–82). Sir Robert Seppings also noted the quality of teak, reporting that "teak is the most durable, but differs very much in quality," and stated that he would "designate Malabar Northern Teak as the most valuable timber in the world for ship-building" (Wadia 1957:183–84). Global trade networks were not so extensive in the late seventeenth century that Indian vessels built of teak would have plied Caribbean waters. The existence of the wood, its origin, and its species are the linchpins in the identification of the shipwreck. In the case of the origin of the wooden structural remains of the *Quedagh Merchant*, the historical documentation again coincides with the archaeological record.

Ballast Stone Analysis

Ballast stones have the ability to provide information not available through other types of investigations (Keith and Simmons 1985). The ballast provides evidence of the history of the *Quedagh Merchant* and where it had been. In order to acquire information from the ballast stones, geological and geographical signatures must be assessed. A small sample of ballast stones were recovered ($n = 14$) from around the site and analyzed in the Geochemistry Laboratory in the Department of Geological Sciences at Indiana University in order to assess their potential origin. The stones were thin-sectioned and underwent testing for rare earth elements and isotopic analysis. The results indicated that the majority of the ballast stones sampled are basalts and, very interestingly, that three of the stones exhibited geographical and geological traits indicative of the Deccan Traps, a large volcanic region located northwest of Surat, India, from which the two rivers on the northern and southern side of the city flow.

Hull Construction

Another very diagnostic feature of the shipwreck is the section of its hull that was excavated in the 2009 field season (figure 5.8). Kidd further testified in regard to the *Quedagh Merchant* that "all her seams are rabbeted" (TNA CO 5/860, fol. 197). Rabbeted seams or joints are a type of tongue-and-groove carpentry technique used in shipbuilding. A seam is "the longitudinal joint between two timbers or planks; the term usually refers to

Figure 5.8. Exposed section of the ship's hull (courtesy of Indiana University).

Figure 5.9. Image of the rabbeted seam and a fastening hole (courtesy of Indiana University).

planking seams, the longitudinal juxtaposition of the edges of the planks in the sides or decks, which were made watertight" (Steffy 1994:279). A rabbet is "a groove or cut made in a piece of timber in such a way that the edges of another piece could be fit into it to make a tight joint" (Steffy 1994:277). European and North American shipbuilders would typically rabbet the first outside plank (or garboard strake) into the keel of the ship. The rest of the planks would be laid end on end, and the seams would be sealed with pitch or adhesive. Kidd's statement that all the *Quedagh Merchant's* seams were rabbeted is yet another indication of Indian shipbuilding. In this case, rather than solely the garboard strake being rabbeted, all the planks and their seams were rabbeted. If all the ship's seams were rabbeted, that alone would make the ship much sturdier and impervious to water.

John Stavorinus, a Dutch rear admiral who visited India on a series of voyages between 1768 and 1771, observed and described this shipbuilding technique at Surat: "they do not put their planks together as we do, with flat edges towards each other, but rabbet them and they make the parts fit into each other with the greatest exactness bestowing much time and attention on this operation . . . after which they unite the planks so firmly and closely with pegs, that the seam is scarcely visible and the whole seems to form one entire piece of timber" (Stavorinus 1798:21). The uncovered section of the hull revealed what could possibly a rabbeted seam, with a fastening hole for a square peg at the corner of the end of the seam (figure 5.9). This type of craft and attention to detail indicates a much longer construction time for the vessel, yet a much longer active life at sea. A peg is a "tapered wooden pin driven into a pre-drilled hole to fasten two members or lock a joint" (Steffy 1994:277). Additional planking uncovered in 2011 showed further evidence of the pegging of planks. J. M. Seppings wrote that "several vessels have lasted, from thirty to fifty years . . . in some particular instances they have run nearly a century" (Wadia 1957:183). Stavorinus also noted that "the tediousness of their method . . . make ship-building very dear here, but, at the same time, their vessels are very lasting and can go to sea for many years, before any repairs of the hull are at all wanted" (Wadia 1957:21–23).

Additional Laboratory Analysis

During excavation in June 2008, one of the cannon was recovered and is being conserved through the process of electrolytic reduction to remove the chlorides and concretions. Initial treatment was initiated at the ONPCS and continued after the cannon was transported to Indiana University in 2010 for ongoing conservation. The cannon was then X-rayed at the Crane Division, Naval Surface Warfare Center, in order to determine if it contained any munitions or shot. The results of the X-rays showed that the cannon did not contain either. The gun was placed in a basic solution of water and soda ash to stabilize and halt the corrosion. Since 2010 the cannon has remained in a basic solution with an average pH of 11 and has undergone electrolytic reduction, a process by which electric current is passed through an object to remove chloride ions (salt) that were introduced while submersed in saltwater. This process stops further corrosion of the artifact and can allow for some recovery of previously corroded metal. Deconcretion of the rocky coralline shell that encased the gun revealed that it had been well preserved since the wrecking event. The researchers were then able to determine the inside diameter and other measurements as well (figure 5.10). In 2011 the cannon was transferred to the Children's Museum of Indianapolis for exhibition. Portions of the wood hull have been recovered and are also undergoing conservation in the museum, including sections of a teak rabbet joint removed from the exterior strake, with evidence of the unique

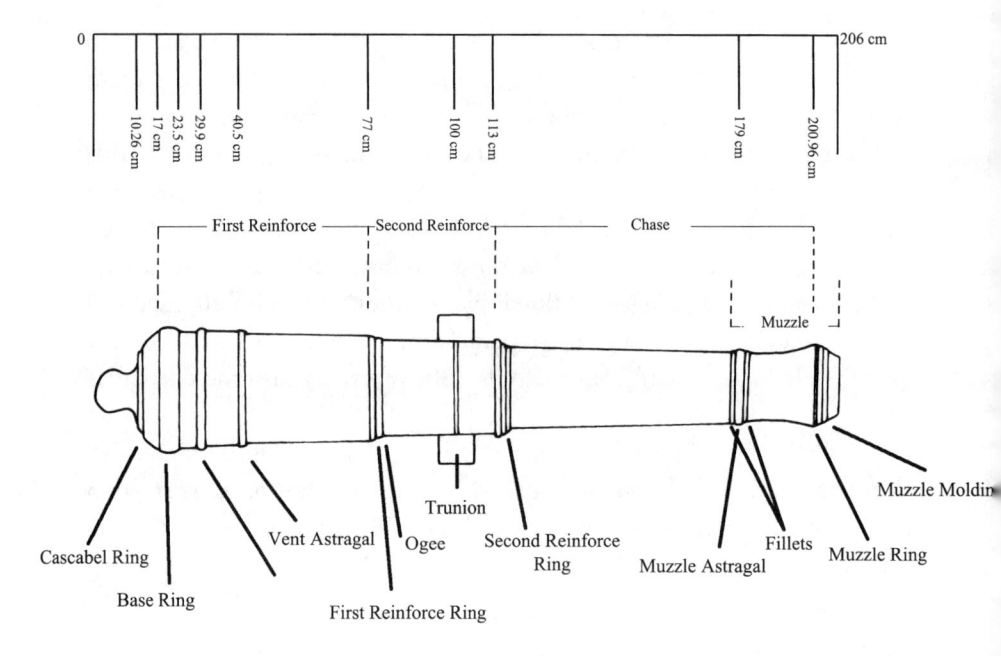

Figure 5.10. Cannon outline with measurements (courtesy of Indiana University).

Figure 5.11. Rabbet seam with peg (courtesy of Indiana University).

fastening techniques indicative of Indian ship construction techniques that Kidd noted in his testimony (figure 5.11).

Public Archaeology and Outreach

The Children's Museum of Indianapolis: Treasures of the Earth Exhibit

The recovered cannon that was transferred to the Children's Museum of Indianapolis is now one of the star attractions of permanent exhibit entitled Treasures of the Earth. This and other shipwreck artifacts have found a home next to an Egyptian tomb and terra-cotta warriors, allowing children and adults to learn more about our shared past and to experience archaeology. The cannon will be exhibited for five years in a wet lab as the conservation treatment continues, allowing visitors to the museum to view and observe this process. Promoted as the "only Pirate cannon recovered from the Caribbean," the exhibit receives over 1.2 million visitors per year and enables conservation of this and other artifacts to be seen in a public venue.

The Captain Kidd Living Museum in the Sea

The wreck of the *Quedagh Merchant* will be left largely in situ as the main feature of the Captain Kidd Living Museum in the Sea, which was developed with funding from the United States Agency for International Development (USAID) as part of a system of regional Marine Protected Areas in partnership with the Secretaría del Estado de Cultura and the Secretaría del Estado de Medio Ambiente y Recursos Naturales in the Dominican Republic. Inaugurated in May 2011, this Living Museum in the Sea will protect both the cultural resources and the associated biodiversity of the site and the surrounding area. It has an appropriate mooring buoy system and efforts to construct an interpretive shelter with a museum-quality reproduction of the recovered cannon, and walking paths connecting to beach entries and the west side of the island are being developed. Local involvement is the key to the success of the usage of this site as an underwater preserve for sustainable tourism use (Beeker 1991). Multilingual underwater guides are being developed (figure 5.12), and workshops continue to be conducted in order to train local stakeholders in site monitoring procedures and interpretation of the site for the purposes of community ownership and the development of cultural heritage tourism. The Living Museum in the Sea will further the goal of promoting sustainable cultural heritage tourism in the southeastern region of the Dominican Republic and allowing the general

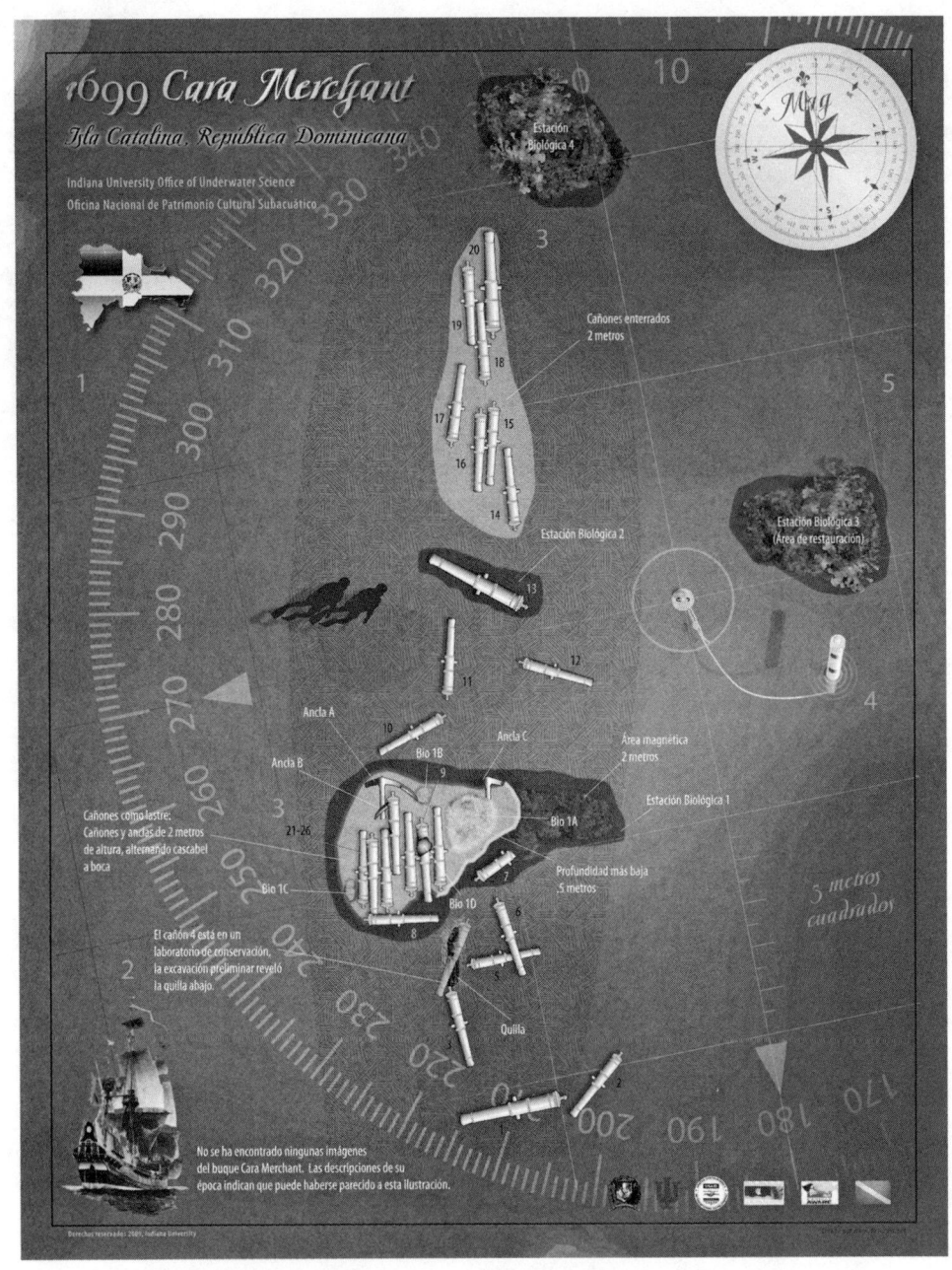

Figure 5.12. Interpretive guide in Spanish for the Captain Kidd Living Museum in the Sea (courtesy of Indiana University).

public to achieve what many archaeologists find so fascinating: being able to interact with history (Hanselmann and Beeker 2008).

Conclusion

For 300 years people have searched for the remains of the *Quedagh Merchant*. The archaeological and archival evidence indicates that the wreck has been found. As the research progresses, it is hoped that more telling information can be obtained from this fascinating glimpse into such a romanticized and fabled history. The most important aspect of the entire project is the preservation of the shipwreck in the Captain Kidd Living Museum in the Sea, which will serve to protect the wreck for the enjoyment and education of future generations, allowing others to take a glimpse into this storied past and visit a real pirate shipwreck.

Acknowledgments

The authors would like to acknowledge our collaborators on this project: Pedro Borrell, Francis Soto, Wilfredo Feliz, and the staff of the Oficina Nacional del Patrimonio Cultural Subacuático of the Secretaría del Estado de Cultura, the Secretaría del Estado de Medio Ambiente y Recursos Naturales, the United States Agency for International Development, Wyndham Viva Dominicus Beach Resort, Project AWARE Foundation, the National Geographic Channel, 62 Blue Productions, the Armenian Nautical Association for the History of Inter-Maritime Trade, the Asociación de Hoteles La Romana–Bayahibe, the California Department of Parks and Recreation, the Children's Museum of Indianapolis, the Lilly Foundation, and the various Indiana University faculty members and students who have participated in the fieldwork.

6

Plundering the Spanish Main

Henry Morgan's Raid on Panama

FREDERICK H. HANSELMANN, TOMÁS MENDIZÁBAL,
AND JUAN G. MARTÍN

The Spanish Main (the continental Spanish colonies in the New World) was rich in natural resources, especially gold and silver. Panama was one of the most crucial waypoints in the shipment of these precious metals. During his fourth and final voyage, Christopher Columbus charted a vast swath of the Caribbean coast of Panama. This resulted in further exploration of these new territories, with the first Spanish incursions on Tierra Firme. These efforts initiated the conquest and colonization that would soon reach most of South America. News of the riches found in these territories spread from the stories of conquistador Vasco Núñez de Balboa's expeditions on the mainland. Spain was eager for more, so Balboa consolidated the first Spanish settlements and established strategic ties with the region's native peoples in order to facilitate the control and exploitation of these extensive territories. In 1511 King Ferdinand appointed him governor of the province. Two years later he became the first European to see the Pacific Ocean from an Atlantic crossing. Due to mistrust in Spain, Balboa was soon replaced by Pedro Arias de Avila, who moved the Spanish settlement to the Pacific side of the isthmus in search of a strategic center to continue the conquest southward and to wrest control of the city from Balboa (Mena 1992).

On August 15, 1519, on the site of a village under the aegis of Chief Cori, Avila founded the city of Panama, a Cueva word meaning fishing place (Castillero Calvo 2006:104). Initially Panama suffered from shortages of labor as a result of the decimated native population and the Spaniards who had run off to participate in the conquest of Peru. Yet the city steadily grew over the course of the sixteenth century as it consolidated its position as a compulsory stepping stone in the trade route that connected the South

American gold and silver mines with Spain. It had a thriving commerce, especially during the gathering of the fleets en route to Europe (Castillero Calvo 1995; Mena García 1984, 1992; Romoli 1987). It was this abundance of wealth that Spain so desperately needed, for by the mid-seventeeth century the empire faced difficulties maintaining control of its drastically increasing debt. At the same time this abundance of wealth called out to those who would seek their fortunes by challenging the Spanish Empire on its own turf. The most successful was the Welsh privateer Henry Morgan, who in 1670 amassed the largest privateer/pirate fleet in the history of the Caribbean. Morgan set sail for Panama. Despite losing his flagship and four other vessels, he made his way across the isthmus and laid waste to the city, achieving the greatest victory of his piratical career. The original Panama City was abandoned, and Morgan's lost ships lay forgotten, buried in the seafloor.

The Legend of Henry Morgan

Sorting through myth and popular perception in order to arrive at historical truth is one of the most intriguing aspects of historical archaeology. That was never more true than in the case of the accounts of many of the most successful privateers/pirates. Captain Henry Morgan was not immune to such exaggerated tales, which continue in our modern era (figure 6.1). Henry Morgan lives on in modern popular culture, from novels by John Steinbeck and James Michener and swashbuckling cinema with Errol Flynn and Tyrone Power to punk rock, reggae, video games, and, of course, the iconic rum. The little historical documentation reveals much about his exploits that led to the creation of his fame and legend.

Beginnings

With the advent of Oliver Cromwell's tenure as the lord high protector of England, he revisited the Elizabethan Western Design, a foreign policy strategy that involved English efforts to assume control of the Spanish colonies in the New World, made famous through the exploits of another English privateer, Sir Francis Drake. To this same end, Cromwell sent a fleet of sixty ships and seven thousand English sailors to attack the Spanish stronghold of Santo Domingo in Hispaniola in 1654, including a nineteen-year-old soldier named Henry Morgan. For twenty days the English forces laid siege to the city, but they were met with heavy resistance, malaria, dysentery, and yellow fever. In an attempt to avoid returning home empty-handed, the

Figure 6.1. Woodcut of Henry Morgan (from Exquemelin 1969).

English set their sights on the sleepy, little-defended island of Jamaica and took it with ease, establishing Port Royal as its capital. Only an estimated two thousand of the original crew survived the first two years of the expedition (Talty 2005). In need of defense and soldiers, Port Royal soon became a haven of privateer and pirate activity as the English government awarded commissions to raid Spanish vessels, cities, and towns in return for protection by serving as the island's ragtag navy and militia. With privateers and buccaneers walking around freely, the influx of gold and silver, and the multitude of taverns and brothels, Port Royal would soon become known as "the wickedest city in the world" (Talty 2005:40). In this atmosphere and environment Henry Morgan came of age and eventually rose to fame.

As we delve into the legend of Henry Morgan, it is necessary to clarify the differences among buccaneers, privateers, and pirates. Buccaneers were one of the earliest forms of pirates in the Caribbean. Named after their method of cooking meat over an open fire learned from the native indigenous groups, buccaneers were hunters who were mostly French in origin and resided on the island of Tortuga, illegally using Hispaniola as their hunting ground. Finding theft on the high seas more lucrative, many sold themselves to the highest bidder, as seventeenth-century mercenaries. These were the men that Morgan typically used as his mercenary army. Privateers are individuals who operate under an official government commission to fight and capture enemy ships, towns, and cities. The term "pirates" was used literally after Morgan's time to describe individuals who rob and commit acts of violence on the sea or shores of the sea.

This chapter discusses historical and archaeological investigations related to an individual famous not only for stunning military victories but also for allegations of what we would consider today cruel interrogatory tactics and torture. Two aspects of Henry Morgan's personality must be deconstructed by analyzing the historic record. From the English perspective, Morgan is an English admiral, hailed as a national hero who restored English pride and was the proverbial straw that broke Spain's back, ultimately forcing it to open its colonies to trade. From the Spanish perspective, Morgan is a thief, murderer, and cutthroat who pillaged Spanish towns and cities for personal gain, often likened to the devil himself. Yet little to no account of Morgan's cruelty exists outside of Alexander Exquemelin's firsthand chronicle (1969) of Morgan's actions against the Spanish. Likewise, Spanish actions against the natives of its colonies as well as its enemies were cruel and barbaric by modern standards. Thus as we delve into the impressive exploits that made Henry Morgan a famous historical figure we must remember that one person's swashbuckling privateer is another's thieving buccaneer.

Mexico to Nicaragua

By 1663 Morgan had risen through the ranks of the privateers and impressed others enough to be given command of his first (albeit small) fleet. Morgan took three ships and 107 men to go "marauding along the coast of Campeche." Their target was Villahermosa (Exquemelin 1969:119). With the intent to "prey upon that nation," they sailed up the river of Tabasco and with the help of native guides marched 300 miles to the settlement (The National Archives, Colonial Office [TNA CO] 1/20, 21). Morgan and his men easily took the city. But upon return to the mouth of the river they discovered that the Spanish had captured their ships, which they used to attack the pirates. The captain reports that they beat off the Spanish "without the loss of a man," yet they had been left stranded in a foreign and hostile land. Soon thereafter the privateers "fitted up two barques and four canoes" and began to paddle north around the Yucatán Peninsula (TNA CO 1/20, 21). Along the way, Morgan and his men continued to plunder any

Spanish settlement that they encountered, noting that thirty men stormed a breastwork at the Río Garta, killing fifteen defenders and taking the rest prisoner. They crossed the Bay of Honduras and resupplied on Roatan Island before sacking the town of Trujillo and acquiring a larger vessel, which they used to sail along the Mosquito Coast to the San Juan River (marking the modern-day border between Nicaragua and Honduras). For the next five days natives of the area again guided Morgan and his men up the river and across Lake Nicaragua, which they noted was a "fair laguna or lake of sweet water, full of excellent fish with its banks full of brave pastures and savannahs . . . where they had as good beef and mutton as any in England." On the fifth night they landed near Granada and marched uncontested into the city's center, "fired a volley, overturned 18 great guns . . . took the sergeant-major's men prisoners, plundered for 16 hours, discharged the prisoners, sunk all the boats, and so came away" (TNA CO 1/20, 21). After sacking Granada, the privateers attacked the town on the island (modern-day Ometepe), captured a 100-ton vessel, and sailed home to Jamaica. It is easy to imagine the shock of the people in Port Royal when Morgan and his men returned rich nearly two years after they had disembarked, with two years' worth of plunder. By the time the campaign was over, Morgan had surpassed Francis Drake's trek across the isthmus ninety-one years earlier and traveled an estimated 3,700 miles, roughly the distance from Los Angeles to Caracas (Talty 2005). The name Henry Morgan became well known, but the captain was only just beginning.

Portobelo

Impressed with Morgan's daring exploits, Sir Thomas Modyford, governor of Jamaica, made him the admiral of the privateers after two years of inactivity following his campaign in Mexico and Central America. The newly minted Admiral Morgan and his latest fleet of ten ships and five hundred privateers set sail again in March 1668 (TNA CO 1/23, No. 53). They were soon successful in capturing Puerto Príncipe in Cuba. The reward was very small, however, much to the crews' consternation, which led to the departure of almost half of the men (Exquemelin 1969; Talty 2005). At a crucial juncture of his piratical career, Morgan remained undaunted and rallied his men, putting out a call for more men and ships and valiantly raising spirits among the remaining crew (Exquemelin 1969; Talty 2005). This led to mustering enough able bodies and vessels to continue the voyage with nine ships and 460 men (Exquemelin 1969). Morgan had so enthralled the men and instilled a sense of victory and impending riches that they sailed without even deciding on a destination, very contrary to pirate code.

When they arrived on the coast of Costa Rica, Morgan made known that he planned to attack Portobelo (the modern spelling of the name), which raised much anxiety and fear among the men. To the English, Portobelo was known as "the terminus of the treasure fleet, the home of the richest merchants of the Indies . . . the key to the even greater riches of Panamá and Peru, one of the King of Spain's most precious jewels in the Indies" (Earle 1981:50). Yet as such it was also known as one of the largest Spanish strongholds on the Main, next to Havana and Cartagena, heavily fortified and bristling with cannon (Talty 2005). After all, even the great Sir Francis Drake could not conquer this Spanish town. He met his death there through illness and was buried at sea in 1596. The mere thought of attempting Portobelo forced the French contingent of Drake's fleet to depart posthaste.

But Portobelo had fallen victim to Spain's ever-thinning budget and overstretched capacity. The city was only fully populated once every one to two years when the treasure fleets arrived to load the gold and silver. In the intervening periods Portobelo was largely a ghost town made up of a motley crew of disenchanted colonists and soldiers waiting on a long overdue paycheck who made the humid, squalid bay their permanent residence. The Spanish squadron at Portobelo was found undermanned with less than half of the total garrison of an estimated 300 soldiers (Earle 1981). Receiving this information from some escaped English captives (privateers themselves) and slaves, Admiral Morgan and his men took advantage of these odds and paddled their canoes toward Portobelo. Beaching their canoes, they hiked the final three miles and silently captured the sentry, yet were fired upon by the first blockhouse. The Spanish soldiers and citizens were abruptly awakened just before dawn on July 11, 1688, to confusion. As the call to arms was issued, Morgan's men charged past the first fortification and into the city, taking possession of it within half an hour. The next day the privateers advanced on the fortification across the bay and forced its surrender. Morgan and his men ransacked the homes and buildings, searching for any trace of gold and silver.

The president of Panama attempted a rescue mission but was forced to retreat due to illness and the strategic advantage that the English privateers held with the captured fortifications and artillery. In the end Morgan settled for a ransom of 100,000 pieces of eight to leave the city, despite having

Figure 6.2. Depiction of Morgan and his men attacking Portobelo (from Exquemelin 1969).

requested 350,000 (Public Record Office, Colonial Office Papers [PRO CO] 1/23, No. 53; Talty 2005; Earle 1981). A month after the privateers took the city, two mules carrying the ransom arrived. Eager to leave the stifling humidity and tropical illness that had begun to plague them, Morgan and his men loaded their prizes, which turned out have an approximate value of 215,000 pesos (counting slaves and merchandise), bringing each of them a small fortune (figure 6.2). The privateers returned to Jamaica to a heroes' welcome. Morgan's fame grew. He was now being talked about throughout England, from the cobbled streets to the highest courts (Earle 1981). To the English eye, the invincible Portobelo had not only been defeated but had been brought to its knees and held for ransom—for a month. To the Spanish, this provided damning evidence of their weakness and inability to control their vast colonies.

Maracaibo

In January 1669 off Isle à Vache or Isla Vaca on the southern coast of modern-day Haiti, Admiral Morgan gathered with the rest of his fleet aboard his new flagship, HMS *Oxford*. The *Oxford* was a frigate with thirty-six guns and the first ship officially sent from England to Jamaica since 1600 with the express purpose of quelling piracy (TNA CO 1/23, No. 96). The gathering brought together pirates from various ports and nations. During the gathering, Morgan's men captured a 24-gun ship named *Le Cerf Volant* from French pirates who had stolen provisions from an English merchantman (TNA CO 1/24, No. 18; Exquemelin 1969; Talty 2005; Earle 1981). With approximately a thousand pirates awaiting orders, Morgan called all of the captains to his chambers, where they held a council of war to determine the next prize. This meeting resulted in the selection of the rich and heavily fortified Spanish city of Cartagena (Talty 2005; Earle 1981). Following proper piratical protocol, the rum bottles were cracked, muskets were fired, and a party was held to celebrate the upcoming campaign. At some point during the festivities an errant spark ignited the powder hold and a huge explosion rocked HMS *Oxford*, throwing chunks of hull, rigging, masts, and bodies into the water. An estimated two hundred men were killed in the explosion, with only twenty surviving (Exquemelin 1969; Talty 2005). Among those who miraculously survived the savage explosion were Morgan and the other captains who had been seated on his side of the table. During the explosion, the table flipped up, blocking most of the shrapnel, while at the same time propelling the men out of the ship into the water (Talty 2005; Earle 1981).

The loss of both the *Oxford* and the men was a blow to Morgan and his designs. While his reputation now bordered on being invincible, he lacked the men and firepower to face Cartagena. Arranging for a second rendezvous after resupplying and acquiring a different ship, Morgan met the remaining men at Saona Island, off the southeastern tip of Hispaniola (modern-day Dominican Republic). With approximately eleven ships, the diminished fleet sailed for three weeks against strong trade winds toward the island of Jamaica. But the fleet was beaten back to the point that three of the ships left the fleet rather than continue the thrashing the vessels were receiving. In addition, because the Spanish were aware of the location of Morgan's fleet, he was unable to resupply his ships. Undaunted, Morgan decided to continue with the remaining five hundred men and eight ships, changing course for the coast of Venezuela (Exquemelin 1969; Talty 2005; Earle 1981). As luck would have it, one of the remaining French captains had participated in the famous raid on Maracaibo led by French pirate Jean L'Ollonais two years before and had extensive knowledge of the coast and lagoon on whose shores the city lay. With disadvantages in artillery and manpower Morgan opted to strike at a known entity and sailed for Maracaibo.

Upon arrival at the channel allowing access into the lagoon Morgan and his men were surprised to find a small Spanish fort guarding the entrance (Thornton 1952; Exquemelin 1969). Morgan's men besieged the fort under heavy cannon fire for an entire day then stormed the structure that night, only to find that the Spanish had deserted and retreated. The privateers stockpiled the remaining ammunition, spiked the cannon, and burned the gun carriages before sailing into the lake toward the city of Maracaibo (Exquemelin 1969). Although the captain attempted to call the citizens of Maracaibo to arms, many gathered what they could and fled the city, leaving it largely abandoned when Morgan and his men arrived. Unsatisfied with what they found in the town, the pirates hunted down as many people as they could. According to Exquemelin, who accompanied Morgan on a number of his ventures (including Panama), the privateers tortured them so that they would disclose the hiding places of other wealth (Exquemelin 1969). Relatives were also ransomed to their families, and the pirates continued to exploit and extract Maracaibo's remaining wealth. Having taken Maracaibo, Morgan and his men continued by exploring the lagoon, which is approximately eighty-six miles long and sixty miles wide, sacking the town of Gibraltar further along the coast and giving it the same treatment as Maracaibo (Earle 1981).

After thirty-eight days of plundering the two towns and rounding up all of the ships in the lagoon, Morgan and his fleet returned to Maracaibo loaded with gold, silver, and fine trade goods, only to receive disheartening news. Three ships of the Spanish Armada of Barlovento, sent in the wake of the Portobelo raid, had blocked the channel and retaken the fort. While Morgan's ships outnumbered the Spanish, he was vastly outgunned. The privateers' ships were largely used for transport and were not well equipped for naval warfare, especially since the loss of *Oxford*. The three Spanish ships were bristling with ninety-four cannon, forty in the Spanish admiral's flagship *Magdalena* alone. Receiving a letter from the admiral offering freedom and safe passage in exchange for the loot, Morgan put it to his men, who voted to fight. The privateers immediately set to readying their vessels for the impending engagement. This included outfitting the largest prize ship, a Cuban merchant vessel captured in the lagoon, as Morgan's flagship, while another was made ready as a fireship (Thornton 1952; Exquemelin 1969; Earle 1981; Talty 2005). After a week of preparations, the privateers sailed straight toward the Spanish fleet and anchored just out of cannon range. After a tense night, the Spanish cut anchors and headed toward the privateers at dawn. Morgan's new flagship led the way, with the fireship right behind. Both sides exchanged fire, with the privateers receiving the brunt of the Spanish firepower. Morgan's flagship approached *Magdalena* and prepared for close-quarter combat. Using grappling hooks, the Spanish were busy pulling the ship in close to engage the insolent privateers. They could see longboats feverishly rowing away and the other privateer vessels beginning to back off. At that moment Morgan's flagship burst into flames. At this point the Spanish realized that what they had thought were men in the early light of day were actually wooden props dressed to appear as men. Morgan had made his flagship the actual fireship, filling the hold with powder, pitch, tar, and dry palm leaves. *Magdalena*, tethered tightly to the now burning ship, also caught fire. The crew, unable to put it out, began to abandon ship. One of the other two ships in the Spanish armada was unable to back off fast enough from the fire and was also consumed, while the other sailed into the lagoon, only to be tracked down and captured by the privateers (Thornton 1952; Exquemelin 1969; Earle 1981; Talty 2005).

The survivors immediately made their way to the fort and waited for the ragtag privateer fleet to approach. In a last-ditch effort to prevent them from entering the channel and escaping, the Spanish made preparations to engage the privateers. At the same time, Morgan had his men salvage what they could from the wreck of *Magdalena*, recovering another 30,000 pieces of eight, which increased the overall take to an approximate value of 250,000 (Exquemelin 1969). At a stalemate and unable to enter the channel and risk being shelled with shot and cannonballs from the fort, Morgan began sending his men ashore in longboats in preparation for an amphibious assault on the fort. The Spanish watched from a distance as the boats hit the beachfront and returned empty. They trained their artillery on the shore in anticipation of the attack. What they did not see was that the men never got out of the boats but merely lay in the bottom of their boats on the row back to their fleet. When dark came and night was upon them, the privateers quietly hauled anchor and drifted with the tide until they were right below the fort. At that point they let out their sails and quickly passed through the channel. The Spanish realized too late that they had been duped, hurrying to train their artillery on the escaping vessels, but little damage was done because the fleet was almost out of range. Once again Morgan had turned the tide on the Spanish and in doing so destroyed the fleet that was meant to quell piracy in the Caribbean. In addition, Morgan had made his crew rich, solidifying the legend that accompanied his name. This legend would allow Morgan to amass what could be the largest fleet of privateers and pirates in the history of the Caribbean, aiding in his final and most daring raid on Panama City.

The Sack of Panama

Upon Morgan's return to Jamaica, the island was alive with the news that the king had ordered that there be no more hostilities against the Spanish, as the two countries were attempting to negotiate a peace. The privateers so loyal to Morgan, who had made a hefty profit from following him, now faced unemployment. While a peace was being negotiated in the courts of Europe, hostilities continued (a result of the time lag for communications between Europe and the Caribbean). Months before the initiation of peace talks between Spain and England, the privateers' actions at Portobelo and Maracaibo had dealt a serious blow to Spanish pride, not to mention the local economy. The Spanish queen took a page from the English playbook and put out a call to all Spaniards in the Caribbean, offering commissions for capturing English ships and towns. When Morgan returned to Jamaica, the English were standing down while the Spanish became more aggressive. This Spanish call to arms led to the capture of several English ships as well as small-scale attacks around Jamaica and fears of a major attack on Port Royal (an event that never occurred). What the Spanish failed to realize was that they had given Henry Morgan and his privateers the perfect excuse to get back to work.

Morgan put out that call for men, proclaiming that they were going to attack a place of such importance that all their fortunes would be made (Exquemelin 1969). Within a matter of days the governors of the Spanish colonies began to receive intelligence of a large fleet that was being put together to attack a major stronghold on the Main. "Hardly was a letter was written which did not report some news of an imminent threat" (Earle 1981, as quoted in Talty 2005:200). The governors of the four richest and largest cities (Santiago, Vera Cruz, Cartagena, and Panama) began to strengthen their defenses, as none knew which target would be hit. Fear was the word of the day, which would ultimately win the battle for Morgan and his men. In a matter of weeks Morgan rendezvoused with his fleet, which numbered 36 ships, 239 guns, and 1,846 men (Livingston 1909), quite possibly the largest privateer/pirate fleet ever amassed in the history of the Caribbean. They set sail for Panama on December 18, 1670.

Morgan and his fleet arrived first at Catalina Island, (modern-day Providencia) and the surrounding islands six days later (TNA CO 1/26, No. 51). They quickly commenced an attack on the Spanish garrison there in order to provision for their assault on Panama. The privateers soon got a small taste of what awaited them in crossing the isthmus to Panama: lack of sufficient food for such a large group. At an apparent stalemate with the Spanish and stuck out in the open in rain and without the food that had been left on the ships, Morgan's men began to grumble. Some talked of desertion (Talty 2005; Exquemelin 1969). In a quick response to the escalating situation, Morgan sent a note to the island's governor to surrender or die. The governor deliberated for two hours before sending his reply. He would surrender on one condition: that his reputation remain intact. To this end the governor explained his plan to Morgan. His ruse required that Morgan and his men attack the two strongest fortifications on the island. Both sides would fire heavily, but into the air. The governor would then arrange to be in transit between the two forts, San Jerónimo and Santa Teresa, at which time he could be captured. Morgan agreed to the plan as long as none of his men were injured. All went as expected: by the end of the night Morgan was in control of the islands (Exquemelin 1969; Talty 2005). The privateers then slaughtered as much meat as they could and stocked up on provisions for the expeditions to come. Morgan also freed the prisoners, recruiting three to four to serve as guides for the trek to Panama (TNA CO 1/26, No. 51; Exquemelin 1969; Talty 2005). With provisions taken care of, the next leg in their journey was the Castillo de San Lorenzo, which guarded the mouth of the Chagres River. Not wanting to alert the Spanish as to the size of his fleet, Morgan sent an advance party of 470 men in five ships to take San Lorenzo (TNA CO 1/26, No. 51).

Castillo de San Lorenzo and the Chagres River

The Chagres River is a very storied part of the landscape. It served as one of the two original passages across the isthmus from the Atlantic to the Pacific for the colonial Spanish (along with the overland mule train route to Portobelo) and is the river that feeds the modern Panama Canal. While exploring the Caribbean coast of Panama, Columbus spent three days in the area of the Chagres, where he traded with the native peoples for gold. He also entered the river's mouth and named it the "Río de Los Lagartos" for the large quantity of alligators observed (Morison 1942:620–21). Hernando de la Serna's expedition upriver by canoe in 1527 proved that the river was navigable. He recommended that a road from Panama be built to link to a local transshipment point at Las Cruces (Anderson 1911:302). In 1528, acting on de la Serna's report, merchants in Panamá petitioned the Crown to fund an alternate route across the isthmus for trade, in addition to the overland mule path to Portobelo, arguing that goods could be carried to the upper reaches of the Chagres and floated down the river in boats. Using slaves, the Spanish cleared the fallen trees and other obstructions in the river (Haring 1918:181–82).

Following two subsequent surveys of the river, the Crown ordered the governor of Panama to spend one thousand gold pesos on clearing the river and erecting a warehouse for goods at the point where the river met the sea in 1534 (Haring 1918:182; Anderson 1911:302). This transformed the river into a partial highway across the Isthmus of Panama (Ward 1993:57–58), facilitating the transportation of goods to and from Panama City. This further strengthened Panama's connections to other Spanish ports via the Pacific Ocean to South America as well as Mexico and Spain's possessions in the Pacific, such as the Philippines. Flat-bottomed barges operated between Cruces and Chagres. One account noted that by 1579 as many as thirty of these craft were in use on the river. In 1534 Phillip II had ordered the construction of fortifications on the cliff overlooking the mouth of the river. Yet he had provided no artillery or armament, making it that much easier for English privateer Francis Drake to sail up the river to attack the town of Cruces in 1571 (Ward 1993). Further fortification of the entrance began in 1597–99 with the construction of a water-level battery, given the name

Figure 6.3. Castillo de San Lorenzo (courtesy of Captain Morgan Rum/Jonathan Kingston).

Castillo de San Lorenzo el Real de Chagres. It consisted of a star-shaped earthwork and wooden-palisaded fort atop the *morro* (cliff) and was first fitted with guns in 1626 (Ward 1993) (figure 6.3). This fortification bristling with cannon guarded the mouth of the river and awaited Morgan's men.

Colonel Joseph Bradley and Morgan's advance party arrived off the coast of the Chagres River and learned that they had lost the element of surprise due to a buccaneer deserter from a previous venture in the nearby region (Talty 2005; Exquemelin 1969). Bradley decided against a frontal attack on the cliff and began ferrying men in canoes to the mainland, four miles from San Lorenzo. Spanish lookouts supplied the castle's commander with updates on the privateers' movements. When Bradley and his men entered the clearing at the back of the fort, they were greeted with a hail of musket fire. Dividing his men into three groups, Bradley had two groups charge the fort through the clearing. Those that reached the wall attempted to lob grenades over the walls but retreated under heavy fire. At nightfall the privateers rallied and charged again, throwing grenades and attempting to dig through the palisade. The fierce battle continued until one of the privateers who had been shot with an arrow in the back removed it, wrapped it in cotton, loaded it in his musket, and fired it into the castle (Exquemelin 1969). The powder ignited the cotton, and the flaming arrow started a fire inside the castle walls that eventually lit two houses on fire. The fire spread and found a powder store (or a loaded bronze cannon according to the Spanish) that exploded and blew a hole in the palisade (Exquemelin 1969; Talty 2005). The privateers swarmed the breach in the castle's defense and pressed their attack. The fire became so intense that the privateers retreated, only to return en masse in the morning and continue the pitched battle (Exquemelin 1969; Talty 2005). The Spanish who did not desert refused quarter and fought to the death, but the privateers proved relentless and finally overcame the Spanish resistance. Bradley, shot in the leg, died ten days later of his wound (Talty 2005; Exquemelin 1969). San Lorenzo would prove to be the true battle for Panama.

Upon receiving news of the victory at Chagres, Morgan sailed for the isthmus, arriving five days after the victory on January 12, 1671. "[W]hereupon I gave orders for ye fleete to follow mee into ye harbour but had ye ill fortune to cast away ye ship that I was in and 4 more but saved ye men" (TNA CO 1671: 1/26, No. 51, 140). Morgan and his flagship, the *Satisfaction*, were the first to run aground on Lajas Reef and hit so hard that the collision brought down the masts and yards and threw sailors into the water (Exquemelin 1969). Four other vessels also grounded before the rest of the fleet was warned and stood off from the reef (TNA CO 1/26, No. 51). The ships caught on the reef "were shattered to pieces," as "the wind was blowing hard across the reef" (Earle 1981:182; Exquemelin 1969). While Morgan writes that no one perished, Exquemelin (1969) writes that ten men drowned, "the sea running very high," as well as the only woman in the fleet, a *bruja* (witch) that Morgan kept with him.

Undaunted, Morgan salvaged what he could, left two hundred men to guard San Lorenzo, and set sail up the Chagres to cross the isthmus to Panama, carrying few provisions in order to travel quickly and lightly (TNA CO 1/26, No. 51). Word of the fall of San Lorenzo reached Panama. A Spanish force of 150 men was sent to ambush them on the river, but Morgan's ruse of sending only 470 to San Lorenzo sparked further Spanish fear when the guerrillas realized the true size of Morgan's forces, which vastly outnumbered their small contingent (Talty 2005). The guerrilla party fled into the mountains, blaming the failure on an incompetent guide. Four days into the passage and beginning to grow hungry, the privateers arrived at a Spanish stockade, only to find that it had been burned and the provisions taken. With the water level running low farther upstream, Morgan and his men were forced to start hiking overland sooner than anticipated. Two hundred men were left behind to guard their trail and protect the canoes for the return trip. The dense, humid jungle took a physical toll on the men, who suffered even more from the food deprivation, eating leather, grass, and what little they could find at the other abandoned Spanish outposts (Exquemelin 1969). Much as at Santa Catalina, the privateers' mood had turned drastically toward desertion, yet none desired to make the return trek through the jungle with nothing to show for it. Upon arrival at Venta de Cruces, the town that was the gateway to the path to Panama, the privateers were dismayed to find more of the same, an empty town with virtually nothing to eat. They continued on the path to Panama, escaped skirmishes with Spanish musketeers and Indians, and on the ninth day emerged at the top of a hill. From there they saw the Pacific Ocean in the distance and the masts of ships in the bay (Talty 2005; Exquemelin 1969). Their elation grew even greater when they saw the herds of cattle grazing in the valley below them and slaughtered them at their leisure, eating as much as they could (Exquemelin 1969; Talty 2005). The men had trekked through the jungle for five days with no food (Talty 2005). Having conquered the jungle and with full bellies, the privateers began their final march to Panama. Arriving just northwest of the city, the privateers halted and set up camp for the night in anticipation of the next day.

Panama

When word reached Panama of Morgan's pending arrival, true fear took hold of the Spanish, evoking all of the superstitions about Morgan and his dreaded privateers. Five hundred men deserted overnight rather than face Morgan and his privateers. Men, women, and children gathered their valuables and weapons and began their exodus from the city. The riches of Panama were stowed in the holds of ships, which then set sail from the harbor to avoid pursuit (Talty 2005). Panama's president, Don Juan de Guzmán, marched his force of 1,200 men out to the savannah west of the city to prepare to meet the privateers. When the Spanish came within sight of the privateers two days later, they were surprised to find a group of approximately 600. Conversely, the privateers were shocked to see that the Spanish forces were nearly double their own (Exquemelin 1969; Talty 2005). Morgan divided his men into three groups, spread out across the top of the hill, and advanced on the Spanish, sending out the best shooters first (Exquemelin 1969). Once the main body of privateers hit the plain, the cavalry attacked. Bogged down in the swampy conditions, the horses were slowed, making the privateers' musket volleys that much deadlier. The infantry forces attempted to aid the cavalry but were pinned down by the other body of privateers. Spanish drovers sent a herd of two thousand wild bulls into the rear of the privateers to break their formation, but the privateers' rear guard broke up and stampeded the bulls. "After two hours' hard fighting, the Spanish cavalry were thoroughly routed; most were dead or wounded, and the rest had fled" (Exquemelin 1969:195). Seeing how the privateers had routed the cavalry, the Spanish infantry began to flee. Still weary from their overland route, the privateers did not pursue them and paused to rest. Their losses were minimal, but more than six hundred Spaniards lay dead on the plain (Exquemelin 1969). After resting a spell, Morgan and his men continued on to the city and had full control within two hours. One of the more curious aspects of the sack of Panama is the fire that supposedly consumed the city during Morgan's raid. Exquemelin writes that Morgan set some of the town on fire, while Morgan reports that the Spanish torched the city upon their retreat to impede the privateers' progress (and protect the departure of the ships with the valuables). Spanish accounts vary. In any case, Morgan and his men held the city for approximately one month, ransoming hostages and trying to accumulate as much wealth as possible before leaving. On March 6, 1671, following Morgan's triumphant return to San Lorenzo from the Pacific, "wee fired the Castle, spiked ye guns and begun our voyage for Jamaica" (TNA CO 1671: 1/26, No. 51, 142). Yet Panama and the rest of the Spanish Main would never be the same. Morgan had shaken the very foundation of the Spanish colonies and their trade. A new city of Panama was soon built farther west along the coast, while the original city was left in ruins.

A Piratical Landscape: Terrestrial and Underwater Archaeological Investigations of Morgan's Final Raid

While the terrestrial and underwater archaeological efforts in regard to Henry Morgan's raid on Panama were initiated separately and a number of years apart, a recent push has been made to integrate the results in order to paint a larger picture of this seminal event in the country's history and place it into the global and social context of its time. The goal of this chapter is to inform readers of the ongoing research efforts, so little theory is directly integrated with the results. Yet the lens through which this aspect of our past is studied adds to our overall understanding. Utilizing a landscape approach on a local level, the focus here is on analyzing the archaeological remains through a framework showing how both the privateers and the Spanish conceptualized, organized, and manipulated their environments and, in turn, how those environments affected their behavior and identity (Branton 2009). On a macro-level or global level, emphasis is placed on using world systems analysis as a means of connecting societies through time within the constructs of the advent of a capitalist world economy (Wallerstein 1980; Orser 2009). Indeed the events that occurred on a local or regional level involving Morgan, British Jamaica, and the Spanish colonies (especially in Panama) were one important aspect in the decline of Spanish hegemony and the ascent of the British Empire and commerce on a global scale. It can also be hypothesized that on this same regional level a piratical landscape exists throughout the Caribbean and the former Spanish Main.

> Buccaneering, usually associated with the dazzling exploits of Henry Morgan, was a source of substantial wealth during the early years of English Settlement in the "Cribey Islands." Morgan and his raiders based themselves in Jamaica after England seized the island from Spain in 1655, and managed over the next sixteen years to sack eighteen cities, four towns, and thirty-five villages in New Spain. They turned an overextended empire to their own purposes and raked in the booty. (Rediker 1987:58)

For the buccaneers and privateers of this time, the Spanish Main was a source of commodities and not simply gold and silver. Slaves, iron, sugar, cloth, and all manner of trade goods could be turned into a profit upon returning to Port Royal. Indeed the local landscape in Panama was shaped by an individual: in the space of three years Henry Morgan laid waste to nearly every significant Spanish city, town, fortification, and village. Careful study of the remains of this human activity aids in better understanding how these events so greatly affected not only Panama on a local level but trade and commerce on an international level, leaving effects that still resound today.

The Ruins of Panama

After several centuries of abandonment the ruins of the old city became part of the nation's heritage with the passing of Law 91 of December 22, 1976, by which the Historical and Monumental Complexes of Panamá Viejo, Portobelo, and Casco Antiguo were created and regulated (Rovira and Martín 2008). In 1995 the Patronato Panamá Viejo (Old Panama Trust) was created, a nonprofit institution composed of government and private sector partners and charged with the management, protection, study, and promotion of the twenty-eight hectares that form the Monumental

Complex (Mendizábal 1999). Today it consists of the Kiwanis Club and HSBC bank from the private sector and the Instituto Nacional de Cultura (INAC: National Institute of Culture) and the National Tourism Authority from the government. Under the Patronato Panamá Viejo's care, the site was included in the World Heritage Site List by the United Nations Educational, Scientific and Cultural Organization (UNESCO) in 2003. It also was able to foster the passing of Law 16 on May 22, 2007, which created the formal boundaries of the site and a buffer zone around it to guarantee its integrity.

Terrestrial Archaeology Efforts

The Patronato Panamá Viejo's permanent onsite archaeology program began in 1995. Most of the archaeological investigations have been linked to architectural conservation and restoration projects for the many masonry ruins scattered throughout the town. Important research interests are colonial funerary practices (Martín and Díaz 2000; Martín 2002c) as well as specialized aspects such as taphonomy (Pereira 2002). With support from a research fund from the National Science, Technology and Innovation Secretariat (SENACYT), the archaeology team carried out a wide program of funerary archaeology between 2007 and 2009 encompassing the Precolumbian and colonial periods, with the participation of Javier Rivera from Universidad del Centro de la Provincia de Buenos Aires (Argentina) and Claudia Rojas from Université de la Méditerranée (France) (Martín et al. 2007; Rojas et al. 2011). The project was also supported by the joint research program with Tübingen University in Germany that took place between 2003 and 2009, with excavations in the ruins of the San Juan de Dios Hospital (Scholkmann et al. 2006).

Paralleling the recovery of the ancient urban layout of the city a joint effort of the Patronato Panamá Viejo's architecture and archaeology departments was undertaken, identifying colonial floor levels and the original alignment of the city streets (Campos and Durán 2006; Martín 2003; Martín and Yanaida 2007). Remote sensing techniques were applied, such as detection through geoelectricity, electromagnetism, and magnetism, which were instrumental in the detection of underground masonry and stone architectural elements (Pastor et al. 2001; Caballero et al. 2004; Patzelt et al. 2007).

In the case of material culture, several different studies have been developed at the onsite laboratories. Worthy of note is the extensive research on Panamanian mayólica (Rovira 1997, 2001b). These studies analyzed the local production of enameled ceramics, from provenance research through trace element analysis as well as a complete study of the distribution of this production in the Americas, with field data from specialists in Chile, Colombia, and Canada (Rovira 2006). This research also includes a specialized identification and definition of the stylistic characteristics of this important ceramic complex (Rovira and Mojica 2007).

Other European ceramic and Sevillian tile samples have been analyzed and documented (Rovira 2001b, 2002a, 2002b), utilitarian ceramics (Rovira 2001a), Creole ceramics (Linero 2001; Zárate 2004; Schreg 2010), red burnished wares known as *búcaros* or vases (Rovira and Gaitán 2010), olive jars (Brizuela 2002), Chinese porcelains (Shulsky 2001), German stoneware (Martín et al. 2008), colonial glass (Sánchez 2002), trimmings and knittings (Martín and Figueroa 2001), and colonial floors (Martín 2001). More recently, the characterization of enameled wares produced in Popayan, Colombia, with the participation of Colombian researchers, has generated a hypothesis on their production as well as on the commercialization of Andean mayólicas on the Pacific American coast (Martín et al. 2007).

Since the end of the 1950s information has been obtained on the Precolumbian occupation of the site, detected within earthworks on a nearby lot close to the Puente del Rey, on the Abajo River (Biese 1964). Decades later the Patronato Panamá Viejo undertook excavations on the Main Square of the town (Plaza Mayor) and other localities such as the site of the modern Visitor Center and at Parque Morelos. These studies have confirmed the extensive and ancient Precolumbian component underneath the whole site, dating from at least the mid-first millennium AD until the Spanish invasion (Martín 2002b, 2002d; Martín and Rodríguez 2006, 2007; Martín and Sánchez 2007; Mendizábal 1999, 2004; Pearson 2006).

The academic character of the archaeology program has also been strengthened by the organization of three field schools (in 2002, 2006, and 2008) with participation of students and young professionals from Panama and abroad who want to specialize in historical archaeology. Five undergraduate dissertations have been published as a result of these field schools (Lanzas 2001; Zárate 2004; Gómez 2007; Sanabria 2007; Garcés 2009) as well as one master's thesis (Belecki 2007), and three doctoral dissertations are in progress (Tübingen University, Columbia University, and Universidad del Centro de la Provincia de Buenos Aires). Also, due to the good results obtained through remote-sensing surveys, the IV Central American

Figure 6.4. Excavation of the Cabildo at the base of the iconic bell tower (courtesy of Patronato Panamá Viejo).

Applied Geophysics School was organized in 2002, together with the Universities of Paris VI, Paris IX, Reims, and Panamá, with a purely archaeological focus and using the equipment in different sectors of Panamá Viejo.

El Cabildo

Near the end of 1995 the archaeology program started to explore the Main Square (Plaza Mayor) and the buildings around it, which include the most emblematic structures of the city and possibly the country, the tower and the cathedral of Panamá Viejo. Next to the cathedral lie the ruins of the Cabildo (or City Hall), where excavations in 1996 aimed to remove the concrete decorations that lay over it and rescue any surviving structures (figure 6.4). The Cabildo was a two-floor masonry building measuring 2 *lumbres* in front by 3 *lumbres* on the side. The colonial *lumbre* was a Spanish construction measurement that is equivalent to roughly 4.1 to 4.3 m.

These efforts resulted in the discovery of the foundations for the perimeter walls of the Cabildo and the remains of the flight of stone stairs that led to the upper floor (Brizuela 1996a, 1996b). On the turn of the stairs to the upper level the excavation team documented the first and only archaeological evidence of the massive fire that is supposed to have destroyed the town. Below the modern earthen surface they first found a stratum composed of debris from a fallen roof: many fragments of bricks, roof tiles, wrought iron nails, and very few ceramics in a soil and ash matrix. Directly underneath the debris level of the fallen roof and upper floor was the third stratum, composed entirely of soil and ash, representing the burned remains as a result of the fire that destroyed the building during the pirate attack of January 28, 1671. The major find on this level was an iron sword now on display at the onsite museum (figure 6.5). Directly beneath the ash level was the stair stone floor, which was blackened by the fire and ash. The masonry walls at the back of the Cabildo and parts of the cobble floors also showed darkened spots, evidence of the fire that took down the building and supposedly the entire town.

In the fifteen years of continuous archaeological excavations at Panamá Viejo since then, these remain the only direct traces of Morgan's attack and the fire that ensued. As those excavations took place, the ruins of houses on the western flank of the Plaza Mayor were also explored, but no traces

Figure 6.5. The sword uncovered during the excavations of the Cabildo (courtesy of Patronato Panamá Viejo).

Figure 6.6. Traces of fire on the excavated steps of the Cabildo (courtesy of Patronato Panamá Viejo).

of ash or fire were found (Mendizábal 1996). Stratigraphic layers without a trace of ash, thick with thousands of fragments of roofing tiles and iron nails, were found directly on top of the stone cobble floors, which indicates that these roofs probably collapsed due to abandonment and lack of upkeep, not because of fire-related destruction. The Terrín family houses, immediately to the north of the Plaza Mayor, were also excavated, revealing no evidence of fire (Mendizábal 1997).

It seems odd that in a late seventeenth century wooden town that suffered major fires and continued to suffer them throughout the eighteenth and nineteenth centuries (even when it moved to its new location in San Felipe) none of the structures around or next to the Cabildo burned down, even when the Cabildo and the cathedral did. These were the most representative buildings of the church and state in the city and obvious targets for the pirates. Yet for all the stories about the conflagration that supposedly destroyed the entire city, no hard evidence has yet to be found of a widespread fire that affected buildings beyond those belonging to the colonial or ecclesiastic authorities (figure 6.6). This contradicts the Spanish account that Morgan burned down the entire city and lends more credence to Morgan's report of trying to put out the flames that the Spanish started upon their retreat, providing an excellent example of how the archaeological record can shed light on questions or misinformation found in the historical record.

Maritime and Underwater Archaeological Efforts

Accounts vary as to whether the stores of the ships were salvaged, but none of the vessels was recovered (figure 6.7). Morgan's flagship *Satisfaction* was originally a fourteen-gun French pirate ship from La Rochelle named *Le Cour Volant* (TNA CO 1669: 1/33, No. 103a). It was first captured by one of Henry Morgan's privateers, Edward Collier, with the ship *Oxford*. Collier brought the vessel to Port Royal, where it was made part of Morgan's fleet and renamed *Satisfaction* (ibid.). Following the explosion and sinking of HMS *Oxford* off Isla Vaca, *Satisfaction* sailed to Campeche then spent eighteen months at sea (TNA 1670: 1/25, No. 51), during which time Morgan took Maracaibo. Upon its return to Port Royal and rendezvous with the rest of the privateer fleet, *Satisfaction* became Morgan's flagship for the voyage to Panama. The vessel was recorded to weigh 120 tons and carried twenty-two guns, the largest ship in Morgan's fleet of thirty-eight ships until the subsequent grounding. The names of the other four vessels that sank are unknown and unrecorded.

Figure 6.7. Aerial image of the Castillo de San Lorenzo, Lajas Reef, and the mouth of the Chagres River (courtesy of Jonathan Kingston).

The Lost Ships of Henry Morgan Project is but one aspect, albeit large, of the Río Chagres Maritime Cultural Landscape Study. In January 2008 with funding from the Waitt Institute, a team of archaeologists conducted the first ever nondisturbance archaeological survey of the submerged cultural resources off the mouth of the Chagres River in the Colón Province of the Republic of Panama. Given the strong northern winds, the surge, and the river current, the team was unable to deploy the magnetometer in selected target areas and therefore relied largely on visual diver survey. The weather also gave the team an understanding of what Morgan might have faced when attempting to sail into the mouth of the river. The waves over the reef were large enough to surf. The divers working below were forced to pause and grab large coralline rocks each time the shadow of a wave's tube loomed over them and crashed, followed by the sudden surge. Despite the weather and setbacks, the survey identified a number of submerged cultural resources, spanning five hundred years of historic maritime activity in and around the Chagres, including a scatter of guns on Lajas Reef that may have belonged to the ships that Morgan lost in 1671.

Guns

The scatter of artifacts found in 2008 consisted of eight coral-encrusted iron guns or cannon, of varied length and size, mapped during the initial survey. Based on observed damage to the surrounding reef by looters, recommendations were made to INAC, which agreed that the guns should be removed before they were lost to strong currents or theft. The team returned in 2010 for recovery of the guns. Significant environmental alterations to the site were noted upon arrival, along with the absence of two of the lightest of the eight cannon. As the most intact cannon remained in situ, looting was ruled out as a cause. Large coralline rocks had tumbled across the site, where none had been in the original 2008 survey. Given the recent strong storms that had passed through the site and the shallow depth, it is hypothesized that the two missing cannon were rolled into the sand bordering the southern edge of the site and subsequently buried. The cannon were recovered using enclosed air-filled liftbags and vessel support. The divers would raise one cannon to the surface, tie it off to the vessel, and then tow it to the shore. During the towing, one diver would stay with the cannon and bag to maintain positive buoyancy and ensure that the lift straps and rigging held. Once at shore the cannon was placed on a sled and pulled gently out of the water with the project vehicle, placed in the truck, and then driven to the marina to await the boom crane. The guns were light

Figure 6.8. Two divers raise a small gun from the seafloor (courtesy of Donnie Reid).

enough that four of the six cannon recovered could be lifted by a group of four (figure 6.8). This process was carried out for each individual cannon (Hanselmann and Delgado 2010).

Following the recovery of the cannons, they were transported and housed in a holding tank at the Smithsonian Tropical Research Institute (STRI) laboratory on Isla Flamenco near Panama City. They were subsequently

Figure 6.9. Image of a gun with concretions removed (courtesy of Captain Morgan Rum/Jonathan Kingston).

transported to the conservation laboratory at the Patronato Panamá Viejo facilities, where the guns are currently undergoing conservation and the concretions that encased the guns are being removed (Hanselmann and Delgado 2010) (figure 6.9).

The size and shape of the cannon suggest that four of them are small deck guns from the sixteenth to seventeenth centuries (Hanselmann and Delgado 2010). They would be breech-loading swivel guns with less than a one-pound range. These rail-mounted antipersonnel weapons could be loaded with shot or grape for close-in fighting. One account from 1644 describes these guns as "Murderers," which are

> small iron or Brass Peeces with Chambers: In Marchant-men they are most used at the Bulkheads of the fore-castle, half-deck, or steeridge; and they have a Pintell, which is put into a stock, and so they stand and are traversed, out of which they use Murdering-shot to scower the Decks, when men enter, but Iron Murderers are dangerous for them which discharge them, for they will scale extremely, and endanger their eyes much with them, I have known divers hurt with shooting them off. (Manwayring 1644:69; Hanselmann and Delgado 2010)

This style of weapon was developed in the sixteenth century and remained in use on both naval and merchant vessels through the seventeenth century, although they were obsolete on English vessels by the eighteenth century (Lavery 1987). This type of gun reentered service during the eighteenth century (ibid.). The typical swivel gun of the eighteenth century varied between 34 and 36 inches in length and 1.5 to 1.75 inches in bore, utilizing shot that weighed either .50 or .75 pounds (Tucker 1989:98; Hanselmann and Delgado 2010).

The guns at Lajas Reef fit within those ranges. One is within a few inches and may be a slightly larger deck gun. The sizes and shapes of the guns suggest smaller weapons, perhaps in the three-pounder range or less, which in English were termed "murderers," "minions," "falcons," "falconettes," and "port-pieces." The sixteenth-century and seventeenth-century guns were considered obsolete in English use by 1635, although some may have continued to be used later into the century (Lavery 1987:103). The heavier guns would have been in position on the gundeck, below the main deck. The type of gun, the date range, and the location of the weapons on Lajas Reef suggest a wreck or wrecks of the sixteenth to seventeenth century and the possibility of an association with the known wrecks of Morgan's ships in 1671 (Hanselmann and Delgado 2010). Other items of consideration include the possible French origin of these guns. A portion of Morgan's fleet was French, and his flagship *Satisfaction* had also been a French vessel in its former life.

As of this writing, concretions from three of these guns have been removed. Two exhibit markings that tell us that their origin is English and date them to the mid- to late seventeenth century (Brown 2012). The third appears to be French in origin. The two English guns that have been deconcreted seem to be falconets (Brown 2012).

> Guns in these small calibers were cast in their hundreds for export and use by merchant ships from the late sixteenth century through to the early eighteenth century. They were the smallest, lightest and cheapest ordnance, were easy to move and took up least space aboard ship. Their production and sales were less regulated by government regulations than the larger caliber guns. However they were always difficult to cast because of the problems of removing a core from such a small gun and they had poor rates of passing proof. (Brown 2012:2)

This points toward the original hypothesis that these guns were thrown overboard when the *Satisfaction* and four other ships from Morgan's fleet ran aground on the reef. As conservation and research of the recovered guns continues, more information will come to light. The guns will later be exhibited in the Hall of Piracy in the Patronato Panamá Viejo's museum.

The Search for the Shipwrecks

With the guns recovered and concurrent with the ongoing conservation, the team conducted two field seasons in 2011 and 2012 of two weeks and eight weeks. For the past two years, the major source of project funding has been a namesake of the admiral himself: Captain Morgan Rum. With significant funding from Diageo, the parent company of the ubiquitous rum, the search for Morgan's ships has advanced by leaps and bounds.

The 2011 field season of the Lost Ships of Henry Morgan Project, albeit very short in duration, resulted in the collection of an enormous and extremely important amount of data through magnetometer survey, diver visual survey, and test excavation. The marine magnetometer survey was conducted at the mouth of the Chagres River and along the Caribbean coast, just west of the river mouth, including the area immediately below Castillo de San Lorenzo, offshore of Lajas Reef, and the mouth of the Chagres River (Hanselmann et al. 2011). The magnetometer is one of the principal detection devices used in underwater archaeological survey. Magnetometers detect and quantify magnetic fields. In hydrographic survey, ferrous or magnetic objects can be located by noting small perturbations, called "anomalies," in the earth's ambient magnetic field (Hanselmann et al. 2011). Ferrous objects cause a localized increase or decrease, usually both, in the ambient magnetic field. Ferrous objects in this context are generally of cultural origin associated with maritime casualty, activity, or depositional sites (Hanselmann et al. 2011). Magnetometers measure and record the total magnetic field intensity in a manner independent of sensor orientation and presence of sediment. In practice, because full-field magnetometers are not influenced by sediment, they are ideal detection devices for submerged cultural materials of ferrous construction on or beneath the seabed (Hanselmann et al. 2011). The team mapped approximately twenty-five square miles of the mouth of the Chagres River and the adjacent coastline, which resulted in ninety-six magnetic anomalies. In order to investigate these anomalies, teams of two or three divers would conduct concentric expanding searches using both visual observation and metal detectors in an attempt to locate the anomaly on or in the seafloor (Hanselmann et al. 2011). The team conducted eleven searches. In some areas the anomaly could not be detected due to deep burial in the sand, and some areas contained material culture. The one area selected for test excavation proved to be a portion

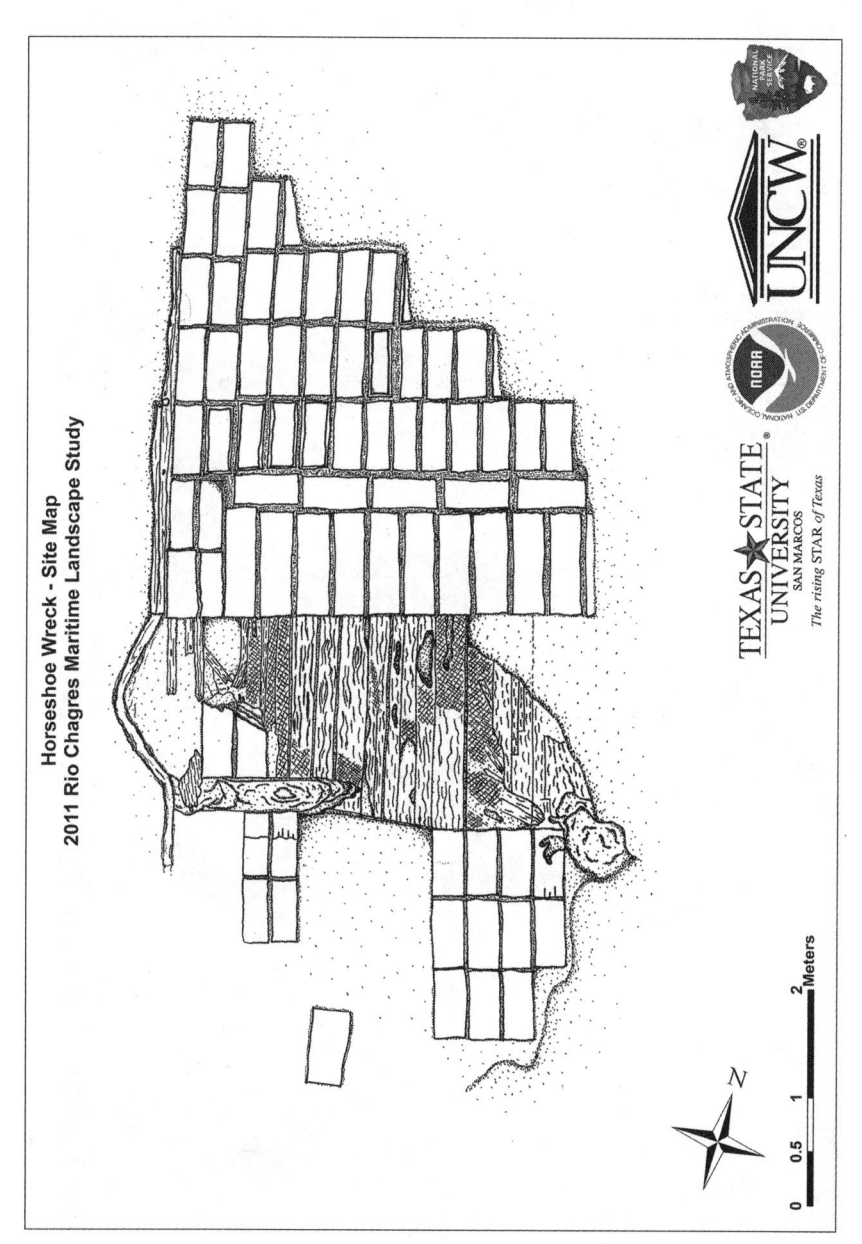

Figure 6.10. 2011 site map (Texas State University/National Park Service).

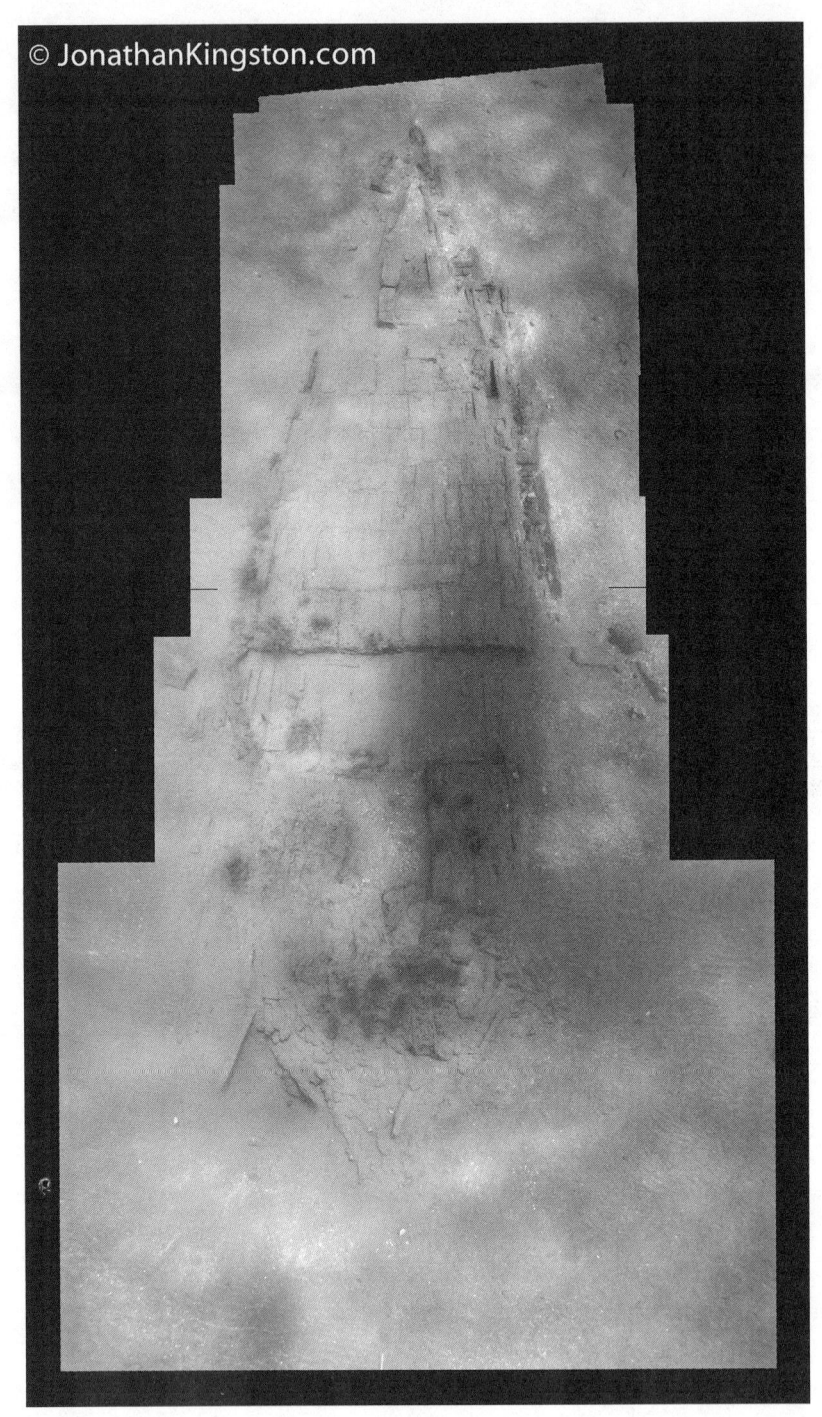

Figure 6.11. Photo mosaic of the shipwreck site.

of a wooden ship hull laden with chests (Hanselmann et al. 2011) (figure 6.10).

The results of the 2012 field season are still in the process of analysis and write-up, yet an expanded magnetometer survey was conducted, excavations continued at the shipwreck site located in 2011, and diver surveys and test excavations commenced at other targets within the project area. A sample of artifacts was recovered from the shipwreck site, indicating that this could possibly be a seventeenth-century Spanish shipwreck. These artifacts include lead cargo seals, muleshoes, two sword blades, a concreted wooden chest, and half of a wooden barrel. Spanish colonists used these items during that period, specifically for overland trade from the Atlantic to Pacific. One of the lead cargo seals was etched with a fleur-de-lis. This is interesting if it turns out to be French, as trade with other nations was strictly prohibited by the Crown. Current analysis of the ship's hull structure suggests that the vessel may not have been masted (figure 6.11). Archival records indicate that a Spanish merchant ship, *Nuestra Señora de Encarnación*, sank in 1681 along with a Spanish salvage barge that was sent to rescue the goods.

Although this is not one of Morgan's lost ships, it helps paint a bigger picture of Spanish life around the time of the privateer attacks. With almost 150 anomalies, only 27 diver searches were conducted. Only two other sites were subjected to test excavation, with limited time due to weather constraints in areas of surge and swell. Much remains to be discovered in the project area. Future efforts on land and underwater include the continuation of the archaeology program at the ruins of Panamá Viejo, the start of terrestrial survey for the battle at the Castillo de San Lorenzo coupled with 3D laser scanning of the fortifications, as well as further underwater investigations into the location and remnants of Henry Morgan's lost ships.

Conclusion

After his exploits in Panama in 1671, Morgan was called back to England and basically given a slap on the wrist. He was allowed to be a free man but was not allowed to travel to Jamaica until 1675, when he returned with a new title: lieutenant governor (Talty 2005; Earle 1981). Morgan retired from politics in 1682 to his 400,000-acre sugar plantation and passed away in 1688 from gout (Talty 2005; Earle 1981). Henry Morgan is quite possibly the most successful privateer of all time, not due to the quantities of gold, silver, and loot that he acquired, but because he retired to enjoy the spoils of his ill-gotten gains, unlike most other pirates. While Morgan's life ended in 1688, his story still continues. The search for the tangible remains of his attacks in Panama on land and underwater has only just begun, with very promising results.

Acknowledgments

The authors of this chapter would like to express their extreme gratitude to the following people and organizations who have assisted and collaborated in this project, without which the project would not have been a success: Diageo/Captain Morgan Rum, the Waitt Institute, the Way Family Foundation, and Charles P. Garrison for project funding; the National Park Service's Submerged Resources Center for project assistance; Captain James Dertien for vessel and logistical support; Julieta de Arango, Jacinto Almendra, Marcelina Godoy, and the staff of Patronato Panamá Viejo; the park rangers with the Autoridad Nacional del Medioambiente; the staff of the Dirección Nacional de Patrimonio Histórico and the Instituto Nacional de Cultura; Shelter Bay Marina and Hotel; Subsalve Liftbags and Halcyon Dive Systems for equipment; Ruth Brown for huge assistance with the analysis of the guns; and finally our good friends and fellow team members James P. Delgado and Dominique Rissolo for starting and supporting the project with us; team member Christopher Horrell for comments on the manuscript; and the rest of our team over the course of the last four years.

7

Ireland's Golden Age of Piracy

History, Cartography, and Emerging Archaeology

CONNIE KELLEHER

Ireland. . . . may be well called the Nursery and Storehouse of Pirates.
Mainwaring and Perrin 1920–22:2:15–16

In the early part of the seventeenth century, piracy was a way of life along the southwestern coast of Munster in Ireland. Such was the nature of this activity at the time that pirates operated openly but not in a haphazard way. The piracy was organized, planned, and, when required, strategically orchestrated. The true nature and full extent of this activity for the southwest of Ireland are difficult to define. Even more difficult is looking at the archaeological record (not hitherto studied for Ireland) to provide cultural evidence on the ground for the activity itself or for the individuals involved. Piracy is synonymous with the "t" word "treasure"; when looking for the cultural remains of piracy, the "t" stands for tenuous, tentative, and tantalizing. The lack of literature on these cultural remains has been previously commented upon (Skowronek and Ewen 2006:4) and is also the case for piracy in Ireland (figure 7.1).

Fortunately a number of contemporary historical sources exist. The High Court of Admiralty papers housed in the National Archives in London contain a large volume of material on piracy for the time in Ireland (Appleby 1992). Another essential source is a treatise on piracy written by a former pirate, Captain Henry Mainwaring, who was a contemporary of the pirates active around the southern coast of Ireland. The "Letter-Book of Sir Arthur Chichester, 1612–14" also includes valuable information (Edwards 1938). Though it primarily contains correspondence by Lord Deputy Chichester dealing with administrative and political issues, it includes

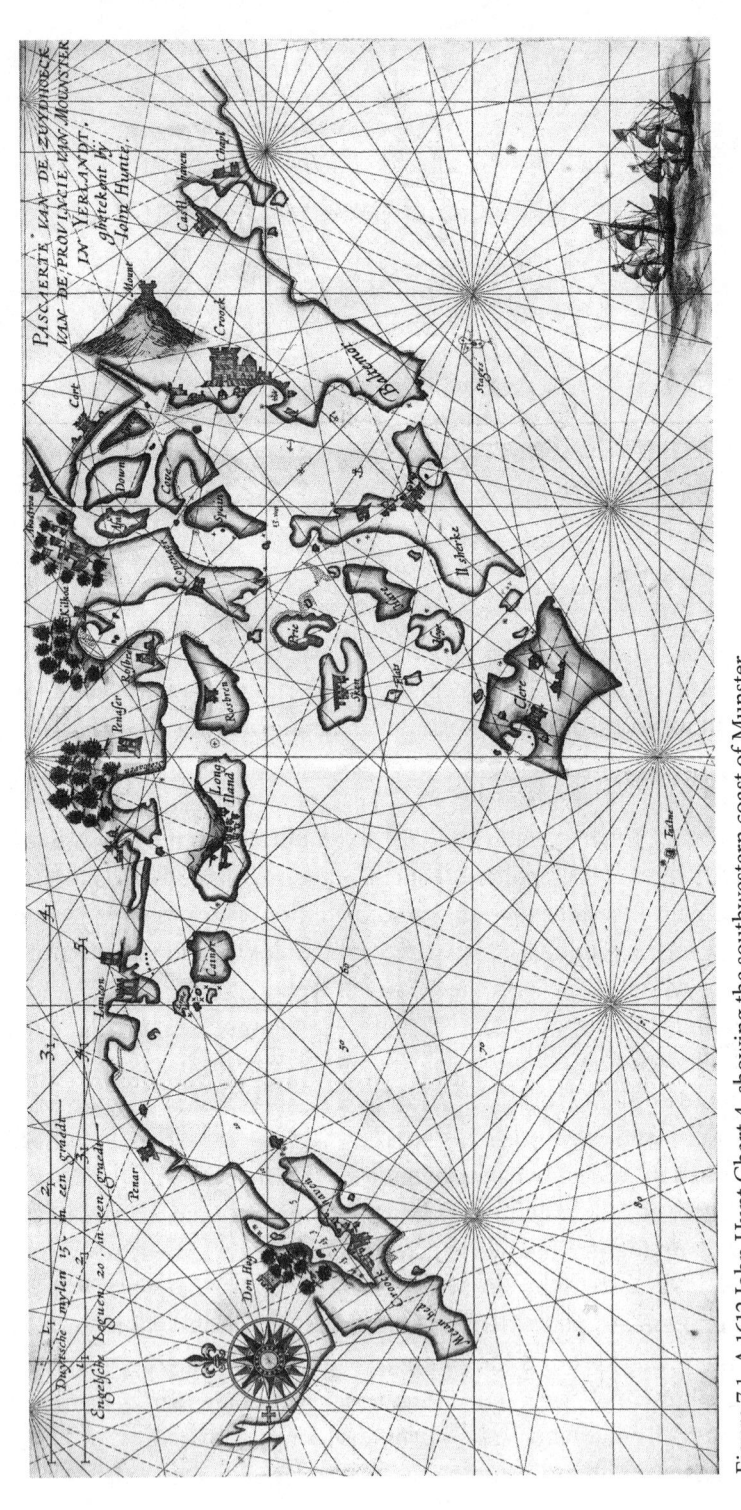

Figure 7.1. A 1612 John Hunt Chart 4, showing the southwestern coast of Munster (by permission of Georg-August-Universität, Göttingen, Germany).

much information on the piratical activity around the coast. The State Papers for Ireland for that period similarly contain a large amount of material relevant to the pirates in the southwest.

A lesser-known chart of the southwest coast of Ireland dating to the year 1612 is a treasure in itself. Written in Dutch, this sea map forms part of a *leeskaart* or sailing directions published by the Dutch East India Company's chief hydrographer, Hessel Gerritszoon, containing four charts and a document written and drawn by the English cartographer John Hunt (written "Hunte" by the Dutch). It clearly states that it is a direct Dutch translation by Gerritszoon of Hunt's pilot. One chart is of the whole of Ireland, two of the east coast, and one of the southwest (though referred to as "the west" within the document). The name of the rutter translates as "Description of the Seacoasts and Ports of Ireland." Its existence appears to have been unknown until its discovery in 1924 in the University Library of Göttingen in Germany (Gerritszoon and Hunt 1612; Cannenburg 1935; Kelleher 2013a:58–60, 2014:349–50).

King James I, after repeated complaints of attacks on their ships by the States General, allowed the Dutch to enter the harbors of West Cork to purge them of pirates (Lords of the Council to Sir Arthur Chichester, September 9, 1611, *Calendar of State Papers Relating to Ireland, of the Reign of James I [CSP], 1611–1614*:101). The document, including the chart, was then commissioned by the Dutch to inform their men-of-war about these "roofhaven" or pirate havens in Ireland (Gerritszoon and Hunt 1612:5; Kelleher 2014) (figure 7.2).

Historical Context

We can begin to get a sense of the extent of the pirate activity in Munster by reviewing the contemporary sources. Lord Henry Danvers, president of Munster between 1607 and 1615, refers to the coast there at the time as "like Barbery, common and free for all" (Danvers to Salisbury, November 20, 1608, *CSP, 1608–1610*:99–100). The practice of piracy was a feature of the maritime landscape of Ireland throughout the early modern period, involving both native Gaelic-Irish lords and visiting predatory mariners. But for a specific period in the early part of the 1600s pirates assumed control on a social, political, and economic level not previously recorded and indeed not seen again thereafter. This can rightly be called Ireland's Golden Age of Piracy (Kelleher 2013a:415–29, 2014).

Figure 7.2. Detail of Dutch ships from 1612 John Hunt Chart 4 (by permission of Georg-August-Universität, Göttingen, Germany).

Three key elements distinguished the pirate activity in the first two decades of the seventeenth-century from earlier and later pirate presences: the intensity of piracy in North Atlantic waters; the level of organization from 1603 onward; and being dominated primarily by English pirates but also including Dutch, French, "Moors," native Irish, and Africans (Senior 1976:49).

Within this confederacy, singular ships and small fleets seem to have been commanded by individual pirates. In turn, these vessels or fleets (numbering two or more ships) cumulatively made up the overall pirate force. The appellation "confederacy" was used when referring to the overall pirate coalition that existed in Ireland at that time (Lords of the Council to Sir Arthur Chichester, November 18, 1612, *CSP, 1611–1614*:302), but this term could also refer to individual pirate captains and their crews. For example, members of the pirate Thomas Coward's crew were referred to as "his confederates" (High Court of Admiralty Papers [HCA] 1610, 13/226:137r). The use of such terminology is suggestive of an alliance that was at the very least semiformal in arrangement, with some semblance of a democratic foundation.

The alliance of pirates (from 1609 onward) had elected commanders: Admiral Richard Bishop, Vice Admiral Peter Easton, and Rear Admiral Thomas Francke. Other individuals also appear to have held positions of authority within the pirate ranks, including John Jennings of Portsmouth (a regular colleague of Bishop), Thomas Coward of Bristol, and Robert Walsingham of London, described as "admiral" of his own ship in Mamora (now

Mehdia/Mehdya on the Moroccan coast) in 1614, which acted as the winter headquarters of the confederacy (Mainwaring and Perrin 1920–22:2:10; Senior 1972:114; Kelleher 2013b:352–53). Others included Robert Stephenson of King's Lynn, described as a "gentleman," and William Baugh, who became rear admiral to Easton after Bishop received his pardon (Appleby 1986:72–73). One of the few pirates referred to as being Irish was Patrick Myagh (later anglicized to Meade). Myagh appears to have come from a long line of settled merchants, whose family had lived in the coastal areas of Munster since the sixteenth century or earlier. Patrick Myagh sailed with Henry Mainwaring to Mamora in 1614. Myagh lived in Crookhaven, west of Baltimore, and commanded his fleet of ships from there (Senior 1972:415; HCA 13/226: 338; Kelleher 2014:359–60) (figure 7.3).

Mainwaring himself in 1612 had set out as a pirate hunter against Easton in Newfoundland but turned pirate as a result of King James's antiprivateering stance. In 1616 he again turned pirate-hunter when he received his pardon from the Crown. Mainwaring's achievements as a commander, which were equally reflected in his success as a pirate, were the primary impetus for pardoning him.

The arrival of so many pirates along the southwest coast of Ireland at the time did not occur in isolation. A number of factors influenced this migration of maritime opportunists to the Munster coastline. Following the Union of the Crowns, when James the VI of Scotland became James I of England, he sought to eradicate both privateering and piracy. He viewed private maritime commerce as just one step away from outright piracy and

Figure 7.3. Crookhaven Harbour, County Cork.

thus outlawed privateers through a series of proclamations revoking all letters of marque and strengthened existing laws against piracy (Steele 1910; Senior 1976:124–52; Murdoch 2010:111–52).

As a consequence of these actions, large volumes of sailors (many previously legitimately employed as mariners in the now dwindling Royal Navy or as commercial privateers) found themselves unemployed in this new era of Stuart peace. With only the sea as their previous experience in gainful employment, increasing numbers of seafarers were now attracted to piracy and foreign privateering ventures as a source of income and, in many cases, the only way of life left open to them. When a further proclamation was issued that outlawed the taking up of foreign commissions by anyone English, the Crown essentially cut the legitimate lifeline to working at sea for hundreds if not thousands of seafarers. These men were left languishing in the ports and harbors of the southern coast of England, looking for any opportunity to go to sea. Many looked to Munster as a place that presented such opportunities (Steele 1910: July 8, 1605: no. 1014; Oppenheim 1914:188–92; Senior 1976:9; Appleby 1990a:2–3).

Only a small number of the various pirates mentioned in the sources provide us with any substantive information about their lives and backgrounds. Clive Senior compiled a comprehensive list of the primary English pirates operating around the coasts of England and Ireland for the early part of the seventeenth century. Some seventy-four of these are recorded as being active along the southern coast of Munster, calling there to trade, revictual, or plunder and primarily to utilize the area as a pirate base. Twenty-one of these pirates are identified as living in the area, either fully settled or amphibiously active as part-time pirates and involved in legitimate work at other times (Senior 1972:appendix 2). It goes without saying, however, that many of the ordinary pirate crews whose names and details did not make it into the contemporary records were more than likely utilizing the coast and may also have settled in the southwest at that time. Numbers presented here therefore are only indicative of what would have been a much higher population of pirates.

The pirate alliance was made up primarily of English mariners of all ranks. Many of them considered themselves to be legitimate descendants of the Elizabethan privateers, who were now involved in piracy by default rather than by desire (MacCarthy-Morrogh 1986:221). Englishman Richard Bishop, for example, reportedly from Yarmouth (HCA 1/47:65v, 1609), who had been elected admiral of the pirates by 1607, had served with distinction under Sir Thomas Norris, lord president of Munster during the closing years of the sixteenth century. He was part of the Irish coast fleet patrolling the area and would thus have been familiar with the Munster coastline.

Earlier Bishop is listed as a captain of the *Black Bishop* of Yarmouth in the year 1591 and seems to have worked as a successful privateer operating out of the south coast of England (Senior 1972:378; Andrews 1964:261). By 1609 Bishop was reportedly commanding eleven pirate ships and over a thousand men in Ireland. His vice admiral, Peter Easton, is said to have entered Villefranche, then part of the Duchy of Savoy in the Mediterranean, with a fleet of nine hundred men (Sir Richard Moryson to Salisbury, August 22, 1609, *CSP, 1608–1610*:277). In the same year Chichester, also writing to Salisbury, recounted that "they are grown to a height of strength and pride that he [Chichester] doubts his endeavours will hardly prevail without the assistance of some of His Majesty's good ships" (August 17, 1609, *CSP, 1608–1610*:273). Bishop had begun his pirating days in the company of another archpirate, John Ward, who remained active in the Mediterranean (Bak 2006). Bishop broke away from Ward in 1608 to head north. He set up his base in Ireland and brought the pirates there into a cohesive alliance (Sir Richard Moryson to Salisbury, August 22, 1609, *CSP, 1608–1610*:277).

Records suggest that Bishop was pardoned sometime around 1611 and is recorded as legitimately settling in West Cork on lands given to him by the local deputy vice admiral, William Hull, who was the linchpin between the pirates and official governance and was most probably an ex-pirate himself (see below). Bishop is said to have built a house "in the English fashion," reflecting the colonial tradition of building in stone or brick, perhaps with two storeys and a slate roof and chimney, to distinguish it from the chimneyless thatched houses of the Irish (Edwards 1938:35; Appleby 1990b:77; Kelleher 2013a:516–17). One of the last references to him in the sources is from the year 1617, when he is described as being fifty-six years of age, "an old pardoned pirate, that lives suspiciously near Limcon and Scull ever plotting with and relieving of pirates" (*Duke of Buccleuch and Queensberry MSS*). In his *General History*, however, Captain John Smith hints at Bishop having ended his days in North Africa: "Bishop was Ancient, and did little hurt." This suggests that by 1629 Bishop had left Leamcon and had perhaps rejoined his old colleague John Ward back in North Africa (Smith 1629:280). It would certainly help to explain why there is no trace of him or a specific house associated with him in the historical or archaeological records for West Cork following his pardon in about 1611.

The Legal Loophole and Official Collusion

A key influencing factor in the targeted expansion of piracy into the southwest was the existence of a legal loophole. This ambiguity meant that anyone accused of piracy could not be tried in Ireland. The accused would have to be extradited to England to stand trial or have a special commission sent over from London to hear charges. If found guilty, the accused would still have to be taken to England to be executed. This was expensive, labor-intensive, and often futile, with many managing to escape along the way during transportation or witnesses being tampered with during the intervening time between capture and trial.

Pirates thus operated relatively untouched in Ireland from a legislative perspective until 1613. In that year the English government sought to bring the law in Ireland into line with law in the rest of Britain. On October 20, 1613, a bill came before the Irish Parliament in Dublin, being passed into law in 1614 as the "Act for the Punishing of Pirates and Robbers at Sea" (Piracy Act 1613; *CSP, 1611–1614*:250, 516; Treadwell 1965:101). Legislation was thus extended to Ireland that allowed both the English central government and Irish Parliament to deal directly with piracy and, more importantly, the pirates themselves on home ground.

The Business of Piracy and Its Allure

During this period the political and economic landscape of Ireland had changed. With the fall of the Gaelic order following the crushing of the Desmond Rebellion in the 1580s and the subsequent defeat of the Spanish at the battle of Kinsale in 1601, remote areas like the southwest that hitherto had been held by the Gaelic-Irish were now open to English settlement (MacCarthy-Morrogh 1986). The plantation of Munster, which commenced in the 1580s, began in earnest during James's administration. Strategic areas began to attract more attention. Coastal locations like West Cork, though outside the official areas of the Plantation Scheme, became the focus for speculation. The ports and harbors in particular were identified for their opportunities to control trade and shipping (Edwards 1938:20–21). The pirates transferred their base of operations from southern England to southern Ireland and arrived en masse from 1603 onward as disenfranchised mariners, merchant adventurers, settlers, and outright predators.

Government officials, including several deputy vice admirals stationed in these remote areas of Munster, facilitated this relocation of pirate operations. These officials operated for the most part within a framework of semiautonomy and inherent self-interest. Such activity was the norm for officers living in isolated areas, as previously attested by acting vice admirals Thomas Killigrew and Richard Hawkins along the Devon and Cornish coastlines in England (Senior 1972:274; Appleby 2009a:70–71). Many of these government officials were themselves to be accused of aiding and abetting the pirates in West Cork (Appleby 1990b; Kelleher 2013a:229–76).

The profits be made from admiralty matters could be substantial. Officers were sent to Ireland, and in particular Munster, to oversee the acquisition of goods and cargoes from ships and in many instances the control of individual ships using the harbors along the southwest coast (Appleby and O'Dowd 1985:317). Humphrey Jobson, who was appointed deputy vice admiral of Munster early in 1607, was as corrupt as Hawkins had been in Devon. Formally secretary to lord high admiral Charles Howard, Earl of Nottingham (who himself was acting vice admiral of Ireland), Jobson had been tasked with investigating reports of corruption in the vice admiralty in Devon in 1606. He would thus have been well informed of the workings of rural politics and familiar with most of the leading pirates there at the time, the majority of whom transferred their attention and activities to Ireland during the first decade of the seventeenth century (Senior 1972:276; Appleby 1990a:83).

Jobson administered his office through assistant deputies, including his brother Richard, and the two of them appear to have acted more on behalf of the pirates than on behalf of the Crown (MacCarthy-Morrogh 1986:217–18). Such was the degree of cooperation between officials (like the Jobsons and the pirates) that the pirates became integrated into local society. A pirate named William Thompson, possibly a Yorkshire man and active along the southern coast of Munster in 1607, apparently became so involved in local business that Jobson engaged him to serve on jury duty during a session of an admiralty court hearing on Sherkin Island (Lord Danvers to the Privy Council, January 1609, *CSP, 1608–1610*:130).

William Hull became deputy vice admiral in Munster from 1607 and held the office for over thirty years thereafter. He was perhaps the primary official "maintainer" of pirates in Munster and presided over what can only be likened to a racketeering business that reaped significant financial rewards (Appleby 1990b). Humphrey Jobson's daughter, Hester, was married to Hull's brother Henry, and indeed such familial relationships appear to have permeated officialdom in the Munster area (Appleby 1990b:78–87; Kelleher 2013a:244–46).

Figure 7.4. Detail from 1612 John Hunt Chart 4, depicting William Hull's fortified house on right and Black Castle on left on Castle Point (by permission of Georg-August-Universität, Göttingen, Germany).

Hull, a Devon mariner, arrived into the West Cork area in the very early part of the seventeenth century and may in fact have been a privateer in his early days (*By the King a Proclamation, 1604*; Appleby 1990b:76–79). This thus raises the prospect that Hull, like Richard Bishop before him, had both prior experiences with the pirates and knowledge of the southern Irish coastline. He may have identified the potential of the area when he visited Leamcon as early as 1601, following receipt of a grant of money from the Crown, possibly for naval services. This would certainly explain his ability to seize opportunities, including liaising with the pirates in Leamcon, where he settled. His coastal estate lay to the west of Schull in County Cork, where Hull leased the lands from the former Gaelic-Irish O'Mahony lords after 1607 and also acquired the lands of Crookhaven from the church (Appleby 1990b:78–79). With Baltimore and Crookhaven, Leamcon became one of the main pirate bases in the Munster coastal region (Kelleher 2013b) (figure 7.4).

From the time that Hull arrived in Cork until the outbreak of the 1641 Rebellion, he became one of the most influential and wealthiest settlers in the locality. He acquired large tracts of land and was directly involved in several business ventures, including trade and fishing. His liaisons with the pirates ensured illicit profits from goods and services throughout his tenure as deputy vice admiral (HCA 1/47:24v; Went 1947; Appleby 1990b).

A number of leading English settlers who arrived in Munster as undertakers (who undertook to settle the area with English settlers) in the Plantation of 1585/86 were equally well placed to take advantage of piratical activities. Thomas Crooke, in Munster by at least 1605, was granted the lands of Baltimore in 1607 after following a protracted legal case involving the hereditary Gaelic-Irish lord of the area, Fineen O'Driscoll, and an Irish Catholic entrepreneur, Walter Coppinger (Kelleher 2007b:138–39; Cotter 2010:44) (figure 7.5).

As early as 1608, however, Crooke was under suspicion of colluding with the pirates in Baltimore. Letters complain about Crooke and his extracurricular commercial activities with individuals in the harbor. Though Crooke was subsequently exonerated, the contemporary accounts at the time contain several entries showing him openly dealing with the pirates: "[Crooke] a chief maintainer and abettor of Coward and other notorious pirates" (Lords of Council to Sir Arthur Chichester, March 8, 1608, *CSP, 1606–1608*:433–34). Certainly Crooke's presence and influence in Baltimore were well known, as depicted by the Dutch in the 1612 chart, where the main castle of Dún na Séad is referred to as "Croock" (Kelleher 2014:82–87) (figure 7.6).

Figure 7.5. Dún na Séad Castle overlooking Baltimore Harbour was the main seat of the Gaelic-Irish O'Driscoll lords. It became the administrative center for Thomas Crooke after 1607.

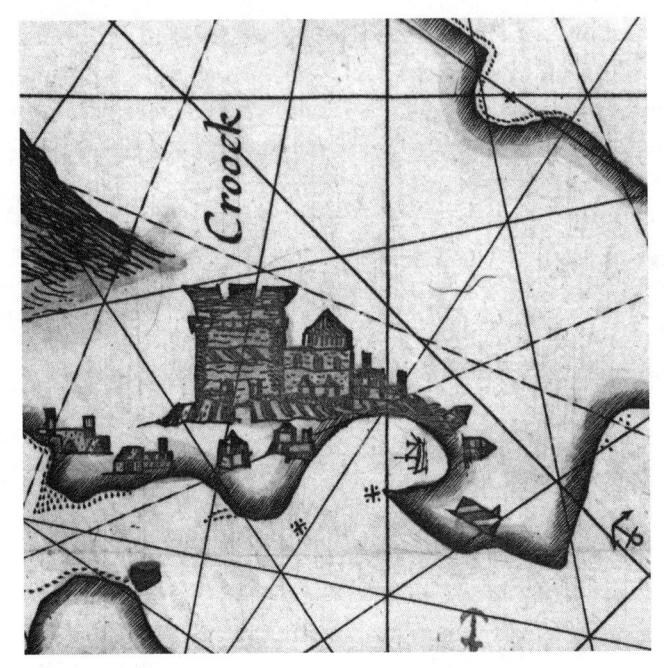

Figure 7.6. Detail from 1612 John Hunt Chart 4, depicting Dún na Séad Castle in Baltimore, referred to as "Croock" on the chart (Gerritszoon and Hunt 1612).

Many more individuals were of course involved in one way or another with facilitating the pirates, including the continued collusion of native Irish rulers and their kin, who learned very quickly that "in order to survive and succeed in this *civilizing* English world and take advantage of the commercial opportunities opening up under the plantation policy, they too needed to change their approach from one of conflict to one of conciliation" (Ohlmeyer 1998:141). This mélange of relationships within all strata of society in West Cork was key to ensuring that the pirates could operate openly and that their bases could successfully function as thriving entrepôts.

Investigating the Invisible

A number of upstanding structures can be directly associated with well-known individual pirates in Ireland. The castles at Rockfleet and on Clare Island, both in County Mayo on the west coast, for example, are linked with the well-known sixteenth-century pirate queen Grace O'Malley (Gránuaile). But first and foremost these were the main residences of the maritime O'Malley chieftains, who were at times regarded as pirates when it suited the agendas of contemporary commentators (Chambers 1998; Appleby 1991:55–59; Gosling, Manning, and Waddell 2007 (figure 7.7).

Similar arguments can be made for the other major Gaelic-Irish maritime lordships at that time, including the O'Donnells in Donegal (Ní Loingsigh 1994) and O'Sullivan-Beare and O'Driscoll clans in Munster (Breen 2005; Kelleher 2007b). While it is acknowledged that these maritime rulers were involved in direct acts of piracy, and indeed at times acted as maritime mercenaries when it suited their purposes, this was a traditional part of Gaelic life revolving around issues of territorial coastal control, economic opportunity, and cultural communication. Piratical events were a tool rather than a dominant theme in their use of the seas bordering their domains (Kelleher 2007b:144–45). The pirates that invaded the southern Munster coast during the first two decades of the seventeenth century were

Figure 7.7. Rockfleet Castle in County Mayo, home to "pirate queen" Gránuaile (by permission of the National Monuments Service, Department of Arts, Heritage & the Gaeltacht).

professional predators, albeit with a pirate code adopted by many that prohibited them from attacking ships belonging to their fellow English. They viewed their actions as a lesser offense, noted by Mainwaring as *pulchrum scelus* or noble crime (Mainwaring and Perrin 1920–22:2:11).

This approach taken by the pirates proved to be a mitigating factor in their subsequent pardoning by the Crown. Claire Schen, in her social study of piracy, suggests that this "forgiveness" of individuals was justified because it advanced colonial and commercial ventures across the Atlantic (Schen 2008). This is corroborated in contemporary sources when the lord deputy writes in favor of pardoning Richard Bishop due to his honorable nature (Lord Deputy to Lord Admiral, June 4, 1610, *Calendar of Carew MSS 1603–1623*:55). Others pardoned were suggested for service overseas to assist with the expansion of the new colonies there: "active men and good mariners, hereafter when time shall wear out their former offences, with better desert in other countries, not troubled so near at hand with their own spoiling, they may return and prove necessary instruments of His Majesty's service" (Sir Richard Moryson to Lord Salisbury, August 22, 1609, *CSP, 1608–1610*:278).

Identifying archaeological evidence for the pirate activity that pervaded the southwest coast in the early 1600s is far more challenging. The essence of these events was surreptitious settlement, established at the same time as the "official" colonial plantation in the area, both of which were influenced by localized sociopolitical and economic factors. Piracy in coastal Munster at that time can thus be viewed as a singular event, though directly linked with the Munster Plantation, with the advent of "peace" under James I and the colonial efforts of England's expanding maritime empire (Appleby 2007:43; Kelleher 2013a:83–93).

Cartographic sources like the 1612 Dutch antipirate chart can assist with the location of possible sites as well as their type and function. Maps from this period have proved to be quite accurate in detail and information, including those by John Hunt (Brain 2011). The 1612 southwest coast chart discussed here is no exception. Though the chart shows obvious skewing of coastal features, John Hunt was clearly someone with knowledge of the coastal topography. The chart is in color, with different shades indicative of the mainland, the islands, and sites on land (Kelleher 2014).

The main pirate bases are highlighted in the chart, providing a rare view of the pirate haunts for that time and indicating the nature of the coastline as it was viewed by contemporary mariners of the day. Bishop settled on lands at Leamcon (shown as "Limcon"). A small settlement cluster appears on the chart east of Leamcon, near where Croagh (pronounced Crewe) harbor is located (figure 7.1). It is tempting to speculate about whether one of these dwellings could be Bishop's house and if so where it was actually located on the ground. We know from William Hull's deposition of 1642 that his lands at Leamcon had "great and strong houses and fishhouses," with tenants paying yearly rents, so settled pirates like Richard Bishop presumably were among these (*Deposition of William Hull, 22 October 1642*:254r).

The challenge lies in identifying the location and nature of the cultural evidence for pirate settlement and differentiating it from the material culture of other settlers, fishers, and native inhabitants. The adoption of a multidisciplinary approach, including the use of history, cartography, folklore, and place-name evidence tied in with archaeological fieldwork, as well as critical assessment of local knowledge, has proved somewhat fruitful. Potential sites are being located that can definitively be said to have been used by pirates and smugglers, though linking material evidence to a specific period (the early seventeenth century) is an ongoing difficulty. The analysis here refers to coastal access points, pending more definitive discussion and comparative evidence. These site types include rock-cut steps, rock-cut platforms, light niches, and coastal pathways, all of which allowed access to and from the coast from the sea (Kelleher 2013b:354–64).

One such site is Dutchman's Cove in Castletownsend. This small cove is located some ten miles east of Baltimore and lies within the main harbor of Castlehaven. Rock-cut steps here lead to the water's edge. They were deliberately hewn out of the bare rock in this secluded spot to provide access from both land and sea, allowing clandestine operations to occur in a controlled and deliberate manner. Niches were cut out of the rock face directly over the steps, inside which were placed lanterns to guide the ships' boats safely to shore. These recesses attest to the link between piracy and smuggling, connecting users of the sea with users of the land. This is the only example currently known of such lantern niches identified in Ireland, though it stands to reason that others must surely exist but await discovery (Kelleher 2013b:361–63) (figure 7.8; I am grateful to Thomas Somerville of Drishane, Castletownsend, for drawing my attention to this site).

Canty's Cove on the northern side of the Mizen Peninsula, in the townland of Dunkelly and overlooking Dunmanus Bay, was presided over by a pirate landlord of native origin. Canty or O'Canty is listed as governing the general area from the latter part of the sixteenth through the first half of the seventeenth century (Hawke 1992:292–98). His first name is disputed but he may have been Gillyneamh, who is recorded as dying in 1633. He could

Figure 7.8. Dutchman's Cove, Castlehaven, with rock-cut steps and lantern niches.

equally have been "Daniell Canty Landlord of Donkelly," who was part of the rebel raid on Leamcon in 1642 (*Deposition of William Hull, 22 October 1642*:253r). This attack, however, had more to do with the general rising during the Irish Rebellion of the Civil War of 1649–53 than with targeted piracy.

Even today the cove retains an air of mystique, with the sands in the harbor stained turquoise from the rich geological veins of copper in the area, giving the place an almost Mediterranean ambience. This is the site of "Canty's House" and garden located on a promontory that looks out over Dunmanus Bay with a full vista of the cove below. A rock-cut platform located below the garden area acted as a pier before the present landing facilities were built in the later nineteenth century. This platform led directly to a set of steps that allowed access to Canty's house. Two sets of rock-cut steps were present. One is known locally as "the pirate steps," while the other (beside the rock-cut platform) gave access to a well for fresh water and to Canty's house and garden. This second set of steps was unfortunately destroyed in recent times when the pier at the cove was being redeveloped. The use of this harbor and the promontory allowed controlled access to facilities ashore, while at the same time aiding in the observation and pillage of passing ships (Kelleher 2013a:31–32, 123–24, 167–71) (figure 7.9).

The use of promontories by pirates has been identified from the earliest times, with these high points in the landscape being ideal locations to act as sentinels for coastal defense and exploitation (Semple 1916:136). Unfortunately, little is known of Canty, with tales of him being clouded in folkloric embellishment and local lore. Dunkelly Castle is reputed to have been located somewhere within the general area, though no above-ground evidence now exists and its actual location remains unknown. The confines of the promontory, however, where Canty's house and garden were located, would have been an ideal spot for such a fortification (Hawke 1992:299–301).

Canty's heyday as a pirate seems to have been during the second and third decades of the seventeenth century, although we cannot say whether this is the same Daniel Canty named in Hull's deposition. Using the term "pirate" for Canty may be inappropriate, however, as his reputation paints him as a lazy, dishonest opportunist who pirated goods from his land base rather than on the high seas. Tradition has it that he would lure passing ships into his cove by sending out his own vessels to greet them with the offer of relief and safe passage. When they came ashore, he invited the captains to dine in his house atop its lofty outcrop. After the consumption of copious amounts of alcohol, he would push them over the cliff and then capture their ships and goods. Little now remains of Canty's house

Figure 7.9. Canty's Cove near Dunmanus Bay, with features indicated.

and garden apart from a series of low walls that have had their stonework robbed over the centuries but outline the perimeter of the promontory cliff edge on all three sides. A larger dividing wall with a doorway opening with a dislodged lintel separates the garden area from a section to its immediate west that could have been a possible courtyard. A house or perhaps a fortified structure may have stood there (Hawke 1992:299–301).

A targeted program of archaeological investigation in this area may help solve the mystery of Canty's Cove. It could provide exciting cultural evidence for the identity of Canty, whether a fortified site once stood here, how such features in the cove are related to each other, and, crucially, whether evidence for pirate activity can be found (Kelleher 2013a:163–70).

Similar rock-cut steps have been found elsewhere, associated with the main pirates' harbors in southwest Ireland but also internationally in direct association with other pirate societies and pirating episodes in the past (for example, Marten 2005:2, 79; Marangou 2006:95–97; Ward 2005:129). While steps may have been used in multiple periods, the nature, extent, and location of such sites can imply a specific use. A set of steps at Gokane Point at the very edge of the headland of Streek Head to the southeast of Crookhaven is such a site (figure 7.10). The steps were hewn out of the bare rock overhanging a cavern and the open sea some one hundred feet below. Their remoteness, precarious position, and strategic location suggest an illicit function (Kelleher 2013b:362–63).

Synonymous with pirates are their ships. We can gain insight into the type of ship preferred by the pirates during the period under study from the contemporary source material. Mainwaring states that the vessels most favored were those known as "Flemish bottoms" or "flyboats." These shallow-drafted, speedy vessels were constructed along the lines of the Dutch *fluyt* or *vlieboot* (Mainwaring and Perrin 1920–22:2:15). They had been modified to a more speedy design toward the end of the sixteenth century, when they traded across the Atlantic to Newfoundland, Africa, and the New World. The Dutch *fluyt* had been first built around 1595 and grew in popularity as the new century began, including being favored by the later Algerian pirates of North Africa (Lane 1998:95). Indeed the High Court of Admiralty papers frequently refer to these "flyboates" as being those most favored by pirates at that time.

The remains of one of these pirate ships may be lying at the bottom of Dunworley Bay in County Cork, linked to the English pirate Robert Nutt, who was active around the southwest coast of Ireland during the 1620s and 1630s. He is recorded as having three ships, one with twenty guns and

Figure 7.10. Pirate steps at Gokane Point, Crookhaven. The location on this windswept outpost implies use by pirates and smugglers.

two with fifteen. Alternatively the wreck may be linked to the infamous Algerian pirate raid on Baltimore in 1631. The wreck, which is early to mid-seventeenth century in date, based on the typology of and markings on the guns on the site, consists of the lower wooden hull structure of a well-constructed vessel. It has a mixture of cast iron muzzle-loaders and wrought-iron breechloading swivel (swing) guns. One recovered medium-caliber falcon has the maker's mark of the English gun-founder John Browne near its touchhole. This along with other features on the gun provides the general date range.

Though the identity of the wreck in Dunworley has yet to be definitively ascertained, the mixture of guns suggests a ship that acquired its armaments from different sources, possibly including those plundered from other ships. Merchant vessels at that time would have had a mixture of guns on board, but the combination of medium-sized muzzle loaders and lighter swivel guns would also fit well as the guns of choice for a pirate ship (Kelleher 2010:143–44). The problem in regard to how to identify this as a pirate-run ship remains. This dilemma has been discussed previously (Babits, Howard, and Brenckle 2006:274–81). While this predicament was highlighted by Wayne Lusardi with respect to the wreck 31CR314 off the coast of North Carolina said to be pirate Blackbeard's ship *Queen Anne's*

Figure 7.11. Recording broken swivel gun on Dunworley Bay wreck site prior to recovery for conservation.

Revenge (Lusardi 2006:216–18), the available evidence for the wreck has been recently well argued to identify it positively as that of the *Queen Anne's Revenge*. The authors discuss the identification of developing patterns through comparison of material with other known pirate wreck sites (Wilde-Ramsing and Ewen 2012). Providing an exact date and identification remains an ongoing difficulty for the Dunworley Bay wreck. But perhaps the diversity of cannon from that site, in association with the historical records for the loss of a pirate vessel in the bay, could be the foundation for a developing pattern. Continued investigation may provide further evidence to support the emerging hypothesis, though caution is still warranted in attributing any identity to the wreck in Dunworley Bay without substantive evidence (figure 7.11).

The Pirate Bases and Cultural Clues

The use of coastlines by geographically astute pirates has been noted. When Ellen Semple (1916) spoke of "environmental determinism" and the concept of "pirate coasts" in locating pirate bases, she was among the first to discuss the judicious use of specific locations by pirates. Similarly, Peter Galvin (1999:8–26) discusses patterns of pillage within the spatial distribution of pirate sites. Analysis of varying influencing environmental factors (including the location of choke points to facilitate the targeting of ships and control of bases, the pirates' relationships with their natural environment, and the use of local resources and engagement in alternative employment within the confines of a specific stretch of coastline) has shown that a cognizance of landscape was central to a successful pirate operation. The location of bases in remote areas outside official settlements and thus beyond central authoritative control was similarly strategic (Pennell 1994:272). The southwest Munster coastline was clearly a prime location for the pirates, their bases, and their theater of operations. Attributing these determining factors to this coastline as highlighted in previous studies fits well into a piratical maritime landscape study in West Cork (Kelleher 2013b:347–66).

While Baltimore, Leamcon, and Crookhaven were the three main bases for the pirates, dotted along the remote stretch of coastline between these bases were dozens of inlets, havens, and little creeks that could be utilized for coastal access as well as the multiple islands within the wider confines of Roaringwater Bay. This coastal landscape provided the ideal base of operations as the seasonal summer refuge for this predatory alliance and eventually as a permanent home for many of the pardoned pirates. No doubt communications and connections were ongoing with other independent pirate harbors at that time (such as at Dutchman's Cove or Canty's Cove, as discussed above), but the main points of power were within the immediate expanse of Roaringwater Bay.

Contemporary commentators referred to certain harbors as being primary bases. William Monson, Royal Naval commander, was given the specific brief to rid the coast of pirates, describing Baltimore as "their headquarters" (Oppenheim 1914:74). Sir Arthur Chichester noted that, "though all of them [the harbors in Munster] be very commodious and safe for pirates to come unto, yet Baltimore is most frequented by them" (Sir Arthur Chichester to the Lords of the Privy Council, March 30, 1608, *CSP, 1606–1608*:447).

Leamcon to the west of Baltimore was called the northern equivalent to Mamora and is sometimes referred to in the sources as Long Island Sound, denoting the main island that lies directly to the south, which was itself a favored haunt. The narrow stretch of water between the island and Leamcon allowed ships to moor safely and provided anchorages for larger vessels. Long Island also ensured protection for Croagh Harbour, to the

Figure 7.12. View of Leamcon looking out toward Long Island and the south Atlantic, showing the inlet to Croagh Harbour and Leamcon Harbour.

immediate east of Leamcon, where the pirates would careen and repair their ships (Bagwell 1909, 104) (figure 7.12).

Crookhaven Harbour became the home base for several of the pirate crews, including Irishman Patrick Myagh and his pirate band, who used it as their main base before the 1614 Dutch attack on the harbor (HCA 13/226: 338; Appleby 1992:285–89). The harbors at Baltimore, Leamcon, and Crookhaven were noted as important markets and supply centers (Appleby 1990b:2). The resident populace, which included locals, settlers, and officials, was more than willing to supply the pirates' needs in what remained a symbiotic relationship, as contemporary sources attest. Henry Skipwith, deputy vice admiral to the Earl of Nottingham, noted that the pirates in Munster "may be enterteyned and kept in those alehouses three moneths or more without payment for anything they take, every pyrate having his factor there for whom hee provideth men and other necessaries against their arrival, and there receweth payment largely for his paynes, soe that it is a perpetuall market for that trafficque." Similarly he detailed that people brought provisions to the pirates from other parts of Ireland under the guise of supplying the fishers of Crookhaven. Henry Cook of Cork brought twenty-two barrels of beer to the pirates at Leamcon (Skipwith, December 2, 1610, *Calendar* of *Carew MSS (1603–1623)*:64).

The southern coast of Ireland thus formed the northern extent of the pirate activity that took in Mamora in northwest Africa and Harbour Grace in Newfoundland, all encompassing the triangular hunting ground of the North Atlantic pirates. It was a seasonal operation, with the pirates following regular courses along the main corridors of the wider and richly laden European trading routes. They would frequent the coast of Ireland during the spring/summer time, from March onward, and leave again to go to Mamora or Newfoundland in August (*CSP, 1608–1610*:371; Edwards 1938:120). Mainwaring referred to Mamora as "the pirates' mecca" and focused his main operations there as well as in Newfoundland rather than in the harbors of Munster, though he did visit Ireland during that period (Mainwaring and Perrin 1920–22:2:40). Mamora provided safe refuge and operated as a free port, where the pirates could trade openly and without fear of capture (Senior 1972:134).

The pirates were equally able to supply their needs (for both supplies and men) in Newfoundland, as they successfully targeted the fishing fleets and land-based fishing enterprises there (Mainwaring and Perrin 1920–22:2:19). Indeed pirates from the earliest stages of migratory settlement in Newfoundland had identified its potential to produce rich rewards in the form of local natural resources and passing merchant shipping. Peter Easton established his main base first in Harbor Grace, where he built a fort that was defended by sixteen guns (Senior 1972:243), and from 1612 onward at Ferryland. The suitability of Ferryland has been well highlighted in the archaeological record, with the excavations carried out by Barry Gaulton and James Tuck providing evidence for the very earliest visiting fishers, traders, and settlement (Gaulton and Tuck 2003:187–88). Easton was there in 1612 with ten ships, and Henry Mainwaring was there in 1614 with a further five ships (Horwood and Butts 1984:11–23; Whitburn 1870:42). Their maritime travels may well have added to the artifactual evidence being discovered there now.

Fleets of ships used the harbors in Munster over time, which suggests that the necessary infrastructure was in place to accommodate such vessels, as in Newfoundland and Mamora. This probably consisted not of shipbuilding facilities but of smaller amenities, such as slipways, landing places, careening and repair service, and, importantly, people with the knowledge and ability to carry out the work. That would no doubt have been well known throughout the maritime community at the time, with local knowledge being a tradable commodity in itself. In 1602 it was reported that in front of Dunalong Castle on Sherkin Island is "a deep pool about half a league over, where infinite numbers of ships may ride [and] a good place to careen ships" (Stafford 1633:216, 584; Kelleher 2007a:195). As noted, Croagh Harbour was used by the pirates for repair and careening needs.

Survey within the general environs of the main bases has provided evidence for some of these facilities, but dating remains indeterminate in the absence of archaeological excavation. Stone mooring posts, more rock-cut steps, eroded slipways, and the basal remains of quays and docks have been identified at Leamcon that certainly represent maritime infrastructure, no doubt for legitimate usage but perhaps facilitating illicit operations too. Indeed a walkover survey of a recently plowed green field area by the foreshore and beside one of the eroded quays produced a sherd from a seventeenth-century Tuscan oil jar, indicative of transatlantic trade and shipping at Leamcon in the past (figure 7.13).

Archaeological evidence for a careening site is to be found in Baltimore, in the Cove area, with rock-cut rope holes, putlog recesses, and beam slots clearly visible. The site is still in use today for mooring vessels. A definitive archaeological study of these site types remains to be done. They were essential to all mariners to ensure the efficient and sustained operation of their ships and critical to the success of any pirate operation. The site in Baltimore lies on the southwest side of Cove strand, by the water's edge. Holes have been cut out of the rock in a number of places along the course of the rockface, interspersed with putlog holes and rock-cut slots to take lengths of timber and beams for scaffolding. For pirates, who needed to ensure that their ships were exposed for the least amount of time, a careening place ideally had to be secluded yet accessible, familiar but not well known. Sites also had to have protection from the prevailing winds and were usually located in areas of calm water, to allow the wooden platforms (hauled close alongside the vessels for the crew to clean the lower hull) to operate properly (Mainwaring and Perrin 1920–22: 2:116–19; Goelet 1986:6–10, 23–36). The site in Baltimore is ideally located in this respect (Kelleher 2103b:356–58).

In Cove the rock-cut holes for the ropes are clearly evident and still in use as mooring holes, along with the putlog holes to take the timber scaffold. It is impossible to say with certainty that the rock-cut features evident today date back to the main period of pirate activity in the area. What can be said is that this is a traditional careening place and as such would more than likely have been in use at the time for the repair and cleaning of vessels. It would certainly have been used by local fishers who operated the pilchard fisheries located within the area of the Cove but was also perhaps

Figure 7.13. Sherd from the handle of a seventeenth-century Tuscan oil jar.

used by the pirates themselves, many of whom were legitimate fishers in Baltimore when not on the high seas plundering passing ships.

The existence of maritime facilities at Leamcon is substantiated by details contained within Sir William Hull's 1642 deposition, where he recounts the loss of up to fifteen seine boats from Leamcon and a "great coasting boat of 12 tonns" (*Deposition of William Hull, 22 October 1642*:254r). Similarly direct references to pirates like William Baugh and William Wollmer bringing captured ships and cargoes of wheat and rye into Leamcon attest to the harbor having at the very least some infrastructure to allow the offloading of cargo (Appleby and O'Dowd 1985:322) (figures 7.14 and 7.15). Rather than being under-resourced remote havens, harbors like Baltimore, Leamcon, and Crookhaven took center stage during this period of heightened clandestine activity.

Conclusion

While the pirate activity in southwest Ireland in the early seventeenth century had a profound social and economic impact locally and regionally,

Figure 7.14. Stone mooring post at Leamcon with evidence of rope wear at base.

its influences were also felt across the wider Atlantic—in North Africa, Newfoundland, and the New World. European shipping, particularly Spanish, Dutch and English, suffered as a consequence. Key pirate players, such as Richard Bishop, were pardoned and may have ended their days in West Cork as legitimate settlers, while Peter Easton refused a pardon and remained a practicing pirate in Newfoundland, ending his days in the Mediterranean.

Historical and cartographic sources provide vivid accounts and illustrative representations of the pirates, their harbors, and where they operated, but we still lack definitive physical evidence for these individuals. Some archaeological sites are emerging (rock-cut steps and platforms, quays and landing stages, careening sites, and indeed potential shipwrecks) that may

Figure 7.15. Basal remains of the "Long Dock" quay and steps at Leamcon Harbour.

have been used by the pirates. While some sites in West Cork can be directly linked to illicit pursuits, the persistent problem of dating remains.

Such sites must be recorded before they are lost to the elements, insensitive development, or general neglect. Many sites, such as the rock-cut steps and platforms, have hitherto not been included in the archaeological record in Ireland. Their spatial distribution, logistics of fashioning, and typological distinctions between sites and their general nature and extent need to be the subject of a formal study not only in Ireland but beyond. Such studies will begin to build a typological and spatial distribution model for these coastal access points that will ensure that comparative research and informed debate can take place, adding to the development of patterns in piracy as suggested by scholars of the subject, along with more recent artifactual material (Hatch 2011).

While historical sources clearly speak about the main pirate havens along the southern coast of Ireland, the identification of cultural evidence is critical to support the historical and cartographic material and add to our understanding of this hidden history. The need for a targeted program of archaeological investigation, in tandem with other disciplinary methodologies such as geophysical or LIDAR survey, may provide some answers. But even with such scientific explorations, results can still remain inconclusive.

Contemporary statements by frustrated government officials reveal that the pirate activity in the southwest in the early part of the seventeenth century was intense, blatant, and economically lucrative: "That which passeth here [in Munster] is rialls of eight, Barbary ducats and dollars and it is thought some treasure is buried on land by these pirates" (Roger Middleton to Robert Cecil, Lord Salisbury, August 22, 1611; *CSP, 1611–1614*:99). The clandestine nature of the pirates and their movements, however, and their intrinsic link with settlement under the Munster Plantation and the process of expanding maritime Atlantic trading empires, leaves us with the equally frustrating task of trying to identify these past peoples in this remote landscape.

How can we identify this part of the coastal landscape of the southwest as a definitive pirate coast and what denotes a pirate ship in shipwreck evidence? Even if settlement evidence is found, how are we to determine who was settler, fisher, or pirate, particularly as so many of the pirates settled legitimately in the area once pardoned? We can glean archaeological evidence for piracy and its attendant smuggling activity along this stretch of the Munster coastline, but pinning this to a specific period continues to be the challenge.

The sociopolitical and physical landscape that ensured the pirates' anonymity and invisibility during their heyday in the southwest seems to persist to the present day. As archaeologists we strive to unravel their continuing mystery and seek a better understanding of this Golden Age of Piracy.

Acknowledgments

The research discussed in this chapter is based upon work funded by the Department of Arts, Heritage and the Gaeltacht (DAHG). The author would like to thank the following individuals, whose support and advice ensured its completion: Professor Jane Ohlmeyer, Department of History, Trinity College Dublin; Fionnbarr Moore, senior archaeologist for the Underwater Archaeology Unit (DAHG); Dr. Elaine Murphy, Dr. James Lyttleton, Professor C. R. Pennell, Dr. John Appleby, and Professor Micheál O'Siochrú for their insights and constructive comments; Dr. Helmut Rohlfing and Georg-August-Universität, Göttingen, Germany; Nigel and Conor Kelleher; and Rob, my own pirate captain. All images are the author's, unless noted otherwise.

8

Shiver Me Timbers!

The Influence of Hollywood on the Archaeology of Piracy

RUSSELL K. SKOWRONEK AND CHARLES R. EWEN

"Pirates": just ask what comes to mind when that word is mentioned and you will hear a litany of peg legs, eye patches, parrots, hooks, and buried treasure. These stereotypes are found in movies, commercials, birthday parties, and toys. While researching our book *X Marks the Spot* we found that many adult women and men still love the images of pirates from their childhoods. We are no different. Pirates and piracy have been a particular fascination of ours throughout our lives. Wondering how pirates came to be such cherished memories began to intrigue us almost as much as the archaeology associated with their sites. Driven by the phenomenal success of the Disney film *Pirates of the Caribbean* we felt the need for a better understanding of the place of piracy in popular culture. To achieve this we started at home.

Shades of Gray—Images from the Past

A pirate's life for me! This phrase, repeated endlessly on Disney's *Pirates of the Caribbean* ride, evokes images that for most of us were formed during childhood: more often than not from films.

It is drizzling and raw outside. The rain-streaked windowpanes gather the weak sunlight of a Saturday afternoon in late fall. In Tenafly, New Jersey, three siblings are trapped with "nothing to do." After the requisite begging they are allowed to turn on the TV in the backroom of the little red Cape Cod house in the suburbs of New York City. This is a time that is unknown to the majority of people alive in the United States in the twenty-first century, a time before remote controls, hundreds of channels, PBS and FOX—and a time before color became the norm. "Mr. Clean" was the only man to sport an earring, and tattoos were rarely seen except on the biceps of sailors and bikers. No personal computers and no computer games existed, and kids were not obese couch potatoes. The President's Council on Physical Fitness did not exist. The life of the Baby Boomers was still relatively insulated. In their short lives two stars had been added to the flag of the United States, a president the age of their fathers had been elected, and Alan Shepard had flown into space.

The children entered the backroom, where their imagination came to life with such early adventure programs as *Ivanhoe*, *Robin Hood*, *Zorro*, and Walt Disney's *Davy Crockett*. Housed in a door-covered ash wood cabinet to protect the screen, the television was an RCA behemoth, made in America. Turning on the set was a sensual experience. The distinctive click of the Bakelite knob was followed by the slight smell of burning ozone as the tubes warmed up and the picture gradually emerged from the center of the screen. Fiddling with the vertical and horizontal controls and the rabbit-ear antenna brought in the gray image of a clock with a pendulum and the distinctive tune of "The Syncopated Clock." The children were happy that they had tuned in just as the channel was about to repeat for the umpteenth time that week Burt Lancaster's 1952 movie *The Crimson Pirate*. Long before anyone dreamed of HBO and repeating films for the convenience of viewers, television stations reran movies time after time. Those children had probably seen parts or all of the film ten times that week. Every time the Spanish had been thwarted by the pirates.

Now, more than fifty years later, the image of that Technicolor film is still burned into our minds as being black and white and on TV. We had succumbed to the allure of Hollywood's sanitized view of pirates who lived to be wealthy old men. These were only somewhat scary bad men, not real enough or scary enough to cause us to lose sleep at night. They were jolly rogues who lived in a Caribbean paradise and stood up to established governments. This, of course, is completely contrary to the reality about pirates, who sometimes tortured their captives and brought fear to the communities that they attacked (for example, Leeson 2009:109–33). As James Parish (1995:1–3) puts it:

> Pirate movies have a special appeal to a wide variety of viewers. Like the equally enduring western movies, pirate pictures deal nostalgically with a bygone, heavily-romanticized era in which derring-do, courage and the right of might rules. Pirates operated on the magically

enticing high seas, away from the confines of traditional land-bound society.

For film makers "it was necessary to blur the distinctions between dastardly cutthroats on the one hand and enviable romantic heroes on the other" (Parish 1995:1–3). Thus these freebooters could be turned into patriotic souls sponsored by a recognized government. As others have asked, how far have these fictional images permeated society and how do they fit with the facts of piracy today and in the past (Cordingly 1995; Cordingly and Falconer 1992)?

The Suppression of Piracy

Most people in this country get their first exposure to piracy in children's literature, such as *Peter Pan* and *Treasure Island*, published in the closing years of the Victorian era. Those first impressions of Jolly Rogers, peg legs, and eye patches never leave us, despite what we learn later. Perhaps this enduring image is so persistent because of the continual parade of pirate literature and movies that passes before us, but we should ask why.

Beginning with the reduction of the North African Barbary States at the turn of the nineteenth century and continuing through the proclamation of the Monroe Doctrine and into the 1830s the United States Navy worked assiduously to clear the Atlantic Ocean and Caribbean Sea of smugglers and pirates, while the Royal Navy did the same in Asia after the defeat of China in the Opium Wars and the establishment of a naval base in Hong Kong. As a result the late nineteenth century world radically changed. The rule of law as dictated by remote governments would regulate trade and thus regulate the lives of the people who were already becoming increasingly regulated in the shift to wage labor in factories.

Pirates, who were so much a part of the accounts of the early eighteenth century (McIlwaine 1928), had largely disappeared by the mid-nineteenth century. In the West the growing strength of the state and industrialists left many longing for an earlier and freer time. Escape would come through literacy.

At the end of the first third of the nineteenth century, after nearly three hundred years of pirate attacks, piracy essentially ceased to exist in American and Caribbean waters and began to enter the world of fiction and legend (Botting 1978:182; Konstam 1999:156–57, 162–65; Saxon 1999).

Pirates in Popular Culture

Over the next fifty years most of the classics of pirate fiction would be written, each with the dichotomy of good and bad. They included W. S. Gilbert and Arthur Sullivan's spoof of young women fantasizing about dashing pirates in the *Pirates of Penzance* (1879); James Barrie's *Peter Pan*, with the evil Captain Hook and the comical Mr. Smee (1928); Rafael Sabatini's *The Sea Hawk* (1915), *Captain Blood* (1922), and the *Black Swan* (1932); Howard Pyle's magnificently illustrated and written *The Book of Pirates* (1921); and the all-time great *Treasure Island* by Robert Louis Stevenson. Published in 1883, the story is a perennial favorite that has been published many times in its original form and in abridged versions, including a comic-book version in the *Classics Illustrated* series (Boyette 1991). Since 1918 more than ten versions of the story have made it to film, including *Muppet Treasure Island* (1996) from Jim Henson Productions; Disney's "update" *Treasure Planet* (2002); an episode of the PBS *Wishbone* television series titled "Salty Dog" (Rocca 1995); and a later book of the same title (Strickland 1997) that cast a Jack Russell terrier in the role of Jim Hawkins. Each version expresses the epitome of scary pirates (Blind Pew, Black Dog, and Israel Hands) and the rough-hewn pirates with a heart of gold ("Captain" Billy Bones and the legendary Long John Silver).

The portrayal of pirates on the silver screen and on television followed the literary stereotypes of Stevenson and those who came after him. From these productions it is clear that Howard Pyle was a key source of inspiration for every costume designer. As far as box office receipts were concerned, it appears that the public became less enchanted with pirates after the 1950s. Nonetheless, Hollywood's love affair with pirate tales has continued, albeit less frequently. New life was breathed into the genre with Johnny Depp's over the top performance as Captain Jack Sparrow in Disney's cleverly marketed *Pirates of the Caribbean: Curse of the Black Pearl*. On its opening day in July 2003 it showed simultaneously in more than 3,200 theaters and earned $13.5 million (Hernandez 2003). By the end of October that same year, it had grossed in excess of $300 million. Its sequels, *Dead Man's Chest*, *At World's End*, and *On Stranger Tides*, have had worldwide revenues of more than $3 billion. Based on these figures and the deluge of pirate-themed merchandise available in stores and online, the pirate genre is back in vogue with the public. We have seen similar Hollywood productions follow Disney's success and capitalize on the public's rediscovered passion for pirates (for example, LEGO pirate play sets, including the *Queen Anne's Revenge*).

In the first sixty years of the twentieth century, no fewer than 100 movies and television programs were made on the topic of pirates (Parish 1995). This period covers the formative years of the Depression and World War II generation and the birth of the Baby Boomers. During the first fifty years of this era, books, radio, and film allowed people to escape the grinding poverty of the Depression and the horrors of World War II. The children who watched and listened to these theatrical performances were voracious readers. Pocketbook editions made to conserve paper and to fit into knapsacks and duffle bags accompanied soldiers and sailors who left their cities and farms and literally went to sea and saw the world. After the war, as work and families limited their mobility, the exotic world that they had experienced was returned to them for a quarter or fifty cents when they read the books of James Michener (1951; Michener and Day 1957), F. Van Wyck Mason (1949, 1957), and others about rogues in paradise, which invariably had a color cover of a swashbuckling pirate and a beautiful "exotic" woman.

Meanwhile in their homes, in the seemingly ever-growing postwar suburbia, the next generation of children, the nascent Baby Boomers, were growing up in a world that was light years away from the bleak tenements of the city and the hard scrabble world of agriculture on a family farm. Technological advances brought television and a growing selection of consumer goods to people who had grown up in want during the Depression. Their goal was never to have their children experience that world. While books and radios had fallen in price and were more readily available, children grew up watching television.

Pirates have fared consistently better on the small screen. There children saw the same movies that their parents had watched in theaters during the 1930s, 1940s, and 1950s as well as adventure television programs based on radio programs (*Gunsmoke*), classic literature (*Ivanhoe*), legends from America's past (*Davy Crockett*), and new technology that had come out of the war (SCUBA diving in *Sea Hunt*). In this era kids and adults continued to "learn" about the dark side of pirates in American history. John Ford's epic *How the West Was Won* (1962) and Disney's *Davy Crockett and the River Pirates* (1956) depict the depredations of pirates against the weak westward-bound pioneers, yet the overall image of pirates is not in the least tarnished. Mass production and the shared experience of having little choice in television shows meant that children across the country grew up with similar experiences in their toys, birthday parties, and images of pirates.

One of the most popular cartoons of the twenty-first century, *SpongeBob SquarePants*, often incorporates pirate themes into its episodes. Today "Who lives in a pineapple under the sea?" has replaced "Way hey blow the man down" as the most recognizable sea chantey. But the piratical iconography in the show (the sinister Flying Dutchman and the pirate-talking, money-grubbing Mr. Krabs) has changed little from the imagery found in the literature of the past century. Many of these images come directly from Barrie's *Peter Pan*. Whether it was Mary Martin or Sandy Duncan flying on the stage, Robin Williams in Steven Spielberg's *Hook* (1991), or the visually impressive *Peter Pan* (2003) from Universal Studios, these images have joined Disney's rerelease of the 1953 animated version of *Peter Pan* in theaters and home video to perpetuate a pervasive image of pirates. This image has given three generations a shared experience. These stereotypic tales were updated and cast in a more mature frame in the 2014 television series *Crossbones* (NBC) and *Black Sails* (Starz). Both of these series focus on adult themes, such as the political intrigue of pirate leadership and the drama of their personal lives.

Theme parks are a third source for pirate stereotypes. Both children and adults are exposed to living, or at least animatronic, effigies of the perceived pirate past. The successful first *Pirates of the Caribbean* movie is based on one of Disney World's most popular attractions. The synergy between the two media is such that the theme park ride was reformatted to mirror the movie's sequel in the summer of 2006. As a special treat at the reopening of the ride, "Captain Jack Sparrow led lighthearted 'pirate training' where kids were invited to join the fun with interactive hi-jinks" (Disney World 2006). The term "hi-jinks" is emblematic of the pirate stereotype. The popular image of pirates' behavior has been softened from mayhem to hi-jinks.

Offsetting this fictional realm is a more "authentic" museum in St. Augustine, Florida, devoted to all things piratical. The St. Augustine Pirate and Treasure Museum boasts "the journal from Captain Kidd's last voyage; one of only two known Jolly Roger flags; and a treasure chest once own by Captain Thomas Tew" (St. Augustine Pirate & Treasure Museum 2015). Besides viewing these authentic pirate artifacts, the visitor also tours a replica of Port Royal and is ushered into the hold of a ship by the animatronic talking head of Blackbeard.

On a more adult level the Treasure Island Hotel and Casino in Las Vegas featured a live battle between a Spanish galleon and a pirate ship in the lagoon in front of the hotel. The pirates always won. Like its Disney counterpart, however, this attraction has been updated. "The Sirens of TI begins with a seventeenth century clash between a group of beautiful, tempting sirens and a band of renegade pirates. With their mesmerizing and powerful song the Sirens lure the pirates to their cove, stir up a tempest strong enough to sink a ship, and transform Sirens' Cove into a twenty first century party; experience music, dance, excitement and seduction—nightly in Sirens' Cove at the front entrance of Treasure Island Hotel and Casino" (Treasure Island Hotel and Casino 2006). Alas, the pirate appeal may be waning: the latest iteration of the Treasure Island Hotel and Casino has the ships sitting in the bay as props and only the Sirens gift shop displaying anything piratical.

Clearly, fictional works have had an addictive influence on our perception of the pirate past. Is there no antidote? Books purported to be "non-fiction" historical studies are perhaps the most enduring media that deal with the romantic notion of pirates. Dozens, perhaps hundreds, of books are touted as the source of information about "who the pirates really were" (for example, Cordingly 1995; Konstam 1999; Rediker 1987). Even the fictional works on pirates often have addenda that discuss the "true" nature of piracy. The Disney DVD of *Treasure Planet* has a bonus feature that the viewer can choose to learn about historical pirates and their ways.

With the distance of history and the softening through adult and children's literature, the atrocities committed by real pirates seem less terrible. Heinous acts of terror become hi-jinks and are more the stuff of adventure stories than actual horrific events. This is undoubtedly due to the imprinting in our minds of the stereotypical images promulgated during childhood. Terms like "scoundrel," "scalawag," "rogue," and even "cutthroat" do not accurately portray the criminal nature of pirates. Indeed these are regarded as positive character traits in the leading male characters in modern romance literature. One exception to this romanticism is a book written by Peter Benchley, the author of *Jaws*. His novel *Island* (1980) captured the terror that genuine pirates must have inspired, because clearly the people of the seventeenth and eighteenth centuries *were* terrified. That is why an instant death sentence was pronounced on anyone choosing to pursue piracy. Not only were they hanged, but their bodies were sometimes tarred and suspended at the entrance to harbors in cages as a warning to others contemplating pursuing a life of piracy. Perhaps use of the term "terrorist" to describe them might resonate more with the modern public, who would then equate pirates with the terrorists' reputation as murdering thieves.

The Golden Age of Piracy

Piracy may be the second oldest profession among state-level societies. Once humans began to use the sea to transport valuable cargoes, others tried to steal those cargoes. Certainly there is documentary evidence of piracy in antiquity: Julius Caesar was captured and held for ransom by pirates (Plutarch 1999). Some have argued that the *Kyrenia* wreck (Katsev 1980, 1987) was sunk by pirates in the Mediterranean, but that case is far from certain. What is lacking is material evidence for piracy, mainly because the archaeology of piracy is not as widespread as piracy itself. All of the sites associated with archaeological literature are primarily products of the Golden Age of Piracy and were excavated by North American or European archaeologists. Fortunately, this is the period that Hollywood chose to portray in movies and television shows, so the focus of the historical context is the Caribbean, North America, and the Indian Ocean.

The riches that the Spaniards hauled out of the New World proved irresistible to many other nations. The French buccaneers were among the first systematically to harass Spanish shipping. By the early seventeenth century they had established a stronghold on Tortuga Island off the north coast of Haiti. By the middle of the seventeenth century the ranks of these freebooters included people of many nationalities and numbered in the thousands.

In 1655 Jamaica was captured by the British. This prompted many of the pirates *cum* privateers to relocate their base of operations to the haven of Port Royal. Over the past fifty years the excavation of this notorious port has been directed by Texas A&M archaeologist Donny Hamilton and others. His research reveals that piracy is less apparent in the archaeological record than it is in the historical record (D. Hamilton 2006). It was during this time that Jean L'Olonnais and Sir Henry Morgan terrified the Spanish Main. The depredations by these pirates fell upon both ships and ports. As a result the Spanish were forced to fortify these ports with imposing stone "castles" and sail their treasure fleets in armed convoys. Even these measures, however, were not entirely successful, as evidenced by the sack of Panamá Viejo by Henry Morgan in 1671 (Mendizábal 1999).

The so-called Golden Age of Piracy was born at the end of the seventeenth century. Though officially discouraged by the European powers, piracy actually increased its scope between 1690 and 1730. The infamous Edward Teach (Blackbeard) and Samuel Bellamy spread their terror up the east coast of North America and beyond in the years following the conclusion of Queen Anne's War in 1714. This era finally drew to a close when powerful merchant interests arose and the national navies became stronger to deal with the policing of increased peacetime trade.

Piracy was not limited to the New World. At the same time pirates were plundering the Americans, others discovered that rich booty was to be had in the Indian Ocean. Captains William Kidd and Richard Condent preyed upon the treasure-laden ships of the Mogul Empire from their base off the coast of Madagascar. The pirates' toll on the shipping of the East India Company brought down the wrath of corporate Britain and essentially ended this pirate reign. The scourge of piracy has never really ended, however, and continues as the bane of honest sailors to this day.

The problem with trying to characterize historical pirates is that piracy has existed for as long as humans have sailed the seas and been found wherever there were vessels to be robbed. How do you characterize piracy through time and space? Hollywood simply falls back on the popular literary stereotype. As archaeologists we try to dispel popular misconceptions about the past by examining the material record that people have left behind, but is it even possible to recognize a pirate in the archaeological record?

The Archaeology of Piracy

In conducting research on piracy two things become abundantly clear. First, historical works about pirates abound; and second, the archaeological literature contains very little about piracy. This is surprising, because since the discovery of what has been touted as the wreck of Blackbeard's flagship dominated the archaeological discussions in North Carolina during the first decade of the twenty-first century. When looking beyond this site, however, only a few other pirate-related sites spring to mind. How can this be if piracy has played such a pervasive role in maritime history?

The historical literature suggests that pirates most often stole commercial cargoes, which they then sold for gold that they promptly spent as fast they could. Yet history is replete with people trying to find pirate buried treasure, even though there is virtually no historical record of pirates' burying their gold. This has not deterred folks from looking for it. Many think that the discovery of a variety of silver and gold coins of differing national origin indicates a pirate ship. That incorrect assumption no doubt stems from Stevenson's *Treasure Island*, where he wrote that Ben Gunn's cave contained

English, French, Spanish, Portuguese Georges, and Louises, doubloons and double guineas and moidores and sequins, the pictures of all the kings of Europe for the last hundred years, strange Oriental pieces stamped with what looked like wisps of string or bits of spider's webs, round pieces and square pieces, . . . nearly every variety of money in the world.

All were valued because the coins' value was based on the actual weight of their respective specie, not on the head or coat of arms struck on the disk.

The Money Pit on Oak Island off Nova Scotia is a good example of a great deal of effort being spent looking for pirate treasure that does not exist. Captain William Kidd, the only pirate who is actually recorded to have buried treasure, on Gardiners Island near his home in New York (Zacks 2002:241–43), allegedly careened his ship in Nova Scotia. Three hundred years later the stories become conflated with Captain Flint's buried booty in *Treasure Island* and voilà, a "mysterious," allegedly booby-trapped pit on the north end of Oak Island becomes the "Money Pit." In 2014 the History Channel started a reality series titled *The Curse of Oak Island,* following Rick and Marty Lagina in their search for treasure. Millions of dollars and at least ten deaths have been attributed to treasure-seekers attempting to find the nonexistent pirate booty. But legitimate pirate treasure *has* been discovered archaeologically.

Pirate booty aplenty was found at the wreck of the *Whydah* off Cape Cod. In the evening of April 26, 1717, the pirate ship *Whydah* ran aground and broke up during a violent gale. All but two of its crew perished, including the captain, Samuel "Black Sam" Bellamy. Just two months earlier the English slaver *Whydah* had offloaded its human cargo at Jamaica and was making its way back home. Bellamy captured the treasure-laden galley, outfitted it with thirty guns, and began plundering his way up the coast of North America until the nor'easter put an end to his depredations (C. Hamilton 2006:131–32).

Treasure salvor Barry Clifford found the *Whydah* off the coast of Cape Cod 261 years after it sank. Excavations were conducted from 1978 until 1989 by the salvors under the guidance of a succession of underwater archaeologists appointed by the state of Massachusetts, including Christopher Hamilton. The identification of the wreck suggested by contemporary documents was confirmed by the recovery of the ship's bell, inscribed "The + Whydah + Gally + 1716," during the 1985 field season. Though virtually all of the ship's hull structure was gone (contemporary records indicate that recovered sections of the hull were burned to recover the iron fittings), over 40,000 artifacts were found scattered across a 24,000 square foot area (C. Hamilton 2006, 133–35).

The identification of the vessel was never a mystery, because documents regarding the salvage abound and the ship's bell was inscribed with the ship's name. But the project was not without controversy. This was especially true in the archaeological community. The collaboration between the archaeologists and the salvors, though performed under legally mandated permit, was viewed as a blasphemy by most underwater archaeologists. Project participants were not permitted to present their findings at professional archaeological meetings at the time. This in part explains the rapid turnover of archaeological "consultants" who saw their careers damaged by the association with the treasure hunters.

Nevertheless, important information was recovered by the project and subsequently published, albeit in limited distribution (Hamilton et al. 1988, 1990) and as a chapter in *X Marks the Spot* (C. Hamilton 2006). Although the ship had been broken up and scattered by the storm, the archaeologists noted that the artifact distribution still reflected the general location of materials on the vessel and provided information on the stages of wrecking (C. Hamilton 2006:157). This information would later prove invaluable in the interpretation of another alleged pirate vessel, the *Queen Anne's Revenge*.

Hamilton also used the data recovered from the wreck to model pirate life and the general practice of piracy. According to him (C. Hamilton 2006:147), "the relationship of the Whydah pirate was egalitarian—or perhaps 'libertarian,' if one emphasizes political orientation—relative to the class-oriented society of early eighteenth century Europe and its colonies." Status was achieved through skill or brute force rather than being assigned by the navy or shipping company. He also noted that even the average pirate had the opportunity to acquire prestige items like "fine pistols" that would cost an ordinary seaman two years' pay (C. Hamilton 2006:149). On a larger scale, piracy played an important role in the dynamics of the world economic system as an expected hazard to shipping, which the various trading nations had to take into account (C. Hamilton 2006:157).

Another pirate project concerns an eighteenth-century shipwreck found off Beaufort inlet along the coast of North Carolina. This wreck was found in 1996 by treasure hunters who were looking for a Spanish treasure ship, *El Salvador*. Unlike the *Whydah*, which is spread over several acres, the Beaufort Inlet Wreck is confined to a relatively small area. This wreck, however, is similar to the *Whydah* in other respects.

According to exhaustive studies on the wreck now identified as the *Queen Anne's Revenge* (Wilde-Ramsing and Ewen 2012), the vessel started out as the slaver *La Concorde* when it was captured by the notorious pirate Blackbeard in the Caribbean toward the end of November 1717. Blackbeard supposedly upgraded the armament to around forty guns and busily began taking prizes in the Caribbean and up the Atlantic Coast of North America. After blockading the harbor at Charleston, South Carolina, and holding the city for ransom, Blackbeard and his growing pirate flotilla proceeded up the coast. In a move viewed by some as an early example of corporate downsizing (Wilde-Ramsing 2006, 162), the *Queen Anne's Revenge* and a smaller sloop, *Adventure*, were run aground in June 1718 off Beaufort Inlet and their crews marooned. Blackbeard commandeered one of the smaller vessels, only to be caught and killed off of Ocracoke Island five months later.

The excavation of the Beaufort Inlet Wreck is controversial for two reasons. First, its association with treasure hunters sent up an immediate red flag with underwater archaeologists. Even though the salvors have little interest in the vessel (there is no treasure on it) and underwater archaeologists employed by the state of North Carolina have conducted virtually all the work on the site, some archaeologists still see an ethical dilemma. The second controversy surrounds the wreck's identification. Several archaeologists felt that the state of North Carolina acted hastily in declaring the wreck to be the *Queen Anne's Revenge*, claiming that the evidence was insufficient to make such a claim (Rodgers et al. 2005; Lusardi 2006).

The identification of the vessel was initially somewhat ambiguous, primarily due to the scant documentary evidence related to the wreck. When the history is sketchy, how can a pirate ship be distinguished from a heavily merchant vessel? It is here that the *Whydah* project provided assistance. Like the *Queen Anne's Revenge*, the *Whydah* was a converted slave ship. Both had offloaded their human cargo when captured by pirates. They both operated in the same general region at the same time. When compared to each other, their archaeological assemblages are remarkably similar. Various cannon, many of them loaded and ready for action, were found on both sites (Wilde-Ramsing and Ewen 2012). A preliminary assessment of the smaller artifacts recovered such as navigation instruments, utilitarian, and personal items show a concurrence as well. Pattern recognition in the artifact assemblage, using a site of known function to interpret a site whose function is not known, is a hallmark of historical archaeology (South 1977).

Pattern recognition is important even at sites with known pirate affiliation. Historically, Port Royal, Jamaica, was the major pirate lair of the Golden Age of Piracy. The "Wickedest City on Earth," as it came to be known, was heavily damaged by an earthquake in 1692 before being destroyed by a hurricane in 1722 and then by another hurricane in 1744. The pirates that are documented to have frequented this port town included the likes of Henry Morgan, Calico Jack Rackham, Anne Bonny, Mary Read, and Bartholomew Roberts. Yet Donny Hamilton (2006, 26), after decades of investigations, was hard pressed to find definitive evidence of their piratical activities: "archaeologically speaking, little has been found that can be attributed exclusively to privateers or pirates. The best archaeological evidence comes from shipwrecks, and even here good historic documentation is essential to identify the ship. Without the written wills, inventories, deeds, and grantor's records that often record partial ownership of vessels used in privateering or trade, there would be little to equate Port Royal with its privateering citizenry." Thus more archaeology is necessary on pirate sites to help define this "pirate pattern" in the archaeological record.

The primary reason why more pirate sites have not been reported in the literature is that they are so hard to identify in the archaeological record. In fact, research (Skowronek and Ewen 2006) has shown that without solid historical documentation most of them would probably not be identified as associated with piracy by their investigators or at least would have their identity debated (compare Lusardi 2006 and Wilde-Ramsing 2006). Most pirate ships began as legitimate sailing vessels before they were captured, so the archaeologist must look to ship modifications and cargo to discern piracy in the past.

Who Were the Pirates Really?

What did it mean to be a pirate and how does the popular perception of piracy today influence our interpretations of piracy in the past? How do we recognize a pirate site in the archaeological record? Are there any archaeological markers that give away a pirate site? If the archaeologist did not have the documentary record to draw from, could a site be positively identified as a pirate shipwreck? In every site associated with pirates the identification was only successful when there was good historical documentation. If the documentation associated with a site is ambiguous or somewhat sketchy, as in the case of the *Queen Anne's Revenge*, then the identification is open to question. Does this rule out the possibility of identifying piracy in the archaeological record?

As professional archaeologists we should not be dismayed. In fact, this is not an uncommon situation in historical archaeology. For example, archaeologists working on plantations sites have been searching for diagnostic artifacts that definitely denote the presence of African American slaves. A single blue bead or cowrie shell does not a slave site make; however, blue beads or cowrie shells in a historical context where slaves are historically recorded to have lived lend credence to such an association. Perhaps this will be the case with pirate sites.

Archaeologists are not as interested in individual artifacts as in patterns in the archaeological record. Each pirate site that is identified, explored, and published takes the archaeologist one step closer to defining such a pattern. Perhaps the pirate ship is characterized by a pattern of armaments, reconfigured mast placement, and a variety of cargo that differs from those of a merchant ship or naval vessel. Early work on pirate land sites suggests that one identifying trait may be the presence of high-status items such as ceramics or clothing-related items in low-status contexts (Finamore 2006; Hatch 2006). If a pattern can be discerned then it would be possible to identify a pirate ship for which no historical record exists. Until we can be sure of our identifications we will not be able to recognize patterns or address questions relating to the "real" lives of pirates and their impact on the larger societies in which they lived.

Until archaeologists can identify the physical world in which pirates sailed we are left with the Hollywood stereotype. This lack of evidence raises the question of whether our image of pirates is completely wrong, a scam perpetrated by the entertainment industry to whitewash past criminals and profit from our ignorance. Some pirates during the late seventeenth and early eighteenth century probably *did* look like Long John Silver; however, many sailors of the period and even naval personnel probably appeared just as sinister. The only harm, if there is any, is in our over-romanticizing these murdering thieves. In 2005 the town of Bath, North Carolina, resurrected an outdoor drama, *Blackbeard: Knight of the Black Flag*. In this bit of revisionist history Blackbeard is portrayed as a basically decent man driven by circumstances and his own personal demons into a life that he did not choose. Does the audience believe this portrayal? Probably not completely, but the authors of bodice-ripping historical romances have been living off the stereotype for generations.

On September 19 the United States observes "National Talk-Like-a-Pirate Day" and Barnes and Noble bookstores across the country offer displays of "pirate" books with a green and cream sign boldly proclaiming, "Ahoy, Matey! September 19th is International Talk-Like-a-Pirate Day." On that day every email or phone call we received sounded as if it was from Blind Pew or Billy Bones. We responded in kind. Indeed it would seem that even the "serious" pirate scholar cannot escape the hype of Hollywood.

9

Signaling Pirate Identity

HEATHER HATCH

The phenomenon that was the Golden Age of Piracy (ca. 1680–1725) grew out of specific historical circumstances. European nations were in the midst of asserting greater direct control over their colonial territories and negotiating a new set of international relationships as they did. Whereas they previously had been more willing to look the other way in the case of freebooters who acted on their own account to forward national interests, these unsanctioned acts of warfare met with greater and greater reprobation and retribution. Those who involved themselves in the trade reacted in part by drawing further away from the society, which now spurned them, and began to identify more strongly with each other. This strengthening of the pirate identity and its distancing from civil society is visible in the ways in which pirates chose to identify themselves. Material culture can speak strongly of cultural and social affiliation: pirates selected and used their goods in ways that marked their separation. One particular marker of identity that pirates wielded handily in this fashion is the flag.

Flags at Sea

Flags are social symbols, and their meaning is inherent in their display (Firth 1973:328). They represent both power and identity and relate these concepts in a positive way that is easy to internalize for in-group members who use and view them. Flags are representations of power and are also capable of rousing allegiance and interest, especially at a national level (Schatz and Lavine 2007:331–33). Much of the limited scholarship surrounding the meaning of flags revolves around national flags. Despite this focus, some of the observations apply to the use of flags in general and to the context of flags used at sea. Raymond Firth (1973:332) discusses sea flags directly when considering the difference between flags as signals ("intended primarily to convey information") and symbols ("meant to express ideas or emotions, often of complex order"). This distinction is interesting and useful, but it is not always obvious or clear cut, as the discussion below reveals.

Flags were often the only method of communicating between ships at sea prior to the development of radio. Historian Marcus Rediker (2004:164) describes them as "markers of property and sovereign power in oceanic zones of tremendous uncertainty." Meaning was conveyed not only through the symbolic imagery on the flags themselves but through their location and context of their use. European nations such as Britain and France had standardized the use of flags for their navies, privateers, and merchant marine by the seventeenth century, and these standards provide a context within which pirate flags and flag use can be understood. While not all ships at sea stuck precisely to the prescribed uses, deviations were conscious manipulations of the established system. French merchantmen, for example, sometimes flew the navy's white flag even though they were banned from doing so to give the impression that they were a king's ship and gain trading advantages (Wilson 1986:19–21, 60–62).

The term "flags" in reference to their use at sea is somewhat problematic. According to a 1685 treatise entitled *Six Dialogues about Sea Services*, "Flags (my Lord) to speak properly, are only those which are borne out in the Tops of Ships, and they serve, as badges, and that as well for the distinctions of Nations, as Officers and Commanders" (Boteler 1688:327). In French and German the words for flags at sea (*pavillons, Flaggen*) are completely different from the words for land flags (*drapeaux, Fahnen*) (Wilson 1986:9). Other types of flags mentioned in Boteler's dialogue are jacks, ensigns (or colors), and pennants. Records from this period, including log books describing encounters with other ships at sea, often provide descriptions of these flags and their uses, giving insights into the crews that flew them.

As the captain in Boteler's dialogue noted, flags are properly only items flown at the masthead of a ship. They were commonly used to communicate, using preestablished signals. Boteler (1688:344–45, 347) gives several examples of these used in the English Royal Navy of his period. They could be used to call meetings between officers on different ships—flying a blue flag from the topmast shrouds of an admiral's ship called a council or war, while a yellow flag from the same position signaled a general captain's meeting. Flags were also used as a system of identification among ships of a fleet. Flying a flag of a certain color or from a certain location, even at a prespecified time of day, could be used as a prompt for others sailing with the fleet to respond in a predetermined way, to guard against infiltration. The Royal Navy formalized many of its flag signals in the 1673 *Instructions*. Nonmilitary ships used flag signals as well but had no common "language" that could be used to communicate between ships of different merchant houses until the nineteenth century (Wilson 1986:82–83).

The ensign (also called the ancient or the colors) was flown from the stern of the ship from the ensign staff through most of the eighteenth century. It was primarily used to signify nationality when ships met at sea. In this sense it was both a signal and a symbol, as the advertised presence of national power: ensigns often included or referenced national flags. The ensign could also be used as a signaling flag: during engagements, the crew would strike the ordinary ensign and "heave out an ensign all over red," a flag known colloquially as the bloody colors (Boteler 1688:333, 349; Wilson 1986:10). The term "colors" could refer specifically to the ensign but was also used to refer to the full complement of ship's flags. Flying the ensign upside-down was generally recognized as a sign of distress (Wilson 1986:82, 109).

The jack, a smaller flag, was flown at the bow. Before around 1720 it was flown above the topsail spritsail. When this sail was phased out of use by 1720, however, a temporary staff was added to display the flag, which was flown only in harbors. While this flag was also used to convey nationality, it had a greater symbolic power as well. The English introduced the Union Jack in 1606 as a way for the king to enforce his rights over the waters of the English Channel. By 1630 it was illegal for ships other than English naval vessels to fly the Union Jack without special permission. As with the example given for the French above, however, English merchants often used this jack illegally to claim tax exemptions at foreign ports (Wilson 1986:16–17).

The last type of flag deserving mention is the pennant, a type generally flown from the mastheads. Pennants are long and tapering in shape but may also be swallow-tailed or blunt. The size, shape, and coloring of pennants all affected their meaning. A long tapering pennant flown from the mast of an English vessel denoted a commissioned naval vessel. Certain ranks of officers had specially appointed flags, which would be flown instead of the commissioning pennant if these officers were on board. The officer would then be named the flag officer and the ship a flag ship. Pennants could also be used for purely decorative purposes, though not all vessels were entitled to fly them. In the eighteenth century the English reserved them solely for the use of naval vessels (Boteler 1688:333–334; Wilson 1986:34).

The importance of color when discussing flags at sea is contextual. The red ensign was a universally recognized battle symbol, as was the white flag of truce. Several nations, including the French and English, used plain red and white flags for other purposes, such as to note rank. The French navy also banned the use of the bloody colors (Wilson 1986:61, 77). Black flags, however, were linked primarily with piracy and were not part of the common complement used and carried by other ships in the seventeenth and eighteenth centuries. While on land black was linked to death, it did not have this meaning at sea, outside of its association with pirates. Flag emblems, placement, and use (such as striking the flag or colors to indicate surrender or deference) were much more significant indicators of meaning than color alone.

Eighteenth-Century Piracy

Piracy in the eighteenth century developed out of particular historical circumstances traceable back to the previous century. In the sixteenth and seventeenth centuries colonial powers such as England and France used privateers or buccaneers in their struggles to undermine Spanish control of the New World. Those who joined the buccaneers came from social underclasses, including interloping hunters expelled from territories claimed by Spain and soldiers who had come to fight for England in Oliver Cromwell's scheme to try to take control of Hispaniola (he wound up with Jamaica as a consolation prize). By the end of the century England sought to gain more direct control of its North American holdings. This new expression of authority left no space for ragtag associations of mariners and soldiers seeking their own fame and fortune.

In his examination of the career and trial of Captain William Kidd, historian Robert Ritchie explains how the infamous pirate was a victim of these changing attitudes toward piracy on behalf of state governments, describing him as a transitional figure. Kidd, a New York Scot, received the king's commission for taking pirates in order to protect the Indian Ocean trade. Richard Coote, the Earl of Bellomont, was Kidd's direct patron. Other powerful members of the Junto, the Whig leaders who then controlled the English government, were silent investors in the enterprise. The captain found no pirates to seize and, through ill luck as much as ill intent, turned to piracy to turn a profit for himself and the investors. Pressure from the East India Company and a change in the balance of power in

London caused the Junto to take a strong stand against pirates and Kidd in particular. As trade networks expanded and the state grew stronger, pirates lost their support from both the government and merchants.

Part of the efforts to control piracy better was expressed through the creation of more robust laws concerning pirate activity and the clarification of legal jurisdiction. The English law on piracy in the seventeenth century came from two 150-year-old statutes enacted during the reign of Henry VIII. These statutes of 1535 and 1536 were passed to facilitate convicting pirates. The statutes mentioned pirates in their preamble but not in their substantive text, which referred specifically to "all Treasons, Felonies, Robberies, Murthers and Confederacies hereafter to be committed in or upon the Sea, or in any other haven, River, Creek or Place where the Admiral or Admirals have or pretend to have Power, Authority or Jurisdiction" (Rubin 1988: 28 Henry VIII c. 15). The king granted commissions to specific people, usually admirals and their deputies, who could then try those crimes as though they had taken place on land. The statutes were unclear as to what the exact jurisdiction of the admiralty included, especially when it came to trying foreigners or crimes committed on the high seas (Rubin 1988:36–38).

The legal conception of piracy in the seventeenth century was confused, but the admiralty primarily used the term in reference to legitimacy and property rights. Pirates were those who seized goods without a legitimate commission to which they had no title claim. This question of legitimacy arose in the case of privateers, and international relations often dictated how it would be answered (Rubin 1988:67–68). The term "piracy" was also linked to the concept of treason. This meant that pirates who rejected loyalty to the English government, which in turn implied that at some point they had loyalty to reject. Once again, jurisdiction was unclear. It was also unclear how the law applied to the English who carried foreign commissions or to legal English privateers who exceeded the bounds of their commissions (Rubin 1988:73, 77–78).

In the seventeenth century the colonies were self-governed and created their own laws. Henry VIII's statutes did not apply, and pirates could not be tried unless the colonies created their own antipiracy laws. Jamaica was the first to do so and passed *An Act for Restraining and Punishing Privateers and Pirates* in 1681. The act made it illegal for the colonists to harbor or trade with pirates and banned English privateers from carrying foreign commissions. In 1684 Governor Thomas Lynch of Jamaica sent a report to the Crown concerning the depredations of pirates throughout the colonies. King James II issued a memorandum that a copy of the law enacted in Jamaica should be sent to all other American colonies with instructions that it should be passed and enforced—he wanted to ensure that England remained a neutral power in the conflicts of other nations (Salley 1928:272–73).

In 1700 Parliament passed a new statute, *An Act for the More Effectual Suppression of Piracy*, to resolve the legal issue. The act's preamble explained the need for the new law: pirates active in remote parts of the world could not be properly tried and punished under the statute of 1536. The act repeated the text of the earlier law but added that now pirates "may be examined, inquired of, tried, heard and determined, and adjudged, according to the Directions of this Act, in any Place at Sea, or upon the Land, in any of his Majesty's Islands, Plantations, Colonies, Dominions, Forts or Factories" (Rubin 1988:11 & 12 William III c. 7 [1700]). The act still required admiralty judges specially commissioned by the king, but it applied the idea of piracy as a felony, punishable by death, throughout the English-controlled world. It also cleared up some of the murky jurisdictional questions of the earlier statute. Pirates could now be tried legally in all the colonies.

Although these changes began even before the turn of the eighteenth century, the outbreak of the War of Spanish Succession (1701–14) meant that their effects were not evident until much later. Piracy did not disappear during this period, but it did decline. The colonial governments now had the power to deal effectively with pirates in their own domains. The royal colonies, at least, had the will to enforce the new laws. Even after the end of the war piracy did not resurge immediately. The postwar economy was strong enough to employ seafarers and discourage them from turning pirate. Enough imported goods were in circulation to meet public demand for a few years, reducing the need to rely on illegal channels of trade and theft. By 1715 the economy had deteriorated, however, and piracy was on the rise again (Rediker 1993:282). Conditions were set for a change in attitude not only toward pirates but also from within that loose community itself.

The most infamous nest of pirates operating after the War of Spanish Succession was in the remains of Nassau in the Bahamas. The Spanish had sacked the town at the beginning of the war. The colonial proprietors never sent anyone to replace the murdered governor and pick up the reins of government. Although some colonists had returned to Nassau by the end of the war, a number of pirate groups followed in their wake (Headlam 1926:332–34). When the Spanish treasure fleet wrecked off the coast of

Florida in 1715, treasure hunters from Jamaica started using Providence as their base of operations. A number of them took to plundering Spanish salvors instead, soon followed by acts of open piracy against some British vessels (Headlam 1930a:139–42).

The politics of this pirate haven highlight some of the differences between old and new generations of pirates: Benjamin Hornigold, an ex-buccaneer, was among the old guard who still refused to prey on British shipping. Hornigold was a mentor to figures such as Blackbeard and Sam Bellamy, who had no such nationalistic tendencies (Johnson 1972:1; Baer 2007c:317). With the new laws in place, it was difficult for pirates to operate under the older model, where loosely worded commissions from governors with questionable authority to issue them provided at least a thin veneer of legitimacy for plundering ships of enemy nations. Older pirates could still feel tied to their nations of origins. Pirates who started their careers in the early eighteenth century had no illusions that their activities would be greeted by their home governments with anything but censure.

On September 3, 1717, secretary of state Joseph Addison wrote the Board of Trade to reveal a three-pronged solution to the Nassau pirate problem. First, the king would send naval ships to patrol the infested waters, as recommended by colonial governors who had been dealing with the problem firsthand. Second, the Crown would issue a royal proclamation of pardon. Third, the board would appoint Captain Woodes Rogers (who had devised the plan) as royal governor of the islands (Headlam 1930b:24). The board sent out the warrants to pardon pirates to the various colonial governors in August 1718 (*Journal of the Commissioners for Trade and Plantation Preserved in the Public Record Office* 1969:425). These pardons gave pirates the opportunity to return to society without suffering any negative consequences for their past actions.

Many pirates accepted the pardon when Rogers arrived in Nassau and settled directly in the Bahamas. Though the new governor complained that they made less than ideal British citizens, they seemed to have at least honestly given up their old ways (Headlam 1930b:372–81). Benjamin Hornigold even turned against his old students and worked as a pirate catcher for the new governor. Thomas Cockram married into the Bahamian community at Harbour Island, taking the hand of the daughter of one of the richest local merchants (Headlam 1926:332–34). Pirates also accepted the offered pardon in other British colonies. Pirate captain Henry Jennings worked closely with authorities in Jamaica to ensure that some of the Bahamian pirates would be given clemency there (Headlam 1930b:170–71). The government guessed that if given the choice either to embrace society or to reject it utterly, many would choose to give up their lifestyle and remain safely in the bosom of society.

Not all pirates made the same choices. Charles Vane was present at Nassau when Rogers arrived and bid the new governor a defiant farewell, slipping out of the harbor under his nose. Edward Teach, also known as Blackbeard, nominally accepted the pardon in North Carolina, after rejecting an opportunity to do so in cosmopolitan Charleston, South Carolina (Brock 1885:273). The Carolinas were under the same proprietary control as the Bahamas. Bath, where Teach settled, was a relative economic backwater. The colony lay beyond the reach and direct influence of the British government, and he found the local officials willing to overlook some questionable actions in exchange for kickbacks. A short while after he took up residence in the colony, Teach brought a French ship full of sugar into port. Governor Charles Eden condemned it as legitimate salvage, and the pirate stored some of the plundered sugar in a barn belonging to Tobias Knight, the colonial secretary (Brock 1885:273). A letter later found with some of Teach's papers implicated the governor as Teach's supporter and was signed "your real ffriend and servant, T. Knight" (Saunders 1968:343–44).

North Carolina, where the primary export products were ships' stores like pitch and turpentine, lacked the economic motivation of richer colonies that cooperated with royal initiatives to eliminate illegal streams of revenue, such as piracy, that would ultimately undermine legitimate enterprise. The government remained corrupt. Individuals who sought to rid themselves of this local menace turned to Virginia, their neighboring royal colony, for support. In response to these appeals lieutenant governor Alexander Spotswood organized a successful expedition to seize the pirate (Brock 1885:273). This episode marks another stage in changes of attitudes toward pirates in this period: even while corrupt governments still saw some advantage in dealing with and harboring pirates, the attitudes of colonial residents were turning against these marauders of the seas. Pirates found themselves socially marginalized to greater and greater extents when they went on the account in the eighteenth century.

Pirate Flags

One of the clearest ways in which those who turned to piracy in the early eighteenth century demonstrated their rejection of their place in the society that more thoroughly rejected them in this period was their use of flags.

Although this may be a reflection of the data available on the subject, the custom of pirate crews using distinctive personalized flags seems to have flourished in the eighteenth century. The earliest personalized pirate flag associated with a specific pirate is the flag of Henry Avery in 1695: a red flag with four silver chevrons flown (probably as an ensign) alongside the St. George's cross. The earliest sighting of a black pirate flag was in 1700, by the captain of the HMS *Poole*, who described it in his log book as "a sable ensign with cross-bones, a death's head, and an hour glass" (Pringle 1953:123). Table 9.1 shows an incomplete list of uses of flags by pirates in the late seventeenth and early eighteenth century that demonstrates the variety that persisted not only in the imagery used but in the ways that different crews employed flags. Despite this variety the information lends itself to some interesting observations.

In terms of the kinds of flags used, where position is definitely described, the ensign is the most common. Proper flags in this sense were also used to identify affiliation—with a particular national navy or a Crown or merchant house. The pirate flags can be viewed in a similar vein to denote association with a particular crew. The second most common location for pirate flags is the ensign. As the flag most explicitly linked to nationality, this is the most significant factor for demonstrating that pirates felt themselves to be outsiders to their homelands. Some pirates still explicitly used national ensigns, however, showing that this attitude was not universal to all crews. In some cases context makes clear that this was a *ruse de guerre*, as in the case of Edward Low's crew, who used Spanish colors to lure in prey and ran up their black flag once escaping the trap became impossible (Johnson 1972:326). Most cases of flag use observed for William Kidd also fall into this pattern (Barlow 1934:470, 491).

Most of our ideas about what messages pirate flags were meant to convey come from contemporary commentary and not from pirates themselves. The most common reading of the flag seems to be that it was intended to incite terror. It appears to have been effective in this role, as the sight of a hoisted black flag often was enough to cause a prize to surrender: "for on the hosting of *Jolly Roger* (the Name they gave to their black Flag) their *French* hearts failed them and they both surrendered without any, or at least very little Resistance" (Johnson 1972:226). Fear was not the only meaning derived from the flag, however. The following passage from William Snelgrave's account of his capture by the pirate crew of Thomas Cocklyn demonstrates the typical attitude: though pirate flags were meant to frighten, outsiders recognized that pirates saw each other's flag as a sign of belonging.

Table 9.1. Use of Flags by Golden Age Pirates

Captain/ Crew	Ship	Date	National Flags	Pirate Flags	Flag Locations	Source
Sam Bellamy	Whydah	1717	king's ensign and pennant			Baer 2007c:303
Stede Bonnet	Royal James	1717		red flag	ensign	Johnson 1972:101; Baer 2007f:329
Thomas Cocklyn		1720		black flag	masthead?	Johnson 1972:174
Christopher Condent	Flying Dragon, Wright	????		pirate's colors	ensign?	Johnson 1972:4
John Cornelius	Morning Star	????	English colors and pennant			
Howell Davis		1720		black flag, pirate's colors	ensign?	Johnson 1972:168, 174, 176
Howell Davis		1720	English colors			Johnson 1972:192
Howell Davis		1720		black flag	masthead?	Snelgrave 1734:198–99
Robert Deal		1718		red flag	masthead?	Baer 2007e:36
Edward England	Indian Queen	1719		black flag, red flag	masthead?	Johnson 1972:118
Henry Every/ Avery		1695	St. George's cross	four silver chevrons, red flag	masthead	Pringle 1953:123
Henry Every/ Avery		1695		red flag	masthead	Pringle 1953:123
William Fly	Elizabeth	1726		black ensign	ensign	Johnson 1972:610, 611, 612
William Fly	Fame's Revenge	1726		black flag	masthead?	Baer 2007d:239, 254, 256; Mather 1726:3, 4
Lewis Guittar	La Paix	1700		red flag	ensign	Rawlinson 1973:273
William Kidd	Adventure Galley	1697	English colors			Barlow 1934:470

(continued)

Table 9.1—*Continued*

Captain/ Crew	Ship	Date	National Flags	Pirate Flags	Flag Locations	Source
William Kidd	*Adventure Galley*	1697	red broad pennant with no cross			Barlow 1934:484
William Kidd	*Adventure Galley*	1697	French ensign			Barlow 1934:491
William Kidd	*Adventure Galley*	1697	French colors			Johnson 1934:446
Captain La Buze/ La Bouse		1720		black flag	ensign?	Johnson 1972:174
Captain Line(s)		1726		black flag, cutlass, figure of a man, pistol		*American Weekly Mercury*, February 22
Edward Low; Harris	*Fancy, Ranger*	1721		black flag	masthead?	Johnson 1972:319, 320
Edward Low; Harris	*Fancy, Ranger*	1722–23		pirate's colors	ensign?	Johnson 1972:329
Edward Low	*Fancy*	1722		pirate colors	ensign?	Barnard 1725:14
Edward Low	*Ranger*	1723		blue flag	masthead	Baer 2007g:176
Edward Low	*Fancy*	1723	Spanish colors	black flag	ensign?	Johnson 1972:326
Edward Low	*Fancy, Ranger*	1723		black flags, red flags	masthead	Baer 2007g:177
Edward Low	*Merry Christmas*	1722–23		black flag, death in red	masthead?	Johnson 1972:334
Edward Low		1723		black flag, dart, death, hourglass, impaled bleeding heart	ensign	Johnson 1972:352
George Lowther	*Delivery*	1723		black flag	masthead	Cordingly 1995:126–27
George Lowther	*Delivery*	1723	St. George's flag			Cordingly 1995:126–127

Captain/ Crew	Ship	Date	National Flags	Pirate Flags	Flag Locations	Source
John Martel	*John and Martha*	1716		cross-bones, death's head, figure of a man, hourglass, sword	ensign	Johnson 1972:68
John Martel		1716		cross-bones, death's head	jack and pennant	Johnson 1972:68
Christopher Moody	unknown ship	1718		black flag	masthead?	Johnson 1972:302
Captain Napin		1717		death's head, hourglass	masthead	*Boston News-Letter*, August 19
Thomas Nichols		1717		bleeding heart, dart		*Boston News-Letter*, August 19
John Quelch		1703	English colors			Baer 2007a:273
John Quelch		1703		dart, death, hourglass, impaled bleeding heart		Pringle 1953:123
Captain Richards	*Revenge*	1717		black flag	masthead?	Baer 2007f:374
Bartholomew Roberts		1720		four blazing balls on a Union flag	masthead	*Boston Gazette*, August 22
Bartholomew Roberts		1720	English colors	black flag, cutlass, death's head	masthead	*Boston Gazette*, August 22; *Boston News-Letter*, August 22; Johnson 1972:216

(continued)

Table 9.1—*Continued*

Captain/ Crew	Ship	Date	National Flags	Pirate Flags	Flag Locations	Source
Bartholomew Roberts		1720–21		"ABH" and "AMH," death's head, figure of a man (Roberts), flaming sword	jack and pennant	Johnson 1972:234
Bartholomew Roberts	*Royal Fortune*	1720–21		black colors	ensign?	Johnson 1972:216
Bartholomew Roberts	*Royal Fortune*	1720–21		black flag	masthead?	Johnson 1972:215, 226, 240
Bartholomew Roberts	*Royal Fortune*	1721	St. George's cross	black flag, crossbones, dart, death, hourglass, impaled bleeding heart	masthead	Johnson 1972:234
Bartholomew Roberts	*Royal Fortune*	1721		black flag	pennant	Johnson 1972:234
Bartholomew Roberts	*Royal Fortune*	1721	king's colors and pennant			Johnson 1972:239
Bartholomew Roberts	*Royal Fortune*	1721		death, figure of a man, flaming sword	masthead	Johnson 1972:245
Bartholomew Roberts	*Royal Fortune*	1721	English ensign and jack	black pennant	masthead	Baer 2007b:77
James Skyrm	*Ranger*	1721	red English ensign, king's jack, Dutch pennant	black flag	masthead	Johnson 1972:240; Baer 2007b:77, 81, 83, 86
John Smith/Gow	*Revenge*	1724	French colors			Johnson 1972:360

Captain/ Crew	Ship	Date	National Flags	Pirate Flags	Flag Locations	Source
John Smith/Gow	*Revenge*	1724	English colors			Johnson 1972:360
Francis Spriggs	*Delight*			black flag, dart, death, hourglass, impaled heart	ensign	Johnson 1972:352
Edward Teach	*Queen Anne's Revenge*	1717–18		black flag	masthead?	Johnson 1972:72; Baer 2007a:375
Edward Teach	*Queen Anne's Revenge*	1718		black flag, death's head	masthead?	*Boston News-Letter*, June 16
Unknown French pirate	*Trompeuse*	1683	white colors		ensign?	Southwell 1698
Unknown French pirate		1717		white flag, death's head	ensign	Cordingly 1995:141
Unknown pirates		1717		death's head	ensign	*Boston News-Letter*, July 22
Unknown—one of Teach's four consorts		1718		black flag, death's head		*Boston News-Letter*, June 16
Unknown—one of Teach's four consorts		1718		red flag		*Boston News-Letter*, June 16
Unknown—one of Teach's four consorts		1718		red flag		*Boston News-Letter*, June 16
Unknown—one of Teach's four consorts		1718		red flag		*Boston News-Letter*, June 16
Unknown		1718		black flag		Johnson 1972:371
Unknown	Unknown sloop	1718		black flag	masthead	*Boston News-Letter*, July 28

(continued)

Table 9.1—*Continued*

Captain/ Crew	Ship	Date	National Flags	Pirate Flags	Flag Locations	Source
Unknown		1723		black flag, dart, death, hourglass, impaled bleeding heart	masthead?	Wilson 1986:46
Charles Vane		1718		red flag	masthead	Baer 2007b:57
Charles Vane	*Lark*	1718		red pennant	masthead	Baer 2007b:56
Charles Vane		1718		black flag*	ensign?	Johnson 1972:138
Charles Vane		1718		black flag	masthead?	Johnson 1972:139; Baer 2007e:35, 36
Richard Worley	*Eagle*	1718		black flag, death's head	complete colors	Johnson 1972:299
Richard Worley	*Eagle*	1718		black flag		Johnson 1972:299, 302
Emanuel Wynn		1700		black flag, crossbones, death's head, hourglass	ensign	Pringle 1953:123

* I am "assigning" a red flag here to Deal and black flag to Vane, as they were sailing together and the witness did not distinguish between the two. There are other reports of Vane using a black flag, so that seemed more likely.

"He [Howell Davis] coming in to *Sierraleon* with her, it put the other two Pirates into some fear, believing at first it was a Man of War: But upon discovering her black flag at the Main-top-mast-head, which Pirate ships usually hoist to terrify Merchant-Men; they were easy in their Minds, and a little time after, saluted one another with Cannon" (Snelgrave 1734:199). Phillip Ashton observed a similar ritual while impressed into Edward Low's crew when their ship, the *Fancy*, reunited with their consort: "But *Low* hoisting his Pirate Colours, discovered who he was; and then, hideous was the noisy joy among the Piratical Crew, on all sides, accompanied with Firing, & Carousing, at the Finding of their Old master, & Companions" (Barnard 1725:14).

An excerpt from the trial of the crew of Bartholomew Roberts related in *A General History of the Pyrates* reveals a similar view and also the law's attitude to the flag at the time: "That this Fight and insolent Resistance against the King's ship was made, not only without any Pretence of Authority more than that of your own private depraved Will, but was done also under a black Flag, flagrantly by that denoting yourselves common Robbers and Traytors, Opposers and Violators of the Laws" (Johnson 1972:258).

Many pirate flags are referred to simply as a black flag. It is not clear if this is simply a convention referring to the most common element that pirates used for their signifiers or if some pirates relied on this most basic form for their message. Black was not commonly used by the navies or merchant houses of the world, so its meaning when encountered at sea was clear. In some cases it is evident that "black flag" is a term of convention, as in the *Boston Gazette*'s report of Edward Teach's ships on June 17–18, 1718: "A large Ship with Black Flags and Death Heads in them." Johnson, the author of the *General History of the Pirates*, seems to have used it as a general term as well, referring to flags by this general term, for example, when describing the flag of one of Bartholomew Roberts's consorts (Johnson 1972:240). Other pirates are noted as using red flags as a base, and one French pirate used white—perhaps as a reference to the white flags of the French navy from this period (Cordingly 1995:142). Where assignment of a flag location is uncertain, this is noted in table 9.1 with question marks, as references to "black flags" may actually denote ensigns and the term "colors" is also ambiguous.

The emblems used by pirates to distinguish their flags are diverse, including skulls (death's heads), crossbones, weaponry (including cutlasses, swords, and pistols) either crossed or wielded by a figure, whole skeletons (the personification of death), hourglasses, impaled and bleeding hearts, figures of men (sometimes meant to represent specific people), darts, and more could all be seen in different combinations. While there are no surviving examples of early eighteenth century pirate flags with good provenience, we do have some contemporary woodcuts, mostly from early editions of the *General History of the Pyrates*. These depictions are as problematic as modern versions, however, because we have is no information about what the artists used for their inspiration.

Descriptions that do survive still provide useful insights into pirate society, and relying on written descriptions can have some advantages as well. In most cases the descriptions of emblems are very precise, so and the language used allows common elements to become readily apparent. This may mask a greater variety in execution, however, and the diversity may be greater than what is known. Table 9.2 identifies the individual elements listed in the flag descriptions examined and their frequency. The most common element, unsurprisingly, is the death's head (eleven), but the next most common are less ubiquitously associated with pirates in modern popular culture: the hourglass (eight), the figure of death (seven), and the impaled bleeding heart (six). The death's head itself occurs as a lone symbol on six of the twenty-one flags described and commonly occurs in conjunction with one or more other elements, such as the hourglass, crossbones, and cutlass. The only other elements that appear on their own are the figure of death, the chevrons, and the blazing balls. The last two only occur once each.

One combination of symbols occurs with sufficient frequency to deserve further mention: the conjunction of the figure of death with an hourglass and an impaled or wounded bleeding heart (often on a dart). It occurs five times in the sample (almost a quarter of the described flags), making it the most common motif used on pirate flags other than the death's head. Johnson (1972:352) refers to this flag specifically as the Jolly Roger: "and a black Ensign was made, which they called *Jolly Roger*, with the same device Captain Low carry'd, *viz*. a white Skeleton in the Middle of it, with a Dart in one Hand striking a bleeding Heart, and in the other, an Hour glass." While this passage demonstrates how contact between crews allowed designs to diffuse throughout the community, there is no direct link among all the crews who used this motif. The first reported use (by John Quelch's crew) in 1703 was not followed by another until 1721 (by Bartholomew Roberts's crew). The second used a slight variation: "The Flag had a Death's Head on it, with an Hour-Glass in one Hand, and cross Bones in the other, a Dart by it, and underneath a Heart dropping three Drops of Blood" (Johnson 1972:234).

The other conjunction of design elements common to the pirate flags described is the figure of a man and a weapon such as a sword, flaming sword, cutlass, or pistol. Whenever a figure of a man appears, he is always wielding at least one weapon and sometimes two: "the way they went to be Tryed was thus, the Commander went at the Head, with about Twenty other Pirates with their Black Silk Flag before them, with the Representation of a Man in full Proportion, with a Cutlass in one Hand, and a Pistol in the

Table 9.2. Frequency of Occurrence of Design Elements on Pirate Flags, 1700–1723

Element of Design	Frequency
"ABH," "AMH"	1
Blazing balls	1
Chevrons	1
Crossbones	4
Cutlass	2
Dart	6
Death/skeleton	7
Death's head	11
Figure of a man	4
Flaming sword	2
Hourglass	8
Impaled bleeding heart	6
Pistol	1
Sword	1

other Extended" (*American Weekly Mercury*, February 22, 1726). In some cases these figures were meant to represent actual pirates (Bartholomew Roberts in particular used two flags with this element meant to represent himself wielding a flaming sword). The crossbones likewise always appears in conjunction with another element (usually a death's head, except in the one example given above). This probably did not carry enough meaning to stand on its own symbolically.

It is notable that so many flags associated with Roberts are described. Five of the twenty-one flags with emblems were flown by him and his fleet. Roberts was a highly successful pirate, and several records of his exploits survive. Johnson covers his career in detail, including the death and the subsequent trial of his crew. A more complete version of the trial was published in London in 1728. It is not necessarily the case that Roberts or his crew used a more diverse array of flags than other pirates—this could be a result of the attention that he and his crew received in their own time. Roberts made particular use of flags, designing some to deliver specific messages, such as creating one in response to government attempts to end his career: "Roberts was so enraged at the Attempts that had been made for the taking of him, by the Governors of *Barbadoes* and *Martinico*, that he ordered a new Jack to be made, which they ever after hoisted, with his own Figure pourtray'd, standing upon two Skulls, and under them the Letters

A.B.H. and *A.M.H.* signifying a *Barbadian*'s and a *Martinician*'s Head" (Johnson 1972:192).

While Roberts and his crew cannot be considered representative of all pirate crews in their use of flags, the fact that they used many of the most common elements (including the impaled and bleeding heart, death's heads, cutlasses, the figure of death, and the figure of a man) reinforces their popularity within pirate society. These flags also demonstrate the personal touches and messages that crews could communicate through their flags.

The association between the imagery on pirate flags and the imagery of death has been noted by other scholars. David Cordingly (1995:139–40) notes that the skull and crossbones appears on gravestones from the period and repeats Marcus Rediker's earlier observation (1993:279–80) that ship captains used it to note the death of crew members. In a later book Rediker notes that other emblems were also apparent in gravestone art and were associated in the Christian world with death and mortality (Rediker 2004:166). This imagery was in use primarily in the late seventeenth century in Britain. It was not limited to use on grave stones but appeared on other mortuary items as well, such as funeral invitations and trade cards, broadsides, and broadsheets. Emblem books, a literary art form combining graphics and prose popular since the sixteenth century, were the source from which much of this imagery originated and was copied. These symbols of mortality, specifically the death's head, crossbones, figure of death (commonly identified by the dart he carried), and hourglass, were preexisting symbols that pirates manipulated to convey their own messages. Some of the images, notably the death's head, had been used on flags of the English Civil War. This tradition may have had roots in other martial traditions (see Young 1995 for examples).

The image of the impaled and bleeding heart that appears on so many pirate flags is a greater mystery, because this is not a motif common to mortuary imagery of the period. The heart did appear in religious contexts and impaled hearts appear in other contexts on broadsides of the period, but none in direct relation to death. Perhaps a straightforward interpretation is best: the image of death with a bloody human heart on the end of his dart was powerful in its own right and could have been extremely effective in inciting terror in the crew of potential prizes. Regardless of whether it was appropriated from religious iconography or some unidentified source or was meant as a more direct threat, the conjunction of the heart motif with the imagery of death is an anomaly in an otherwise straightforward borrowing of familiar images from other media.

Pirates used their flags not only as a form of psychological warfare but to represent themselves to each other and society at large. Death was the penalty for piracy, so pirates in the eighteenth century lived on borrowed time: they were already dead to society. Their flags show their acceptance of this fate and of their place outside society. They used rites of passage such as signing of the articles to induct newcomers into this liminal state of social death. Their choice of emblems reflects their awareness and acceptance of that status. It is perhaps one of Roberts's flags that best represents this: "it had the Figure of a Skeleton in it, and a man pourtray'd with a flaming Sword in his Hand, intimating a Defiance of Death it self" (Johnson 1972:245). Although Johnson interprets the flag as a defiance of death, other possibilities exist. The figure holding the flaming sword represents Roberts himself, much as in another of his known flags, and the conjunction of symbols represents his acceptance and even camaraderie with both the concept and personification of death. Other pirates chose their flags for similar reasons. Though they intended their flags as threats to society at large, by their deployment they also intended the flags as a symbol of identity. Feared because of their actions and the stigma of their social status, pirates pressed their advantage by appropriating symbols of death familiar to eighteenth-century society and presenting them in a new context that flaunted their outsider status, striking terror in the hearts of their prey.

10

Artifacts That Talk Like Pirates

Jolly Roger Iconography and Archaeological Sites

KENNETH J. KINKOR

Relatively few writers on pirates have resisted the temptation to regale readers with swashbuckling exploits. To that end pirate crews are typically portrayed as ad hoc aggregations of predators, motivated by greed, adventurism, or simple perversity and isolated from other social influences. Writers emphasize the lurid details of the pirates' crimes and not the motivations for those crimes, focusing on the events of their voyages and not on the context of those voyages. More attention is paid to pirate personalities than to pirate principles.

In recent decades, however, the historiography of piracy has recognized that piracy did not occur in a social vacuum and that pirates of the seventeenth and eighteenth centuries were essentially a subculture within the larger social unit. Contrary to their popular image as misanthropic "lone wolves of the sea," strong sentiments of group cohesion, solidarity, and commonality of interest, if not a common ideology, existed among the Brethren of the Coast. This is reflected in part by adoption of symbols such as the infamous Jolly Roger as a means of visible distinction.

Piracy was not an articulate movement, and we have no first-person explanations of the "inner meaning" of the Jolly Roger. Nonetheless, its design elements can be examined in terms of the subculture of piracy as well as in terms of the larger social order.

The infamous skull and crossbones design began as a religious symbol, appearing frequently as gravestone art. Its debut as a flag was on a banner attached to a trumpet blown by "King Death" in a 1607 *Totentanz* (Dance of the Dead) portrait (Hill 1920:56). In 1626 peasant rebels carried "black banners bearing a death's head and the words 'It Must Be' because, as they grimly knew, the revolt would probably mean death for its leaders whether they won or lost" (Wedgewood 2005:206-7). A banner during the English Civil War sported a skull and a triumphal laurel wreath with the motto "One of These," meaning "Death or Victory" (Adair 1983:93). Sailors were also familiar with the practice of commanders, who would draw a skull and crossbones as a marginal sign in ship's logs to record a death (Hill 1920:56).

Nowadays the skull and crossbones is simply a symbol of death. Death was inseparably linked to resurrection in Christian theology, however, until at least the early twentieth century. Without the crucifixion there could be no resurrection and no eternal life. Bones in general have been seen as the "seeds of the body," symbols of resurrection analogous to the chrysalis, while crossed thigh bones signify vital procreative force (Cirlot 1962:29, 285).

Membership in a pirate crew was tantamount to legal death: piracy was punished by outlawry—being put outside the protection of the laws of the land. Anyone could beat, rob, or even kill an outlaw with impunity, and apprehended pirates were denied full due process of law. The link between outlawry and the Jolly Roger in popular perception is shown by a mutineers' plot to "hoist Jolly *Robin* [emphasis added] and the Cross Bones at the mast-head and go a-pirating in the East Indies" (Starkey 1990:186).

The original implications of the skull and crossbones motif seem to have marked a process of protorevolutionary self-transformation within pirate crews. Many pirates described themselves as "marooners" or "maroons" (Johnson 1972:342), a term implying the radical separation of an individual from established society, whether voluntary or involuntary. This may be why many crews, including the *Whydah* pirates, refused to take married men. They wanted men who could discard old values and attachments in favor of a new loyalty to their "brethren" as sworn through their articles (Rediker 1987:260-61, 286-27).

While it is unlikely that an underwater archaeological team will ever resurrect the remnants of a Jolly Roger flag from a pirate shipwreck site, this does not mean that the skull and crossbones motif need necessarily be absent from a pirate shipwreck site.

In 1984 a team led by underwater explorer Barry Clifford discovered the site of the 1717 shipwreck of the pirate ship *Whydah* off Cape Cod, Massachusetts. Built in 1715, the *Whydah* had been a slave-transport prior to its capture by pirates led by Samuel Bellamy. A significant portion of over 100,000 artifacts recovered to date in this ongoing project consists of colonial Spanish silver coinage.

Some of these coins were drilled so they might be worn—whether on a necklace, on a bracelet, or stitched directly to clothing is unknown. In some instances, however, the drill hole was deliberately positioned so that the Spanish cross on the obverse of the coin was approximately 45 degrees off perpendicular, producing an appearance similar to the skull and crossbones. The number of coins so adapted precludes coincidence, so it appears that piratical loyalty to the Jolly Roger even extended to proud personal adornment.

Like the skull and crossbones, other design elements of Jolly Roger had internal as well as external messages and might be likewise found in other media at archaeological sites.

Depictions of full skeletons ("anatomies") invoked the Dance of Death theme. They not only menaced intended victims: pirates, as social rebels, undoubtedly relished popular *Totentanz* depictions of "King Death" claiming the lives of the rich and powerful.

The hourglass informed victims that they had little time to decide whether to fight or surrender. To a pirate, however, it may have been a reminder of the transience of life. According to Bart Roberts, "a merry Life and a short one, shall be my Motto" (Johnson 1724:244). At least one pirate aboard the *Whydah* may have seen things the same way, as shown by an hourglass carved into the bowl of a pewter spoon.

The wounded heart motif is not only a design element of the Jolly Roger but is also found on a hand-carved wax seal matrix recovered from the *Whydah* site (figure 10.1).

Similar in shape and proportion to the heart depicted on this seal are worked stones from other sites associated with piratical activity. One such stone was found at the reputed "Pirates' Bank" site on Oak Island, Nova Scotia, while others are reported from Haiti and Madagascar (O'Connor 1978:45, 168). Barry Clifford recorded a similar stone heart carved in relief at a terrestrial site associated with pirates near Ile Ste. Marie, Madagascar, in 2000.

In Puritan iconography the heart was associated with the soul triumphant (Ludwig 1966:69). The wounded heart design therefore suggests death, danger, destruction, loss, or mourning, thus punctuating the warning conveyed by the black flag to potential victims.

Depictions of weapons such as swords or "darts of death" aggressively threatened violence in the event of resistance but also conveyed a sense of fatalism. In European iconography in general, as well as Freemasonry in particular, "The Sword Pointing at a Naked Heart" design demonstrates

Figure 10.1. Wax seal with wounded heart motif.

inexorable justice. The darts of death likewise signify fate, destiny, or nemesis. In early English almanacs these darts are often portrayed as the unerring weapons of King Death.

Prepared for defeat and death, many pirates rejected surrender. The crew members of Richard "Dirk" Chivers knew that they "were sure to be hanged if taken, and that they would take no quarter, but would do all the Mischief they could" (*Calendar of State Papers: Colonial Series* [*CSPCS*] 16:115). Others saw themselves "going on in their Voyage to Hell, whither they all were bound" (Snelgrave 1734:227). Some of the men of Roberts likewise said that "if they should ever be over-power'd, they would set Fire to the Powder with a Pistol, and all go merrily to Hell together" (Johnson 1972:217).

The very name "Jolly Roger" may itself reflect this nihilistic fatalism. "Old Roger" was a synonym for the devil during the early eighteenth century (Pringle 1953:123–25). Malcolm Cowley (1933:328) argued that, having declared war on the entire world, pirates "believed they were also rebels against God . . . [in] a sort of naïve Satanism resembling that of the Middle Ages," representing a very profound rejection of society.

Jolly Roger's interlocking symbols—death and resurrection, the brevity of life, violence, and heartache—"simultaneously pointed to meaningful parts of the seaman's experience, and eloquently bespoke the pirates' own consciousness of themselves as preyed upon in turn" (Rediker 1987:279).

232 · Kenneth J. Kinkor

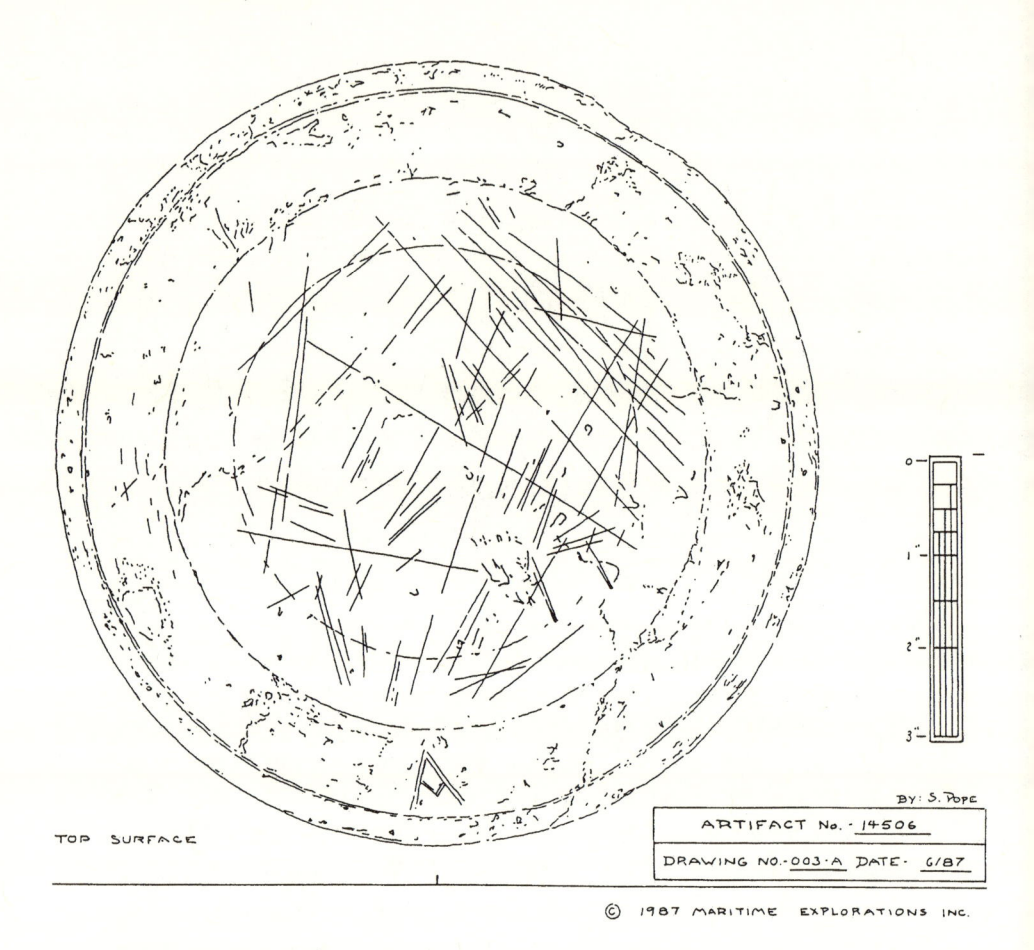

Figure 10.2. Pewter plate.

The Jolly Roger prompted not only feelings of martyrdom, however, but also thirst for revenge. For "as pirates—and only as pirates—these men were able to fight back beneath the somber colors of 'King Death' against those captains, merchants, and officials who waved banners of authority" (Rediker 1981:223).

In examining artifact iconography to determine whether or not an archaeological site was associated with pirates in the seventeenth and eighteenth centuries it is also necessary to consider symbols that are not themselves specifically piratical but nonetheless could have been transmitted by pirates. This is the case for a pewter plate (Artifact #14506, figure 10.2) recovered from the site of the wreck of the *Whydah Galley*.

The top of the plate is covered with random knife marks, while both sides have deliberately inscribed carvings. Aside from probable lack of access to relatively expensive pewter by common sailors, stringent shipboard discipline supports the presumption that these pictographs were not inscribed by a merchant seaman (Rediker 1987:215–35) but rather by a pirate prior to the wreck of the *Whydah Galley* on April 26, 1717.

On the bottom of the plate, to the left of the maker's mark, is a hand-inscribed cross-hatched rectangle, reminiscent of the British Union Flag, next to an L-shaped carving representing the British pound sterling mark.

The top of the plate contains an interlaced compass and square design. While the compass and square were used independently as early as the Crusades, there are no other instances before 1750 where the two are interlaced (Coil 1961:633). This mark is therefore the earliest representation of the hallmark of Freemasonry, its terminus post quem being almost two months before the formal advent of Grand Lodge Freemasonry on June 24, 1717.

While there are other viable hypotheses for the origin of this mark, these are obviated by the presence of other *Whydah* artifacts with Masonic symbols. As mentioned, the hourglass carving on the spoon has Masonic affinities. A hand-crafted brass seal matrix with a trefoil-design handle (see figure 10.1) has also been recovered. The face of the seal is an oval containing the previously mentioned wounded heart motif flanked by the moon in its waxing and waning phases. Above is a "Blazing Star" representing the sun with rays of light radiating outward. This appears to be a variant of the "Fixed Star" symbol of ancient astrology (Walker 1988:68), the probable precursor of an important symbol in Freemasonry called the "Star of Direction," the "Blazing Star," or the "Glory in the Center" (Coil 1961:98–99).

The appeal of such a symbol to a mariner is obvious. Flags used by pirate captains Anstis and Thomas Cocklyn included "four blazing Balls" (*Boston Gazette*, August, 22, 1720), and one of Thomas Anstis's vessels was the *Morning Star* (Johnson 1972:289).

A symbol related to the Masonic "Blazing Star" may be the "Rising Sun," an old Masonic emblem after which many lodges were named in the eighteenth and early nineteenth centuries. This was also the name of William Moody's pirate ship in 1719 (Hannah 1952:115; Coil 1961:528; The National Archives of the United Kingdom, Colonial Office Papers [TNA CO] 152/12, No. 136v).

It should also be noted that Freemasons not only employed the skull and crossbones as devices on tombstones, elements of Lodge decoration, and ornaments on personal regalia during this period but also used it as an initiation symbol in some of their ritual degrees or orders (Baigent and Leigh 1989:129–130; Hannah 1952:131, 199, 202–7; Coil 1961:626; Jones 1967:307; Stevenson 1988:160–61).

Some of the tenets of Freemasonry would have been quite attractive to eighteenth-century pirates. Certainly they would have found the Masonic belief in "Liberty, Equality, Fraternity" quite congenial. Like the piratical "floating commonwealths," Masonic lodges "could become, in effect, private exercises in self-government" (Jacob 1981:12, 35, 45, 49). Nonetheless, the concept of a Masonic lodge aboard a pirate ship understandably strains credulity.

Can these marks be accounted for as the product of an individual Freemason? The partner of Samuel Bellamy was one Palgrave Williams, a former goldsmith from an upper-class family in Newport, Rhode Island. Newport was also the home of a Masonic Lodge whose foundation reportedly dated to the mid-1600s. The Williams family belonged to a Baptist congregation that appears to have included members of this lodge (TNA CO 137/11, No. 45iii; Katz 1988:161–63, 171; Moriarty 1915, 1948, 1951).

Or were these the doodlings of an anonymous Freemason who fled the unsuccessful Rising of 1715 and thereafter turned pirate? Over six hundred Scottish prisoners were shipped to America as rebel-convicts. Did one of the no less than twelve Fergusons among them, for example, escape servitude to become the pirate surgeon recorded aboard the *Whydah Galley*? (*CSPCS* 29:309–15; TNA CO 137/11, No. 45iii).

There is another explanation.

Whether a criminal organization or a secret society, a deviant subculture mirrors pertinent conditions and tensions within the larger social unit. Two distinct subcultures may therefore mirror each other insofar as they may commonly reflect such conditions and tensions (Jacob 1981:184). We have little evidence for direct interaction between Freemasonry and early eighteenth century piracy. But connections between the iconography of piracy and similar symbolic elements in Freemasonry may be accounted for by the existence of a "third mirror" as a transmitting medium between the other two phenomena. Jacobitism—the amorphous pro-Stuart exile movement of the seventeenth and eighteenth centuries—may have acted as this third mirror.

Many scholars have identified linkages between Jacobitism and Freemasonry. Indeed Freemasonry became associated with the Stuarts as early as the Restoration (Monod 1990:300). Some view the exiled Stuart court as the main source of the "Scottish Rite" form of Freemasonry (Jacob 1981:209).

Downplaying subversive episodes in their organization's history, some Masonic scholars minimize or completely deny such connections (for example, Coil 1961; Hamill 1986). Other scholars, however, take a moderate position.

> [L]odges were, on the whole, remarkably supportive of established institutions of church and state. Yet they could also house divisive, or oppositional, political perspectives. They could be loyal to the Hanoverian and Whig order, yet they could also at moments show affiliation with radical interests, whether republican or Jacobite, and, possibly by the end of the century, Jacobin. (Jacob 1981:50–51)

The emphasis of the lodges on secrecy, loyalty, and elitism fostered an operational template adaptable to a variety of ideological stances (Stevenson 1988:7). As one historian puts it: "There is no question but that the Jacobites had a crucial influence on the development of Freemasonry—to such an extent, indeed, that later witnesses went so far as to describe freemasonry as a gigantic Jacobite conspiracy" (McLynn 1985:140).

Evidence suggests that the outbreak of piracy in the early eighteenth century may itself have been in part a by-product of Jacobite intrigue. Per royal order, issuance of privateering commissions by colonial governors without specific and express orders from the king was prohibited (Steele 1986:198, 206). Governor Archibald Hamilton of Jamaica nonetheless issued such commissions in late 1715 to a number of Caribbean adventurers, ostensibly to capture Spanish "pirates."

These privateers then used the commissions as authority for attacks on innocuous Spanish and French merchant shipping, including a Spanish treasure salvage expedition off Florida. This incident ignited an outbreak of piracy that was not fully extinguished until the late 1720s.

The most prominent of these renegade privateer captains was one Henry Jennings, who may have been related to Jacobite exiles Sir William Jennings and his son, likewise named William (Gooch 1978:278; Bromley 1987:162). Jennings and Samuel Bellamy consorted together early in 1716. This connection may explain later testimony from one of Bellamy's crew that "they had got a Commission from King George [sic]"—and why another wryly commented: "We will stretch it to the Worlds end" (*The Trials of Eight Persons* 1717:10).

Together with veiled accusations of Jacobite sympathies, Governor Archibald Hamilton was accused of direct collusion with the renegade privateers (*CSPCS* 29:158viii). He was promptly removed from office and recalled to London to account for his actions (Peterson 1975:370–75). Despite damning evidence of complicity, the charges against Lord Hamilton were eventually dropped.

Lord Hamilton had interesting relatives, at least eight of whom were royalists or Jacobites. He may have belonged to Hamilton Lodge, of which David Crawford, secretary to the Duchess of Hamilton, was a member in 1698 (Stevenson 1988:204). One of Archibald's brothers, Lord George Hamilton, was a distinguished army general who assisted the Earl of Mar in raising the highlands for the Stuart cause in 1715. Despite his prominent role in the Rising, he was eventually pardoned and went on to establish a Masonic lodge in Switzerland (McLynn 1985:140).

Governor Archibald Hamilton issued the privateering commissions nearly four months *after* the news of the Spanish wrecks had reached Jamaica. Had his sole motivation been personal gain, he could easily have moved far more quickly in arranging matters with the Jamaican captains. But sending mail from southwest England to Jamaica averaged a mere eight weeks (Steele 1986:30). Could Hamilton's dealings with the privateers have been prompted by news from his brother George of the imminent rebellion and its desperate need for funds? Were the Jamaican privateers intended as potential reinforcements for an embryonic Jacobite navy? If Lord Hamilton shared his family's Masonic affiliations, could he have passed these along to some of the privateers, together with his pro-Jacobite sympathies? Was Henry Jennings another conduit to the Jacobites in furtherance of this scheme?

Some pirates of the early eighteenth century certainly held strong Jacobite sympathies. In March 1718 a Jacobite naval officer, George Cammock, reported to the exiled Stuart court that the pirates at New Providence "did with one heart and voice proclaim James III for their King" and asked for a Jacobite "Captain-General" to direct their efforts against the Hanoverians. Cammock proposed that he be put in command of the pirates in the Bahamas to take and hold those islands in the king's name (Craton 1962:100). Associated with Cammock was an Irishman named Richard Holland who was later accused of committing piracy in the West Indies under Spanish auspices (Johnson 1724:48, 637).

When Bellamy's crew conscripted a carpenter, "one of the Pirates hearing him lament his sad condition, said, Damn him, He was a Presbyterian Dog, and should fight for King James etc." (*The Trials of Eight Persons* 1718:20). When Bellamy's crew styled themselves "Robin Hood's Men" they knew that Robin Hood not only robbed from the rich to give to the poor but supported the rightful king against a tyrannical usurper (Holt 1982:156–57, 162–63, 183–85; Faller 1987:121).

Another one-time shipmate of Bellamy's was the notorious Blackbeard. The name of his flagship, *Queen Anne's Revenge*, may have echoed Jacobite grievances as a sarcastic retort to "Queen Anne's Bounty," a royal relief fund for financially distressed Anglican ministers (Green 1970:124–25).

Associates of Blackbeard, Stede Bonnet's crew toasted "the Pretender's Health, and hoped to see him King of the English Nation" (South Carolina Court of Vice-Admiralty 1719:166). Their ship was dubbed the *Royal James*. A prisoner of Thomas Cocklyn's pirate crew indignantly reported that they toasted "the Pretender, by the name of King James the Third, and thereby I found they were doubly on the side of the Gallows, both as Traitors and Pirates" (Snelgrave 1734:216–17).

An especially argumentative member of Ned Low's crew picked a quarrel by asking a prisoner who was king:

> I answer'd, In my Opinion, he that wears the Crown, is certainly King while he keeps it. Well, says he, and pray who is that? Why, says I, King George at present wears it. Hereupon he broke out in the most outrageous Fury, damning me, and calling me Rascally Son of a B——; and abusing his Majesty in such a virulent Manner, as is not fit to be repeated, asserting, with bitter Curses, that we had no King . . . swearing and cursing his Majesty in the most outrageous Terms, and asserting the Pretender to be the lawful King of Engl. & c. (Dow and Edmonds 1968:178–80)

A suspected pirate captain, Richard Tookerman or Tuckerman, did not hesitate to fire cannon to celebrate the Pretender's birthday—despite the presence of Royal Navy captain Edward "Old Grog" Vernon in the harbor (*Acts of the Privy Council*, March 25, 1723, 43–44). Tookerman had been an associate of Stede Bonnet before going on to work with the pirate combine led by Bartholomew Roberts, who was a "pupil" of the Welsh pirate Howell Davis (Johnson 1972:221). At one time or another the Davis/Roberts pirate flotilla included vessels such as the *King James*, the *Royal Rover* (echoing the popular song "Jamie the Rover"?), and the *Sea King* (Johnson 1972:175; TNA CO 152/13 No. 282).

By mid-1718 the British government was putting serious pressure on the pirates in the West Indies. Many consequently fled to the Indian Ocean. Some of these pirate vessels included the *Royal James* (Johnson 1972:115), *Flying King* (Johnson 1724:116), *King James* (Snelgrave 1734:280–81; Luntley 1721), *Wyndham Galley* (Snelgrave 1734:262–64), and *Duke of Ormonde* (Luntley 1721). The last two vessels were named after prominent Tories who had defected to the Jacobite cause in 1715.

Conspiracy theory is seductive. Despite mutual interconnections, Jacobitism, Freemasonry, and piracy are clearly distinguishable from each other in both goals and methods. A pirate might toss off a wistful toast to King James "over the water," a zealous Jacobite émigré might exploit politically disaffected pirates for the "Good Old Cause," and both may have found in the secret organization and esoteric mysticism of Freemasonry a sympathetic ideology in their mutual resistance to the established sociopolitical order, but this does not negate the differences among these groups. Instead these interconnections show how social, economic, political, and religious tensions in early eighteenth century British society produced strange bedfellows—as well as strange inscriptions on pewter utensils.

11

Pirates as Providers

KATHLEEN DEAGAN

Pirate: a person who attacks and robs ships at sea

Piracy in Spanish colonial America was very much a double-edged sword. While colonial residents and officials dreaded pirate attacks on the coastal towns and treasure fleets of the Spanish Main, they also relied in many ways on the material products of piracy and smuggling to sustain their local economies and daily lives. This chapter is concerned with the ways in which colonial residents in the Spanish colonies coped with the conundrum of an essential, but illegal, economic mechanism, and how their consumption practices mediated both social practice and social identity. It also serves as a cautionary illustration of the inherent difficulties in trying to understand piracy and contraband from an archaeological perspective.

The definition of piracy itself can be problematic. Here I use the standard dictionary definition of a pirate as "a person who attacks and robs ships at sea," in that it permits a broadly situational perspective on piracy. This construction does not distinguish between privateers (who attacked and robbed ships with the sanction of a state government) and the popularly conceived notion of pirates as lawless ruffians with no national affiliation or sanction. Certainly this distinction did not give comfort to those being attacked and robbed at sea—the attackers were undoubtedly seen as pirates regardless of their license to steal.

Although the treasures of American gold and silver en route to Spain provoked the famously pirate-plagued seafaring of the Spanish Main, Spain's imperial economic system was the principal contributor to nearly universal smuggling and contraband goods in the colony. The system was structured by the principles of mercantilism. Economic strength was sought by strictly controlling colonial production and exchange in order to encourage the exportation of raw materials from the colonies to Spain and of manufactured goods from Spain to the colonies. The colonies were theoretically not to develop either industries or external exchange networks. Commerce was strictly regulated by a monopoly that restricted trade in the colonies to Spain itself. All goods had to be shipped from Spain, by Spanish-licensed merchants, in Spanish-licensed ships (for comprehensive discussions of Spain's colonial economic policies and problems, see Haring 1966; Hoffman 1980; Lang 1975; Walker 1979).

This system was spectacularly unsuccessful. Spain was consistently unable to provide the manufactured goods needed by the American colonists, so the residents of Spanish America turned to illicit trade with foreigners to survive. Historians of the Spanish colonial economy have shown that virtually none of the Iberian colonies in America could adequately subsist by relying on legal supply systems and that illicit trade was an essential part of colonial economic life (Cohen 2003; Grahn 1997; McAllister 1984:236; Moya Pons 1998:43–50; Pijning 1997; Thompson 2010; Wright 1970).

The dependency on contraband material throughout the Spanish colonies is well established at the community scale in written texts, but they reveal considerably less about how the distribution and consumption of illegal goods was played out within communities. Historical archaeology's privileged position at the intersection of textual, archaeological, and iconic lines of evidence, however, makes it uniquely appropriate for addressing undocumented consumption of illegal goods at a variety of social scales from households to regions.

In order to take full advantage of this position, it is essential that historical archaeologists address questions that can only be answered through the articulation of both material and textual information. In Spanish Florida, for example, it does not require reference to the archaeological record to demonstrate that trade in contraband probably existed there or to suggest the periods during which it probably occurred. These conclusions, as discussed, already have been established by textual evidence.

Other, more interesting questions about illicit trade in Spanish Florida, however, cannot be answered by textual information alone. Patterns of exchange and consumption of illicit material items provide useful archaeological points of entry into understanding social relationships and expressions of social identity. For instance, did these community-wide trends in contraband activity represent a homogeneous economic behavior across diverse social classes, economic levels, and ethnic affiliations in the community? Could this tell us anything significant about society and the economy within colonial St. Augustine? Exploring these questions requires a consideration of illicit trade at a household level, rather than on a community-wide scale.

Problems in Studying Contraband

Approaching contraband in the households of Spanish Florida is not unproblematical, given the complex issues of recognition and periodicity. Recognition of contraband material is particularly difficult, depending to a large extent on temporal control of individual archaeological deposits (Deagan 2007; Newquist 2007; Skowronek 1992). Although Spain prohibited trade between the American colonies and English, Dutch, and French merchant ships, it did not prohibit the purchase of goods manufactured in those countries, as long as they arrived on Spanish-licensed ships. In other words, it was generally not the items themselves that indicated contraband activity but rather how, through whom, and when they got into the community. From the mid-sixteenth century onward, the majority of manufactured goods arriving on Spanish-licensed legal supply ships were in fact of non-Spanish production. The legal Spanish trade with America (particularly during the eighteenth century) was supplied and controlled by Dutch, English, French, Portuguese, and German merchants resident in Andalusia (Chaunu and Chaunu 1957; Haring 1966:286; Vicens Vives 1969:402, 434–36; Lang 1975:50–52; Pulido Bueno 1993). It has been estimated by Spanish economic historians that by 1700 only about five percent of the goods shipped from Cádiz were of Spanish origin, with Spanish contributions consisting principally of wine, oil, some cloth, wax, and iron (Usher 1932:203–5; Walker 1979:15–16).

Foreign materials that under normal conditions might be considered contraband also arrived in Spanish Florida through a variety of other legal means (Deagan 2007; Johnson 2003; Thompson 2010). These included the sale of foreign cargoes captured through Spanish privateering and temporary legal dispensation to trade with foreigners as economic relief (Bushnell 1982:89; Johnson 2003) as well as foreign merchant ships that Spain permitted to call annually in Mexico as part of the *asiento* contract to provide slaves to the Spanish colonies. The *asiento* ships were also permitted to bring their own trade goods for sale in the colonies. Portugal held the *asiento* until 1640; the French had the privilege from 1640 to 1713; and the English from 1713 until 1739 (Haring 1966:268–69).

Given the variety of legal mechanisms by which foreign goods might have entered the colonies, how can we actually distinguish foreign items that arrived illegally from those that arrived legally? The foregoing discussion suggests that this cannot be done at the scale of individual objects or types of objects (except perhaps in very rare individual cases). Understanding what material goods were illegal at any given time requires deep historical contextualization at a local level, a precise understanding of economic regulations and flow of goods, tightly controlled archaeological contexts, and precisely dated material culture.

With proper contextual control, we should be able to study illicit origins archaeologically by careful articulation of multiple archaeologically connected factors, including: (1) artifact origins (where artifacts were produced); (2) artifact periodicity (dates of artifact production and use); (3) trade periodicity (dates during which objects of various national origins should have been available only illegally or, conversely, only legally); and (4) archaeological context (when and how artifacts were deposited into the archaeological record).

St. Augustine, Florida

St. Augustine, Florida, provides an ideal case study for exploring archaeology's potential role in eliciting new information about illicit economic activity. St. Augustine is not only very well documented historically but also provides a very large, diverse, and temporally controlled body of archaeological data. Established in 1565 to challenge the French Huguenot presence in Florida, and surviving to guard the route of the homebound Spanish fleets, the settlement remained a subsidized presidio (a fortified military town supported by a government subsidy) until 1763.

On the very fringes of empire, and with no significant natural resources for exploitation or trade, St. Augustine was among the most economically disadvantaged colonies in Spanish America. It had almost no direct trade between Florida and Spain, and few ships other than those of the garrison itself ever called at St. Augustine. As a presidio Florida was supported by a government subsidy supplied by Crown-mandated fees in Mexico City until 1707, in Puebla from 1707 until 1740, and in Cuba after 1740. The system was plagued by money shortages, shipwrecks, pirate attacks, spoiled food, and inflated costs of goods. In many years the *situado* (annual supply ships) simply never arrived in St. Augustine (Bushnell 1994; Halbirt 2004; TePaske 1958; Harman 1969).

For the citizens of St. Augustine, turning to whatever economic opportunities were presented to them—regardless of legality—was only common survival sense. Those opportunities were considerably enhanced after 1670, when the English (enemies of Spain) established Charlestown and provided a potential, if illegal, source of European goods for St. Augustine. St. Augustine resident took enthusiastic advantage of that source (for extended discussions of this and the ensuing Anglo-Spanish interaction, see Bolton and Ross 1968; Gillaspie 1961; Oatis 2004; Runyon 2005; TePaske 1958, 1964; Wright 1970).

To explore contraband trade in the Spanish households of St. Augustine, I have followed Carl Halbirt's (2004) initiative by examining the relative proportions of Spanish-tradition versus non-Spanish Old World tableware ceramics in contexts deposited between 1650 and 1760 (a more detailed discussion of methods and caveats used in this study can be found in Deagan 2007). Included in this category are vessels used at the table for serving and consuming as well as the wares and types that occur consistently and principally in tableware forms (table 11.1).

Table 11.1. Ceramics Occurring as Tablewares in St. Augustine Households, 1650–1750

Spanish-Tradition Origin	Begin	End	English/Northern European Origin	Begin	End
San Luis Polychrome Majolica	1650	1750	English Soft Paste Porcelain	1745	1800
Aranama Polychrome Majolica	1750	1800	Delftware, Blue and White	1650	1790
Abó Polychrome Majolica	1650	1750	Delftware, Plain	1640	1800
Castillo Polychrome Majolica	1680	1710	Delftware, Polychrome	1570	1790
Puebla Polychrome Majolica	1650	1725	Delftware, Manganese Sponged	1708	1790
Puebla Tradition Majolica, White	1700	1800	Astbury Ware	1725	1750
Puebla Blue on White Majolica	1700	1750	Agateware	1740	1775
Huejotzingo Blue on White Majolica	1700	1850	Whieldon Ware	1740	1770
Unidentified Puebla Majolica	1650	1800	Staffordshire Slipware	1675	1770
Aucilla Polychrome Majolica	1650	1700	Jackfield Ware	1740	1790

(*continued*)

Table 11.1—*Continued*

Spanish-Tradition Origin	Begin	End	English/Northern European Origin	Begin	End
Mount Royal Polychrome Majolica	1650	1700	Nottingham Stoneware	1700	1810
San Agustín Blue on White Majolica	1700	1730	White Salt-Glazed Stoneware, Plain	1720	1790
El Morro Ware	1550	1750	White Salt-Glazed Stoneware, Molded	1740	1770
Rey Ware	1725	1825	Scratch-Blue White Salt-Glazed Stoneware	1735	1775
Black Lead-Glazed Earthenware	1700	1770	Rhenish-Type Gray Stoneware Mugs	1700	1775
Guadalajara Polychrome	1650	1800	Elers-Type Ware	1690	1790
Mexican Red Painted Ware	1550	1750			
French Origin			**Asian Origin**		
			Porcelain, Blue and White Underglaze Chíng	1644	1912
Faience, St. Cloud Polychrome	1675	1766	Porcelain, "Chinese Imari"	1700	1780
Faience, Provence Blue on White	1725	1765	Porcelain, White	1640	1750
Faience, Brown Rouen	1740	1790	Porcelain, Monochrome Brown	1700	1780
Faience, Plain	1675	1775			
Faience, Brittany Blue on White	1750	1770	General range: TPQ determined by specific motifs when present		
Faience, Normandy Blue on White	1690	1775	Stamped or incised		
Faience, Seine Polychrome	1690	1765			

Sources: Dates for Spanish-tradition and Asian wares follow the sources provided by Florida Museum of Natural History (2004); dates for French faience follow Waselkov and Walthall (2002); dates for English-tradition wares follow Miller et al. (1999) and Noël Hume (2002).

I focus specifically on tableware ceramics for this particular problem for several reasons:

1. All such tableware ceramic types in St. Augustine were imported.
2. They are one of the few artifact categories recovered in substantial numbers for which we can determine both the country of origin and the dates of manufacture or use.
3. They were accessible to and used by all people in the colony. Although the kinds of tablewares may have varied in cost and quality, the fact of tableware use does not. They therefore present a direct representation of both community-wide and household-specific cultural practice and cultural choice.
4. Ceramics are one of the only classes of nonperishable material that was produced and exported in Spain and Spanish America during the colonial period. Virtually all classes of nonceramic items found typically on colonial sites (glassware, buttons, pins, scissors, common jewelry, religious items, kitchen implements, tools) were imported to Seville or Cádiz from France, England, Germany, and Holland and re-exported to America throughout the colonial era (Torre Revello 1943; García-Baquero González 1976; Walker 1979:234–37; Pulido Bueno 1993). Tableware ceramics therefore represent perhaps the only material category that can reflect a true consumer choice between Spanish-tradition and non–Spanish-tradition goods in colonial Florida.

The utility of using tableware ceramics as proxies for legal versus illicit trade is further underscored by Mitch Marken's study (1994) of pottery found on seventeen Spanish shipwrecks dating between 1500 and 1800. He identified a wide variety of ceramic wares from production centers in Spain, Italy, and Mexico but did not find pottery produced in other European centers. The absence of non-Spanish ceramics in these vessels reflects the probability that ceramics from Germany, France, England, and Holland were rarely transported on Spanish merchant vessels (Marken 1994).

Assessing Periodicity

Although all of the Spanish colonies were subject to the same economic policies and trade restrictions, the actual periodicity of legal versus illicit trade was specific to individual communities. Periodicity for St. Augustine based on documentary sources is summarized in table 11.2, suggesting that

Table 11.2. Political Events and Related Periods for the Legal Entry of English and French Goods into St. Augustine

Date	Event	Legal French Goods	Legal English Goods
1765	Spain cedes Florida to England, 1763		
1760			X
1755			X
1750	Havana Company provisions St. Augustine directly from New York and Charleston		X
1745			
1740			
	War of Jenkins' Ear, 1739–43		X
1735			X
1730			X
1725			X
1720			X
1715			X
1713	Treaty of Utrecht, 1713: English receive trade *asiento* in Spanish colonies (1713–50)	X	
1710	St. Augustine *situadista* (transporter) in Mexico forced to accept boatload of porcelain in place of money and goods for the St. Augustine *situado* (annual subsidy)	X	
1705		X	
1700	Bourbon ascendancy in Spain War of Spanish Succession: French receive trade *asiento* in Spanish colonies, 1701–13	X	
1695			
1690			
1685			
	1683–84: St. Augustine supplied legally by English merchants in New York and Carolina		X
1680			
1675			
1670	Charleston established		
	Treaty of Madrid: Spain recognizes legitimacy of England's Caribbean colonies. England agrees to suppress illegal trade with Spanish colonies		

English goods, including ceramics, could have legally entered St. Augustine almost continuously from 1713 until Spain's entry into the French and Indian War in 1762. The highest probability of English goods entering the town illegally would have been before about 1715 and possibly between 1739 and 1750. French goods could have entered legally between 1702 and 1713, but there were few legal mechanisms for entry of French goods before 1702 or after 1713.

The materials used in this study include the excavated remains from 136 undisturbed, closed context features from six domestic sites and one religious site that represent a cross section of St. Augustine's eighteenth-century households by income, ethnic origin, and occupation (table 11.3). The deposits were all either trash-filled pits or barrel wells and were either single-event or very short-term deposits. They were excavated between 1973 and 1994 by the Florida State University and University of Florida field schools and contained a total of 5,468 ceramic tableware artifacts of European or Euro-American origin.

Table 11.3. Sites and Households Used in This Study

Site	Residents	Affiliation	Occupation	Income
Palm Row Site (Sa-36-4)	Francisco Ponce de León	Elite *criollo*, old family	Sergeant major of the Florida Garrison	960 pesos
Avero Site (Sa-7-5)	Antonia de Avero and her husband, Joaquín Blanco	Elite *criollo*, old family	Keeper Of the Royal Storehouse	590 pesos
De Hita Site (Sa-7-4)	Gerónimo de Hita y Salazar and Gertudis de Avero	Elite *criollo*, old family	Cavalryman	264 pesos
De Mesa Site (Sa-7-6)	Antonio de Mesa	Nonelite *criollo*, new family	Customs harbor guard	180 pesos plus ship fees
De la Cruz Site (Sa-16-23)	María de La Cruz	Mestizo/Indian	Soldier	130 to 170 pesos
Fatio Site (Sa-34-2)	Cristóbal Contreras	Canary Islander Peninsular	Merchant from Spain	?
Convento de San Francisco (8sa42)	Multiple	Franciscan friars (Spanish and *criollo*)	Friars	?

Table 11.4. Terminus Post Quem Groups for Archaeological Deposits Used in This Study

TPQ	Determining Artifacts
1650	Puebla Polychrome Majolica, San Luis Polychrome Majolica, Abó Polychrome Majolica, Guadalajara Polychrome Earthenware
1675–80	St. Cloud Polychrome Faience, Combed Staffordshire Slipware, Castillo Blue on White Majolica, Nottingham Stoneware, Elers-Type Red-Bodied Stoneware
1700	Puebla Blue on White Majolica, Huejotzingo Blue on White Majolica, San Agustín Blue on White Majolica, Rhenish-Type Gray Stoneware Mugs, Normandy Blue on White Faience, Seine Polychrome Faience
1720–25	Plain White Salt-Glazed Stoneware, Rey Ware, Astbury Ware, Provence Blue on White Faience
1735–40	Molded White Salt-Glazed Stoneware, Whieldon Ware, Brown Rouen Faience, Agate Ware, Jackfield Ware
1745–50	Aranama Polychrome Majolica, English Porcelain, Scratch Blue Salt-Glazed Stoneware

Note: This table does not reflect all datable ceramic types included in the sample but only those types that occurred as the latest-dating item in a deposit, thereby providing the terminus post quem date for that deposit. Dates for Spanish-tradition and Asian wares follow the sources provided by Florida Museum of Natural History (2004); dates for French faience follow Waselkov and Walthall (2002); dates for English-tradition wares follow Miller et al. (1999) and Noël Hume (2002).

Each feature deposit was assigned a terminus post quem (TPQ) based on stratigraphic association and the latest-dating item in that provenience. These dates—based primarily upon what we know independently about the dating of artifacts—determine the periodicity of the archaeological record and obviously both constrain and bias the ways in which we can look at trends through time (table 11.4). Terminus post quem reflects only the date after which a deposit entered the ground and furthermore assumes that ceramics were acquired, used, and deposited shortly after they were first produced. This troubling assumption might be mitigated by calculating a mean ceramic date for each deposit; in this sample however, many of the deposits lacked a sufficient number of tightly dated ceramic types to make such a determination valid. The dates assigned to the archaeological deposits based on TPQ are thus probably skewed to slightly earlier than their actual deposit in the ground, a probability of which we should remain mindful when articulating these data with events dated by documentary sources.

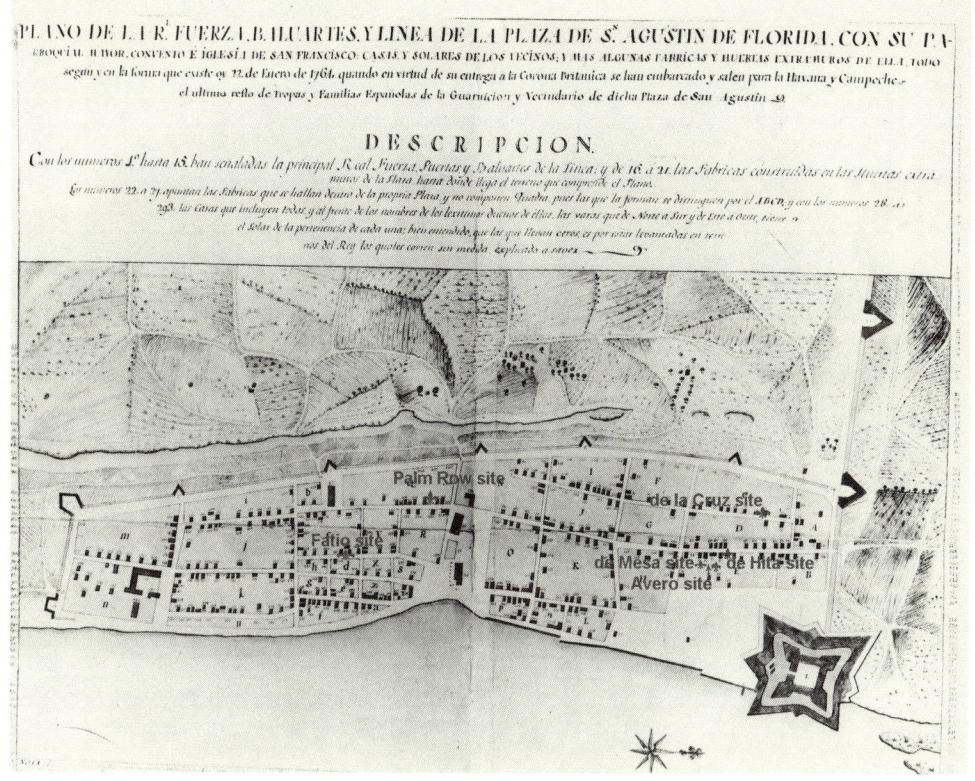

Figure 11.1. Locations of study sites shown on the 1764 Puente map.

In the absence of more refined temporal tools the TPQ-based chronology does offer a framework (albeit crude in comparison to documentary periodicity) for assessing temporal change.

The Households

The households used in this study include members of the prestigious old *criollo* families (those of Spanish descent but raised in the Americas), a wealthy government official, low-ranking members of the garrison, a mixed Indian-Hispanic household, a well-to-do merchant, and a Franciscan monastery. The income for most of these households is independently documented (Deagan 1983:44; Scardaville and Ganong n.d. [1975]). It should be pointed out that the occupants of specific sites are identified by reference to a property map made in 1764 at the end of the first Spanish occupation (Puente 1764) (figure 11.1). In many cases, no additional information about potential earlier site occupants has yet been located through documentary

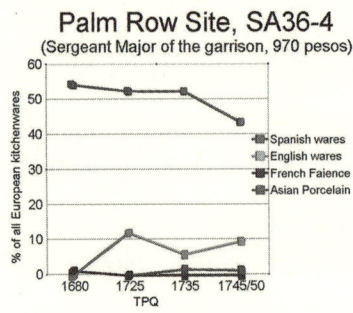

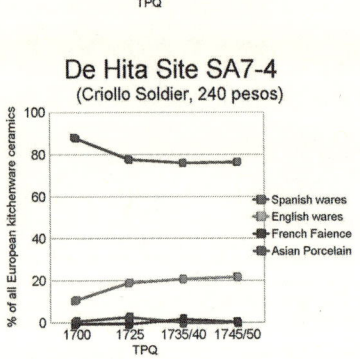

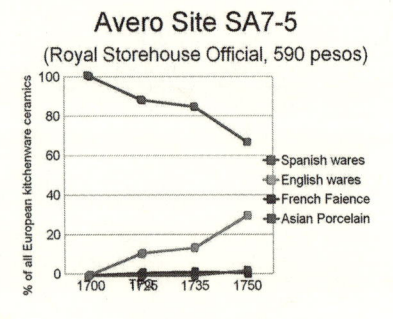

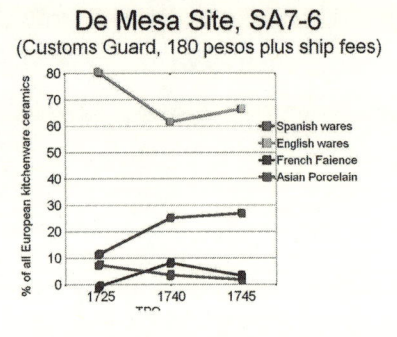

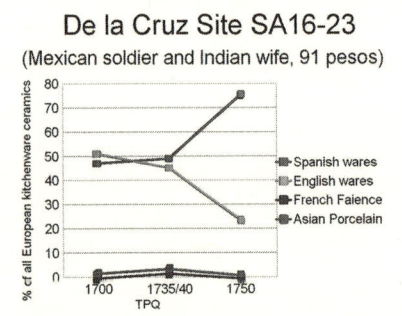

Figure 11.2. Trends in the origins of tableware ceramics in St. Augustine households, 1650–1760.

research. It is therefore possible that other families occupied some of these sites during the early years of the eighteenth century.

This possibility is somewhat mitigated in that property among this group is well documented to have been held in the family, passed along as dowries for daughters (Parker 1999). Spanish St. Augustine, like most Spanish towns, is furthermore well documented as organizing residential spaces along class and ethnic lines (Bond 1995; Deagan 1982). If some of these sites did have earlier household occupants than those currently documented, those occupants very likely would share economic and class affiliations with later Spanish period residents. The sites and their known residents are summarized in table 11.3.

Figure 11.2 and table 11.5 show the ceramic trends for each of these households. Those from the *criollo* sites (Ponce de León, Avero, and De Hita y Salazar) are very similar throughout the eighteenth century, despite marked differences in income. The occupants of all these sites, as noted above, were all members of old *criollo* families, each headed by a government official or member of the military garrison. Spanish-tradition ceramics, although declining through the century, consistently made up the majority of tableware ceramics in these households. Foreign ceramics (predominantly English) were infrequent at the beginning of the century, when it was unlikely that English ceramics were entering the colony legally. By TPQ 1735, the proportion of foreign wares in these households rose to nearly 20 percent of the ceramic assemblages, corresponding to the peak period of privateering in St. Augustine and the legal sale of English prizes (and their cargoes) captured by Spanish pirates.

These points of rough convergence in the archaeological and documentary records (that is, consistently low proportions of non-Spanish wares in the household assemblages during periods when non-Spanish wares should have been illegal) may suggest that the *criollo* military families did not engage in illicit traffic as a regular and important means of acquiring goods, perhaps for reasons of identity reinforcement.

This trend is even more sharply pronounced in the assemblage of the Franciscan friars at the Convento de San Francisco (table 11.5). Spanish-tradition tablewares here consistently account for 90 percent or more of the assemblage through all periods until 1745–50, when English goods became available through the *situado*. The friars, whose material needs were supplied to them (rather than selecting them themselves), may well reflect the composition of legal goods in the colony most strongly.

Although not directly part of this study, Ingrid Newquist's assessment (2007) of the excavated tableware assemblage of Convento de San Francisco in Santo Domingo (ca. 1556–1700) showed a similar pattern of consumption. Here the excavated contexts were chronologically grouped by stratigraphy into three categories: ca. 1600, ca. 1635–50, and ca. 1675–1700. The proportion of Spanish-tradition tablewares (as a percent of all tablewares) in these three periods was 96 percent ca. 1600, 100 percent ca. 1635–50, and

Table 11.5. Imported European-Tradition Tablewares in Eighteenth-Century St. Augustine Households

PALM ROW SITE (SA-36-4) (SERGEANT MAJOR OF THE GARRISON, 960 PESOS INCOME)

	1680* #	1680* %	1725 #	1725 %	1735–40 #	1735–40 %	1745–50 #	1745–50 %	TOTAL #
Spanish wares	63	90	12	75	298	81	75	69	448
English wares	5	7	3	19	34	9	26	24	68
French faience	2	3	1	6	26	7	4	4	33
Asian porcelain	0	0	0	0	10	3	3	3	13
TOTAL	70	100	16	100	368	100	108	100	562

AVERO SITE (SA-7-5) (ROYAL STOREHOUSE OFFICIAL, 590 PESOS INCOME)

	1700 #	1700 %	1725 #	1725 %	1735–40 #	1735–40 %	1745–50 #	1745–50 %	TOTAL #
Spanish wares	26	100	80	0.88	207	0.84	67	0.67	380
English wares	0	0	10	0.11	34	0.14	30	0.30	74
French faience	0	0	1	0.01	4	0.02	1	0.01	6
Asian porcelain	0	0	0	0	0	0	2	0.02	2
TOTAL	26	100	91	100	245	100	100	100	462

DE HITA SITE (SA-7-4) (CRIOLLO CAVALRY SOLDIER, 240 PESOS INCOME)

	1700 #	1700 %	1725 #	1725 %	1735–40 #	1735–40 %	1745–50 #	1745–50 %	TOTAL #
Spanish wares	274	88	48	77	621	76	1020	76	1963
English wares	35	11	12	19	174	21	291	22	512
French faience	0	0.00	0	0.00	19	2	12	1	31
Asian porcelain	4	1	2	3	6	1	11	1	23
TOTAL	313	100	62	100	820	100	1334	100	2529

DE MESA SITE (SA-7-6) (Customs Guard, 180 pesos income plus ships' fees)

	1700 #	1700 %	1725 #	1725 %	1735–40 #	1735–40 %	1745–50 #	1745–50 %	TOTAL #
Spanish wares	3	12	5	13	75	25	55	27	138
English wares	22	88	31	79	185	62	134	66	372
French faience			0		25	8	8	4	33
Asian porcelain			3	8	15	5	5	2	23
TOTAL	25	100	39	100	300	100	202	100	566

DE LA CRUZ SITE (SA-16-23) (Hispanic-Indian Family, ca. 150 pesos income)

	1700 #	1700 %	1725** #	1725** %	1735–40 #	1735–40 %	1745–50 #	1745–50 %	TOTAL #
Spanish wares	25	47	25	46	44	45	60	70	129
English wares	26	49	1	49	47	48	25	29	98
French faience	1	2	0	2	2	2	0	0.00	3
Asian porcelain	1	2	1	3	5	5	1	1	7
TOTAL	53	100	27	100	98	100	86	100	237

FATIO SITE (Spanish Merchant, Income Unknown)

	1700 #	1700 %	1725 #	1725 %	1735–40 #	1735–40 %	1750 #	1750 %	TOTAL #
Spanish wares	36	65	25	93	254	68	71	72	386
English wares	8	15	1	4	101	27	23	23	133
French faience	5	9	0		1	0.00	2	2	8
Asian porcelain	6	11	1	4	16	4	3	3	26
TOTAL	55	100	27	100	372	100	99	100	553

(*continued*)

Table 11.5—*Continued*

CONVENTO DE SAN FRANCISCO (Franciscan Monastery)

	1650 #	1650 %	1700 #	1700 %	1720–25 #	1720–25 %	1745 #	1745 %	TOTAL #
Spanish wares	44		252	94	32	89	51	81	28
English wares	5	90	10	4	4	11	9	14	2
French faience		10	1	.00			1	2	379
Asian porcelain			6	2			2	3	8
TOTAL	49	100	269	100	36	90	63	100	417

* No proveniences with TPQ 1700 were excavated.
** No proveniences with TPQ 1725 were excavated. Graph line value extrapolated between 1700 and 1735 percentage values.

76 percent during the 1675–1700 period (data from Newquist 2007:table 1). The absence of potentially illegal non-Spanish tablewares is particularly striking in Santo Domingo, which was notorious in illegal trade activity (see Wright 1970:346). The parallel to Franciscan convent in St. Augustine, although perhaps coincidental, is intriguing.

The reluctance on the part of the garrison *criollos* and the religious orders to incorporate foreign and possibly illegal goods into their households stands in sharp contrast to the household of Antonio de Mesa, the harbor guard with six children. His is the only household in the sample in which non-Spanish wares consistently outnumber Spanish ceramics throughout the century. It is likely that his position as a customs guard afforded ample and enhanced access to goods from both prizes and illicit trade. If so, it was an opportunity of which he took considerable advantage. This can be seen in the dramatically high proportions of English and French tableware ceramics in his household through the eighteenth century, regardless of prevailing regulations about illegal foreign trade. This is also one of the clearest examples of probable traffic in contraband that we can reasonably suggest from St. Augustine's archaeological record.

The low-income occupants of the mestizo De la Cruz site had a notably different ceramic kitchenware assemblage from either the *criollo* military households or the harbor guard. During the early decades of the eighteenth century, when English goods were largely illegal, the proportions of English and Spanish pottery were roughly the same. This implies some participation in or access to contraband trade. After TPQ 1735, however, the proportion of Spanish wares increased quite dramatically and the English wares decreased equally dramatically. This period (after 1735–40) corresponds to the phase of peak legal availability of English goods through sales of privateer prizes. It appears that members of this family significantly incorporated English ceramics into their household while they were illegal but did not acquire or use nearly as many of the English kitchen wares during the period when they were presumably more available and for sale—whether owing to poverty or to preference. Perhaps once goods became legal and entered the commercial marketplace, they were more costly and difficult to obtain for low-income families.

The household assemblage of Spanish Canary Islander Cristóbal Contreras (at the Fatio site) may suggest yet other kinds of engagement with contraband trade. The archaeological data from the site suggest that the occupants may have engaged in contraband trade—or the acquisition of contraband goods—between the establishment of Charlestown in 1670 and the War of Spanish Succession in 1702. Between those dates there was a steady increase in English tablewares and a steady decrease in Spanish tablewares, in a period during which no legal mechanism for the entry of English goods to the colony existed. This was followed by a sharp reversal in this trend between about TPQ 1700 and TPQ 1725, roughly corresponding to the War of Spanish Succession against England.

As was characteristic of the community-wide trend, the very low proportion of English wares during this period suggests that the war inhibited the site's inhabitants from engaging in (or perhaps from wanting to engage in) trade with the English. The household nevertheless sharply increased its consumption of English ceramics again after TPQ 1725, when English goods became legally available through the sale of English prizes in St. Augustine. Private merchants quite likely did not have access to this government-sanctioned and government-controlled trade and had to rely instead on the legal markets of Havana and Mexico, where Spanish-tradition wares prevailed.

After 1750 English goods were openly and legally available to St. Augustine through arrangement with the Royal Havana Company, which supplied the St. Augustine *situado* goods through official arrangement with merchants in Charlestown and New York. Despite this post-1750 availability of legal English goods through the *situado*, the assemblage from the Contreras merchant shows a decrease in English wares after 1740 and a concomitant increase in Spanish tablewares. In this the household departs from the trends shown at all of the other households (except for that of the mestizo De la Cruz site). This may well be a function of Contreras's merchant status. Private merchants quite likely did not have access to this government-sanctioned and controlled trade and had to rely instead on the legal markets of Havana and Mexico, where Spanish-tradition wares prevailed.

Summary: Household Contraband

Viewing the archaeological assemblages of these individual households through the lens of trade periodicity may suggest how people of diverse origins, occupations, and incomes engaged with contraband trade as part of their economic and social household strategies. Consumption of contraband played out quite differently among the households in this study and seems to have been contingent not only on economic access but also on relative positions of social identity and social privilege and the attitudinal values that reinforced those positions.

It is possible, for example, that members of the old *criollo* families connected to the garrison, as well as the Franciscan friars, may have shared a set of values and practices regarding illicit trade that discouraged their participation in it. This is suggested by the consistently low proportions of non-Spanish wares in their household assemblages during periods when these non-Spanish wares should have been illegal.

Households that differed from the garrison *criollo* mainstream in economic capacity, cultural origin, or occupation, however, did not conform to those practice or, presumably, to garrison *criollo* values regarding contraband. They seem instead to have engaged in contraband trade as a systematic part of their individual household strategies, according to the degree to which they were presented with or excluded from the opportunity do so. The low-income Hispanic-Indian family, for example, seems to have favored foreign goods when they were illegal and not on the open market, possibly because of restricted access to the mainstream economic life of the town. The harbor guard, in contrast to his criollo neighbors, took full advantage of his position to secure foreign goods—both legal and illegal—throughout his occupation, seemingly unhindered by a value system that emphasized legal mandates.

A Cautionary Conclusion

Understanding the ways in which consumption of contraband played out across a diverse community is a truly historical archaeological question that cannot be answered by reference to texts or archaeological material alone. As in the original version of this study (Deagan 2007), however, the conclusions reached in this effort to understand contraband trade through archaeology are couched in methodological caveats and cautions. Many of these are common to all historical archaeological projects, including taphonomic factors operating on sites and document collections, biases in sampling sites and documents, and bias in the compression and quantification of archaeological or documentary observations. But other difficulties are specific to the study of contraband and have to do with the need to organize archaeological data in discrete time intervals that are established through textual information about illicit trade.

The ability to correlate the essentially temporally relative archaeological record with the much more detailed and essentially chronometric periodicity of the textual record is especially problematic. This has largely to do with archaeology's relatively crude tools of chronology that limit the capacity to achieve a precise periodicity of data comparable to that of text-based accounts. Even when working with undisturbed, single-episode deposits, we are normally restricted to such imprecise and relative dating tools as stratigraphy, terminus post quem, midpoints, and formula dates in establishing the chronology of deposits within a site. The most precise of these tools, such as terminus post quem, are in turn biased by our often imperfect understanding of date ranges for material items as well as by issues of time lag, heirlooming, redeposition, disturbance, and so on. Most of us feel fortunate if we can confidently order deposits even in ten-year increments. Despite a theoretical climate that often does not favor "artifact studies," a great deal more research needs to be done in this area in order to achieve a more refined periodicity, as such examples of rigorous primary research have demonstrated (Miller et al. 1999; Noël Hume 2002; Shlasko 1989; Waselkov and Walthall 2002).

That said, the study of illicit commerce in households of eighteenth-century St. Augustine suggests certain reliable conclusions:

1. Archaeological efforts to understand the ways in which the use of contraband reveals social dynamics seem most productive at a household scale of inquiry. Community-wide characterizations are more likely to reify existing textual accounts than to reveal new information. A household focus can reveal how people with specific economic, occupational, religious, ethnic, and social identities engaged in contraband as a strategy, within the larger system of regulations that defined contraband for the community. This can help establish and inform the shape and limits of economic possibility and lead to a more nuanced understanding of the structure, opportunity, and dynamics of economic practice within a community.

2. Practices and expressions of contraband consumption at any scale are highly local. Although all of the Spanish colonies were subject to the same economic policies and trade restrictions, the circumstances of individual places shaped the actual configurations of illicit trade in a manner unique to each community. The strategies used in St. Augustine, Pensacola, Hispaniola, Caracas, and Buenos Aires, for example, were highly distinct, although they all shared the same set of imperial regulations (Cohen 2003; Deagan 1995; Newquist 2011; Roberts 2010; Schávelzon 2000). Local economic

networks, shipping routes, proximity to non-Spanish settlements, and relative isolation from trade centers and international conflicts all shaped the contours of illicit trade for every community. Exploration of similarities and differences in how the households in these communities managed the problem of illicit but necessary economic activity has not yet been carried out through rigorous comparative archaeological analysis, but it offers a potentially productive focus for historical archaeology in the Spanish Americas.

3. Archaeological studies of household and community practice related to illicit trade also hold an untapped potential for framing studies of colonial resistance and economic development related to emergent American identity and, ultimately, the separation of colonies from their imperial centers.

12

Recognizing a Pirate Shipwreck without the Skull and Crossbones

COURTNEY PAGE AND CHARLES R. EWEN

Introduction

The image of a pirate is well ingrained in the minds of the public. Yet many of the stereotypical images—"the [Jolly Roger] flag, eye patch, wooden leg, and hook" (Babits et al. 2006:274)—are just not good indicators of a pirate (and do not preserve in the underwater environment anyway). Piracy is a behavioral act and does not survive physically in the archaeological record (Babits et al. 2006:276). Because pirates differ from merchants primarily in the legality of their actions, the difference in what was owned by a pirate and what was owned by a merchant is difficult to discern. Pirate attire appears very similar to the clothing of other mariners. Pirates followed the changing fashions just as merchants and naval officers did (Babits 2001:9). Possessions such as tobacco pipes and wine bottles may not look any different on a pirate ship than they do on a merchant ship. But they may differ in quantity.

Rather than analyzing differences in individual artifact types as an indicator of piracy, this chapter explores the possibility of using the differences in artifact frequency or patterning to illuminate the behavioral differences between the crews of pirate and nonpirate ships. We look at the artifact assemblages of the pirate vessels *Queen Anne's Revenge* (1718) and *Whydah* (1717), dating to the Golden Age of Piracy (ca. 1680–1730), and contemporary nonpirate ships: the naval ship HMS *Invincible* (1758) and the slave ship *Henrietta Marie* (1700) (table 12.1). We hypothesize that artifacts representing illicit commercial and aggressive behavior will have the highest frequency among pirate vessels.

Table 12.1. Categories Used to Organize Artifact Assemblages and Artifact Types in Each Category

Category	Artifact Type
Arms and armament	Ammunition, artillery, personal arms
Personal effects	Clothing, pastimes, tobacco items, accessory, jewelry, toiletries
Cargo	Container, treasure, jewelry, commodity, community use
Kitchen	Tableware, galley/storage
Tools and instruments	Fabric working, maintenance, navigation and surveying, fishing, medicinal, sharpening, miscellaneous

History

Queen Anne's Revenge

After starting out as a French privateer in 1710, *La Concorde* operated as a French slave ship between 1713 and 1718 (Wilde-Ramsing 2009:109–11). In July 1717 *La Concorde* left Africa on its third voyage with at least five hundred African slaves, bound for Martinique. In November 1717 pirates under the command of Edward Teach, more commonly known as Blackbeard, captured the vessel near the island of St. Vincent, releasing the French crew and many of the slaves on the island of Bequia and providing them with a smaller sloop (Lusardi 2006:196; Wilde-Ramsing 2009:114). Keeping the larger slave ship and many of the slaves for himself, Blackbeard increased the armament of the vessel and changed the name to *Queen Anne's Revenge*, sailing it as his flagship for about seven months. Upon arrival at Topsail Inlet off the coast of Beaufort, North Carolina, in June 1718, the ship ran aground and wrecked on an outer sandbar (Lusardi 2006:197).

The wreck was discovered in 1996 off the Beaufort Inlet in North Carolina by treasure salvors searching for a Spanish treasure ship (figure 12.1). Control of the project was turned over to the North Carolina Underwater Archaeology Branch, which began systematic excavation and research in the fall of 1997. Excavation, conservation, and data analysis have been ongoing since then (Wilde-Ramsing 2006:164–66). An assemblage of over 240,000 artifacts was used for this research.

262 · Courtney Page and Charles R. Ewen

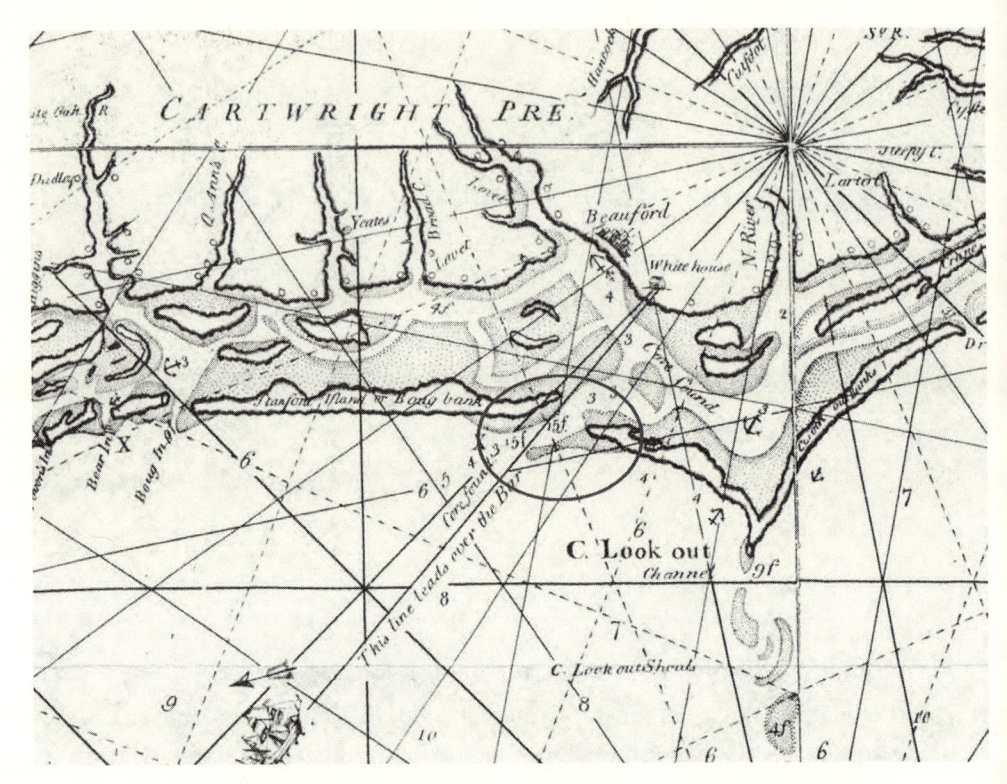

Figure 12.1. Approximate location of the wreck of *Queen Anne's Revenge* on James Wimble's 1738 map of eastern North Carolina (Digital Collections, East Carolina University, http://digital.lib.ecu.edu/1068).

Whydah

The history of the *Whydah* paralleled the *Queen Anne's Revenge* in many respects. It, too, was a slave ship operating between England and Africa and the Caribbean. After completing the first two legs of a voyage in February of 1717, *Whydah* was returning home loaded with sugar, indigo, quinine, and revenues from slave sales when it was captured by "Black" Samuel Bellamy in the northern Bahamas. Bellamy, like Blackbeard, set the *Whydah* crew free and sailed north along the coast of North America, headed for Richmond Island in present-day Maine. But the *Whydah* came to a much more violent end. In late April 1717 the vessel became caught in a heavy northeaster. Winds smashed the vessel into a shoal and capsized it. Only two crew members survived the wreck (C. Hamilton 2006:131–32).

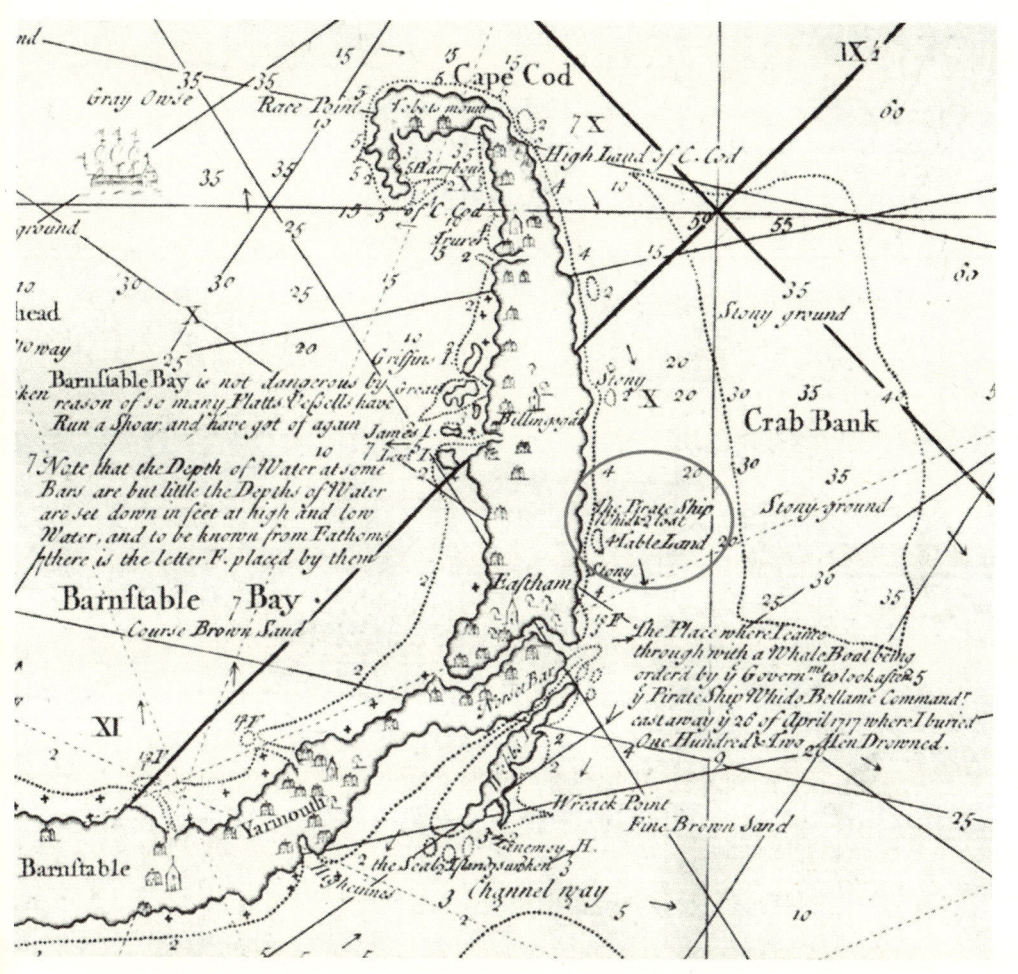

Figure 12.2. Approximate location of the wreck of *Whydah* off the coast of Cape Cod on Cyprian Southack's map of the New England coast. The specific location of the wreck was marked by Southack, just east of Eastham (Norman B. Leventhal Map Center, Boston Public Library, http://maps.bpl.org/id/10064).

Again like *Queen Anne's Revenge*, *Whydah* was discovered by treasure salvors (figure 12.2). The search for the wreck of *Whydah* began in 1978, and archaeological testing occurred between 1983 and 1987. Full excavation began in 1988, with recovery of 21,000 artifacts in the first field season alone (C. Hamilton 2006:134–35). By 1992 the project had recovered over 106,000 artifacts.

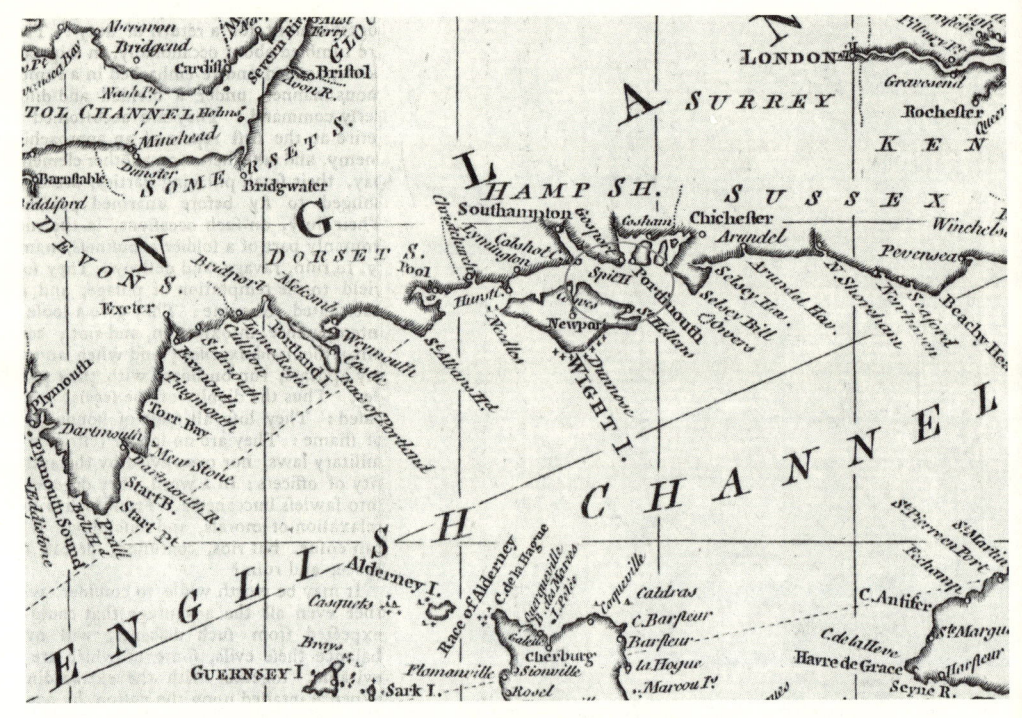

Figure 12.3. Approximate location of the wreck of HMS *Invincible* in the Solent Straight near Portsmouth, England, on Thomas Kitchin's 1758 map of the English Channel (Open Access Maps, New York Public Library, http://maps.nypl.org/warper/maps/13910).

HMS *Invincible*

The HMS *Invincible* was a French-built naval ship, completed and launched in 1744. It was captured by British admiral Lord George Anson in 1747 near Cape Finisterre, on the west coast of Spain. Because the ship was the second of a new design of French 74-gun naval ships considered superior to the English naval ships, it was utilized as a model for English ship construction (Bingeman 2010:6–7). *Invincible* was considered an unlucky ship, as several damaging incidents occurred over the ship's lifespan. The final incident happened as the vessel left Portsmouth: an anchor became stuck, and strong winds and waves caused the ship to run aground on Horse Sand Tail in the Solent Straight, off the coast of England (Bingeman 1981:154–55).

The wreck was discovered in May 1979 by a fisher in the Solent Straight (figure 12.3). The remains of the shipwreck were later identified in 1981 by

Commander John Bingeman, who directed the excavation. Artifacts were recovered during the summer of 1979, but official excavation did not begin until May 1980 in partnership with Bingeman (Bingeman 1981:155–56). A complete inventory of the excavation from 1980 to 1991 contains over 10,000 artifacts.

Henrietta Marie

The *Henrietta Marie* first appears in the documentary record in 1697, marking the ship's voyage from London to the Bight of Biafra and then to Barbados. It arrived in Barbados in July 1698, successfully returning to London at the end of that year. The Barbados shipping records state that *Henrietta Marie* was a foreign-built, London-registered vessel. At this time the ship was considered an "interloper": an independent slave ship operating outside the monopoly of the Royal African Company. In 1698, however, the "Act to Settle the Trade to Africa" imposed a 10 percent tax on the cargo of all independent slave ships to be paid to the Royal African Company (Moore and Malcolm 2008:26–27). Under this tax, *Henrietta Marie* made a second slave voyage, arriving in Jamaica in May 1700. On the return voyage to England the ship ran aground on New Ground Reef in the Dry Tortugas, off Key West, Florida (Moore and Malcolm 2008:21).

The wreck of *Henrietta Marie* was discovered in 1972 by treasure salvors (figure 12.4) during the search for the Spanish treasure galleon *Nuestra Señora de Atocha*. Onsite investigations continued through 1973, but excavation was suspended after that season to focus work on the discovered *Atocha*. A subcontractor of the original company picked up excavations in 1983, recommencing excavations that April, with a second subcontractor continuing through March 1985. Thereafter work continued sporadically until September 1991. Six years of excavation yielded over 1,100 artifacts.

Methodology

For an effective comparison of the patterns of onboard behavior for each vessel, the assemblages were divided into categories based on the functional attributes of the artifacts that reflect their crew's behavioral activity. The categories for this study are based on the organizational categories developed for the *Queen Anne's Revenge* project (Wilde-Ramsing 2009:95–100). The analysis of these artifacts makes it possible to discern patterns in the artifact assemblages by vessel and compare and contrast them.

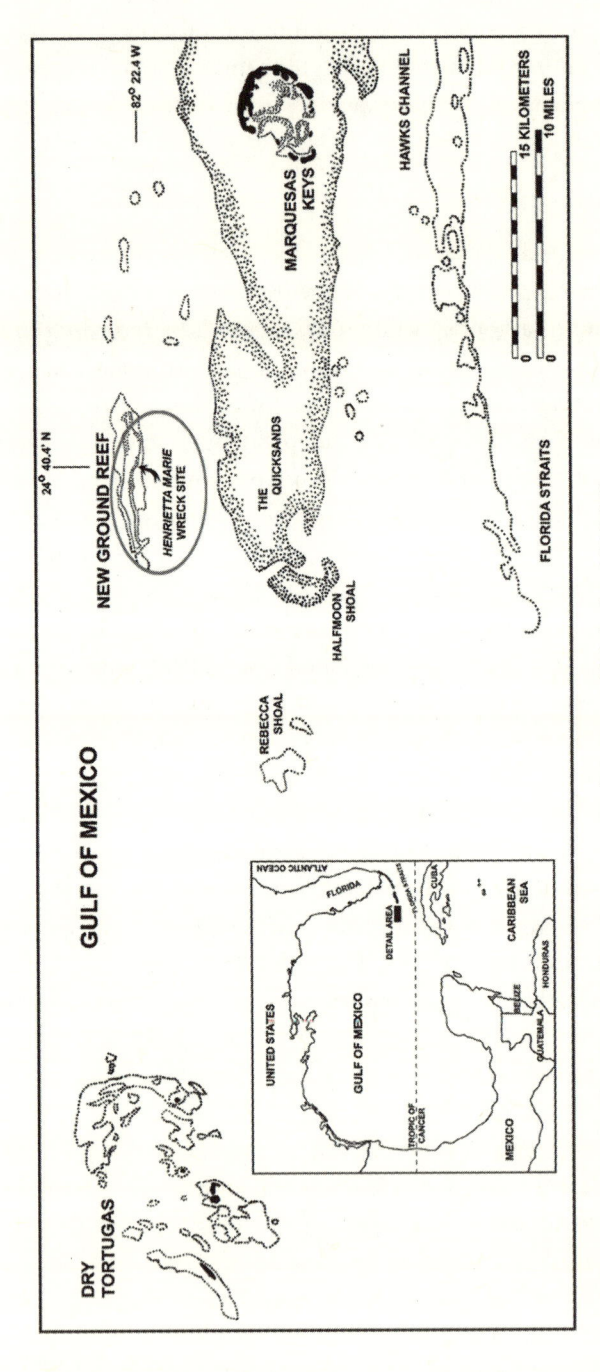

Figure 12.4. Location of the wreck of *Henrietta Marie* (Moore and Malcolm 2008:22).

Artifact Categories

The category Arms and Armament contains things related to weaponry, including ammunition, cannon, and cannon accessories (ramrod, vent pick, tompion, apron, and so forth) and personal arms (firearms and edged weapons). This category reflects the offensive and defensive capabilities of the ship and its crew.

The category Personal Effects contains items that would have been privately owned and used by an individual, excluding small arms. Personal attire in the form of jewelry and clothing, smoking and recreational materials, and writing accoutrements are all included in this group. These artifacts may suggest the status of the crew or the types of personal belongings that they possessed as well as their personal habits.

The category Cargo Items includes wooden and ceramic storage containers, treasure (coins, gold dust, ingots, and so forth), commodities (including slaves, as represented by shackles), and items for community use (chamber pots and hammock parts).

The category Kitchen contains artifacts involved in food preparation and consumption: cooking and serving materials, faunal remains, and fuel. The variety and volume of these objects found on a ship may reveal the status of the crew members and their standard of living in board ship.

The category Tools and Instruments covers a wide variety of materials associated with activities aboard the ship. Tools related to ship maintenance, medicine, navigation, sharpening, fishing, sewing, and navigation are included in this group. The proportions of these categories of artifacts may suggest the extent to which the crew members had to obtain their own food or keep their tools and ship functional. Artifacts related to the architecture and basic functioning of the ship (such as wood planks, sail cloth, and rigging) were excluded from this study because they are necessary to all ships, regardless of type. The artifact inventories from the four shipwrecks were analyzed and the artifact assemblages compared by type and category.

Totals for each artifact type, subcategory, and category were obtained. A percentage value was calculated for each subcategory within the overarching category for intrasite comparisons. The proportion represented for each category was calculated for intersite comparisons. Because of the overwhelming percentage of ammunition artifacts in the assemblages, the logarithm of each overarching category was derived to discern finer-grained differences.

Important Considerations

Several variables in this study were difficult to control. The sizes of the artifact assemblage and their dates were problematic, given the limited availability of published reports on early eighteenth century wrecks. Ethnicity has been limited to British crews, but the dates during which these ships operated and the locations to which they sailed were somewhat varied.

Factors such as how the ship wrecked and what happened to the site in the ensuing years alter the types and frequencies of artifacts that occur on each shipwreck. The initial process of wrecking affects the number and distribution of artifacts. For example, the *Whydah* was torn apart in a violent storm and is now spread across an area of about one acre (C. Hamilton 2006:131). In extreme cases of surface disintegration, the more buoyant items do not have a chance to become waterlogged and will float away from the wreck (Muckelroy 1978:166). The *Queen Anne's Revenge* and HMS *Invincible*, in contrast, ran aground, making it possible for the crew members to take objects with them as they left or to return for important or valuable items shortly after the grounding. After some time those porous items that remained trapped inside the ship would become waterlogged and sink (Muckelroy 1978:166).

A study by Keith Muckelroy (1978:163–64) of wrecks in the British Isles suggests that the topography and the texture of the sedimentary deposits (coarse gravel or fine sand) of the seabed where the wreck occurred correlate strongly with the preservation quality of archaeological remains. Those sites deposited on a seabed with a low slope and finer sediments are more likely to preserve archaeological remains relatively intact. The general aquatic environment, such as water temperature, favors the preservation of some perishable artifacts, such as clothing or wooden objects. The *Whydah* and HMS *Invincible* are found in cooler waters in the northern Atlantic, while the *Queen Anne's Revenge* and *Henrietta Marie* lie farther south in the much warmer Gulf Stream. Hurricanes, natural seabed movements, and dredging displace artifacts, which negatively affects their preservation and recovery.

Scavenging or salvaging of the wrecks for valuable items by contemporary locals and later sport-divers during the 200-plus years since deposition also skews the artifact frequencies. The degree to which salvaging affects the site is related to its location and depth. Greater depths in remote locations are more accessible in modern times with sophisticated methods, while a shallow and visible wreck would not likely be left alone (Muckelroy

1978:166). Finally, the excavation techniques and duration for each project affect the quantity of artifacts recovered and the quality of the record-keeping. Still, these caveats apply to most archaeological projects. While they definitely affect the comparisons made, any significant differences between the assemblages should be apparent and suggestive of the need for further investigation.

Results

As expected, the Arms and Armament category for the pirate ships and naval vessels has percentages of greater than 80 percent of their total assemblage. The merchant ship has a percentage less than 50 percent, which is much smaller than that of the other vessels, although it is still the largest category. *Henrietta Marie* has the highest frequency of cargo-related artifacts (over 23 percent). *Queen Anne's Revenge* and HMS *Invincible* have a frequency of about 6 percent, while *Whydah* has a frequency over twice that of its pirate comparison (table 12.2; figure 12.5). Although the remainder of the *Henrietta Marie* assemblage is noticeably different, the variations in the Personal Effects, Kitchen, and Tools and Instruments categories for the *Queen Anne's Revenge*, *Whydah*, and HMS *Invincible* are more difficult to discern. Because the data are swamped by the large percentage values of the Arms and Armament category among these three ships (table 12.2), the logarithm of all categories was taken to reduce the noise and better define other patterns (figures 12.6 and 12.7).

Table 12.2. Artifact Frequencies for Each Shipwreck (in Percentages)

	Queen Anne's Revenge	Whydah	HMS Invincible	Henrietta Marie
Arms and armament	92.765	83.574	81.315	41.696
Personal effects	0.032	0.329	4.015	0.524
Cargo	6.779	15.698	6.042	23.164
Kitchen	0.317	0.164	3.040	32.255
Tools and instruments	0.107	0.235	5.589	2.360

270 · Courtney Page and Charles R. Ewen

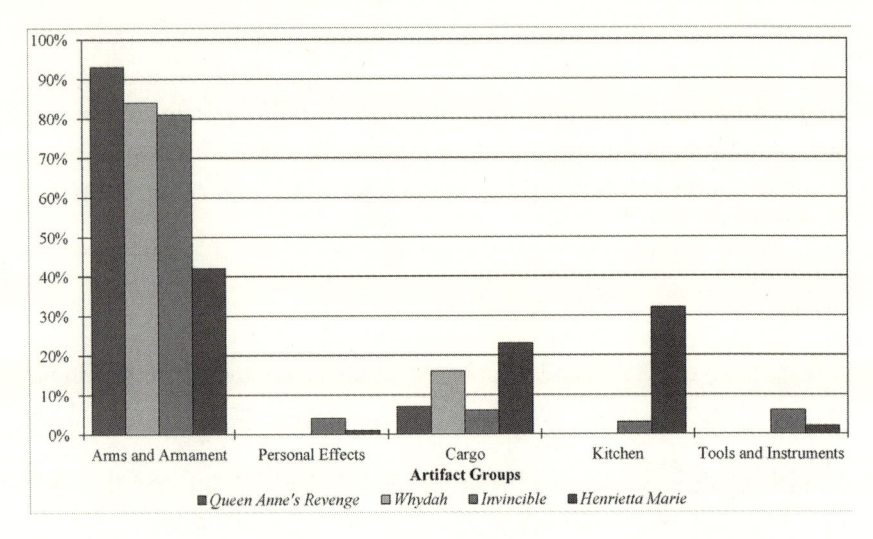

Figure 12.5. Graphic representation of artifact frequencies for each shipwreck by category.

A base 10 logarithmic value equals the exponent by which 10 is multiplied to obtain the original value. The equation is used to reduce the range of difference between category values. With the logarithms displayed, the patterns (if they exist) become more apparent (figure 12.8). The frequency of Personal Effects artifacts appears more similar among the *Queen Anne's*

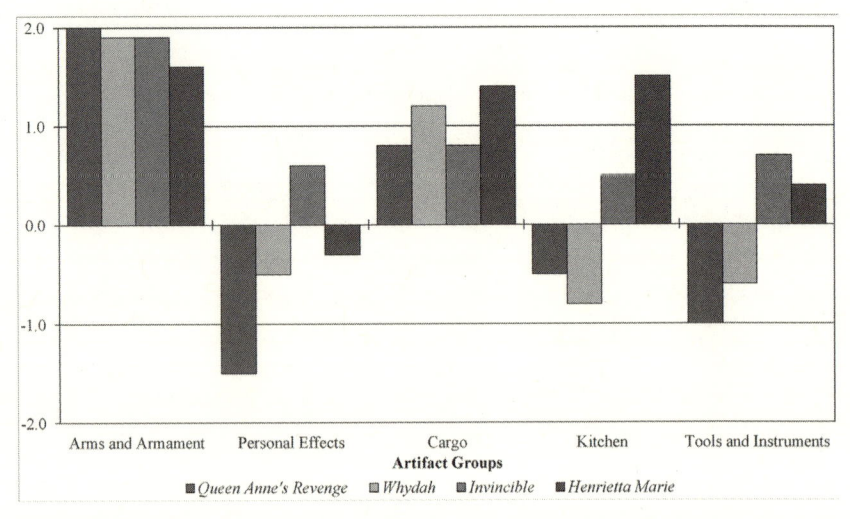

Figure 12.6. Graphic representation of the logarithm of artifact frequencies for each shipwreck by category.

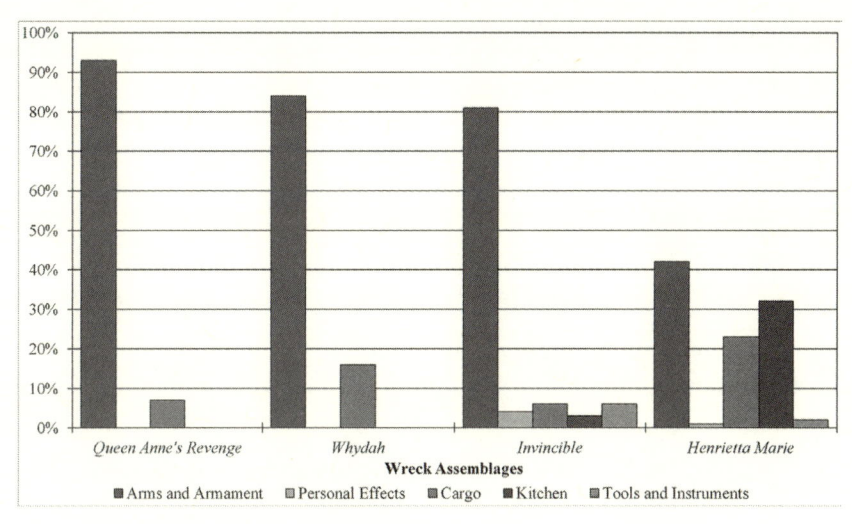

Figure 12.7. Artifact frequencies by ship.

Revenge, *Whydah*, and *Henrietta Marie* assemblages, but the frequency of Personal Effects artifacts of HMS *Invincible* is greater (table 12.3). While the frequencies of artifacts of the Kitchen and Tool and Instruments categories of the pirate assemblages differ, all the frequencies are less than the frequencies of the naval and merchant ship assemblages.

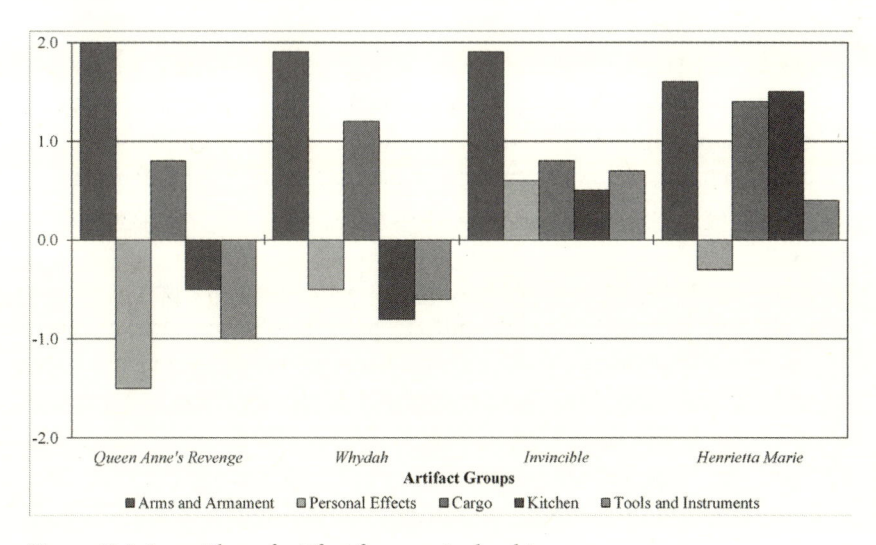

Figure 12.8. Logarithm of artifact frequencies by ship.

Table 12.3. Logarithm of Artifact Frequencies for Each Shipwreck

	Queen Anne's Revenge	Whydah	HMS Invincible	Henrietta Marie
Arms and armament	1.967	1.922	1.910	1.620
Personal effects	-1.494	-0.483	0.604	-0.280
Cargo	0.831	1.196	0.781	1.365
Kitchen	-0.499	-0.785	0.483	1.509
Tools and instruments	-0.971	-0.628	0.747	0.373

Discussion and Conclusions

When considered across all categories, the assemblage of the *Henrietta Marie* appears the most different of the four vessels. While similarities are apparent between the pirate and naval ship assemblages, the *Queen Anne's Revenge* and *Whydah* are more similar to each other than either is to HMS *Invincible*. This becomes more evident after a visual examination of the frequency logarithms (figure 12.8). An Arms and Armament artifact frequency greater than 80 percent shared by the *Queen Anne's Revenge*, *Whydah*, and HMS *Invincible* seems to suggest their similar aggressive function. The *Henrietta Marie*, however, has an Arms and Armament artifact frequency of less than 50 percent (though it is still its highest category). While merchant ships would need to be armed enough for defense, their main purpose was commerce, and traded cannon space for larger cargo capacity.

The artifact frequencies for the Cargo category are more similar for the *Queen Anne's Revenge*, *Whydah*, and HMS *Invincible* than for the *Henrietta Marie*. A consideration of the artifact frequencies within that category, however, shows differences between the ship functions. Treasure (gold and silver artifacts) represents over 88 percent of the artifacts of the Cargo category for the *Whydah* and the *Queen Anne's Revenge* but less than 1 percent of HMS *Invincible* artifacts in this category, which consist almost entirely of containers (barrel pieces and ceramic vessel sherds), suggesting a need for storage space. Items in the Cargo category on the *Henrietta Marie* are represented by only 11 percent treasure, while the rest of the artifacts in this category are heavily represented by shackles and a few elephant tusks (over 76 percent). This seems to suggest the commercial function of the merchant ship, while the pirate ships would need to balance cargo capacity with offensive capability.

The significant difference in Cargo artifact frequencies between the *Whydah* and the *Queen Anne's Revenge* may be a factor of the wrecking process. While treasure artifacts represent over 85 percent of both Cargo assemblages, over 50 percent of the *Whydah* treasure consists of coins, which went down with the ship, whereas 98 percent of the *Queen Anne's Revenge* treasure is gold dust, which would be difficult for sailors to recover. The grounding of the *Queen Anne's Revenge* would have allowed the sailors to retrieve their coins and as much of the valuable gold dust as possible, leaving behind only small grains that had fallen into the cracks of the ship.

While pirate ship assemblages may differ from those of other types of shipwrecks, it is not possible to discern a definitive artifact pattern for pirate shipwrecks based on these data. Though the sample size is inadequate, this study represents an initial assessment of a collection of data that can be modified and corrected as additional comparable shipwrecks are excavated and more data are collected. A sample size of two is hardly a definitive representation of pirate ships, but it can serve as the basis for further research when studying ships of unknown function or identity. With more data, a clearer pattern may be developed that can provide a basis not only for vessel identification but also for studying behavioral distinctions within this special population of seafarers.

13

Parting Shot

CHARLES R. EWEN

> In an honest service there is thin commons, low wages, and hard labor; in this, plenty and satiety, pleasure and ease, liberty and power; and who would not balance creditor on this side, when all the hazard that is run for it, at worst, is only a sour look or two at choking. No, a merry life and a short one, shall be my motto.
> Bartholomew "Black Bart" Roberts (Johnson 1972:244)

The thread running through our previous volume, *X Marks the Spot*, was how can you tell a pirate from an ordinary sailor? What is it that distinguishes the pirate in the archaeological record? The underlying theme continues in this volume. Do we reach a definitive answer? No, but I think that after reading the preceding chapters we are closer to being able to appreciate and study piracy in the past.

Again, this volume is not so much a history of piracy as an anthropology of piracy. It is a study of piracy from its material culture and linking those artifacts to past behaviors. You might think of the cases in this book as episodes in the series *CSI: Tortuga*, as archaeologists pore over the material evidence to answer questions about the nature of pirate ships and those who sailed them.

Some sites (such as *Queen Anne's Revenge*, *Fiery Dragon*, and *Ranger*) discussed in *X Marks the Spot* are revisited in this volume. This was a result of more work and a firmer identification of the wrecks. Establishing the identity of the wrecks allowed more and different questions to be asked. New discoveries have been added as well. Most of the effort, however, was spent in establishing the identity of Captain Kidd's *Quedagh Merchant*, Black Bart's *Ranger*, and Henry Morgan's vessel.

As the data from positively identified pirate sites accumulate, researchers have been able to delve more deeply into what it means to be a pirate. The last five chapters in this book examine the idiosyncrasies of pirate life in both fact and fiction and attempt to find some commonalities among all pirates.

Revisiting Wrecks

The second chapter revisits the wreck of the alleged *Queen Anne's Revenge*, Blackbeard's flagship. In *X Marks the Spot* we presented two chapters on this wreck that argued for and against the identification with the notorious pirate. Now Mark U. Wilde-Ramsing and Linda F. Carnes-McNaughton present a compelling case that the intervening years have indeed produced a preponderance of evidence linking the wreck to Blackbeard. With the identity established, they address questions concerning the status and ethnicity of the crew members and what life may have been like on a pirate ship.

John de Bry and Marco Roling give us an update on the *Fiery Dragon*, further confirming its identity and exploring other wrecks in the area. They provide the setting for piracy in the latter days of the Golden Age of Piracy, when it had moved from the Caribbean to the Indian Ocean. It is interesting to note the parallels between the lives of pirates in these widely divergent locales, giving some credence to the existence of a "pirate pattern" that characterizes their lifestyle.

The story of Black Bart's *Ranger* told by Chad M. Gulseth is technically a new one, but we did cover Port Royal in the last volume. This chapter shows how archaeology, when combined with a study of the historical record, can tell us a larger story than either considered individually. It also gives us the rest of the story of how Port Royal survived the devastating earthquake only to suffer further catastrophes decades later.

New Discoveries

The tale of the discovery and identification of the *Quedagh Merchant* is much like that of the *Queen Anne's Revenge*. Frederick H. Hanselmann and Charles D. Beeker examine the historic evidence and then test the archaeological evidence against it. The identification of East Indian materials and construction techniques makes a compelling case for the ship being the *Quedagh Merchant*. As such it serves as a tangible link to the incredible story of the rise and fall of William Kidd.

Henry Morgan's raid on Panama was certainly one of the signature moments in the history of the Golden Age of Piracy. Frederick H. Hanselmann,

Tomás Mendizábal, and Juan G. Martín provide a thorough retelling of the sacking of Panama as well as the early exploits that made Henry Morgan's reputation and eventually resulted in his knighthood. The ongoing archaeology, while not yet rewriting history, is beginning to scale back some of the hyperbole and correct the historical record.

When we think of the Golden Age of Pirates, it takes place in the southern Atlantic/Caribbean from the later seventeenth century into the early eighteenth century. Connie Kelleher tells of an earlier Golden Age in the north Atlantic. Her contribution on pirates in Ireland represents early work on a hitherto little studied arena of piracy. Here she calls upon the documentary record and what has been revealed on previous sites as perhaps the only way to connect these locales with piracy.

Pirate Life

"Shiver Me Timbers!" examines pirate stereotypes through time as they are portrayed in literature and film. These images, which mostly derive from Robert Louis Stevenson's *Treasure Island*, are impossible to shake. But are they wrong? Probably not entirely, as we find out, but they could apply to many sailors of the period. They were a scruffy lot. The following chapters on pirate life look at the artifacts and iconography that are attributed to "real" pirates.

Heather Hatch looked at one of the most iconic of all pirate characteristics, the Jolly Roger. She goes beyond the mere emblems of a pirate ship to analyze their meaning and uses. She also avoids the general assignment of flags to particular pirates, discussing their symbolic meaning to piracy in general and how they were used to distinguish friend from foe.

The late Kenneth J. Kinkor continues the examination of the symbolism of pirate flags as well as a bit more obscure iconography. He discusses graffiti and images scratched onto artifacts recovered from the pirate ship *Whydah*. Some Masonic symbols are clearly present, which Kinkor also connects to the Jacobite Uprising in Scotland. While his suggestion is not conclusive, he certainly offers plenty to keep conspiracy theorists busy looking into the connections of Jacobitism, Freemasonry, and piracy.

Kathleen Deagan reverses the perspective: from the pirates to their victims or, in the case of St. Augustine, customers. This is a cautionary tale on being careful not to use the archaeological record uncritically. Fortunately, the archaeology and the documentary research conducted at Saint

Augustine have been meticulous, allowing Deagan to determine when the presence of non-Spanish items was the product of illegal activity as opposed to secondary trade. The result is a picture of how pirates were tolerated by the residents of that remote Spanish outpost and even welcomed by some.

Courtney Page and I attempt to distinguish a pirate from an ordinary sailor. This might be possible by defining a "pirate pattern" in the artifacts. No single artifact by itself would identify a pirate or a ship. Unfortunately, the sample size for pirate ships is low, and no pattern jumps out. Future pirate finds may add to the database, making a pattern more apparent. Or perhaps a true historical archaeological approach will always be necessary, combining archaeological and historical records to identify these pirate sites. Unfortunately, not all potential sites are found and excavated by archaeologists.

Investigating Pirate Sites

In *X Marks the Spot* we noted that working with treasure hunters was something that most archaeologists would only do under duress. Many view the word "collaboration" with the same disdain that the French Resistance felt during World War II. To be a collaborator becomes a mark of shame rather than cooperation. This antipathy is something that the average history buff has trouble comprehending. Perhaps a historical analogy with the eighteenth-century Caribbean might make this conflict more understandable.

Let us equate data with treasure. For the archaeologist that is exactly what treasure is: a category of data that helps us understand the site. The treasure can indicate a wreck's identity, chronological placement, place of origin, route, nationality, and even destination. In short, it helps the archaeologist learn more about the site and its inhabitants. Archaeologists analyze, interpret, and publish the data. This is their currency in the business of academia. Archaeologists can be equated with royal governments who regulate the trade in knowledge and keep it in circulation.

Treasure salvors operate outside of the controls of the realm of academia. They also see data as treasure, but it is their use of the data and its disposition that bother the archaeologists. The treasure salvors see themselves as privateers, going after treasure that would be lost to the elements or in environments too costly for the academic archaeologist to recover. They are willing to share the data with the Crown (the archaeological regulators), but their cut is the treasure itself. Rather than being reviled, they feel that they should be knighted or at least accepted as peers of the realm for recovering these data.

The archaeologists, in contrast, see the treasure hunters not as allies in the quest to preserve the data but as pirates who are only in it for themselves and thus deprive the academy and the general public of the treasure that is theirs by right. The data are removed from circulation, often by means that compromise the integrity of the sites. The consequences of these activities by these treasure hunters are as scary to the archaeologist as Blackbeard was to commercial shipping in the Caribbean and along the eastern seaboard of North America.

For many treasure hunters the concern for context is overridden by the concern for treasure. To archaeologists the context of the artifact/treasure is paramount. Context provides meaning. Destroying the context through expedient recovery methods results in the loss of much of the wreck's story. The dispersal of the artifacts through sale to disparate parties compounds the loss and makes it impossible to reanalyze the artifacts when new questions and techniques arise.

The penalty for collaborating with treasure hunters is very nearly as dire as the penalty for collaborating with pirates in the eighteenth century. No archaeologists are killed, but their careers often are. Many archaeologists feel so strongly about the preservation of the data that those who seek to remove it from circulation are not allowed to publish in scholarly journals or to present papers on their work at professional conferences lest others think that they, too, can loot underwater wrecks. Thus we have a situation with little middle ground. Those archaeologists who have sought to work with treasure hunters in order to recover data that would otherwise be lost have found themselves consigned to the fate that befell Captain William Kidd. Kidd was initially recruited to hunt pirates but fell afoul of circumstances and politics and was hung as a pirate himself. The careers of some archaeological colleagues in essence have been executed, tarred with an ethical brush, and hung up as a warning to those who would dare usurp the data.

Fortunately, the data in this volume are not ill-gotten gains. Russ and I, for the moment, are safe from the gibbet. The chapters once again have demonstrated how difficult it is to identify a pirate site without both archaeology and the historical record. Our authors also show that we have much to learn about the lives of pirates, which tended to be, as "Black Bart"

Roberts is supposed to have said, short but merry. The Golden Age of Piracy may have been too short to leave a fully developed pirate culture that is clearly recognizable in the archaeological record. Still, with so few pirate sites upon which to draw, every new site brings us new insights. Perhaps a more definitive "pirate pattern" will emerge in the next volume.

References Cited

Abbreviations

APC	*Acts of the Privy Council*, Cornell University Library, Ithaca, N.Y.
BL	British Library, London, UK
BNA	British National Archives and Maritime Museum, Portsmouth, UK
CAOM	Centre des Archives d'Outre-Mer, Aix-en-Provence, France
CSPCS	*Calendar of State Papers: Colonial Series*
DNA	Dutch National Archives, The Hague, Netherlands
HCA	High Court of Admiralty Papers, The National Archives, London, UK
IOR	India Office Records, Public Record Office, London, United Kingdom
PRO CO	Public Record Office, Colonial Office Papers, London, UK
SHD	Service Historique de la Défense, Vincennes, France
TNA CO	The National Archives of the United Kingdom (formerly Public Record Office), Colonial Office Papers, London, UK

Archives

British Library, London, UK (BL)
British National Archives and Maritime Museum, UK (BNA)
    ADM 1/2242
    ADM 51/954
    ADM L/S/564
    CO 137/14
    T 70/4
    T 70/922
    T 701225
Centre des Archives d'Outre-Mer, Aix-en-Provence, France (CAOM)
Dutch National Archives, The Hague, Netherlands (DNA)
High Court of Admiralty Papers, The National Archives, London, UK (HCA>
    HCA 1/47, fol. 24v: *Deposition of William Hull, 1609.*
    HCA 1/47, fol. 65: *Examination of Richard Parker of London, 13 December 1609.*
    HCA 13/226, fol. 137: *Mayor and Aldermen of Bristol to Sir Daniel Dun Judge of the High Court of Admiralty, 20 September 1610.*
    HCA 13/226, fol. 338: *Deposition of Edward Davenant, 1 October 1614.*

India Office Records, Public Record Office, Kew, United Kingdom (IOR)
Public Record Office, Colonial Office Papers, London, UK (PRO CO)
Service Historique de la Défense, Vincennes, France (SHD)
The National Archives of the United Kingdom, Colonial Office, London, UK (TNA CO)

Documentary Sources

Acts of the Privy Council, March 25, 1723. Public Record Office, London.

Anonymous. 1701. *The Arraignment, Tryal, and Condemnation of Captain William Kidd for Murther and Piracy*. London: J. Nutt.

Atkins, John. 1723. *A Full and Exact Account of the Tryal of All the Pyrates, Lately Taken by Captain Ogle, on Board the Swallow Man of War, on the Coast of Guinea*. Warwick, England: Privately Printed by J. Roberts.

———. 1735. *A Voyage to Guinea, Brazil, and the West-Indies; In His Majesty's Ships, the Swallow and Weymouth*. Reprint London: Frank Cass, 1970.

By the King: A Proclamation against Pirats, 1608. London: Deputies of Robert Barker, Printer to the Kings Majestie: http://eebo.chadwyck.com.elib.tcd.ie/search.

By the King: A Proclamation for the Search and Apprehension of Certaine Pirates, Giuen at our Pallace of Westminster the xij.Day of Nouember 1604. London: Robert Barker, Printer. 2nd ed.: Society of Antiquaries, STC/8363, STC/1875:25: http://eebo.chadwyck.com.elib.tcd.ie/search.

Deposition of William Hull: 22 October 1642. Trinity College Library. Deposition ID: 839001: 824253r225: http://www.1641.tcd.ie.

Dosset, Pierre. 1718. *La Concord de Nantes* Plundered and Taken by Pirates. Archives Départementales de Loire-Atlantique, Série B 4578, fols. 56v–57v. Nantes, France.

Duke of Buccleuch and Queensberry MSS: Report on the Manuscripts of the Duke of Buccleuch and Queensberry, Preserved at Montagu House, Whitehall, 1, 1483–1778: http://sources.tannerritchie.com.elib.tcd.ie.

Ernaut, François. 1718. *La Concorde de Nantes* Plundered and Taken by Pirates. Archives Départementales de Loire-Atlantique, Série B 4578, fols. 56v–57v. Nantes, France.

Falconer, William. 1780. *A Universal Dictionary of Marine: Or a Copious Explanation of the Technical Terms and Phrases Employed in the Construction, Equipment, Furniture, Machinery, Movements, and Military Operations of a Ship*. Reprinted as *Falconer's Marine Dictionary* in 1970. New York: Augustus M. Kelley.

Gerritszoon, H., and John Hunt. 1612. *Beschrijvinghe van de Zeecusten ende Havenen van Yerlandt/Description of the Seacoasts and Ports of Ireland*. Georg-August-Universität, SUB Göttingen, 4 H BRIT P III, 6 RARA: 23 pages, including 4 charts of Ireland.

Hawkins, Richard. 1724. Letter of Richard Hawkins to One of His Owners April 24, 1724. In *The Political State of Great Britain for the Year 1724*, edited by Abel Boyer, pp. 147–51. Vol. 28. London: T. Warner.

Johnson, Charles. 1972 [first published in 1724]. *A General History of the Robberies and Murders of the Most Notorious Pirates*. Edited by Manuel Schonhorn. Columbia: University of South Carolina Press.

Luntley, Richard. 1721. *The Last Speech and Dying Words, of Richard Luntley, Carpenter Aboard the Eagle Snow, Who Was Executed within the Floodmark at Leith, upon the 11th January 1721, for the Crimes of Piracy and Robbery*. Edinburgh: n.p.

Mesnier, Charles. 1717. A Letter from the Intendant of Martinique Describing the Capture of *La Concorde*, December 10. AN Col C8a (8A) 22 (171) Fo447. Centre des Archives d'Outre-Mer, Aix-en-Provence, France.

Moseley, Edward. 1733. A New and Correct Map of the Province of North Carolina by Edward Moseley, Late Surveyor General of the Said Province 1733, Showing Settlements, Inhabitants, Soil Conditions, Rivers, and Principal Products, with Insets Showing "Port Brunswick or Cape Fear Harbour," "Port Beaufort or Topsail Inlet," "Ocacock (Ocracoke) Inlet," "Explanation," and "Directions for Ocacock (Ocracoke) Inlet." North Carolina Department of Archives and History, Raleigh.

Piracy Act 1613 (11, 12, and 13 Jas I, c. 2, 1613–15): http://www.irishstatutebook.ie/isbc/pui1613.html.

Puente, Elixio de la. 1764. Plano de la Real Fuerza, baluarte y línea de la Plaza de St. Augustín de la Florida. Manuscript copy, P. K. Yonge Library of Florida History, University of Florida, Gainesville.

Snelgrave, William. 1734. *A New Account of Some Parts of Guinea and the Slave-Trade.* Reprint London: Frank Cass and Co., 1971.

South Carolina Court of Vice-Admiralty. 1719. *The Tryals of Major Stede Bonnet and Other Pirates.* London: Benjamin Cowse.

Stafford, Thomas. 1633. *Pacata Hibernia or a History of the Wars in Ireland during the Reign of Queen Elizabeth, 1602.* Edited by Standish O'Grady. Reprint London: Downey and Company, 1896.

The Trials of Eight Persons Indited for Piracy & c. of Whom Two Were Acquitted, and the Rest Found Guilty: At a Judiciary Court of Admiralty Assembled and Held in Boston, within His Majesty's Province of the Massachusetts Bay in New England, on the Eighteenth of October 1717, and by Several Adjournments Continued to the 30th. Pursuant to His Majesty's Commission and Instructions, Founded on the Act of Parliament Made in the 11th and 12th of King William IIId. Intitled An Act for the More Effectual Suppression of Piracy. 1718. Boston: Printed by B. Green, for John Edwards, and sold at his Shop in King's Street, 1718.

The Tryals of Major Stede Bonnet and Other Pirates. 1719. London: Benjamin Cowse.

Wimble, James. 1738. Chart of His Majestie's Province of North Carolina. North Carolina Department of Archives and History, Raleigh

Newspapers

American Weekly Mercury
Boston Gazette
Boston News-Letter
New England Courant (Boston)

Secondary Sources

Adair, John. 1983. *By the Sword Divided.* London: Century Publishing.

Anderson, C.L.G. 1911. *Old Panama and Castillo Del Oro.* New York: North Rover Press.

Anderson, Robert T. 1965. From Mafia to Cosa Nostra. *American Journal of Sociology* 71:302–10.

Andrews, K. R. 1964. *Elizabethan Privateering: English Privateering during the Spanish War, 1585–1603*. Oxford: Oxford University Press.

Anonymous. 2010a. Captured Somali Pirates "Dead"—Russia. Electronic document: http://www.news.com.au/world/captured-somali-pirates-dead-russia/story-e6fr-fkyi-1225865292229.

———. 2010b. Somali Pirates Captured and Released by Russian Navy "Have Died." Electronic document: http://www.telegraph.co.uk/news/worldnews/piracy/7713375/Somali-pirates-captured-and-released-by-Russian-navy-have-died.html.

Appleby, John C. 1986. The "Affairs of Pirates": the Surrender and Submission of Captain William Baugh at Kinsale, 1611–1612. *Journal of the Cork Historical and Archaeological Society* 91:68–84.

———. 1990a. A Nursery of Pirates: The English Pirate Community in Ireland in the Early Seventeenth Century. *International Journal of Maritime History* 2(1):1–27.

———. 1990b. Settlers and Pirates in Early Seventeenth Ireland: A Profile of Sir William Hull. *Studia Hibernica* 25:76–104.

———. 1991. Women and Piracy in Ireland: from Gráinne O'Malley to Anne Bonny. In *Women in Early Modern Ireland*, edited by M. MacCurtain and M. O'Dowd, pp. 53–68. Edinburgh: Edinburgh University Press.

———. 1992. *A Calendar of Material Relating to Ireland from the High Court of Admiralty Examinations, 1563–1641*. Dublin: Irish Manuscripts Commission.

———. 2007. The Problem with Piracy in Ireland, 1570–1630. In *Pirates?: The Politics of Plunder, 1550–1650*, edited by C. Jowitt, pp. 41–55. New York: Palgrave Macmillan.

———. 2009. *Under the Bloody Flag: Pirates of the Tudor Age*. Stroud: History Press.

Appleby, John C., and Mary O'Dowd. 1985. The Irish Admiralty: Its Organization and Development, c. 1570–1640. *Irish Historical Studies* 24(96):299–326.

Arango, J. de, Félix Durán, Juan Guillermo Martín, and Silvia Arroyo (editors). 2007. *Panamá Viejo: De la aldea a la urbe*. Panama City: Patronato Panamá Viejo.

Arnade, Charles. 1962. The Avero Story: An Early St. Augustine Family with Many Daughters and Many Houses. *Florida Historical Quarterly* 40:1–34.

Arnold, J. Barto, III. 1977. Site Test Excavations Underwater: The Sequel to the Magnetometer Survey. *International Journal of Nautical Archaeology* 6(1):21–26.

Arnold, J. Barto, III, and Carl Clausen. 1975. A Magnetometer Survey with Electronic Positioning Control and Calculator Plotter System. Paper presented to the International Conference on Underwater Archaeology, Charleston, South Carolina.

Babits, Lawrence E. 1998. I Just Know It's a Pirate: Popular Imagery, Contemporary Details and Actual Fact. In *Underwater Archaeology, Proceedings of the 31st Conference on Historical and Underwater Archaeology*, edited by Lawrence E. Babits, Catherine Fach, and Ryan Harris, pp. 61–66. Rockville, Md.: Society for Historical Archaeology, Rockville.

———. 2001. Pirates. *North Carolina Maritime Museum Tributaries* 11:7–13.

Babits, Lawrence E., Joshua B. Howard, and Matthew Brenckle. 2006. Pirate Imagery. In *X Marks the Spot: Archaeology of Piracy*, edited by Russell K. Skowronek and Charles R. Ewen, pp. 271–81. Gainesville: University Press of Florida.

Baer, Joel H. 2007a. *The Arraignment, Tryal, and Condemnation, of Capt. John Quelch, and Others of His Company, &c. for Sundry Piracies, Robberies, and Murder, Committed upon the Subjects of the King of Portugal, Her Majesty's Allie, on the Coast of Brasil, &c.*

In *British Piracy in the Golden Age: History and Interpretation, 1660–1730*, edited by Joel H. Baer, 2:263–88. 4 vols. London: Pickering and Chatto.

———. 2007b. *A Full and Exact Account of the Tryal of the Pyrates Lately Taken by Captain Ogle, on Board the Swallow Man of War, on the Coast of Guinea*. In *British Piracy in the Golden Age: History and Interpretation, 1660–1730*, edited by Joel H. Baer, 3:73–166. 4 vols. London: Pickering and Chatto.

———. 2007c. *The Trials of Eight Persons Indited for Piracy &c. Of Whom Two Were Acquitted, and the Rest Found Guilty*. 2007. In *British Piracy in the Golden Age: History and Interpretation, 1660–1730*, edited by Joel H. Baer, 2:293–319. 4 vols. London: Pickering and Chatto.

———. 2007d. *The Trials of Sixteen Persons for Piracy, &c. Four of Which Were Found Guilty, and the Rest Acquitted*. 2007. In *British Piracy in the Golden Age: History and Interpretation, 1660–1730*, ed. Joel H. Baer, 3:235–58. 4 vols. London: Pickering and Chatto.

———. 2007e. *The Tryals of Captain John Rackham and Other Pirates . . . Who Were All Condemn'd for Piracy, at the Town of St. Jago de la Vega, in the Island of Jamaica, on Wednesday and Thursday the Sixteenth and Seventeenth Days of November 1720. As also, the Tryals of Mary Read and Anne Bonny, alias Bonn*. 2007. In *British Piracy in the Golden Age: History and Interpretation, 1660–1730*, edited by Joel H. Baer, 3:7–66. 4 vols. London: Pickering and Chatto.

———. 2007f. *The Tryals of Major Stede Bonnet, and Other Pirates*. 2007. In *British Piracy in the Golden Age: History and Interpretation, 1660–1730*, edited by Joel H. Baer, 2:325–80. 4 vols. London: Pickering and Chatto.

———. 2007g. *Tryals of Thirty-Six Persons for Piracy, Twenty-Eight of Them upon Full Evidence Were Found Guilty, and the Rest Acquited. At a Court of Admiralty for Tryal of Pirates, Held at Newport within His Majesties Colony of Rhode-Island and Providence-Plantations in America*. In *British Piracy in the Golden Age: History and Interpretation, 1660–1730*, edited by Joel H. Baer, 3:171–92. 4 vols. London: Pickering and Chatto,

Bagwell, R. 1909. *Ireland under the Stuarts and during the Interregnum*, 1:1603–42. 4 vols. London: Longman, Green, and Company.

Baigent, Michael, and Richard Leigh. 1989. *The Temple and the Lodge*. New York: Arcade.

Bak, Greg. 2006. *Barbary Pirate: the Life and Times of John Ward, the Most Infamous Privateer of His Time*. Stroud: Sutton Publishing.

Barlow, Edward. 1934. *Barlow's Journal of His Life at Sea in King's Ships, East and West Indiamen and Other Merchantmen from 1659 to 1703*. Transcribed by Basil Lubbock. London: Hurst and Blackett.

Barnard, John. 1725. *Ashton's Memorial: An History of the Strange Adventures and Signal Deliverances of Mr. Philip Ashton*. Boston: Samuel Gerrish.

Barrie, James Mathew. 1904. *Peter Pan* (play). Produced in London.

Beeker, Charles D. 1991. Recognizing a Renewable Resource: The Public and Shipwrecks. On file, Indiana University Office of Underwater Science, Bloomington.

Beeker, Charles D., and Frederick H. Hanselmann. 2009. The Wreck of the *Cara Merchant*: Investigation of Captain Kidd's Lost Ship. In *ACUA Underwater Archaeology Proceedings 2009*, edited by Erika Laanela and Jonathan Moore, pp. 219–26. Columbus: PAST Foundation.

Belecki, H. 2007. Spanish Inheritance and Cultural Adaption: Small Finds from Panamá La Vieja. Master's thesis, Tübingen University, Germany.

Benchley, Peter. 1980. *Island*. New York: Doubleday.

Bianco, Barbara A., Christopher R. DeCorse, and Jean Howson. 2006. Chapter 13: Beads and Other Adornment. In *New York African Burial Ground Archaeology Final Report*, pp. 382–417. Washington, D.C.: Howard University Press.

Biese, Leo. 1964. *The Prehistory of Panamá Viejo*. Smithsonian Institution Bureau of American Ethnology Bulletin, 191. Anthropological Papers 68. Washington, D.C.: Smithsonian Institution, Government Printing Office.

Bingeman, John. 1981. Solent: HMS *Invincible* (1758) Wreck Site. *International Journal of Nautical Archaeology and Underwater Exploration* 10(2):154–56.

———. 2010. *The First HMS Invincible (1747–58): Her Excavations (1980–1991)*. Oxford: Oxbow Books.

Blair, David. 2008. Somali Pirate Port Becomes Boom Town. Electronic document: http://www.telegraph.co.uk/news/worldnews/africaandindianocean/somalia/3479001/Somali-pirate-port-becomes-boom-town.html.

Blok, Anton. 1972. The Peasant and the Brigand: Social Banditry Reconsidered. *Comparative Studies in Society and History* 14(4):494–503.

Bolton, Herbert E., and Mary Ross. 1968. *The Debatable Land: A Sketch of the Anglo-Spanish Contest for the Georgia Country*. New York: Russell and Russell.

Bond, Stanley. 1995. Tradition and Change in First Spanish Period (1565–1763) St. Augustine Architecture: A Search for Colonial Identity. Ph.D. diss., Anthropology Department, New York State University at Albany. Ann Arbor, Mich.: University Microfilms International.

Boteler, Nathaniel. 1688. *Colloquia Maritima: or Sea-Dialogues*. London: William Fisher and Richard Mount.

Botting, Douglas. 1978. *The Pirates*. Seafarers Series. Alexandria, Va.: Time-Life Books.

Boucaud, Philippe. 2010. Pewter Found Aboard *Queen Anne's Revenge*. Syndicat Français des Experts Professionnels en Oeuvres d'Art. Manuscript on file, North Carolina Underwater Archaeology Branch, Kure Beach.

———. 2011. Research Pertaining to the Pewter Porringer (QAR2350). Syndicat Français des Experts Professionnels en Oeuvres d'Art. E-mail (July 11, 2011) on file, *Queen Anne's Revenge* Lab, North Carolina Office of State Archaeology, Greenville.

Boudriot, Jean, and Hubert Bertia. 1993. *The History of the French Frigate, 1650–1850*. Rotherfield, East Essex: Jean Boudriot Publications.

Boyette, Pat. 1991. Adaptation of Robert Louis Stevenson's *Treasure Island* (comic book). Classics Illustrated No. 17. Chicago: Berkley Publishing Group and First Publishing.

Brady, W. Maziere. 1863. *Clerical and Parochial Records of Cork, Cloyne and Rose*. Vol. 1. Dublin: Alexander Thom Publishers.

Brain, Jeffrey P. 2011. The John Hunt Map of the First English Colony in New England. *Northeast Historical Archaeology* 31(1):69–74.

Branton, Nicole. 2009. Landscape Approaches in Historical Archaeology: The Archaeology of Places. In *International Handbook of Historical Archaeology*, edited by Teresita Majewski and David R. M. Gaimster, pp. 51–65. New York: Springer.

Breen, Colin. 2005. *The Gaelic Lordship of the O'Sullivan Beare: A Landscape Cultural History.* Dublin: Four Courts Press.

———. 2007a. *An Archaeology of Southwest Ireland, 1570–1670.* Dublin: Four Courts.

———. 2007b. The Post-Medieval Coastal Landscape of Bantry and Beara. In *The Post-Medieval Archaeology of Ireland 1550–1850,* edited by A. Horning, R. O'Baoill, C. Donelly, and P. Logue, pp. 205–19. Wicklow, Ireland: Wordwell.

Brizuela, Alvaro. 1996a. *Arqueología histórica en las ruinas de la Antigua Ciudad de Panamá.* Conference at Anthropology Faculty, University of Xalapa, Mexico, December 10, 1996.

———. 1996b. Informe final de excavación en El Cabildo, San José, Hospital de San Juan de Dios, Calle Obispo. Unpublished report for Patronato Panamá Viejo, Panama City.

———. 2002. Las peruleras del pozo de casas Terrín (Panamá La Vieja): Propuesta tipológica inicial de los bordes. *Arqueología de Panamá La Vieja—Avances de Investigación, época colonial* (August 1):135–55. Patronato Panamá Viejo, Panama City.

Brock, R. A. (editor). 1885. *The Official Letters of Alexander Spotswood, Lieutenant-Governor of the Colony of Virginia, 1710–1722.* Vol. 2. Richmond: Virginia Historical Society.

Bromley, John Selwyn. 1987. The Jacobite Privateers in the Nine Years War. In *Corsairs and Navies: 1660–1760,* pp. 140–65. London: Hambledon.

Brown, Ruth. 2007. Bronze Signaling or Saluting Gun, Second Report (No. 090). Unpublished report for *Queen Anne's Revenge* Conservation Lab, East Carolina University, Greenville, N.C.

———. 2009. QAR Breechblocks, Preliminary Report (No. 122). Unpublished report for *Queen Anne's Revenge* Conservation Lab, East Carolina University, Greenville, N.C.

———. 2012. Report No. 159—Panama 3. On file, Meadows Center for Water and the Environment, Texas State University, San Marcos.

Brown, Ruth, and Robert Smith. 2005. Report Number 047, Iron Gun 173. Unpublished report for *Queen Anne's Revenge* Conservation Lab, East Carolina University, Greenville, N.C.

Burgot, Daniel. 2008. Armements de la famille Montaudouin: Grand armateus nantais. Electronic document: http://archive.is/QWifc.

Burnett, John S. 2002. *Dangerous Waters: Modern Piracy and Terror on the High Seas.* New York: Dutton.

Bushnell, Amy T. 1982. *The King's Coffer: Proprietors of the Spanish Florida Treasury, 1565–1702.* Gainesville: University Press of Florida.

———. 1994. *Situado and Sabana: Spain's Support System for the Presidio and Mission Provinces of Florida.* Anthropological Papers Number 74. New York: American Museum of Natural History.

Butler, Lindley S. 2000. *Pirates, Privateers, and Rebel Raiders of the Carolina Coast.* Chapel Hill: University of North Carolina Press.

Caballero, O., Juan Guillermo Martín, and Alexis Mojica. 2004. Prospecciones geofísicas y arqueológicas para la recuperación de la traza urbana de Panamá La Vieja: El caso de la calle de Santo Domingo. *Revista Geofísica* 60:43–64.

Calendar of Carew MSS (1603–1623), Preserved in the Archiepiscopal Library at Lambeth. Vol. 6. Edited by J. S. Brewer and W. Bullen. London, 1873.

Calendar of State Papers Relating to Ireland, of the Reign of James I, 1606–1608. 1874. Vol. 12. Edited by C. W. Russell and J. P. Prendergast. Ontario, Canada: TannerRitchie Publishing/St. Andrews, Scotland: University of St. Andrews, Scotland. Online at http://www.tannerritchie.com.

Calendar of State Papers Relating to Ireland, of the Reign of James I, 1608–1610. 1874. Vol. 13. Edited by C. W. Russell and J. P. Prendergast Ontario, Canada: TannerRitchie Publishing/St. Andrews, Scotland: University of St. Andrews. Online http://www.tannerritchie.com.

Calendar of State Papers Relating to Ireland, of the Reign of James I, 1611–1614. 1877. Vol. 15. Edited by C. W. Russell and J. P. Prendergast. Ontario, Canada: TannerRitchie Publishing/St. Andrews, Scotland, University of St. Andrews. Online at http://www.tannerritchie.com.

Calendar of State Papers Relating to Ireland, of the Reign of James I, 1615–1625. 1880. Vol. 15. Edited by C. W. Russell and J. P. Prendergast. Ontario, Canada: TannerRitchie Publishing/St. Andrews, Scotland: University of St. Andrews. Online at http://www.tannerritchie.com.

Callahan, John E., J. William Miller, and James R. Craig. 2001. Ballast Stones from North Carolina Shipwreck 003BUI, the *Queen Anne's Revenge*: Hand Specimen, X-Ray, Petrographic, Chemical, Paramagnetic and 40K-40Ar Age. *Southeastern Geology* 40(1):49–57.

Campos, J., and Félix Durán. 2006. La traza urbana colonial de Panamá Viejo: Su recuperación. *Canto Rodado* (Patronato Panamá Viejo) 1:41–64.

Cannenburg, W. Voorbeijtel. 1935. An Unknown "Pilot" by Hessel Gerritsz, Dating from 1612. *Imago Mundi* 1:49–51.

Carnes-McNaughton, Linda. 2007a. The Perusal of Personal Gear from 31CR314. Paper presented at the Society for Historical Archaeology, Williamsburg, N.C.

———. 2007b. Tobacco Pipe and Tool Analysis from 31CR314, *Queen Anne's Revenge* Shipwreck Site. *Queen Anne's Revenge* Shipwreck Project Research Report and Bulletin Series, QAR-B-07-04, North Carolina Department of Cultural Resources, Raleigh.

———. 2008. Galley Goods from the *Queen Anne's Revenge* Shipwreck Site 31CR314. Paper presented at the Southeastern Archaeological Conference, Charlotte, N.C.

Carnes-McNaughton, Linda, and Mark U. Wilde-Ramsing. 2008. Preliminary Glassware and Bottle Analysis from Shipwreck 31CR314, *Queen Anne's Revenge* Site. *Queen Anne's Revenge* Shipwreck Project Research Report and Bulletin Series, QAR-R-08-02. North Carolina Department of Cultural Resources, Raleigh.

Caruana, Adrian B. 1994. *The History of English Sea Ordnance, 1523–1875: Volume I: 1523–1715, The Age of Evolution.* Rothfield, UK: Jean Boudriot.

Cascoigne, J'm. 1724. *An Exact Plan of Chocolata Hole and the South End of the Town of Port Royal in Jamaica.* Copy in Texas A&M University Collection of Port Royal Maps, College Station.

Cashion, Jerry. 1998. Remarks for delivery at the Museum of Albemarle. Manuscript, Research Branch, North Carolina Archives and History, Raleigh.

Castillero Calvo, Alfredo. 1995. *Conquista, evangelización y resistencia.* Panama City: Editorial Mariano Arosemena, Instituto Nacional de Cultura.

———. 1999. *La ciudad imaginada: El Casco Viejo de Panamá*. Panama City: Ministerio de la Presidencia.

———. 2004. *Destrucción de Panamá La Vieja y fundación de la nueva Panamá*. Historia General de Panamá 1(2). Panama City: Comité Nacional del Centenario de la República.

———. 2006. *Sociedad, economía y cultura material: Historia urbana de Panamá La Vieja*. Panama City: Patronato Panamá Viejo.

Castro, F. V. 2005. *The Pepper Wreck: A Portuguese Indiaman at the Mouth of the Targus River*. College Station: Texas A&M University Press.

Chambers, Anne. 1998. *Granuaile: The Life and Times of Grace O'Malley*. Dublin: Wolfhound Press.

Chaunu, Pierre, and Huguette Chaunu. 1957. *Séville et l'Atlantique (1504–1650), Vol. 6, Le movement des navires et des merchandises entre l Espagne et l'Amérique, de 1504 à 1650*. Paris: Ecoles Practiques de Hautes Etudes, SEVPEN.

Cirlot, J. E. 1962. *A Dictionary of Symbols*. Translated by Jack Sage. New York: Philosophical Library.

Cohen, Jeremy. 2003. Informal Commercial Networks, Social Control, and Political Power in the Province of Venezuela, 1700–1757. Ph.D. diss., Department of History, University of Florida, Gainesville. Ann Arbor: University Microfilms International.

Coil, Henry W. 1961. *Coil's Masonic Encyclopedia*. New York: Macoy Publishers and Masonic Supply.

Cooke, R. G., Diana Carvajal, Juan Guillermo Martín, and Alexandra Lara. 2008. Diversidad cultural y biológica del archipiélago de las perlas en el periodo precolombino: Informe de avance. Unpublished report on file at Secretaría Nacional de Ciencia, Tecnología e Innovación, Panama City.

Cordingly, David. 1995. *Life among the Pirates: The Romance and the Reality*. London: Little, Brown.

———. 1996. *Under the Black Flag: The Romance and the Reality of Life among the Pirates*. New York: Random House.

Cordingly, David, and John Falconer. 1992. *Pirates: Fact and Fiction*. New York: ARTABRAS.

Cotter, E. 2010. Dún na Séad Castle: An Early 17th Century House at Baltimore, Co. Cork. *Journal of the Cork Historical and Archaeological Society* 115:31–54.

Cowley, Malcolm. 1933. The Sea Jacobins. *New Republic* (February 1):327–29.

Craton, Michael. 1962. *A History of the Bahamas*. London: Collins.

Deagan, Kathleen. 1976. *Archaeology at the Greek Orthodox Shrine*. Florida State University Notes in Anthropology, Vol. 16. Tallahassee: Florida State University.

———. 1982. St. Augustine: America's First Urban Enclave. *North American Archaeologist* 3(3):183–205.

———. 1983. *Spanish St. Augustine: The Archaeology of a Colonial Creole Community*. New York: Academic Press.

———. 1991. Historical Archaeology's Contribution to Our Understanding of Early America. In *Historical Archaeology in Global Perspective*, edited by Lisa Falk, pp. 97–112. Washington, D.C.: Smithsonian Institution Press.

———(editor). 1995. *Puerto Real: The Archaeology of a Sixteenth Century Spanish Town in Hispaniola*. Gainesville: University Press of Florida.

———. 2002. *Artifacts of the Spanish Colonies of Florida and the Caribbean, 1500–1800, Vol. 2, Portable, Personal Possessions*. Washington, D.C.: Smithsonian Institution Press.

———. 2007. Eliciting Contraband through Archaeology: Illicit Trade in Eighteenth-Century St. Augustine. *Historical Archaeology* 41(4):96–114.

de Bry, John. 2006. Christopher Condent's *Fiery Dragon*. In *X Marks the Spot: The Archaeology of Piracy*, edited by Russell K. Skowronek and Charles R. Ewen, pp. 100–130. Gainesville: University Press of Florida.

Delgado, James P., Frederick H. Hanselmann, and Dominique Rissolo. 2009. Submerged Cultural Resource Reconnaissance, Mouth of the Río Chagres and Approaches, República de Panamá. Submitted to the Instituto Nacional de Cultura, República de Panamá. On file, Waitt Institute, La Jolla, California.

———. 2011. The Richest River in the World: The Maritime Cultural Landscape of the Mouth of the Río Chagres, República de Panamá. In *The Archaeology of Maritime Landscapes*, edited by B. Ford, pp. 233–45. New York: Springer.

De Maisonneuve, Bernard, and Mireille De Maisonneuve. 1991. *Le Maidstone*. N.p.: Arhims.

Desroches, J. P. 1992. In *Du Tage à la Mer de Chine*. Exhibition catalogue. Paris: Musée National des Arts Asiatiques-Guimet.

Disney World. 2006. Pirates of the Caribbean. Electronic document: http://disneyworld.disney.go.com/wdw/parks/attraction Detail?id=PiratesoftheCaribbeanAttractionPage.

Dow, G. F., and J. H. Edmonds. 1968. *The Pirates of the New England Coast: 1630–1730*. Reprint New York: Argosy-Antiquarian.

Downing, Clement. 1737. *A Compendious History of the Indian Wars*. London: T. Cooper.

Ducoin, Jacques. 2001. Compte rendu de recherches dans les Archives Françaises sur le navire nantais *La Concorde* capturé par des pirates en 1717. Manuscript on file, North Carolina Department of Cultural Resources, Division of Archives and History, Raleigh.

Earle, Peter. 1981. *The Sack of Panamá: Captain Morgan and the Battle for the Caribbean*. New York: Thomas Dunne Books.

Edwards, R. D. 1938. Letter-Book of Sir Arthur Chichester, 1612–14. *Analecta Hibernica* 62(8):3–178.

Exnicios, Joan M. 2006. On the Trail of Jean Lafitte. In *X Marks the Spot: The Archaeology of Piracy*, edited by Russell K. Skowronek and Charles R. Ewen, pp. 31–43. Gainesville: University Press of Florida.

Exquemelin, Alexander O. 1969. *The Buccaneers of America*. Translated by Alexis Brown. New York: Dover.

Faller, Lincoln B. 1987. *Turned to Account: The Forms and Function of Criminal Biography in Late Seventeenth and Early Eighteenth Century England*. Cambridge: Cambridge University Press.

Fay, Bernard. 1935. *Revolution and Freemasonry: 1680–1800*. Boston: Little, Brown.

Feinman, Gary M. 1997. Thoughts on New Approaches to Combining the Archaeological and Historical Records. *Journal of Archaeological Method and Theory* 4(3–4):367–77.

Finamore, Daniel. 2006. A Mariner's Utopia: Pirates and Logwood in the Bay of Honduras.

In *X Marks the Spot: The Archaeology of Piracy*, edited by Russell K. Skowronek and Charles R. Ewen, pp. 64–80. Gainesville: University Press of Florida.

Firth, Raymond. 1973. *Symbols, Public and Private*. Symbol, Myth, and Ritual Series, edited by Victor Turner. Ithaca, N.Y.: Cornell University Press.

Flemming, Gregory N. 2014. *At the Point of a Cutlass: The Pirate Capture, Bold Escape, and Lonely Exile of Philip Ashton*. Lebanon, N.H.: ForeEdge, University Press of New England.

Florida Museum of Natural History. 2004. Historical Archaeology Digital Ceramic Type Collection. Electronic document: http://www.flmnh.ufl.edu/histarch/gallery_types/.

Foster, Sir William. 1924. *A History of the Indian Wars by Clement Downing*. London/New York: Humphrey Milford/Oxford University Press.

Frothingham, Alice. 1941. *Hispanic Glass*. New York: Hispanic Society of America.

Galvin, Peter R. 1999. *Patterns of Pillage: A Geography of Caribbean-Based Piracy in Spanish America, 1536–1718*. New York: Peter Lang.

Garcés, A. 2009. Loza panameña, mayólica europea: Diferencias sociales en dos contextos arqueológicos de la primera ciudad de Panamá. Undergraduate thesis, Departamento de Antropología, Universidad del Cauca, Colombia.

García-Baquero González, Antonio. 1976. Cádiz y el Atlántico (1717–1778): El comercio colonial español bajo el monopolio gaditano. Diss., Escuela de Estudios Hispano-Americanos, CSIC, Excelentísima Diputación Provincial de Cádiz, Cádiz, Spain.

Gaulton, B., and James A. Tuck. 2003. The Archaeology of Ferryland, Newfoundland until 1696. In *Avalon Chronicles: The English in America, 1497–1696*, p. 8. Ferryland, Canada: Colony of Avalon Foundation.

Gettleman, Jeffrey. 2011. Taken by Pirates. *New York Times Magazine*, October 5.

Gilbert, W. S., and Arthur Sullivan. 1879. *Pirates of Penzance* (play). Produced in New York.

Gill, Conrad. 1961. *Merchants and Mariners of the 18th Century*. London: E. Arnold.

Gillaspie, William Roscoe. 1961. Juan de Ayala y Escobar, Procurador and Entrepreneur: A Case Study of the Provisioning of Florida, 1683–1716. Ph.D. diss., Department of History, University of Florida, Gainesville. Ann Arbor, Mich.: University Microfilms International.

Goddio, Franck, and Evelyne Jay Guyot de Saint Michel. 1999. *Griffin: On the Route of an Indiaman*. London: Periplus.

Goelet, Michael P. 1986. The Careening and Bottom Maintenance of Wooden Sailing Vessels. Master's thesis, Texas A&M University, College Station.

Gómez, Carlos. 2007. Continuidad cultural en torno a las creencias religiosas coloniales. Undergraduate thesis, Universidad de Panamá.

Gooch, L. 1978. Catholic Officers in the Navy of James II. *Recusant History* 14:276–80.

Gosling, P., C. Manning, and J. Waddell. 2007. *New Survey of Clare Island, 5: Archaeology*. Dublin: Royal Irish Academy.

Grahn, Lance. 1997. *The Political Economy of Smuggling: Regional Informal Economies in Early Bourbon New Granada*. Boulder, Colo.: Westview Press.

Green, David. 1970. *Queen Anne*. New York: Scribner.

Grey, Charles. 1933. *Pirates of the Eastern Seas: 1618–1723*. Port Washington, N.Y.: Kennikat Press.

Gulseth, Chad M. 2012. An Underwater Archaeological Survey by the Texas A&M University Nautical Archaeology Program in Port Royal Harbor, College Station.

Halbirt, Carl. 2004. La Ciudad de San Agustín: A European Fighting Presidio in Eighteenth-Century La Florida. *Historical Archaeology* 38(3):33–46.

Hamill, Stephen. 1986. *The Craft: A History of English Freemasonry*. Leighton Buzzard, Bedfordshire: Crucible.

Hamilton, Christopher E. 1992. Final Report of Archaeological Data Recovery: The *Whydah* Shipwreck Site WLF-HA-1. The *Whydah* Joint Venture and U.S. Army Corps of Engineers, South Chatham, Mass.

———. 2006. The Pirate Ship *Whydah*. In *X Marks the Spot: The Archaeology of Piracy*, edited by Russell K. Skowronek and Charles R. Ewen, pp. 131–59. Gainesville: University Press of Florida.

Hamilton, Christopher E., James R. Reedy Jr., and Kenneth Kinkor. 1988. Final Report of Archaeological Testing, the *Whydah* Shipwreck, Site WLF-HA-1. Report Submitted to the Massachusetts Board of Underwater Archaeological Resources, the U.S. Army Corps of Engineers, and the Advisory Council on Historic Preservation. South Chatham, Mass.

———. 1990. The 1989 Annual Report of Archaeological Data Recovery, the *Whydah* Shipwreck, Site WLF-HA-1. Report Submitted to the Massachusetts Board of Underwater Archaeological Resources, the U.S. Army Corps of Engineers, and the Advisory Council on Historic Preservation. South Chatham, Mass.

Hamilton, Donny. 1982. Unpublished Port Royal dive logs. Surveys conducted by Sharon Braunagel, Robyn Woodward, Roger Smith, and Lisa Shuey. Port Royal, Jamaica.

———. 2006. Pirates and Merchants: Port Royal, Jamaica. In *X Marks the Spot: The Archaeology of Piracy*, edited by Russell K. Skowronek and Charles R. Ewen, pp. 13–30. Gainesville: University Press of Florida.

Handler, Jerome S. 2006. On the Transportation of Material Goods by Enslaved Africans during the Middle Passage: Preliminary Findings from Documentary Sources. *African Diaspora Archaeology Newsletter* (December).

Hannah, Walton. 1953. *Darkness Visible*. London: Augustine Press.

Hanselmann, F. H., and Charles D. Beeker. 2008. Establishing Marine Protected Areas in the Dominican Republic: A Model for Sustainable Preservation. In *ACUA Underwater Archaeology Proceedings 2008*, edited by Susan Langley and Victor Mastone, pp. 52–61. Columbus: PAST Foundation.

———. 2015. The Wreck of the *Quedagh Merchant*: An Indian Merchantman Captured by Captain Kidd. In *Shipwrecks around the World: Revelations of the Past*, edited by S. Tripati, pp. 56–71. New Delhi, India: Kaveri.

Hanselmann, F. H., and James P. Delgado. 2010. The Río Chagres Maritime Landscape Study: 2010 Cannon Recovery Field Report. Submitted to the Instituto Nacional de Cultura, Dirección Nacional de Patrimonio Histórico, República de Panamá. On file, Meadows Center for Water and the Environment, Texas State University, San Marcos.

Hanselmann, Frederick H., James P. Delgado, and Dominique Rissolo. 2009. The Maritime Cultural Landscape of the Chagres River, Panamá: A Preliminary Survey of More Than 500 Years of Maritime Activity. In *ACUA Underwater Archaeology Proceedings 2009*, edited by E. Laanela and J. Moore, pp. 37–49. Columbus: PAST Foundation.

Hanselmann, F. H., Bert Ho, and Andres Diaz. 2011. Río Chagres Maritime Cultural Landscape Study: The Lost Ships of Henry Morgan Project 2011 Field Report. Submitted to the Instituto Nacional de Cultura, Dirección Nacional de Patrimonio Histórico, República de Panamá. On file, Meadows Center for Water and the Environment, Texas State University, San Marcos.

Haring, Clarence Henry. 1918. *Trade and Navigation between Spain and the Indies in the Time of the Hapsburgs*. Cambridge, Mass.: Harvard University Press.

———. 1966. *Trade and Navigation between Spain and the Indies*. Gloucester, Mass.: Peter Smith.

Harman, Joyce. 1969. *Trade and Privateering in Spanish Florida, 1762–1763*. St. Augustine: St. Augustine Historical Society.

Harress, Christopher. 2013. Secret Flow of Somali Piracy Ransoms: 179 Hijacked Ships Generated Some $400M in Payments since 2005: So Where Has It All Gone? Electronic document: http://www.ibtimes.com/secret-flow-somali-piracy-ransoms-179-hijacked-ships-generated-some-400m-payments-2005-so-where-has.

Harris, Jane E. 2000. Eighteenth-Century French Blue-Green Bottles from the Fortress at Lousibourg, Nova Scotia. In *Studies in Material Culture Research*, edited by Karlis Karklins, pp. 44–48. Ottawa, Canada: Society of Historical Archaeology.

Hassan, Mohamed Olad, and Jill Lawless. 2009. Pirate Hold British Couple on Ship. *Monitor* (McAllen, Texas), October 20,7B.

Hatch, Heather. 2006. Arrrchaeology: Investigating Piracy in the Archaeological Record. Master's thesis, Department of History, East Carolina University, Greenville, N.C.

———. 2011. Material Culture and Maritime Identity: Identifying Maritime Subcultures through Artifacts. In *The Archaeology of Maritime Landscapes, When the Land Meets the Sea* 2, edited by Ben Ford, pp. 217–32. New York: Springer.

Hawke, John. 1992. Canty's Cove—Legend and History. In *The Mizen Journal 5* (Selections from the *Mizen Journal*, 1993–2004), pp. 292–302. Skibbereen, Ireland: Design and Print.

Headlam, Cecil, ed. 1926. *Calendar of State Papers, Colonial Series, America and West Indies, 1712–1714*. Vol. 27. London: Her Majesty's Stationery Office.

———(editor). 1930a. *Calendar of State Papers, Colonial Series, America and West Indies, 1716–1717*. Vol. 29. London: Her Majesty's Stationery Office.

———(editor). 1930b. *Calendar of State Papers, Colonial Series, America and West Indies, 1717–1718*. Vol. 30. London: Her Majesty's Stationary Office.

Heintzelman, Katherine, and Jennifer Rainey Marquez. 2013. Captain Courageous: Tom Hanks and Capt. Richard Phillips. Electronic document: http://parade.condenast.com/157589/katherineheintzelmanjenniferraineymarquez/the-making-of-a-hero-what-tom-hanks-learned-playing-capt-richard-phillips.

Hellmer, John. 2010. Oh Boy, Russian Navy Gives Hell to Somali Pirates. Electronic document: http://www.businessinsider.com/russian-navy-attacks-somali-pirates-2010-5#ixzz1A0dyl3ak.

Henry, Nathan. 2008. Ship's Artillery and Implications. Paper presented at the Southeastern Archaeological Conference, November 12–15, 2008, Charlotte, N.C.

———. 2009. Analysis of Armament from Shipwreck 31CR314, *Queen Anne's Revenge* Site.

Queen Anne's Revenge Shipwreck Project Research Report and Bulletin Series, QAR-B-09-01, North Carolina Department of Cultural Resources, Raleigh.

Hernandez, Gred. 2003. Disney's "Pirates" Hoists Victory Flag. *San Francisco Chronicle*, July 12.

Hill, S. Charles. 1920. *Episodes of Piracy in the Eastern Seas, 1519–1851*. Indian Antiquary, vols. 48 and 49. Bombay, Indian Antiquary.

Hobsbawm, E. J. 1972. Social Bandits: Reply. *Comparative Studies in Society and History* 14(4):503–5.

Hoffman, Paul. 1980. *The Spanish Crown and the Defense of the Caribbean, 1535–1585*. Baton Rouge: Louisiana State University Press.

Holt, J. C. 1982. *Robin Hood*. New York: Thames and Hudson.

Hornsby, P.R.G., R. Weinstein, and R. Homer. 1989. *Pewter: A Celebration of the Craft, 1200–1700*. London: Museum of London.

Horwood, H., and E. Butts. 1984. *Pirates and Outlaws of Canada, 1610–1932*. Toronto: Doubleday.

Jacob, Margaret C. 1981. *The Radical Enlightenment: Pantheists, Freemasons, and Republicans*. London: Unwin and Allen.

Jiménez, M., and Richard Cooke. 2001. Análisis faunístico de los restos excavados en las Casas de Terrin (Panamá La Vieja): Una aproximación a la dieta y a la ecología. *Arqueología de Panamá La Vieja—Avances de investigación*, época *colonial* (Patronato Panamá Viejo) (August 1):89–126.

Johnson, Sandra. 2003. External Connections. In *Presidio Santa María De Galve: A Struggle for Survival in Colonial Spanish Pensacola*, edited by Judith Bense, pp. 315–40. Gainesville: University Press of Florida.

Jones, Mervyn. 1967. Freemasonry. In *Secret Societies*, edited by Norman MacKenzie. London: Aldus.

Journal of the Commissioners for Trade and Plantation Preserved in the Public Record Office (JCTP). 1969. Klaus Reprint. Nendeln, Liechtenstein: Kraus-Thompson Organization.

Katsev, Michael. 1980. A Cargo from the Age of Alexander the Great. In *Archaeology under Water: An Atlas of the World's Submerged Sites*, edited by Keith Muckleroy, pp. 42–43. New York: McGraw-Hill.

———. 1987. The Kyrenia Ship Restored. In *The Sea Remembers: Shipwrecks and Archaeology*, edited by Peter Throckmorton, pp. 55–59. New York: Weidenfield and Nicolson.

Katz, David S. 1988. *Sabbath and Sectarianism in Seventeenth-Century England*. New York: Leiden.

Keith, Donald J., and Joe S. Simmons III. 1985. Analysis of Hull Remains, Ballast, and Artifact Distribution of a 16th-Century Shipwreck, Molasses Reef, British West Indies. *Journal of Field Archaeology* 12(4):411–24.

Kelleher, C. 2007a. The Fort of the Ships. In *From Ringforts to Fortified Houses: Studies of Irish Monuments in Honour of David Sweetman*, edited C. Manning, pp. 195–208. Wicklow, Ireland: Wordwell.

———. 2007b. The Gaelic O'Driscoll Lords of Baltimore, Co. Cork: Settlement, Economy, and Conflict in a "Maritime" Cultural Landscape. In *Gaelic Ireland: Lordship in Medieval and Early Modern Ireland*, edited by L. Doran and J. Lyttleton, pp. pp. 130–59. Dublin: Four Courts Press.

———. 2010. The Dunworley Bay Shipwreck: 17th-Century Evidence for Piracy and Slavery in Ireland? In *ACUA Underwater Archaeology Proceedings 2010*, edited by C. Horrell and M. Damour, pp. 138–45. Advisory Council on Underwater Archaeology.

———. 2013a. The Confederacy of Pirates in Early Seventeenth-Century Southwest Ireland—Trade, Plunder and Settlement: A Historical and Archaeological Study. Ph.D. diss., Trinity College Dublin.

———. 2013b. Pirate Ports and Harbours of West Cork in the Early-Seventeenth Century. *Journal of Maritime Archaeology* (Special issue: The Social Archaeology of Ports and Harbours) 8(2):347–66.

———. 2014. Depicting a Pirate Landscape: The Anti-Pirate Chart from 1612 and Archaeological Footprints on the Ground. *Journal of Irish Archaeology* 22:77–92.

Kennedy, Helen. 2009. Piracy Big Boon to Somalia Economy: Hotels, Restaurants Sprout in Port of Eyl in Pirates' Presence. Electronic document: http://www.nydailynews.com/news/world/piracy-big-boon-somalia-economy-hotels-restaurants-sprout-port-eyl-pirates-presence-article-1.360682#ixzz326paW4BX.

Kidd, Kenneth E., and Martha A. Kidd. 1982. A Classification System for Glass Trade Beads for the Use of the Field Archaeologists (1970). In *Proceedings of the 1982 Glass Bead Conference*, edited by Charles F. Hayes III, pp. 45–89. Rochester, N.Y.: Rochester Museum and Science Center.

Kisch, Bruno. 1965. *Scales and Weights: A Historical Outline*. New Haven: Yale University Press.

Konstam, Angus. 1999. *The History of Pirates*. New York: Lyons Press.

Kottmann, A. 2006. Implementación de un sistema de información geográfico (SIG) en las ruinas de Panamá Viejo. Unpublished report, DAAD research scholarship. On file at Patronato Panamá Viejo, Panama City.

Kritzler, Edward. 2008. *Jewish Pirates of the Caribbean*. New York: Doubleday.

Kwass, Michael. 2014. *Contraband, Louis Mandrin and the Making of a Global Underground*. Cambridge, Mass.: Harvard University Press.

Lane, Kris E. 1998. *Pillaging the Empire: Piracy in the Americas, 1500–1750*. New York: M. E. Sharpe.

Lang, James. 1975. *Conquest and Commerce: Spain and England in the Americas*. New York: Academic Press.

Lange, F. W. 1999. *Los recursos culturales, coloniales, históricos y contemporáneos en el* área *San Lorenzo/Ft. Sherman*. Panama City: USAID.

Lanzas, G. 2001. Clavos coloniales, siglos XVI y XVII: Panamá La Vieja. Undergraduate thesis, Universidad de Panamá.

Lavery, Brian. 1987. *The Arming and Fitting of English Ships of War, 1600–1815*. London: Conway Maritime Press.

Lawrence, Richard W. 2008. An Overview of North Carolina Shipwrecks with an Emphasis on Eighteenth-Century Vessel Losses at Beaufort Inlet. *Queen Anne's Revenge* Shipwreck Project Research and Bulletin Series, QAR-R-08-01, North Carolina Department of Cultural Resources, Raleigh.

Lawrence, Richard W., and Mark U. Wilde-Ramsing. 2001. In Search of Blackbeard: Historical and Archaeological Research at Shipwreck Site 0003BUI. *Southeastern Geology* 40(1):1–9.

Lee, Robert E. 1974. *Blackbeard the Pirate: A Reappraisal of His Life and Times*. Winston-Salem, N.C.: John F. Blair.

Leeson, Peter T. 2007. An-*arrgh*-chy: The Law and Economics of Pirate Organization. *Journal of Political Economy* 115(61):1049–94.

——. 2009. *The Invisible Hook: The Hidden Economics of Pirates*. Princeton: Princeton University Press.

Leibbrandt, H.C.V. 1896. *Precis of the Archives of the Cape of Good Hope: Journal, 1699–1732*. Cape Town: Richards, Government Printers.

Linero, M. 2001. Cerámica criolla: Muestra excavada en el pozo de las Casas de Terrin. *Arqueología de Panamá La Vieja—Avances de investigación*, época *colonial* (Patronato Panamá Viejo) (August 1):149–63.

Little, Barbara J. 2007. *Historical Archaeology: Why the Past Matters*. Walnut Creek, Calif.: Left Coast Press.

Livingston, Noel B. 1909. *Sketch Pedigrees of Some of the Early Settlers in Jamaica: Compiled from the Records of the Court of Chancery of the Island with a List of the Inhabitants in 1670 and Other Matter Relative to the Early History of the Same*. Kingston, Jamaica: Educational Supply Company.

Lizé, Patrick. 2006. Piracy in the Indian Ocean. In *X Marks the Spot: The Archaeology of Piracy*, edited by Russell K. Skowronek and Charles R. Ewen, pp. 81–99. Gainesville: University Press of Florida.

Long, G. 1967. Archaeological Investigation at Panamá La Vieja. Master's thesis, Department of Anthropology, University of Florida, Gainesville.

Ludwig, Allen I. 1966. *Graven Images: New England Stonecarving and Its Symbols, 1650–1815*. Middletown, Conn.: Wesleyan University Press.

Lusardi, Wayne R. 2006. The Beaufort Inlet Shipwreck Artifact Assemblage. In *X Marks the Spot: The Archaeology of Piracy*, edited by Russell K. Skowronek and Charles R. Ewen, pp. 196–218. Gainesville: University Press of Florida.

Lyon, Eugene, and Barbara Purdy. 1982. Contraband in Spanish Colonial Ships. *Itinerario: Journal of the Institute of European Expansion* (Leyden, The Netherlands) 6:2.

MacCarthy-Morrogh, M. 1986. *The Munster Plantation: English Migration to Southern Ireland, 1583–1641*. Oxford: Clarendon Press.

Macleod, Murdo. 1984. Spain and America: The Atlantic Trade, 1492–1720. In *Cambridge History of Latin America, Vol. 1, Colonial Latin America*, edited by L. Bethell, pp. 341–88. Cambridge: Cambridge University Press.

MacNeill, Ben Dixon. 1958. *The Hatterasman*. Winston-Salem, N.C.: John F. Blair.

Mainwaring, G. E., and W. G. Perrin. 1920–22. *The Life and Works of Sire Henry Mainwaring*. 2 vols. Navy Records Society.

Manwayring, Henry. 1644. *The Sea-Mans Dictionary: or, an Exposition and Demonstration of All the Parts and Things Belonging to a Shippe: Together with an Explanation of All the Termes and Phrases Used in the Practique of Navigation*. London: G. M. for John Bellamy.

Marangou, C. 2006. Carved Rocks, Functional and Symbolic (Lemnos Island, Greece). In *Prehistoric Art: Signs, Symbols, Myth, Ideology, XV World Congress (Lisbon)*, edited by L. Oosterbeek, M. Otte, L. Remacle, and D. Seglie, pp. 93–101. BAR Series 2009. Oxford: BAR.

Maritime Research Society. 1924. *Pirate's Own Book*. Publication No. 4. Salem, Mass.: Maritime Research Society.

Marken, Mitch. 1994. *Pottery from Spanish Shipwrecks, 1500–1800*. Gainesville: University Press of Florida.

Marten, M. G. 2005. Spatial and Temporal Analyses of the Harbor at Antiocha ad Cragum. Master's thesis, Florida State University.

Martín, Juan Guillermo. 2001. Pisos coloniales en Panamá La Vieja: Una manera de afianzar el status. *Arqueología de Panamá La Vieja—Avances de investigación, época colonial* (Patronato Panamá Viejo) (August 1):225–38.

———. 2002a. Estructuras arquitectónicas, bienes muebles y adornos personales: Alternativas de ostentación en la antigua ciudad de Panamá. *Revista de Antropología y Arqueología* 13:61–72.

———. 2002b. Excavaciones arqueológicas en el Parque Morelos (Panamá La Vieja). *Arqueología de Panamá La Vieja—Avances de investigación, época colonial* (Patronato Panamá Viejo) (August 2):203–229.

———. 2002c. Funerales en Panamá La Vieja: Existen patrones en la América colonial? *Arqueología de Panamá La Vieja—Avances de investigación, época colonial* (Patronato Panamá Viejo) (August 2:94–103).

———. 2002d. Panamá La Vieja y el Gran Darién. *Arqueología de Panamá La Vieja—Avances de investigación, época colonial* (Patronato Panamá Viejo) (August 2):230–50.

———. 2003. Panamá La Vieja: La recuperación de su traza urbana. *Revista de Arqueología Americana* 22:165–83.

———. 2007. La cerámica prehispánica del parque Morelos: Un ejercicio de caracterización tecnológica. *Canto Rodado* (Patronato Panamá Viejo) 2:45–68.

———. 2009. Arqueología de Panamá La Vieja: Del asentamiento prehispánico a la ciudad colonial. Ph.D. diss., Universidad de Huelva, Huelva, Spain.

Martín, Juan Guillermo, Ana Caicedo, Bibiana Etayo, Alejandra Garcés, and Paola Sanabria. 2007. Producción y comercialización de cerámicas coloniales en los Andes: El caso de las mayólicas de Popayán. *Boletín del Gabinete de Arqueología* (Bogotá, Colombia) 6:28–39.

Martín, Juan Guillermo, and Claudia Díaz. 2000. Enterramientos coloniales en la Catedral de Panamá La Vieja: Un ejercicio de reafirmación de las creencias religiosas. *Trace* 38:80–87.

Martín, Juan Guillermo, and Paula Figueroa. 2001. Pasamanería colonial: El arte de trenzar y anudar hilos. *Arqueología de Panamá La Vieja—Avances de investigación, época colonial* (Patronato Panamá Viejo) (August 1):215–24.

Martín, Juan Guillermo, and Félix Rodríguez. 2006. Los moluscos marinos de Panamá Viejo: Selectividad de recursos desde una perspectiva de larga duración. *Canto Rodado* (Patronato Panamá Viejo) 1:85–100.

Martín, Juan Guillermo, and Claudia Rojas. 2008. Arqueología funeraria de Panamá Viejo-Informe de Avance. FID07–004. Document on file at Secretaria Nacional de Ciencia, Tecnología e Innovación, Panama City.

Martín, Juan Guillermo, and Luis Alberto Sánchez. 2007. El istmo mediterráneo: Intercambio, simbolismo y filiación social en la bahía de Panamá, durante el período 500–1000 D.C. *Arqueología del Area Intermedia* 7:113–22.

Martín, Juan Guillermo, and T. Yanaida. 2007. La escala urbana como unidad de análisis: Métodos y estrategias de investigación para la recuperación de la traza urbana de la antigua ciudad de Panamá. In *Escalas menores-Escalas mayores: Una perspectiva arqueológica desde Colombia y Panamá*, edited by L. G. Jaramillo, pp. 95–108. Bogotá, Colombia: Universidad de los Andes.

Martín, Juan Guillermo, A. Zeischka-Kenzler, H. Mommsen, and Aline Kottmann. 2008. Gres: La sutil presencia alemana en la Panamá colonial. *Canto Rodado* (Patronato Panamá Viejo) 3:65–94.

Marx, Robert. 1968. Excavation of the Sunken City of Port Royal: December 1965–March 1968. a Preliminary Report, Institute of Jamaica, Kingston.

———. 1973. *Port Royal Rediscovered*. New York: Doubleday.

Mason, F. Van Wyck. 1949. *Cutlass Empire*. Garden City, N.Y.: Doubleday.

———. 1957. *Captain Nemesis*. New York: Pocket Books.

Mather, Cotton. 1726. *The Vial Poured Out upon the Sea: A Remarkable Relation of Certain Pirates Brought unto a Tragical and Untimely End. Some Conferences with Them, after Their Condemnation. Their Behaviour at Their Execution*. Boston: T. Fleet for N. Belknap.

McAllister, Lyle N. 1984. *Spain and Portugal in the New World, 1492–1700*. Minneapolis: University of Minnesota Press.

McIlwaine, Henry Read. 1928. *Executive Journals of the Council of Colonial Virginia*. Richmond: D. Bottom.

McLynn, Frank. 1985. *The Jacobites*. Boston: Routledge and Kegan Paul.

McNinch, Jesse E., Arthur C. Trembanis, John T. Wells. 2005. Scour and Burial at Shipwreck 31CR314. *Queen Anne's Revenge* Shipwreck Project Research Report and Bulletin Series, QAR-R-07-03. North Carolina Department of Cultural Resources, Raleigh.

McNinch, Jesse E., John T. Wells, and Thomas G. Drake. 2001. The Fate of Artifacts in an Energetic, Shallow-Water Environment: Scour and Burial at the Wreck Site of *Queen Anne's Revenge*. *Southeastern Geology* 40(1):19–27.

McNinch, Jesse E., John T. Wells, and Arthur C. Trembanis. 2006. Predicting the Fate of Artefacts in Energetic, Shallow Marine Environments: An Approach to Site Management. *International Journal of Nautical Archaeology* 31(1):1–20.

Mena García, M. 1984. *La sociedad de Panamá en el siglo XVI*. Excma. Diputación Provincial de Sevilla, Sección Historia, Vo Centenario del Descubrimiento de América, Seville: Hon. Provincial de Sevilla.

———. 1992. *La ciudad en un cruce de caminos (Panamá y sus orígenes urbanos)*. Seville: Escuela de Estudios Hispano-Americanos de Sevilla.

Mendizábal, Tomás. 1996. Informe de Excavación: Casas de la Plaza, temporada de campo abril–septiembre. Unpublished report on file at Patronato Panamá Viejo, Panama City.

———. 1997. Excavaciones en las Casas Terrín, enero a junio. Unpublished report on file at Patronato Panamá Viejo, Panama City.

———. 1999. Current Archaeological Research in Panamá Viejo, Panamá. *Papers for the Institute of Archaeology* 10:25–36.

———. 2004. Panamá Viejo: An Analysis of the Construction of Archaeological Time in Eastern Panamá. Ph.D. diss., Institute of Archaeology, University College London, University of London.

Mettas, Jean. 1978. *Répertoire des expéditions négriè françaises au XVIII siècle*. Paris: Société Française d'Histoire d'Outre-Mer.
Michener, James A. 1951. *Return to Paradise*. New York: Bantam Books.
Michener, James A., and A. Grove Day. 1957. *Rascals in Paradise*. New York: Bantam Books.
Miller, George, Patricia Stamford, Ellen Shlasko, and Andrew Madsen. 1999. Telling Time for Archaeologists. *Northeast Historical Archaeology* 29:1–22.
Miller, J. William, John E. Callahan, James R. Craig, and Caitlin Blum. 2007. 31CR314 Ballast. Paper presented at the 40th Conference on Historical and Underwater Archaeology, January 9–14, 2007, Williamsburg, Va.
Mintz, S. W. 1986. *Sweetness and Power: The Place of Sugar in Modern History*. New York: Penguin.
Monod, Paul K. 1990. *Jacobitism and the English People: 1688–1788*. Cambridge: Cambridge University Press.
Mookerji, R. K. 1962. *Indian Shipping*. Calcutta: Kitab Mahal.
Moore, David D., and Corey Malcolm. 2008. Seventeenth-Century Vehicle of the Middle Passage: Archaeological and Historical Investigations on the *Henrietta Marie* Shipwreck Site. *International Journal of Historical Archaeology* 12:20–38.
Moore, Simon. 1987. *Spoons, 1650–1930*. Colchester, Buckinghamshire: Shire Publications.
———. 2001. Blackbeard's *Queen Anne's Revenge*. *Tributaries* 11:49–64.
Moriarty, George. 1915. John Williams of Newport, Merchant, and His Family. *Genealogical Magazine* (December).
———. 1948. Additions and Corrections to Austin's Genealogical Dictionary. *American Genealogist* (April).
———. 1951. Notes on Block Islanders of the Seventeenth Century. *New England Genealogical Magazine* (January–December).
Morison, Samuel Eliot. 1942. *Admiral of the Ocean Sea: A Life of Christopher Columbus*. Boston: Little, Brown.
Moss, David. 1979. Bandits and Boundaries in Sardinia. *Man* 14(3):477–96.
Moya Pons, Frank. 1998. *The Dominion Republic: A National History*. Princeton: Markus Wiener Publishers.
Muckelroy, Keith. 1978. *Maritime Archaeology*. Cambridge: Cambridge University Press.
Murdoch, Steve. 2010. *The Terror of the Seas?: Scottish Maritime Warfare, 1513–1713*. Leiden, Netherlands: Brill Publications.
Newland, James D. 1997. The Disciplinary Viewpoint from History and Its Application to Historical Archaeology. *Proceedings of the Society for California Archaeology* (San Diego) 10:110–15.
Newquist, Ingrid M. 2007. Contracted International Trade as an Archaeological Red Herring: Material Indications of Illicit Trade in the Colonial Commerce of Santo Domingo. Master's thesis, Anthropology, University of Florida, Gainesville.
———. 2011. Contraband in the Convento? Material Indications of Trade-Relations in the Spanish Colonies. In *Islands at the Crossroads: Migration, Seafaring, and Interaction in the Caribbean*, edited by L. Antonio Curet and Mark W. Hauser, pp. 87–103. Tuscaloosa: University of Alabama Press.
Newsom, Lee A., and Regis B. Miller. 2009. Wood Species Analysis of Ship's Timbers and Wood Items Recovered from Shipwreck 31CR314, *Queen Anne's Revenge* Site. *Queen*

Anne's Revenge Shipwreck Project Research Report and Bulletin Series, QAR-R-09-01, North Carolina Department of Cultural Resources, Raleigh.

Ní Loingsigh, M. 1994. An Assessment of Castles and Landownership in Late Medieval North Donegal. *Ulster Journal of Archaeology* 57:145–58.

Noël Hume, Ivor. 1969. *Glass in Colonial Williamsburg's Archaeological Collection*. Colonial Williamsburg Archaeological Series. Williamsburg, Va.: Colonial Williamsburg Foundation.

———. 1970. *A Guide to Artifacts from Colonial America*. New York: AA Knopf.

———. 2002. *If These Pots Could Talk*. Philadelphia: Chipstone Foundation.

Oatis, Steven. 2004. *Colonial Complex: South Carolina's Frontiers in the Era of the Yamsee War, 1680–1730*. Lincoln: University of Nebraska Press.

O'Connor, D'Arcy. 1978. *The Money Pit: The Story of Oak Island and the World's Greatest Treasure Hunt*. New York: Coward, McCann, and Geoghegan.

Ohlmeyer, J. 1998. "Civilizing of Those Rude Partes": Colonization within Britain and Ireland, 1580s–1640s. In *The Origin of Empire*, edited by N. Canny, pp. 124–47. Oxford: Oxford University Press.

Oppenheim, M. 1914. *The Naval Tracts of Sir William Monson in Six Books*. London: Navy Records Society.

Orser, Charles E. 2009. World-Systems Theory, Networks and Modern-World Archaeology. In *International Handbook of Historical Archaeology*, edited by Teresita Majewski and David R. M. Gaimster, pp. 253–68. New York: Springer.

Paesie, Rudolf. 2008. *Lorrendrayen op Africa*. Amsterdam, Netherlands: De Bataafsche Leeuw.

Parish, James Robert. 1995. *Pirates and Seafaring Swashbucklers on the Hollywood Screen*. Jefferson, N.C.: McFarland.

Parker, Susan R. 1999. The Second Century of Settlement in Spanish St. Augustine, 1670–1763. Ph.D. diss., Department of History, University of Florida, Gainesville. Ann Arbor, Mich.: University Microfilms International.

Pastor, L., R. Vanhoeserlande, N. Florsch, I. Florsch, J. Toral, J. González, M. Lezcano, and A. Mojica. 2001. Prospección arqueogeofísica en Panamá La Vieja: Presentación de casos. *Arqueología de Panamá La Vieja—Avances de investigación, época colonial* (Patronato Panamá Viejo) (August 1):43–61.

Patel, Samir S. 2013. Pirates of the Original Panama Cana. *Archaeology Magazine* (March/April) 66(2):30–37.

Patzelt, A., A. Kottmann, and M. Waldhör. 2007. Prospección geoeléctrica en la ciudad colonial de Panamá Viejo: Técnicas, mediciones y primeros resultados de las excavaciones. *Canto Rodado* (Patronato Panamá Viejo) 2:23–44.

Pawson, Michael, and David Buisseret. 2000. *Port Royal, Jamaica*. Barbados, Jamaica, Trinidad and Tobago: University of the West Indies Press.

Pearson, G. 2006. La industria lítica prehispánica de Panamá Viejo: Hacia una caracterización tipológica y tecnológica (Patronato Panamá Viejo) *Canto Rodado* 1:133–56.

Pennell, C. R. 1994. The Geography of Piracy: Northern Morocco in the Mid-Nineteenth Century. *Journal of Historical Geography* 20(3): 272–82.

Pereira, G. 2002. Análisis de un entierro encontrado en la iglesia del convento de las monjas de la Concepción de Panamá La Vieja. *Arqueología de Panamá La Vieja—Avances de investigación* (Patronato Panamá Viejo) (August 2):104–12.

Peterson, Mendel. 1975. *The Funnel of Gold*. Boston: Little, Brown.

Phillips, Richard, with Stephan Talty. 2010. *A Captain's Duty, Somali Pirates, Navy SEALS, and Dangerous Days at Sea*. New York: Hyperion Books.

Pijning, Ernst. 1997. Controlling Contraband: Mentality, Economy and Society in Eighteenth-Century Rio de Janeiro. Ph.D. diss., Johns Hopkins University, Baltimore.

Pirates of the Caribbean. 2011. In *Pirate Medicine: Pestilence and Pain during the Golden Age of Piracy*. Electronic document: http://Pirates.Hegewisch.net/Pestilence_Pain.

Plutarch. 1999. *Roman Lives: A Selection of Eight Roman Lives*. Translated by Robin Waterfield. Oxford: Oxford University Press.

Pringle, Patrick. 1953. *Jolly Roger: The Story of the Great Age of Piracy*. New York: Norton.

Pulido Bueno, Ildefonso. 1993. *Almojarifazgos y comercio exterior en Andalucía durante la época mercantilista, 1526–1740: Contribución al estudio de la economía en la España moderna*. Huelva, Spain: Artes Gráficos Andaluzas.

Purmer, D., and A.H.N. van der Wiel. 2006. *Handboek van de Nederlandse provinciale muntslag, 1573–1806, van de voormalige provincies, steden en heerlijkheden, alsmede de gouden, zilveren en koperen afslagen*. Langweer: Nederlandse Vereniging van Munthandelaren.

Pyle, Howard. 1921. *The Book of Pirates*. New York: Harper and Brothers.

Pyle, Howard, and Merle Devore Johnson (editors). 1921. *Howard Pyle's Book of Pirates: Fiction, Fact and Fancy concerning the Buccaneers and Marooners of the Spanish Main*. New York: Harper and Brothers.

Rankin, Hugh F. 1960. *The Pirates of Colonial North Carolina*. Raleigh: Division of Archives and History, North Carolina Department of Cultural Resources.

Rawlinson, A. 1973. Deposition of Joseph Man. Bodleian Library, MS Rawlinson A. 271, fol. 44b. In *Privateering and Piracy in the Colonial Period: Illustrative Documents*, edited by J. Franklin Jameson, pp. 273–74. New York: August M. Kelley.

Rediker, Marcus. 1981. "Under the Banner of King Death": The Social World of Anglo-American Pirates, 1716–1726. *William and Mary Quarterly* (3rd Series) 38:203–27.

———. 1987. *Between the Devil and the Deep Blue Sea: Merchant Seamen, Pirates, and the Anglo-American Maritime World, 1700–1750*. Cambridge: Cambridge University Press.

———. 1993. *Between the Devil and the Deep Blue Sea: Merchant Seamen, Pirates and the Anglo-American Maritime World, 1700–1750*. Canto Edition. Cambridge: Cambridge University Press.

———. 2004. *Villains of All Nations: Atlantic Pirates in the Golden Age*. Boston: Beacon Press.

Ritchie, Robert C. 1986. *Captain Kidd and the War against the Pirates*. Cambridge, Mass.: Harvard University Press.

Rivkin, David B., Jr., and Carlos Ramos-Mrosovsky. 2010. A Better Way to Deal with Pirates. Electronic document: http://www.washingtonpost.com/wp-dyn/content/article/2010/12/08/AR2010120806188.html.

Rocca, Mo. 1995. *Salty Dog: The Adventures of Wishbone*. (teleplay). Richardson, Tex.: Big Feats! Entertainment.

Rodgers, Bradley A., Nathan Richards, and Wayne R. Lusardi. 2005. "Ruling Theories Linger": Questioning the Identity of the Beaufort Inlet Shipwreck. *International Journal of Nautical Archaeology* 34(1):24–37.

Rogozinski, Jan. 2000. *Honor among Thieves: Captain Kidd, Henry Every, and the Pirate Democracy in the Indian Ocean.* Mechanicsburg, Pa.: Stackpole Books.

Rojas, C. M., J. Rivera-Sandoval, and J. G. Martín-Rincón. 2011. Paleoepidemiology of the pre-Columbian and Colonial Panamá Viejo: A Preliminary Study. *Bulletin et Memoires de la Societe Anthropologie* 23:70–82.

Romoli, Kathleen. 1987. *Los de la lengua de Cueva: Los grupos indígenas del Istmo Oriental en la época de la conquista española.* Bogotá, Colombia: Instituto Colombiano de Antropología, Instituto Colombiano de Cultura, Ediciones Tercer Mundo.

Rovira, Beatriz. 1997. Hecho en Panamá: La manufactura colonial de mayólicas. *Revista Nacional de Cultura* (nueva época) 27:67–85.

———. 2001a. Cerámicas ordinarias torneadas procedentes de un contexto de finales del siglo XVI y principios del SXVII. *Arqueología de Panamá La Vieja—Avances de investigación, época colonial* (Patronato Panamá Viejo) (August 1):117–48.

———. 2001b. Presencia de mayólicas panameñas en el mundo colonial: Algunas consideraciones acerca de su distribución y cronología. *Latin American Antiquity* 12(3):291–303.

———. 2002a. Las cerámicas esmaltadas al estaño de origen europeo: Una aproximación a la etiqueta doméstica en la Colonia. *Revista de Antropología y Arqueología* 13:6–25.

———. 2002b. Paredes no tan desnudas . . . La muestra de azulejos sevillanos del sitio de Panamá La Vieja. *Arqueología de Panamá La Vieja—Avances de investigación* (Patronato Panamá Viejo) (August 2):167–83.

———. 2006. Caracterización química de cerámicas coloniales del sitio de Panamá Viejo: Resultados preliminares de la aplicación de activación neutrónica experimental. *Canto Rodado* (Patronato Panamá Viejo) 1:101–31.

Rovira, Beatriz, and Felipe Gaitán. 2010. Los búcaros: De las indias para el mundo. *Canto Rodado* (Patronato Panamá Viejo) 5:39–78.

Rovira, Beatriz, and Juan Guillermo Martín. 2008. Arqueología histórica de Panamá. La experiencia en las ruinas de Panamá Viejo. *Vestigios* 1(2):7–34.

Rovira, Beatriz, and Jazmín Mojica. 2007. Encrucijada de estilos: La mayólica panameñan gustos cotidianos en el Panamá colonial (siglo XVII). *Canto Rodado* (Patronato Panamá Viejo) 2:69–100.

Rubin, Alfred P. 1988. *The Law of Piracy.* Newport, R.I.: Naval War College Press.

Runyon, Shane. 2005. The Founding of Georgia and Spain's Fight for the Frontier, 1732–1740. Ph.D. diss., Department of History, University of Florida, Gainesville. Ann Arbor, Mich.: University Microfilms International.

Sabatini, Rafael. 1915. *The Sea Hawk.* Philadelphia: Lippincott.

———. 1922. *Captain Blood: His Odyssey.* New York: Houghton Mifflin.

———. 1932. *Black Swan.* New York: Houghton Mifflin.

Salley, Alexander S., ed. 1928. *Records in the British Public Records Office Relating to South Carolina 1663–1710.* Vol. 1. Columbia, S.C.: Crowson-Stone Printing.

Sanabria, P. 2007. Transformaciones en cultura-ambiente generadas por la introducción de los animales domésticos a Panamá durante la Colonia. Undergraduate thesis. Universidad del Cauca.

Sánchez, Néstor. 2002. Artefactos de vidrio en Panamá La Vieja. *Arqueología de Panamá La Vieja—Avances de investigación* (Patronato Panamá Viejo) (August 2):156–66.

Saunders, William L. (editor). 1968. *Colonial Records of North Carolina*. Vol. 2. New York: AMS Press.

Saxon, Lyle. 1999. *Lafitte the Pirate*. Gretna, La.: Pelican Publishing Group.

Scardaville, Michael, and Overton Ganong. N.d. (1975). Historical Report on Block 7, Lot 4, St. Augustine. Unpublished manuscript on file, Historic St. Augustine Preservation Board, St. Augustine, Florida.

Schatz, Robert C., and Howard Lavine. 2007. Waving the Flag: National Symbolism, Social Identity, and Political Engagement. *Political Psychology* 28(3):329–55.

Schávelzon, Daniel. 2000. *The Historical Archaeology of Buenos Aires: A City at the End of the World*. New York: Kluwer Academic/Plenum Publishers.

Schen, Claire. 2008. Breaching "Community" in Britain: Captives, Renegades, and the Redeemed. In *Defining Community in Early Modern Europe*, edited by Michael J. Halvorson and Karen E. Spierling, pp. 229–46. Cambridge, UK: MPG Books.

Schmidt, Peter R., and Stephen A. Mrozowski. 1993. Documentary Insights into the Archaeology of Smuggling (1988). Reprinted in *Documentary Archaeology in the New World*, edited by Mary C. Beaudry, pp. 32–42. New York: Cambridge University Press.

Scholkmann, B., R. Schreg, A. Kottmann, I. Martínez, and A. Zeischka. 2006. El Hospital San Juan de Dios, Panamá Viejo: Nota preliminar acerca de las investigaciones arqueológicas. *Canto Rodado* (Patronato Panamá Viejo) 1:65–83.

Schreg, R. 2010. Panamanian Coarse Handmade Earthenware as Melting Pots of African, American and European Traditions? *Postmedieval Archaeology* 44(1):135–64.

Schuyler, Robert L. 1977. The Spoken Word, the Written Word, Observed Behavior and Preserved Behavior: The Contexts Available to the Archaeologist. In *The Conference on Historic Sites Archaeology*, edited by Stanley South 10(20):99–120.

The Sea-Man's Vade Mecum: The Duty of the Clerk, Pilot, Mate, Surgeon, and Sea-Men of a Ship, according to the Custom of France. 1707. Reprint 1996. Electronic document: http://www.bruzelius.info/Nautica/Personnel/Vademecum(1707)_p133.html.

Sekulich, Daniel. 2009. *Terror on the Seas: True Tales of Modern-Day Pirates*. New York: Thomas Dunne Books, St. Martin's Press.

Semple, Ellen C. 1916. Pirate Coasts of the Mediterranean Sea. *Geographical Review* 2(2):134–51.

Senior, Clive. 1972. An Investigation of the Activities and Importance of English Pirates, 1603–40. Ph.D. diss., Bristol University.

———. 1976. *A Nation of Pirates: English Piracy in Its Heyday*. New York: David and Charles Newton Abbot.

Shepherd, Stephen. 1983. The Spanish *Criollo* Majority in Colonial St. Augustine. In *Spanish St. Augustine: The Archaeology of a Colonial Creole Community*, edited by Kathleen Deagan, pp. 65–97. New York: Academic Press.

Shlasko, Ellen, 1989. Delftware Chronology: A New Approach to Dating English Tin-Glazed Ceramics. M.A. thesis, Department of Anthropology, College of William and Mary, Williamsburg, Virginia.

Shulsky, L. 2001. Porcelana china de sitios coloniales españoles del sur de Norteamérica y el Caribe. *Arqueología de Panamá La Vieja—Avances de investigación, época colonial,* (Patronato Panamá Viejo) (August 1):203–14.

Skowronek, Russell K. 1982. The Patterns of Eighteenth-Century Frontier New Spain: The 1722 Flota and St. Augustine. Master's thesis, Department of Anthropology, Florida State University, Tallahassee.

———. 1992. Empire and Ceramics: The Changing Role of Illicit Trade in Spanish America. *Historical Archaeology* 26(1):109–18.

———. 2006. X Marks the Spot—Or Does it? In *X Marks the Spot: The Archaeology of Piracy,* edited by Russell K. Skowronek and Charles R. Ewen, pp. 282–98. Gainesville: University Press of Florida.

Skowronek, Russell K., and Charles R. Ewen (editors). 2006. *X Marks the Spot: The Archaeology of Piracy.* Gainesville: University Press of Florida.

Smith, Aaron. 2011. *The Atrocities of the Pirates: A Faithful Narrative of the Unparalleled Suffering of the Author during His Captivity among the Pirates* (1824). New York: Skyhorse Publishing.

Smith, Captaine [sic] John. 1629. The Bad Life Qualities and Conditions of Pyrats; and How They Taught the Turks and Moores to Become Men of Warre. In *The General Histories of Virginia, New-England and the Summer Iles, Divided into Sixe Books,* 2:279–82. Reprint London: Franklin Press, 1819.

Smith, Steven D., James B. Legg, Brad Lieb, Charles R. Cobb, Chester DePratter, and Tamara S. Wilson. 2013. Ackia and Okla Tchitoka: Defining Two 1736 Battlefields on the French-Chickasaw War, Tupelo, Mississippi. South Carolina Institute of Archaeology and Anthropology, Columbia.

Snodin, Michael. 1982. *English Silver Spoons.* London: Letts.

South, Stanley. 1977. *Method and Theory in Historical Archaeology.* New York: Academic Press.

Southerly, Chris, Sarah Watkins-Kenney, and Mark Wilde-Ramsing. 2007. Full Recovery Plan for North Carolina Archaeological Shipwreck Site, August 2007 update. Manuscript on file, North Carolina Underwater Archaeology Branch, Kure Beach.

Southwell, Philip. 1698. Official Papers. SOU 18. National Maritime Museum, Greenwich.

Starkey, David. 1990. *British Privateering Enterprise in the Eighteenth Century.* Exeter: University of Exeter Press.

St. Augustine Pirate & Treasure Museum. 2015. Electronic document: http://thepiratemuseum.com/.

Stavorinus, J. S. 1798. *Voyages to the East Indies.* Vol. 3. London: G. G. and J. Robinson/Pater-Noster-Row.

Steele, Ian K. 1986. *The English Atlantic 1675–1740: An Exploration of Communication and Community.* New York: Oxford University Press.

Steele, R. 1910. *Tudor and Stuart Proclamations, 1485–1714.* Oxford: Clarendon Press.

Steffy, J. R. 1994. *Wooden Ship Building and the Interpretation of Shipwrecks.* College Station: Texas A&M University Press.

Stevenson, David. 1988. *The Origins of Freemasonry: Scotland's Century, 1590–1710.* Cambridge: Cambridge University Press.

Stevenson, Robert Louis. 1949. *Treasure Island* (1883). Reprint New York: Random House.

Strickland, Brad. 1997. *Salty Dog: The Adventures of Wishbone.* Allen, Tex.: Big Red Chair Books.

Talty, Stephan. 2005. *Empire of Blue Water: Captain Morgan's Great Pirate Army, the Epic Battle for the Americas, and the Catastrophe That Ended the Outlaws' Bloody Reign.* New York: Crown Publishers.

TePaske, John R. 1958. Economic Problems of the Florida Governors. *Florida Historical Quarterly* 36:42–52.

———. 1964. *The Governorship of Spanish Florida, 1700–1763.* Durham: Duke University Press.

Terry, C. S. 1901. *The Chevalier de St. George and the Jacobite Movement in His Favour: 1701–1720.* London: D. Nutt.

Thompson, Amanda D. R. 2010. A New Economic Framework for Spanish Colonial Outposts: An Ethnohistoric Example from Presidios of Santa Maria de Galve and Isla Santa Rosa. *Florida Anthropologist* 63(2):62–78.

Thornton, H. P. 1952. The Modyfords and Morgan. *Jamaican Historical Review* 2:36–60.

Torre Revello, José. 1943. Merchandise Brought to America by the Spaniards (1534–1586). *Hispanic American Historical Review* 23(4):773–80.

Treadwell, V. 1965. House of Lords in the Irish Parliament. 1613–1615. *English Historical Review* 80(314):92–107.

Treasure Island Hotel and Casino. 2006. The Sirens of TI. Electronic document: http://www.treasureisland.com/pages/ent_sirens.asp#view (no longer available).

Trembanis, Arthur C., and Jesse E. McNinch. 2003. Predicting Scour and Maximum Settling Depths of Shipwrecks: A Numeric Simulation of the Fate of *Queen Anne's Revenge.* In *Proceedings of Coastal Sediments '03.* Clearwater Beach, Fla.: ASCE Press.

Tucker, Spencer. 1989. *Arming the Fleet: U.S. Navy Ordinance in the Muzzle Loading Era.* Annapolis: Naval Institute Press.

Turley, Hans. 1999. *Rum, Sodomy and the Lash, Piracy, Sexuality, and Masculine Identity.* New York: New York University Press.

Usher, Abbott P. 1932. Spanish Ships and Shipping in the Sixteenth and Seventeenth Centuries. In *Facts and Factors in Economic History: Articles by Former Students,* edited by E. F. Gay, pp. 189–213. Cambridge, Mass.: Harvard University Press.

Vicens Vives, Jaime. 1969. *An Economic History of Spain.* Translated by Frances M. López Morillas. Princeton: Princeton University Press.

Wadia, Ardeshir Rutonjee. 1957. *The Bombay Dockyard and the Wadia Master Builders.* London: R. A. Wadia.

Walker, Barbara G. 1988. *The Woman's Dictionary of Symbols and Sacred Objects.* New York: Harper and Row.

Walker, Geoffrey J. 1979. *Spanish Politics and Imperial Trade, 1700–1789.* Bloomington: Indiana University Press.

Wallerstein, Immanuel. 1980. *The Modern World-System II: Mercantilism and Consolidation of the European World-Economy, 1600–1750.* New York: Academic Press.

Ward, Cheryl. 2005. Rough Cilicia Maritime Archaeological Project 2004: Preliminary Report. *Andolu Akdenizi Arkeoloji Haberleri 2005* 3:126–30.

Ward, Christopher. 1993. *Imperial Panama: Commerce and Conflict in Isthmian America, 1550–1800.* Albuquerque: University of New Mexico Press.

Waselkov, Gregory A., and John A. Walthall. 2002. Faience Styles in French North America: A Revised Classification. *Historical Archaeology* 36(1):62–78.

Waterbury, Jean P. (editor). 1999. *Denses and Defenders at St. Augustine. A Collection of Writings by Luis Rafael Arana.* El Escribano, Vol. 36. St. Augustine: St. Augustine Historical Society.

Watkins-Kenney, Sarah. 2006. Report on the Cask Assemblage from Shipwreck NC-31CR314. Draft report, December 15. Manuscript, North Carolina Underwater Archaeology Branch, Kure Beach.

———. 2008. Beaufort Inlet Shipwreck (31CR314) 1997–2007: Casks and Pewter. Paper presented at the Southeastern Archaeological Conference, Charlotte, N.C., November 12–15, 2008.

Webster's New Collegiate Dictionary. 1981. Springfield, Mass.: G. and C. Merriam Co.

Wedgewood, C. V. 2005. *The Thirty Years War.* New York: New York Review Books.

Wells, John T., and Jesse E. McNinch. 2001. Reconstructing Shoal and Channel Configuration in Beaufort Inlet: 300 Years of Change at the Site of *Queen Anne's Revenge. Southeastern Geology* 40(1):11–18.

Welsh, Wendy, and Mark Wilde-Ramsing. 2008. Final Report on Peering into a Pirate's Trove: A Proposal to Conduct High Definition Radiography on Concretions from the *Queen Anne's Revenge* Shipwreck Site. National Geographic Expeditions Council Grant No. EC0259-05. Report on file, North Carolina Underwater Archaeology Branch, Kure Beach.

Went, A.E.J. 1947. Sir William Hull's Losses in 1641. *Journal of the Cork Historical and Archaeological Society* 52:55–68.

Whitburn, T. 1870. *Westward Hoe for Avalon: In the New-found-land, as Described by Captain Richard Whitbourne, of Exmouth, Devon, 1622.* London: Sampson Low, Son and Marston.

Wilde-Ramsing, Mark U. 1998. A Report on the 1997 Archaeological Investigations at North Carolina Shipwreck Site 0003BUI. In *Underwater Archaeology: Proceedings of the 31st Conference on Historical and Underwater Archaeology*, edited by Lawrence E. Babits, Catherine Fach, and Ryan Harris, pp. 54–60. Rockville, Md.: Society for Historical Archaeology.

———. 2005. A Stratified Site Sampling Research Plan for the 2005–2006 Investigations and Recovery at North Carolina Archaeological Shipwreck Site 31CR314. Manuscript on file, North Carolina Underwater Archaeology Branch, Kure Beach.

———. 2006. The Pirate Ship *Queen Anne's Revenge*. In *X Marks the Spot: The Archaeology of Piracy*, edited by Russell K. Skowronek and Charles R. Ewen, pp. 160–95. Gainesville: University Press of Florida.

———. 2009. Steady as She Goes . . . A Test of the Gibbs' Model Using the *Queen Anne's Revenge* Shipwreck Site. Ph.D. diss., Program in Coastal Resource Management, East Carolina University, Greenville.

Wilde-Ramsing, Mark U., and Charles R. Ewen. 2012. Beyond Reasonable Doubt: A Case for *Queen Anne's Revenge*. *Journal of Historical Archaeology* 46(2):110–33.

Wilde-Ramsing, Mark U., and Joseph M. Wilde-Ramsing. 2008. Report on "HIS Maria" Bell Recovered from 31CR314. *Bell Tower* 66(4):23.

Wilson, Timothy. 1986. *Flags at Sea.* London: National Maritime Museum.

Wright, J. Leitch. 1970. *Anglo-Spanish Rivalry in Eastern North America*. Athens: University of Georgia Press.
Young, Alan (editor). 1995. *Index Emblimaticus: The English Emblem Tradition, Vol. 3: Emblematic Flag Devices from the English Civil Wars, 1642–1660*. Toronto: University of Toronto Press.
Zacks, Richard. 2002. *The Pirate Hunter: The True Story of Captain Kidd*. New York: Hyperion.
Zárate, Diana. 2004. La cerámica con engobe rojo en Panamá Viejo (1519–1671): Caracterización y análisis. Undergraduate thesis, Universidad de los Andes–Bogotá.

Contributors

Charles D. Beeker has been directing the Indiana University Academic Diving Program since 1984 and the Underwater Science Program since 1991. A registered professional archaeologist and PADI master instructor, he has been an IU faculty member with the School of Health Physical Education and Recreation (HPER) since 1980 and an adjunct faculty member in the Department of Anthropology since 2002. He was appointed to the Marine Protected Areas Federal Advisory Committee in 2005 and is responsible for the creation and implementation of numerous underwater parks and preserves in the states of Florida and California as well as in the Cayman Islands and Dominican Republic.

Linda F. Carnes-McNaughton currently serves as archaeologist/curator for the Cultural Resources Management Program at Fort Bragg, where she has been since 2003. Before that, she worked as the archaeology supervisor for the Historic Sites Section, North Carolina Department of Cultural Resources, for twelve years. She received a B.A. in anthropology from Georgia State University then began graduate work at University of Tennessee. She completed her doctoral degree in anthropology at the University of North Carolina at Chapel Hill in 1997. As a material culture specialist, she contributes to the *Quenn Anne's Revenge* Shipwreck Project as a volunteer, providing analysis of ceramics, glass ware, pipes, beads, jewelry, clothing items, and other small finds.

Kathleen Deagan is distinguished research curator of archaeology and adjunct professor of Anthropology at the University of Florida's Florida Museum of Natural History. She received her Ph.D. in 1974 from the University of Florida. After teaching in the Florida State University Anthropology Department for eight years, she joined the University of Florida faculty in 1982. Deagan is the author of eight books and more than sixty-five scientific papers. She was named an "Alumna of Outstanding Distinction" by the University of Florida in 1998 and is a recipient of the Society for Historical Archaeology's J. C. Harrington Award for Lifetime Distinction in Historical Archaeology.

John de Bry is the director of the Center for Historical Archaeology. He is a paleographer specializing in sixteenth- through eighteenth-century French, Spanish, and English manuscripts. As a historical archaeologist, Dr. de Bry has also participated in a number of field excavation projects in the United States, the Caribbean, South America, and the Philippines. He holds an M.A. in history and a doctorate in post-medieval history.

Charles R. Ewen received his Ph.D. at the University of Florida in 1987. He joined the faculty at East Carolina University in 1994 and is a full professor in the Department of Anthropology as well as director of the Phelps Archaeology Laboratory. He was elected to the presidency of the Society for Historical Archaeology in 2012.

Chad M. Gulseth is currently reconstructing the French ship *Ranger* of the pirate Bartholomew Roberts as part of his master's thesis at Texas A&M University. He received an undergraduate degree at the University of Wisconsin–La Crosse in archaeology, before which he spent four years in the Marine Corps Infantry and did three tours in Iraq.

Frederick H. "Fritz" Hanselmann is a research faculty member at the Meadows Center for Water and the Environment at Texas State University. He holds two master's degrees and is a doctoral candidate at Indiana University.

Heather Hatch is a Ph.D. student in the Nautical Archaeology Program at Texas A&M University. Her research focuses on archaeological approaches to identity and maritime communities. She has two M.A. degrees, in European historical archaeology from the University of Sheffield and in maritime history from East Carolina University, both of which have allowed her to explore her long-standing interest in pirates and piracy in an academic framework.

Connie Kelleher is a Ph.D. candidate at Trinity College Dublin. She is also a lecturer at University College Cork.

Kenneth J. Kinkor had been the historian for the *Whydah* Project since 1986. He wrote and lectured extensively on piracy, smuggling, and other aspects of New England maritime history. He passed away shortly after completing the chapter for this volume.

Juan G. Martín is an anthropologist at the National University of Colombia and received his Ph.D. at the University of Huelva, Spain. He has extensive experience in historical archeology, participating and managing projects in Panama, Colombia, and Cuba. He coordinated the Panama Viejo Archaeological Project from 2000 to 2010. Martín is a member of the editorial board of *Canto Rodado* in Panama, the scientific committee of Vinculos in Costa Rica, and editor for Latin America for *Historical Archaeology*. He is currently the director of the

Archaeological Museum of Universidad del Norte (MAPUKA) in Barranquilla, Colombia, and is in charge of several national and international projects, including "The City Invincible," an underwater archaeology research program in Cartagena de Indias Bay.

Tomás Mendizábal is an archaeologist contractor for the Panama Canal Authority. He has a Ph.D. from the Institute of Archaeology at the University College London and is responsible for research, documentation, and management of cultural resources detected during the Expansion Program of the Panama Canal.

Courtney Page is a graduate student at East Carolina University. She works as a conservator at the *Queen Anne's Revenge* Conservation Lab at Greenville, North Carolina.

Marco Roling is an independent researcher from the Netherlands, focusing on the Dutch maritime expansion of the seventeenth and eighteenth century. He has a degree in archaeology and computer science and is currently working as a cultural heritage digitization expert.

Russell K. Skowronek (Ph.D., Michigan State University), a research associate of the Smithsonian Institution, is interim associate dean, School of Interdisciplinary Programs and Community Engagement, College of Liberal Arts, and professor of anthropology and history at the University of Texas–Rio Grande Valley, where he serves as the director of the Community Historical Archaeology Project with Schools. He is the author or editor of several books, including *X Marks the Spot: The Archaeology of Piracy* (with Charles R. Ewen), *HMS Fowey Lost and Found* (with George Fischer), *Beneath the Ivory Tower: The Archaeology of Academia* (with Kenneth Lewis), and *Recovering a Legacy: The Ceramics of Alta California* (with M. James Blackman and Ronald L. Bishop), all published by the University Press of Florida, as well as *Situating Mission Santa Clara de Asís: 1776–1851, Documentary and Material Evidence of Life on the Alta California Frontier*.

Mark U. Wilde-Ramsing formerly served as North Carolina's deputy state archaeologist in charge of the Underwater Archaeology Branch. He began his career with the state in 1978 and has directed archeological investigations on the *Queen Anne's Revenge* shipwreck site since its discovery in 1996. A graduate of Wake Forest University and the Catholic University of America, Wilde-Ramsing completed his doctorate in coastal resource management at East Carolina University in 2009.

Index

Page numbers marked with f refer to figures and those marked with t refer to tables.

Adventure, 204
Adventure Galley, 57, 112, 114, 119, 121
Adventure Prize, 114. See also *Quedagh Merchant*
Alcohol, 181
Anchors, 26, 37, 117, 119
Anson, George, 264
Anstis, Thomas, 233
Archaeological record: material culture data, 7; patterns in, 205; pirates and, 14, 260, 274, 276
Ashton, Philip, 3, 222,
Asiento, 241, 246t
Avery, Henry, 216

Ballast: related to *Fiery Dragon*, 66–67, 69, 71, 82–83; related to *Quedagh Merchant*, 119, 123–25; related to *Queen Anne's Revenge*, 15, 30; related to *Ranger*, 104–5, 107–9
Baltimore, 169, 174–76, 179, 183, 185–86, 188–89
Bandits, 7
Barcaderas, 9–10
Barges, 9, 144
Barrie, James, 196, 198
Bathymetry system, 24
Baugh, William, 169, 189
Bay of Honduras, 4, 9, 136

Beads, 22, 30–31, 35, 206
Beaufort (North Carolina), 20, 28
Beaufort Inlet, 15, 19–20, 24, 32, 35, 54, 203–4, 261; charts of, 25f; See also *Queen Anne's Revenge*
Beeker, Charles D., 12, 275
Belize. *See* Barcaderas.
Bellamy, Samuel, 12, 200, 202, 214, 217t, 229, 234–37, 262
Bellomont, Earl of, 112, 211; and the arrest of William Kidd, 114; as governor, 112
Benchley, Peter, 199
Billy Bones, 196, 207
Bingeman, John M., 265
Bishop, Richard, 168–71, 174, 178–79, 190
Black Sails, 198
Black Swan, 10, 196
Blackbeard, 12, 29–30, 40, 55, 98, 201, 206, 214, 237, 261–62; and activities in North Carolina of, 19–20, 215; and blockade of Charleston's port, 19, 44, 204; and capture of *La Concorde*, 18–20, 204, 261; in Caribbean, 19, 204; death of, 204; and Ocracoke Island, 204; pardon for, 215; in relation to *Queen Anne's Revenge*, 17, 275. *See also* Teach, Edward
Blackwood. *See* Logwood
Blake, Emmanuel, 105
Blunderbuss. *See* Musketoon barrel
Bolton, Henry, 114, 117, 121–22
Bonnet, Stede, 217t, 237
Bonny, Anne, 205

Book of Pirates, 196
Bottles: glass onion, 108; wine, 34, 35, 40, 86f
Boucanier, 5
Boucaud, Philippe, 44, 48
Bowen, John, 12
Bradley, Joseph, 145–46
Brethren of the coast, 5, 228–29. *See also* Pirates
Bronze: bell, 32, 37–38, 39f; cannon, 146
Brown, John, 183
Brown, Ruth R., 164
Buccaneers, 4–5, 145, 149, 135, 200, 211, 214; base on Tortuga Island, 5; definition of, 5, 134

Campeche (Yucatán), 135, 155
Campechewood. *See* Logwood
Cannonballs, 83, 85, 104, 142
Cannons, 15: in Chagres River, 156–58; in Ilot Madame, 84–85; on the *Fiery Dragon,* 59, 60, 67, 83–85; on the *Quedagh Merchant,* 112, 114–15, 117, 119, 121–23, 127, 128f, 129; on the *Queen Anne's Revenge,* 19, 26, 28–30, 32–35; on the *Whydah,* 30. *See also* Shot
Canty, Daniel, 180–81
Canty, Gillyneamh, 179
Canty's Cove, 179, 181f, 182, 185; Canty's House, 180–81
Cape Cod, 87, 193, 202, 229, 263f
Cape Finisterre, 264
Cape of Good Hope, 59–60
Cape Verde, 59–60
Captain Blood, 10, 196
Captain Hook, 196
Captain Philips. See Somali Pirates.
Careening, definition of, 58
Carnes-McNaughton, Linda, 34, 41, 275
Cartagena, 137, 139–40, 143
Cascoigne, James: maker of Port Royal map, 100, 105
Castillo de San Lorenzo, 144–46, 155f, 163
Ceramics, 151; frequencies of, 248, 250t, 252t-254t; Spanish tableware, 245, 251.

See also Chinese porcelain; Delftware; Majolica; Stoneware
Chagres River, 144–46, 156, 160
Chichester, Arthur, 165, 171, 185
Children's Museum of Indianapolis, 127, 129
Chinese porcelain, 58, 71, 72f, 85f, 151; as date marker, 83; and Emperor Wanli, 77; on *Fiery Dragon,* 74–78; and Guangzhou (Canton), 76; and Jingdezhen, 75; and Kangxi period, 60, 62, 75; as Kraak, 76; and phoenix motif, 76;
Chivers, Dirk, 62, 231
Clifford, Barry, 202, 229–30
Cocklyn, Thomas, 216, 233, 237
Cockram, Thomas, 214
Coins, 32, 73, 83, 201–2, 272; silver, 35, 230. *See also* Ducats; Gold
Collier, Edward, 155
Columbus, Christopher, 132, 144
Compagnie des Indes Orientales. *See* French East India Company
Compagnies Welvaren, 60
Condell, John. *See* Condent, Christopher
Condent, Christopher, 201; on the *Fiery Dragon,* 12, 57, 59; as negotiator, 61; pardoned, 61; and pirate flag of, 217t; on Saint Mary's Island, 60–61; and settled in France, 62
Condent, Richard. See Condent, Christopher.
Condon, John. *See* Condent, Christopher
Condon, William. *See* Condent, Christopher
Congdon, John. *See* Condent, Christopher
Connor, John. *See* Condent, Christopher
Continuous sites. *See* Muckelroy, Keith
Cook, Henry, 186
Coote, Richard. *See* Bellomont, Earl of
Cordingly, David, 226
Corsair, 4–5
Coward, Thomas, 168, 175
Crawford, David, 236

Crawford-Hitchins, Diana, 45
Crimson Pirate, 194
Croagh Harbour, 185, 188
Cromwell, Oliver, 133, 211
Croock. See Dún na Séad.
Crooke, Thomas, 175
Crooker, 61
Crookhaven, 169, 174, 182–83, 185–86, 189
Crossbones, 198
Culliford, Robert, 62
Curse of Oak Island, 202

Danvers, Henry, 167
Davis, Howell, 94, 217t, 222, 237
Davy Crockett and the River Pirates, 194, 197
Deagan, Kathy, 13, 276–77
De Bry, John, 275
de Zeebloem, 59
Defensive fortifications. See Fortifications
Delftware, 243t
Depp, Johnny, 8, 196
Disney, 196, 199; *Treasure Planet*, 196, 199; Pirates of the Caribbean (attraction), 198; *Pirates of the Caribbean* (film), 8, 10, 193, 196, 198
Downing, Charles, 61
Drake, Sir Francis, 4, 133, 136–37, 144; and attack on St. Augustine, 13; as bogeyman, 13
Ducats, 73–74, 192
Ducoin, Jacques, 18, 36
Dún na Séad, 175, 176f
Dunworley Bay wreck, 183–84, 184f
Dutchman's Cove, 179, 180f, 185

East India Company, 59–60, 76, 112, 114, 167, 201, 211
Easton, Peter, 168–69, 171, 187, 190
Eden, Charles, 215
Ek. *See* Logwood
El Salvador, 203
Every, Henry, 217t
Ewen, Charles R., 13, 54
Exquemelin, Alexander, 135, 140

Fame, 60; renamed as *Fiery Dragon*, 60
Fastenings, 37, 54, 107, 126f, 127, 129
Fiery Dragon, 57, 274–75; ballast stone from, 66–67; burning of, 61; Chinese porcelain from, 71, 74–79; cowrie shells from, 71, 72; and Dutch construction tradition, 69, 71; identification of as pirate ship, 12, 57; ivory figurine from, 81–82; organic material from, 79–80; photo mosaic of, 68f; test excavation of, 67, 69
Finamore, Daniel, 9
Firth, Raymond, 209
Flags: at sea, 208–11; emblems, 223–27, 225t; flag use, 217t–222t
Flemmish Bottoms. See Flyboats.
Flyboats, 182
Flying Dragon, 59–60
Ford, John, 197
Fortifications, 9, 64, 137, 143, 145, 149, 163, 181; strengthening of, 13, 144
Fort Macon: and cannonballs, 29
Francke, Thomas, 168
Freebooters, 195, 200. *See also* Pirates
Freemasonry, 230, 233–35, 238, 276
French East India Company, 112
Futtocks, 37, 69, 71, 73, 88, 104, 107, 108t

Galvin, Peter R., 185
Gaulton, Barry, 187
Gerritszoon, Hessel, 167
Gilbert, W.S., 196
Gokane Point, 182, 183f
Gold: as coins, 32; as dust, 26, 31, 35; as ingots, 267; as nuggets, 31
Golden Age of Piracy, 57, 64, 92, 93, 110, 200, 205, 208, 260, 275–76, 279; in Ireland, 165, 167, 192
GPS, 66
Gránuaile. *See* O'Malley, Grace.
Grande Terre, 9
Greater Antilles, 114
Great Mahomet, 62–63, 66, 83, 87, 91
Great Ranger. See *Ranger*.
Great Red Island. *See* Madagascar

Grenades, 40, 145
Gulseth, Chad M., 275

Hamilton, Archibald, 235–36
Hamilton, Christopher, 202–3
Hamilton, D. L., 10, 100, 105, 109, 200, 205
Hammond, George, 33
Hanselmann, Frederick H., 12, 13, 275
Harbour Grace, Newfoundland, 187
Hatch, Heather, 14, 276
Havana (Cuba), 3, 137, 256
Hawkins, Jim, 196
Hawkins, Richard, 173
Henrietta Marie, 260; artifacts of, 269–73, 269t, 270f-271f,
Hispaniola, 5, 9, 13, 30, 110, 115–17, 133–34, 140, 211, 258. *See also* Santo Domingo
HMS Invincible, 260; artifacts of, 269–73, 269t, 270f-271f, 272t; history of, 264; wreck site of, 264f, 268
Hobsbawm, E. J., 7
Hook, 198
Hornigold, Benjamin, 214
Howard, Charles, 173
Hull, William, 171, 173, 174, 179, 189; and fortified house, 174f
Hunt, John, 166f, 167, 168f, 174f, 176f, 178

Ile aux Forbans. *See* Pirate's Island
Ile Sainte-Marie, 9, 63, 112, 230
Illicit trade, 13, 240; archaeological record of, 242, 251, 255, 260; as contraband in Caribbean and Spanish Florida, 240–59; supply system and, 240
Ilot Madame: charts of, 65f; on Saint Mary's Island, 63–64, 66, 71, 92
Indian Ocean, 4, 58, 62, 110, 112, 200–201, 211, 238, 275; arrival of pirates in, 59
Indiana University, 115, 117, 118, 125, 127
Institute of Nautical Archaeology (Texas A&M), 105
Instructions, 210
International Maritime Bureau, 2

Ireland: pirates of, 165, 168–69
Island, 199
Israel Hands, 196

Jacobitism, 234–38, 276
Jamaica National Heritage Trust, 105, 109
Jennings, Henry, 214, 235–36
Jennings, John, 168
Jennings, William, 235
Jobson, Humphrey, 173
Johnson, Charles, 93, 223–25, 227
Jolly Roger, 95, 97, 194–95, 198, 216, 224, 228, 276; on coins, 230; symbolism of, 229–32

Kelleher, Connie, 10, 276
Khan, Ibrahim, 62
Khan, Muklis, 114
Kidd, William, 4, 57, 62, 110, 111f, 113f, 198, 201, 211–12, 216; business venture of, 112; conviction of, 5, 114; granted commission to hunt pirates, 4, 112; hanging of, 114, 278; as pirate, 114; and the *Quedagh Merchant*, 12, 110, 112, 114, 274–75; and testimony of, 116–17, 119, 129; treasure of, 202
Killigrew, Thomas, 173
Kinkor, Kenneth J., 14, 276
Knight, Tobias, 215
Kyrenia, 200

La Buse, Oliver, 91
La Concorde, 12, 30, 37, 44, 204; background history of, 17, 18, 261; final voyage of, 18; renamed, 18, 54–55; as slave trader, 18, 35–36
Lafitte, Jean, 10
Lafitte, Pierre, 10
Lajas Reef, 146, 155–56, 159–60
Langrage, 28. *See also* Cannons
Lawes, Nicholas, 100
Leamcon: as pirate base, 174, 178–80, 185–86, 188–89, 190f, 191
Leeson, Peter, 6

Lewis Hulk, 100, 109
Libbey, Joseph, 3–4
Little Ranger, 94, 95, 95f, 100, 102, 105, 109
Logwood, 9
L'Olonnais, Jean, 200
Long John Silver, 196, 206
Lost Ships of Henry Morgan Project, 156, 160
Low, Edward "Ned," 3, 216, 218t, 222, 237
Lusardi, Wayne, 183
Lynch, Sir Thomas, 212

MacNeill, Ben Dixon, 6
Madagascar, 57, 58, 60, 92, 201, 230; book on, 89; women of, 91
Magdalena, 141
Magnetometer, 156, 160, 163, 284. *See also* Remote sensing
Mainwairing, Henry, 165, 169, 178, 187
Maison d'Autriche, 78
Majolica, 243t-244t, 248t; Andean, 151; Panamanian, 151
Mamora, Africa, 168–69, 185, 187
Mandrin, Louis, 5–6
Martín, Juan G., 13, 276
Marx, Robert, 102, 104–5, 109
Mary Rose, 45
Mason, F. Van Wyck, 197
Maynard, Robert, 6–7, 29
McBride, David, 9
Meiboom, 59
Mendizábal, Tomás, 13, 276
Mettas, Jean, 18
Michener, James, 133, 197
Miller, Regis, 37
Mississippi River, 10
Mocha Frigate, 62, 66, 83, 87, 91
Modyford, Thomas, 136
Mollusks, bivalve, 58, 104
Monroe Doctrine, 195
Monson, William, 185
Moore, William, 112
Morgan, Henry, 134–35, 163, 200, 205, 274; as lieutenant-governor of Jamaica, 163; and the raid on Maracaibo, 140–42, 155; in Mexico and Nicaragua, 135–36; as privateer, 133; and the raid on Portobelo, 137, 138f, 139; and the sack of Panama, 13, 142–48, 154, 275–76
Mosquito Coast, 136
Mountaudoin, Rene: as owner of *La Concorde*, 36
Muckelroy, Keith, 268
Munster, 165, 167, 170, 172–75, 177–78, 185–87, 192
Muppet Treasure Island, 196
Murder, 29, 62, 91, 135, 158–59, 199, 206, 213
Musketballs, 97, 104
Musketoon barrel, 29, 32, 54
Myagh, Patrick, 169, 186

Nash, James, 60
Natierre, 41
National Talk-Like-a-Pirate Day, 206–7
Navigation instruments, 204, 261t, 267
New Orleans, 9–10
Newsom, Lee A., 37
Nicaragua, 135–36
Norris, Thomas, 170
North Carolina, 6, 28, 54, 183, 201, 204, 215, 262f; and Bath, 206; and Beaufort, 15, 203, 216; and Ocracoke Island, 204
North Carolina Department of Cultural Resources, 56
North Carolina Underwater Archaeology Branch, 261
Nostra Senhora de Cabo: capture of, 62, 91; release of viceroy from, 62
Nuestra Señora de Atocha, 265
Nutt, Robert, 182

Oak Island, 202, 230
Ocracoke. *See* North Carolina
Ogle, Chalenor, 94, 96f, 97, 99–100
Old Port Royal. *See* Roatan
O'Malley, Grace, 176, 177f
Oxford, 139–41, 155

Page, Courtney, 13, 277
Panama Viejo: archaeology at, 150–51, 163; artifacts from, 151; Main Square (Plaza Mayor), 152–54; ruins of, 149–50; sack of, 142–48, 200. See also Morgan, Henry.
Parish, James Robert, 194,
Personal effects, 261t, 267, 269–71, 272t
Peter Pan, 195–96, 198
Pewterware, 33, 35, 41, 47
Photo mosaic technique, 67, 68f, 71, 162f
Pipes, smoking, 30–31, 34–35, 72t, 107, 108t, 260
Piracy: in the Caribbean, 5, 19, 58, 134, 142–43, 149, 195, 204, 275–76; definition of, 4; in the Indian Ocean, 9, 58–59, 62, 110, 201, 211, 238, 275; legends of, 93, 115, 133–34, 142; modern incidents of, 2, 3, 9, 10–12; suppression of, 195, 213; and Treaty of Madrid, 246t; as terrorism, 199
Pirates: Black Dog, 196; Blind Pew, 196; as caricatures, 8; comics of, 196; definition of, 135; images of, 94f, 111f, 113f, 134f, 138f; modern, 2, 3, 9, 10–12; as romantic myth, 7. *See also names of individual pirates*
Pirate's Island, 9, 89
Pirates of Penzance, 196
Pirogues, 91
Pistol, 93, 97–98, 203, 218t, 223–24, 225t, 231
Port Royal, 5, 99–100, 149, 155, 275; and artifacts of, 102, 104; and earthquake (1692), 109, 205, 275; excavations of, 10, 12, 102, 103f; and hurricane (1722), 99–100, 205; and map of Chocolata Hole, 101; as mercantile center, 10; as pirate haven, 10, 134, 200, 205
Privateer: British, 10, 110, 135–37, 139–19, 211, 212; definition of, 4, 135; and French, 36, 211, 261; in Jamaica, 10, 139, 149, 236; in Mexico, 136; and Spanish, 241, 251; and suppression of, 169–70
Providence, 214

Public Records Office, National Archives, 116
Puritans, 14, 230
Pyle, Howard, 11, 11f, 11f, 196

Quedagh Merchant, 12, 110, 112, 131, 274–75; and archaeological investigations of, 115; and artifacts of, 119, 121–22, 260; and ballast of, 124–25; and Captain Kidd Living Museum in the Sea, 129, 130f, 131; and historical documentation, 116–17; and rabbeted seams, 125–27; and shipwreck of, 119–21, 120f; and site map of, 118f; and wood sample analysis of, 123–24
Queen Anne's Revenge, 15, 107, 183–84, 237, 265, 275; archaeological site plan of, 21f, 27f; and artifacts, 15, 20, 22, 26, 29–54, 269–73, 269t, 270f-271f, 272t, 274; bell from, 32, 37–39; and ceramics, 34–35, 41, 43–44; and environmental impacts on wreck, 20, 24; excavations of, 20, 261; and history of, 261; and hull construction of, 36; hull structure of, 26, 37; identification of, 12, 15, 17, 203–5; impact of hurricanes on, 268; intentional grounding of, 204; initial fieldwork on, 15, 20; iron artifacts of, 26, 29; LEGO play set, 197; location of, 15, 16f; remains of, compared to Whydah, 30; and wreck site, 20, 24, 262f, 268
Queen Anne's Revenge Conservation Laboratory, 22
Queen Anne's War. *See* War of Spanish Succession

Rackham, Calico Jack, 205
Ranger (also known as *Great Ranger*), 12, 95, 97, 99–100, 274–75; archaeological survey of, 105; artifacts of, 104, 107–9; and ballast, 105; excavations of, 104; in Port Royal, 100, 102, 104; and site plan of, 106f

Read, Mary, 205
Rediker, Marcus, 209, 226
Remote sensing: and LIDAR, 191; and magnetic gradiometer, 26
Ribbon, silk, 52, 58, 60–61, 89, 91, 112, 116, 224
Rich Island. *See* Roatan
Rigging, 3, 28, 102, 104, 107, 108t, 139, 156, 267
Río Chagres Maritime Cultural Landscape Study, 13, 156; site map of, 161f
Ritchie, Robert C., 211
Rivera, Javier, 150
Roaringwater Bay, 185
Roatan, 4, 9, 136
Robert, Sieur, 89, 91
Roberts, Bartholomew, 93, 97–98, 205, 230–31, 278; flags used, 223, 225–26; and his pirating career, 93–94; and *Ranger*, 12, 94f, 274–75; and *Royal Fortune*, 94, 94f
Rock-cut Steps, 179, 180f, 182, 183f, 188, 190–91, 191f
Rockfleet Castle, 177f
Rogers, Woodes: as governor of Nassau, 214–15
Rojas, Claudia, 150
Roling, Marco, 275
Royal African Company, 95, 265
Royal Fortune, 94, 96–97, 99–100, 102, 105, 109
Rupee, 60

Sabatini, Rafael, 10, 196
Sainte-Marie Island. *See* Saint Mary's Island
Saint Mary's Island, 57, 77; discovery of, 57; famous pirates on, 62; life on, 89–91; map of, 64f, 90f; merchants on, 58, 91; as pirate base, 58, 60–61, 89; as strategic location, 89
Santiago (Cuba), 143
Santo Domingo, 13, 119, 133, 251, 255
Satisfaction, 146, 155, 159

Schen, Claire, 178
Schuyler, Robert L., 5
Sea Hawk, 196
Semple, Ellen, 184
Senior, Clive, 170
1722 Wreck, 104, 109. See also *Ranger*
Ship construction, 36, 37, 55, 67, 69, 79, 107, 117, 123; and architecture, 91; and Indian shipbuilding, 123, 125–27, 129
Ship modifications, 205
Shot: bar, 28; cannon bag, 30; lead, 15, 22, 29, 30, 87; solid, 29
Side scan sonar, 63, 66
Silk. *See* Ribbon, silk
Silver. *See* Coins
Skipwith, Henry, 186
Skowronek, Russell K., 1, 193
Slaves, 31, 149; and African, 36; and artifacts of, 31, 206; and ships, 17–18, 30–31, 35–36, 43, 55, 96, 202, 204, 229, 260–62, 265
Smith, Aaron, 3
Smith, John, 171, 220t-221t
Smithsonian Tropical Research Institue (STRI), 157
Smuggling, 10, 13–14, 179, 192, 195, 239; on Grand Terre, 9; in Hispaniola, 5. *See also* Illicit trade
Snelgrave, William, 216
Soldado, 62–63
Solent Strait, 264
Somalia, 9–10
Somali pirates 2–3, 11–12
Sonar survey, 66
Southack, Cyprian, 263f
Spain: and annual fleets, 241–42; and asiento with England, 241; economic weakness of, 239–40; and New World colonies, 132, 239–40; and trade networks, 240, 259; and treasure ships, 203, 261
Spanish Main, 132, 137, 149, 200, 239
Sparrow, Jack, 196, 198
Spongebob Squarepants, 198

St. Augustine, 242, 276–77; and Non-Spanish trade goods, 243t–244t, 245, 246t, 247–56; and ceramics from, 245, 250t, 252t-254t, 255–57; and households, 249, 255–56; and illicit trade, 242–59; Spanish privateers in, 241, 251; and trade with Cuba, 242
St. Augustine Pirate and Treasure Museum, 198
Statues, 80–81, 80f-81f
Stevenson, Robert Louis, 93, 196, 201, 276
Stiles, John, 33
Stoneware, 35, 151
Sullivan, Arthur, 196
Surat, 60, 62, 122–26
Swallow, 94, 97, 99–100

Tableware. *See* Ceramics; Chinese porcelain; Delftware; Majolica; Pewterware; Stoneware
Tar, 18
Taylor, John, 91
Taylor, John (pirate), 62, 91
Teach, Edward, 6, 12, 18, 29, 200, 215, 221t, 223, 261. *See also* Blackbeard
Teredo worms. *See* Mollusks, bivalve
Tew, Thomas, 198
Thompson, William, 173
Tompion, wooden, 29, 267
Tools, carpenter, 36, 43, 261t, 267, 269, 272t
Topsail Inlet, 20. *See also* Beaufort Inlet
Tortuga Island, 5, 134; buccaneer settlement on, 9, 200
Totentanz, 228, 230
Treasure: hunters, 8, 115, 203–4, 214, 277–78; stories of buried, 115, 192, 193, 201–2
Treasure Island, 93, 195–96, 201–2, 276
Treasure Island Hotel and Casino, 198–99

Treasure salvors, 204, 261, 263, 265, 277–78; collaborating with, 203, 278; and ethics, 278
Treaties: Madrid, 246t; Utrecht, 246t
Triangle of Trade, 18
Tuck, James A., 187
Tuckerman, Richard, 237

Underwater site formation, 120–21
Urethral syringe, 35, 44

Vane, Charles, 215

Walshingham, Robert, 168
War of Jenkins' Ear, 246t
War of Spanish Succession, 18, 36, 201, 213, 256
Wars. *See names of individual wars*
Ward, John, 171
Weights, 45–46
Whydah, 30, 54, 83, 87, 202, 204, 229–30, 233; alternation to, 262; artifacts of, 260, 269–73, 269t, 270f-271f, 272t, 276; and bag shot, 30; bell of, 203; cannon of, 30; history of, 229, 262–63; movement of artifacts in, 203, 268; as predator, 83; and sinking of, 267; and site of, 12, 203, 263f, 268
Whydah Galley, 232, 234
Wilde-Ramsing, Mark, 55, 275
Williams Palgrave, 250
Williams, Robin, 198
Wishbone, 196

X Marks the Spot: The Archaeology of Piracy, 8, 15, 17, 22, 35, 44, 193, 202, 274–75, 277

Zephyr, 3